Musica Practica

The Psychoanalysis of
Artistic Vision and Hearing
by Anton Ehrenzweig   978-1138874961

The Rational and Social Foundations
of Music
by Max Weber

The Languages of Art   978-0915144341
by Nelson Goodman

The Hidden Order of Art   978-0520038455
by Anton Ehrenzweig

V

Musica Practica

The Social Practice of Western Music
from Gregorian Chant to Postmodernism

————◆————

MICHAEL CHANAN

VERSO
London · New York

First published by Verso 1994
© Michael Chanan 1994
All rights reserved

3 5 7 9 10 8 6 4 2

Verso
UK: 6 Meard Street, London W1F 0EG
USA: 29 West 35th Street, New York, NY 10001-2291

Verso is the imprint of New Left Books

ISBN 1-895984-905-9
ISBN 1-85984-005-1 (pbk)

British Library Cataloguing in Publication Data
A catalogue record for this book is available from the British Library

Library of Congress Cataloging-in-Publication Data
Chanan, Michael.
Musica practica : the social practice of Western music from
Gregorian chant to postmodernism / Michael Chanan.
p.   cm.
Includes bibliographical references and index.
ISBN 1-85984-905-9. — ISBN 1-85984-005-1 (pbk.)
1. Music and society.   2. Music—History and criticism.
I. Title.
ML 3795.C42   1994
306.4'84—dc20
94–19901
CIP
MN

Typeset by MHL Typesetting Ltd, Coventry
Printed and bound in Great Britain by
Biddles Ltd, *www.biddles.co.uk*

For Titon and Julio
and in memory of my mother

Contents

Acknowledgements

Plates 1−6 are reproduced by kind permission of the British Museum. Plate 8 is reproduced by permission from *The New Grove Dictionary of Musical Instruments*, ed. Stanley Sadie (London: Macmillan, 1984). Plate 9 is Copyright 1965 Universal Edition; reproduced by permission. Plate 10 is Copyright 1974 Jugend und Volk; reproduced by permission of Julia Logothetis.

SCENARIO

Music . . . was bestowed for the sake of harmony. And harmony, which has motions akin to the revolutions of the soul within us, was given by the muses . . . not as an aid to irrational pleasure (as is now supposed), but as an auxiliary to the inner revolution of the soul, when it has lost its harmony, to assist in restoring it to order and concord with itself.

PLATO
fourth century BC

We shall now proceed to the consideration of harmonics and its parts. It is to be observed that in general the subject of our study is the question, in melody of every kind what are the natural laws according to which the voice places the intervals? For we hold that the voice follows a natural law in its motion . . .

ARISTOXENUS
third century BC

When they say the planets sing, they seem to be ignorant of what sound is.

JEAN DE GROUCHY
c.1300

The man that hath no music in himself,
Nor is not moved with concord and sweet sounds
Is fit for treasons, stratagems and spoils;
. . .
Let no such man be trusted

SHAKESPEARE
The Merchant of Venice V.i, 1596

Now divine air! Now is his soul ravished! Is it not strange that sheeps' guts should hale souls out of men's bodies?

SHAKESPEARE
Much Ado About Nothing III.iii, 1598

Without music no State could survive

Molière's Music Maser in
Le Bourgeois Gentilhomme, 1670

As long as we choose to consider sounds only through the commotion they stire in our nerves, we shall never have the true principles of music and of its power over our hearts. Sounds in the melody do n ot act solely as sounds, but as signs of our affections . . .

ROUSSEAU
(1712—78)

The two valets sit at the top of the table, but at least I have the honour of being placed above the cooks.

MOZART
(1756—91)

Speak to Goethe about this, tell him to listen to my symphonies, for then he will admit that music is the only entrance to that higher world of knowledge which, though it embraces a person, a person cannot grasp.

BEETHOVEN
(1770—1827)

A singer who sings like a bird is an unproductive worker. When she sells her song, she is a wage earner or merchant. But the same singer, employed by someone else to give concerts and bring in money, is a productive worker because she directly produces capital.

KARL MARX
(1818—83)

The passions enjoy themselves in the form of music.

NIETZSCHE
(1884—1900)

> You language where all language
> ends. You time
> standing vertically on the motion of mortal hearts.
> Feelings for whom? O you the transformation
> of feelings into what?

RILKE
(1875—1926)
To Music

I prefer a few notes from an Egyptian shepherd's pipe; he is part of the landscape and hears the harmonies not mentioned in your treaties.

DEBUSSY
(1862—1918)

If we compose music, we are also composed by history.

LUCIANO BERIO
(born 1925)

PART I

Introduction

1

Prologue: the Puzzle of Music

There's a nineteenth-century silhouette drawing which shows the great composers lining up in heaven to pay homage to their acknowledged master, Beethoven. The scene is eternal. It would be much the same if drawn today, only the queue would be longer. Imagine the conversation which passes between them as they wait. Beethoven has accepted the honour with a mixture of satisfied self-esteem and humility, for he protests with complete sincerity that 'Handel is the greatest of us all'. Handel, of course, won't hear of it; in any case he's too busy arguing with Verdi about Italian opera and nationalist politics which, cosmopolitan that he is, he barely understands. Bach, on the other hand, has rejected his own nomination by Mendelssohn and a host of camp followers from Palestrina to Busoni, on the grounds that all he did was to the greater glory of God and no man should usurp God's honour. Berg and Bartók are both embarrassed by the proceedings, indeed they're embarrassed to be there at all, in a heaven they don't believe in. Meanwhile Mendelssohn is somewhere in the middle of the queue heatedly discussing the metaphysics of musical expression with Stravinsky. You simply can't put words into music, he says. If someone asks me to explain a piece of music, he says, I tell them I can't do it, not because the music's too vague but because words are too vague. Haydn, overhearing, chimes in that someone once asked him if any of the movements of his symphonies were about anything special and he'd replied, yes, there was one, but he couldn't remember which, nor what it was about. And as he laughs, Mozart smiles wistfully to Schubert, as if to say, 'Dear old Papa Haydn, he never really ever suffered, did he?' Schubert smiles in agreement, as he pens a new song on the back of the invitation card.

Meanwhile, Wagner is sulking in a corner, peeved that the only person who nominated him for the seat of honour was Bruckner, yet even now Bruckner has wandered off somewhere, looking for Bach, to continue their yesterday's conversation about the monumental architecture of proper church music. Brahms is contentedly chatting in another corner with Charles Ives about polyphony, eager to learn as ever but completely bewildered. Stravinsky is trying, without much luck, to explain to Mendelssohn that it's not a question of how *precisely* music expresses something because music doesn't actually express anything. Our delight in music, he says, is like the delight we feel in the contemplation of the interplay of architectural forms. In any case, he adds, I really agree with Bach. I didn't compose *The Rite of Spring*, I was merely the vessel through which it passed. Not far away, Mahler is busily trying to teach a group of angels to sing the music from the last movement of his Fourth Symphony. Music, Stravinsky continues, is for me the justification for all things. The music, Mahler shouts back at him, in a spirit of mischief, is not in the notes, and all the angels laugh. Now *that's* how I want you to sing, Mahler says, turning back to them.

Then a strange figure enters; nobody's quite sure who he is. Permit me to introduce myself, he says. Adrian Leverkühn, by grace of Thomas Mann out of T.W. Adorno. Ah yes, someone says, you're the, um, 'hero' of *Dr Faustus*, I don't think you should really be here. Quite so, says the newcomer, can anyone tell me where to find Schoenberg?

'Let me tell you,' says Leverkühn when he finds his prey, listening in rapture to Mahler's angels, 'Let me tell you, I incline more and more to the admission that there is something very odd indeed about this music of yours. A manifestation of the highest energy — not at all abstract, but without an object, energy in a void, pure ether — where else in the universe does such a thing appear? We Germans have taken over from philosophy the expression "in itself", we use it every day without much idea of the metaphysical. But here you have it, such music is energy itself, yet not as idea, rather in its actuality. I call your attention to the fact' — he looks around him with a devilish grin on his face — 'that this is almost a definition of God. *Imitatio Dei* — I am surprised it is not forbidden.'[1]

Schoenberg is about to reply, but Saint Cecilia calls the proceedings to order.

What is it about music that lends itself to such fantasies? What embarrasses us about it? Why does it seem so difficult to talk about music in social and historical terms? Why does it seem to resist the kind of understanding and interpretation to which the other arts lend themselves so much more readily?

Western civilization proclaims its music as one of its proudest achievements. The sociologist Max Weber was only elaborating upon a view that has been widely held when he spoke of it in the Introduction to *The Protestant Ethic and the Spirit of Capitalism*:

The musical ear of other peoples has probably been even more sensitively developed than our own, certainly not less so. Polyphonic music of various kinds has been widely distributed over the earth. The co-operation of a number of instruments and also the singing of parts have existed elsewhere. All our rational tone intervals have been known and calculated. But rational harmonious music, both counterpoint and harmony, formation of the tone material on the basis of three triads with the harmonic third; our chromatics and enharmonics, not interpreted in terms of space, but, since the Renaissance, in terms of harmony; our orchestra, with its string quartet as a nucleus, and the organisation of ensembles of wind instruments; our bass accompaniment; our system of notation, which made possible the composition and production of modern musical works, and thus their very survival; our sonatas, symphonies, operas; and finally, as means to all these, our fundamental instruments, the organ, piano, violin, etc.; all these things are known only in the occident, although programme music, tone poetry, alteration of tones and chromatics, have existed in various musical traditions as means of expression.[2]

The unique properties of Western music (an explanation of the technicalities will come later) are for Weber part of a cluster of qualities resulting from the application of the same rational and systematic principles that produced Western capitalism itself. Capitalism, he holds, has to do with the restraint — that is to say, the rational tempering — of the irrational impulse to acquisition. By itself, he believes, the pursuit of gain, of money, of the greatest possible amount of money, is not yet capitalism. Capitalism is something more — the pursuit of profit, forever renewed by a special type of enterprise in which business is separated from household, corporate from personal property, and most important of all, for the calculations of capitalism are dependent on it, where the rational organization of 'free labour' is introduced. The achievements of Western music have depended no less on calculation as a means for the rational organization of labour in the production of music. In particular, the Western system of notation has allowed what the composer-conductor Lukas Foss once called the very unmusical idea of dividing what is essentially indivisible — music — into two separate processes: composition, the making of music, and performance, which is also the making of music. Through notation, composition becomes a calculable procedure based on comprehensible principles in a manner otherwise impossible, by which often very large forces in various combinations can be organized in harmonious co-operation. But there is a price. Western notation deals poorly with certain aspects of musical expression, like dynamics, attack and timbre, which cannot be calculated in the same way and given fixed values: their values are relative. At best, therefore, they are indicated by means of codes written alongside the stave, which are necessarily approximate and suggestive rather than precise and prescriptive. They do not disappear from performance, of course, but notation demotes them, they cease to carry any structural significance, and in some cases they are even repressed.

From this point of view the achievements of Western music begin to seem, if not the result of the same principles, then at least like a symbolic representation of what Western capitalism proclaims itself to have achieved in the social organization of production. An idealization, to be sure, since the truth is that the capitalist mode of production is constructed on a base not of harmonious, but of dissonant and antagonistic relationships. In fact, like every art-form, music is a site where as well as the dialogue of individual voices, competing ideologies engage in battle to express themselves, often through a kind of artistic guerrilla warfare. But this is largely obscured by the dominant modes of public discussion of music, which fail to see the links between music and society.

One of the problems is that the calculable procedures of Western music are responsible for a difficulty which has severely limited the socio-historical investigation of music. Music has long possessed a technical terminology which is frequently the envy of scholars of the other arts because of its apparently clear and unambiguous terms of reference. The language of this theory is so technical, however, that it's almost as impossible for someone with no formal education in music to read a piece of musical analysis as it is for someone who is not a chemist to read a research paper in chemistry. Partly, then, for the benefit of the non-specialist reader, but also because it in any case suits my purpose, I shall assume no prior technical knowledge in my approach to the musical material — only general knowledge of common terminology, and an average acquaintance with the musics of different styles and periods. This, after all, corresponds to the state of our music culture in the 1990s, which consists in a never-ending pot-pourri of the music of every historical period and every culture of the globe churned out by every speaker system and headphone set in sight, in which even television commercials lift their music from the classical record catalogues — in short, the fluid heterogeneous mix of styles dissociated from their origins which characterizes what has come to be called the postmodern condition. So one way or another, the likely reader of this book will probably have heard nearly all the music I talk about, even if only in the background, on the soundtrack of daily life in the metropolis. And in that case, it is only a question of identifying what is already familiar.

The conditions which dominate the public discussion of music were described by a young American composer, Elie Siegmeister, in a pamphlet published by the Workers' Music Association in 1938:

> While in literature the ivory tower, art-for-art's-sake theory is no longer accepted, this concept still prevails with regard to music, which is still considered

largely as a vague, intangible experience, unrelated to all other experiences, whose chief function is to entertain, uplift, provide subjective emotional satisfaction to each individual in his own way ... In present-day musical criticism there is no general agreement on the nature and function of music, its place in society, or contemporary problems.[3]

A spiritual view of music therefore holds sway, problematic not because it is spiritual but because it includes the notion that music comes from a source of which we are ignorant, points to something beyond (and thus serves as an excellent substitute for religion), and remains unaffected by material conditions. Not only is this attitude still dominant, but so is the corollary which Siegmeister observed:

... if these doctrines are unhesitatingly accepted by those concerned with music, as for the most part they actually are, musicians will not question the social bases of the conditions under which they work, nor the social function of their work. The public, too, will patiently accept the musical status quo, believing that since music is unrelated to material conditions, and is, furthermore, entirely the affair of a few individuals, they, as the mere audience, cannot possibly have any influence on the development of the art. Composers will go on creating in the same way for the same people, contemplating the 'inner soul' and never questioning the society under which such activity is doomed to frustration in advance.

Conversely, the spread of a realistic, social view of music would be dangerous to those for whom the confusion and mysticism of the present viewpoint is valuable. Once we begin to look upon this art as part of the social organism, we are rudely awakened out of the idyllic dream-world of the romantic biographers and radio commentators ... We find that, as in other fields, capitalism has created the most magnificent apparatus for the production, distribution and consumption of music that the world has ever seen: yet this apparatus is so riddled with contradictions basically economic in origin that it negates its own potentialities ...[4]

Exactly the same argument is presented by the editors of a much more recent book called *Music and Society*, who contend that as long as music is regarded as a purely autonomous activity, then the apparatus, including the technologies and the institutions, which determine what is performed, published, recorded and broadcast, remain in crucial ways invisible (or inaudible).[5] They are merely the channels through which the composer's subjectivity comes into contact with that of the listener, and the mystical union of composer and listener admits of no actual mediation. However, once the processes of mediation become matters for discussion, they believe, the components of that mystical union fall apart, adding that perhaps the most disturbing loss that then occurs is the dissolution of the traditional construct of subjectivity itself.

But there are powerful ideological reasons why music should retain what the cultural theorist Edward Said calls its 'reticence, mystery, or allusive silence'. Musician and layperson, he says, both collude in sustaining this condition, which disconnects it from its worldly context and 'symbolises its autonomy as an art'.[6] Indeed the idea of a form of expression purged of the temporal and contingent concerns of daily life is highly seductive. Supported by the long tradition, going back to Pythagoras, which assimilates music to the laws of mathematical harmony and proportion and places it in the realms of 'pure knowledge', music provides a special kind of ideological reassurance. It becomes the last refuge of 'authentic' values in an age given over to the clash of rival ideologies in which all ideology is seen as flawed.

These themes crop up in various ways in the pages which follow. There is no sense in denying music's subjectivity, but if the experience of music is subjective then this subjectivity is not so spontaneous and naïve as usually supposed, but is constructed by the subject's own social, cultural and historical situation and self-interest. As for the autonomy of music, it is relative. On the one hand, each artistic medium is an independent mode of expression with its own logic and its own laws of development. On the other, this logic is constrained, again by social, cultural and historical factors. The problem is that such external determinants are always symbolically coded, frequently in paradoxical ways.

Another aspect of our highly capitalized and technologized music industry is that as music comes to be heard more in the background than played for personal diversion, the widespread practical knowledge of music which comes from its educated amateur practice has been displaced and demoted. It is part of this syndrome that the integral place occupied by music in liberal humanist education has been lost, and music has become an increasingly isolated technical study. The process has been accompanied by distinctive cultural effects. On the one hand, musicians, who since the early nineteenth century have been trained increasingly in conservatoires, have become progressively more ignorant of the general developments of intellectual thought. Hence the impression given by the discipline of musicology of being intellectually retarded: as Said observes, even the best musicologists 'seem not to have kept pace with many of the great advances made in other branches of humanistic interpretation' such as linguistics, anthropology and semiotics.[7] On the other hand, the exponents of those developments have themselves grown less and less familiar with music, especially as the accomplishments of amateur musicianship diminished after the First World War. The centrality of the musical experience for the modernist movement at the beginning of this century — evidence the work of writers and poets like Proust, Mann, Rilke, Eliot and Joyce — seems to have been lost, partly because the academic industry which interprets them for later generations is lacking the necessary knowledge of music to understand it. It is deeply symptomatic that almost none of the numerous books which have appeared in the last few years on the question of postmodernism makes even passing reference to music. Max Weber's advanced technical knowledge of music is thus a reminder of a different age; today, figures like Edward Said, a literary scholar who sports the musical knowledge of the good amateur pianist, are almost unique, at any rate in English-speaking academia.

Indeed the twentieth century seems to have witnessed a near breakdown in critical knowledge of one of the central arts of Western society, even though music itself continues to play a crucial role in cultural life. The latter is amply registered in the responses it unceasingly evokes not only from dancers and choreographers but also from poets, writers, plastic artists and film-makers, all involved in parallel aesthetic endeavours and always eager to collaborate with composers. Nonetheless, intellectual discussion of music has frequently remained entrapped in an idealist, sometimes sub-Hegelian discourse, even in the one modern scholar for whom its social dimensions were always paramount, Theodor Wiesengrund Adorno. Philosopher, sociologist and trained musician, Adorno was one of the first to perceive how the industrialization of culture over the past hundred years or so has not only markedly extended the social reach of the high musical tradition but at the same time transformed the conditions of listening. For Adorno this process distorted the very enjoyment of music, because the process of commercialization ends up by fetishizing certain qualities and features at the cost of others, not only in the music directly produced under commercial conditions but in the old music which the music industry feeds on too. It is inevitable that a good part of this book should consist in a dialogue with Adorno's extensive writings on music.

Seventy-odd years since Adorno first wrote about music, a more adequate and realistic 'social view of music' has finally begun to develop. His ideas are now more widely discussed, at least in intellectual circles, and the dialogue with Adorno is now also a dialogue with a range of writers who have taken up the same issues. There is no single dominant paradigm among these new approaches. They are the work of sociologists, anthropologists, semiologists, social historians, economists and even a few musicologists, which include a number of feminist studies. My own approach ranges between them. I also survey incursions into music by thinkers like Claude Lévi-Strauss, Roland Barthes and Umberto Eco, who remind us that Anglo-Saxon culture is more compartmentalized than European culture. All in all, the phenomenon of music is so diverse and kaleidoscopic that as our interest moves from one area of investigation to another, there is no individual theoretical framework and no single discipline which can adequately comprehend it. (If the reader identifies this as a trait of postmodernist theory, so be it. However it should not be taken to imply adherence to other theoretical positions with which I do not concur.)

Weber provides a crucial starting point. He did not conceive the Western musical idiom in the same way that wittingly or unwittingly most of its theorists have done for centuries: as a complete, logical and closed system. He argued that the Western musical system of harmony and chords is constructed on a contradiction between its method of rationalization and the intractable irrationality of what may be called its material basis in nature — in other words, the facts of acoustical physics. Only by constructing scales and devising methods of tuning which suppress certain oddities in the physical behaviour of sound did the fullest development of harmonic chordal music become possible. The argument is contained in a compact and highly technical essay, *The Rational and Social Foundations of Music*.[8] Unfortunately never completed, it was published a year after his death in 1921 but written around 1911 — the same year as another and towering work of musical theory which perhaps surprisingly it turns out to complement, namely, Schoenberg's *Harmonielehre* ('Treatise on Harmony').[9] This book, at the time the most comprehensive analysis yet of the idiom that had dominated Western music since about 1600, completely overturned the ideological view of Western music as a closed system by portraying it as a dynamic and continuing evolutionary process.

Harmonielehre has nothing directly to do with the twelve-tone (or dodecaphonic) method of composition for which Schoenberg later became notorious, and which was not formulated until the early 1920s, although as we shall later see, it explains a good deal about how he got there. It is decisively informed, however, by the new psychological currents of thought of its place and time. Since this was Vienna at the beginning of the century, it is presumably not an accident that Schoenberg, although he was no Freudian, evinces profound consideration for the unconscious, and the role its creative powers have played in constantly expanding the frontiers of harmony, until eventually the system began to disintegrate under its own weight and the astounding result was atonality. That is, technically, the abandonment of harmony and the key system which had operated since the Renaissance. It also seemed to produce a rejection of the tunefulness of all music since prehistoric times, but Schoenberg rejected this charge; and indeed nowadays our hearing has been transformed and it's much easier to hear the melody in atonal music. Of course tonality never disappeared; it was more as if music split up into an avant-garde who rejected the vernacular, and everyone else, who in one form or another retained it. Albeit an over-simplification, this bifurcation helps to define our subject: the trajectory of Western music coincides with the rise and fall of a unitary system conventionally known as harmony, from its pre-Renaissance origins down to the end of the nineteenth century. But in the twentieth century this unique firmament has suffered dislocation and displacement by a new plurality. It turns out, then, first that this trajectory is not a linear one, and secondly that the radical shifts which have occurred over the past hundred years or so raise large question marks over its previous sense of direction, not only by undermining long-established traditions and creating new and quite open possibilities, but also by rediscovering facets of music which the high musical tradition of European civilization had repressed.

I begin this book with a section entitled *The Shaping Forces of Music*, which examines the underlying conditions behind the evolution of the Western musical tradition: the presence of music in the community, the role of the Church, the development and effects of notation; I also look at the fundamental question of music and psyche. This is an alternative approach to that of established musicological authorities, who describe a tradition based on written scores and therefore far too restricted. They also tend to pass over in silence another crucial issue: the sense of separation between Western and other musics which first developed in the early Renaissance, when modern notation was established and the ancient modes began giving way to the characteristic European scales of major and minor. The technical basis for this scale system goes back to the ancient Greeks, the first Europeans to calculate the proportions of the notes which divide the octave. It was they who originated the system of modes inherited by medieval Europe, from whose decay the Renaissance sense of harmony then emerged. These underpinnings are examined in Part IV, *Musical Engineering*, in the course of an inquiry into the evolution of musical instruments.

This discussion of instruments as technology is preceded by a section on *The Political Economy of Music*. One of my main concerns is to examine the scope of external determinants upon musical form and style, the nature of the social forces which condition our musical traditions. If Western music, in the course of its trajectory, takes on the aspect of a symbolic representation of Western capitalism, this is because music is always — among other things — an expression of actual or ideal social relations. There are certain affinities between the forms of music making and those of society. Pierre Boulez, for example, composer-conductor and leader of the post-war avant-garde, has remarked on the suspicious similarity of the symphony orchestra to a factory, with the conductor as a kind of managing director. He is not the only one to notice the comparison; actually, the first person to observe an analogy between the orchestra and the factory was Karl Marx. And more recently, a similar suggestion has been made, from a somewhat different political perspective, by Crawford H. Greenewalt,

President of the Du Pont Corporation. 'Perhaps the best analogy to an executive's job', he says, 'is that of the symphony conductor under whose hand a hundred or so highly specialized and yet very different skills become a single effort of great effectiveness.'[10] In short, the groups which musicians constitute, the relations they engage in when playing or performing, these are analogues either of existing patterns of social relations, or else their idealization, their ideological refraction. It is not for nothing that from Plato to John Cage, music has been an agent of utopian thinking in all its various guises.

Music seems in this respect to belong to the social superstructure, the political, legal, religious, aesthetic and philosophical, or in short, ideological forms, in which, according to Marx, humanity becomes conscious of historical conflict and fights it out.[11] I am not speaking here of the stereotyped Marx, the economic determinist, the denuded figure of vulgar Marxism, or what Sartre described as lazy Marxism, which sees the superstructure as nothing more than the effect of the economic base, determined by economic forces to which it can be reduced − this has nothing to do with the present study. That now discredited approach is merely mechanistic, and largely a product of the institutionalization of Marx's writing by official communist ideology. The effect was to clamp dialectical thinking within rigid categories, from which those who contested the orthodox interpretation did not by any means manage to escape themselves. As a result, much of what Marx wrote remained buried from sight even after previously unpublished texts became available. Among these neglected texts are a number of passages where Marx, in order to illustrate some economic process, uses music as an example. As we shall later see, these passages are often highly suggestive, hinting at a subtlety in the economic moulding of cultural production which at the end of the twentieth century is more critical than ever.

Economic forces do not determine but they condition very strongly and are reinforced by ideological effects. The character of Western music is therefore only intelligible on condition that we give proper economic account of it. Music is an economically productive field in its own right, which duplicates on a smaller scale the structure of the social and economic macrocosm to which it belongs. If we wish to evaluate the present highly critical situation of music, we must analyse the history of the productive apparatus which it began to acquire the moment music printing arrived, turning music into a commodity and creating a new market. The relationship which ensues within the development of music from that moment on between economics and aesthetics is far more complex than proponents of the base/superstructure model have generally allowed. For, while the economic development of music is embedded within the development of the general forces of production which surround it, its development is heavily conditioned by its own peculiar nature as an aesthetic product, whose essential features enable it repeatedly to escape direct determination and fulfil its own immanent laws.

The labour expended in musical creation, as in all forms of cultural production, is peculiar: it cannot be fully and properly quantified, it is not essentially susceptible to control by managements. The result is that the art-form always makes for a somewhat peculiar commodity, in which the essential value is determined by non-economic factors. But each form of cultural production also manifests peculiarities which depend on the material characteristics of the form in question. There are characteristic differences here between the performing arts, which before the twentieth century could only realize exchange value through gate-money, the fine arts, which produced unique originals whose market price is essentially speculative, and literature, which since the invention of printing was mass produced. But there is one underlying common factor: artistic creation works according to its own timetables and cannot be reduced to the sale of average labour-power. A crucial consequence is that the need of the body politic to constrain it calls forth ideological pressures designed to force or induce the artistic creator to conform. As a result, the process is mediated by a whole variety of factors which orthodox approaches fail to acknowledge, factors which all need careful study in order to gauge their effects. Furthermore, in the last hundred years the mediation of music has radically changed through the startling mutation of its commodity forms brought about by new means of reproduction and diffusion — technologies whose properties are actually far from mechanical.

The following section on instruments, called *Musical Engineering*, is intended to answer one of the most curious omissions in orthodox histories of music. The historical development of musical forms and styles is intricately related to the changing mode of production of music, which affects the relations of production in various ways. This refers not only to how the musical ensemble is organized but also to such factors as who the musicians are employed by and the way they are paid, the purposes for which music is used, the places where it is performed and the size and composition of the audience. These things all contribute to determining the forms and styles of the age. But at the same time, as the so-called early music movement has vividly demonstrated, the musical idiom is also conditioned by the kinds of instruments upon which musicians play (and as we shall see, the way they are tuned). Bach, played on period instruments directed from the harpsichord, is almost a different composer from a performance of the same work by a symphony orchestra under a traditional conductor with the continuo played on a piano. Instruments, however, depend in turn upon the techniques and forms of technology employed in their manufacture. Yet in spite of the growing number of period instrument

makers, and their knowledge of old forms of artisanal production, the
question seems hardly to have entered the ken of academic musicology, still
less of popular commentators. Generally it is only the electrical and
electronic which are thought of as technological, and scant attention is paid
to technological (and economic) factors in the history of traditional
instruments. The two chapters which make up Part IV are intended to
point to a more adequate approach to these issues. The question of modern
electrophonic instruments is then taken up in the last section of the book.

This last section is devoted to *Music in the Age of Electro-acoustics*. The
industrialization of music, which brought about the critical condition
described by Siegmeister and Adorno, involved an unprecedented
mutation in musical experience, a transformation in musical life insepar-
able from the effects of modern technology. The story begins with the
introduction of mechanical reproduction, which starts to impact upon
musical life around the turn of the nineteenth century; there follows the rise
of radio broadcasting after the First World War, and the introduction of the
film sound-track. After the Second World War comes the multiplication
and perfection of recording and transmission systems which is still going
on: LP, magnetic tape, stereo, audio cassette, compact disc, digital
recording; and the convergence with television, video and the computer
chip. Economically this is a tale of repeated expansion, recession and
regeneration, and the transformation of the music business and its markets
through the development of novel forms of consumption.

The gramophone record, descended from the primitive phonograph
patented by Edison in 1877, is not only a new commodity in itself, but for
the first time turns the performance of music, previously intangible, into a
vendible object. The aesthetic effects of this transformation were already
multiplying when the gramophone was joined by radio. The seeds of
broadcast radio were planted in the years leading up to the First World
War, reaching fruition after the war as an indirect result of wartime
military investment. The development of amplification and the loudspeaker, not to mention the improvement of the microphone, was also to
benefit the phonograph, and by the mid-1920s the record industry began to
fight back against radio with the introduction of electrical recording and a
huge improvement in the quality of recorded sound. In consequence, radio
and records fell upon each other rapaciously. Radio fed off records to fill up
airtime, while records were attracted to radio as an aural showcase. After
heavy battles had been fought over the questions of copyright, both media
also provided important additional sources of income for publishers and
composers.

In the course of this process, the age-old dialogue of musical
communication was radically upset. Above all, the technique of reproduction — mechanical, electrical or electronic — creates a distance, both

physical and psychic, between performer and audience that simply never existed before, which produces new ways for music to be heard and allows the listener totally new ways of using it. In the words of Walter Benjamin's crucial essay on the subject, 'The Work of Art in the Age of Mechanical Reproduction', the effect is to put a copy of the original into situations which are out of reach of the original itself, like a choral performance played in a drawing room.[12] Nowadays, being further down the same road, we can listen to opera while travelling on the underground, Bach while driving along the motorway, or Mahler while flying high above the ocean. Not to mention John Coltrane, Ravi Shankar, Youssou N'Dour or Los Van Van. Even if the work in itself were to remain untouched in this process, the quality of its presence is reduced and diminished, like the image of a landscape on a television screen. In short, the technique of reproduction detaches the musical work from the domain of the tradition which gave birth to it, and destroys the aura which signals its authenticity. A mutation of musical communication has occurred in which live performance has become a mere adjunct to most people's musical experience, which now comes to them overwhelmingly through loud-speakers and even earphones. This is the condition which Pierre Schaeffer, pioneer of *musique concrète*, called acousmatic: sounds which one hears without seeing their source. In the acousmatic world, the integrity of the musical work, its intimate unity with the time and place of performance, perhaps the most essential aspect of what Benjamin called its aura, has been destroyed. Music has become literally disembodied, and the whole of musical experience has been thrown into a chronic state of flux. And in these circumstances, in which ubiquitous mechanical reproduction pushes music into the realms of noise pollution, it often seems that musical values must inevitably become relative.

But the process is not entirely negative. Bartók, one of the first ethnomusicologists to make field recordings, once said that listening to phonographic recordings was like examining musical objects under a microscope. This recalls something else Benjamin observed, about the way film enriched our perception in a manner comparable, he said, to Freudian theory. Before Freud,

a slip of the tongue passed more or less unnoticed. Only exceptionally may such a slip have revealed dimensions of depth in a conversation which had seemed to be taking its course on the surface. Since *The Psychopathology of Everyday Life* things have changed. This book isolated and made analysable things which had heretofore floated along unnoticed in the broad stream of perception. For the entire spectrum of optical, and [with the addition of sound to film] now also of acoustical, perception, the film has brought about a similar deepening of apperception. It is only an obverse of this fact that behaviour items shown in a movie can be analysed much more precisely and from more points of view than those presented in paintings or on the stage.[13]

Recording has had the same effect on musical apperception. It has radically changed the way in which music is heard by the inner ear, so to speak, and not just by throwing the production of music on the mercy of the market: at the same time, our hearing has been gradually reawakened to dimensions of musical expression repressed by the hegemony of notation, marginalized or even expelled from the civilized Western musical idiom, like the quarter tones and microtonal inflections which Bartók discovered in Eastern European and Mediterranean folk music.

Is it an accident that over the same period as the introduction of the new technology of reproduction, music experienced a revolution in its every aspect? That figures like Debussy, Schoenberg, Berg, Webern, Bartók and Stravinsky turned it inside out and upside down, which not only left it utterly transformed but also became paradigmatic for the whole modernist movement? I hardly want to suggest that technology was the sufficient cause of this transformation, but neither is it neutral, or merely secondary to aesthetic and spiritual processes. The rupture of the musical language is often understood as the explosion of an internal crisis in artistic expression brought on by the artist's growing alienation. It was long conceived essentially as a product of the relation between psychology and technique, combined with the susceptibilities of a fateful *fin-de-siècle* — a conception largely produced by the shared time and place of birth of modernism and psychoanalysis. But a hundred years later, on the eve of the millennium, immersed in a new global cultural crisis, the modernist revolution reveals new aspects and now appears above all as a pivotal episode in the continual process of modernization, a process synonymous with capitalism especially since the industrial revolution.

To follow David Harvey's incisive analysis of *The Condition of Postmodernity*, the roots of the process are found in the transformation of daily experience through the compression of time and space which is integral to the development of industrial capitalism, from steamships, railways and the telegraph, to jet air travel, communications satellites and the digital computerization of information. What popular language calls the media are implicated as both symptoms and agents of this process. As modern technologies of communication have progressively shortened the horizons of time and space, 'so we have [had] to learn how to cope with an overwhelming sense of *compression* of our spatial and temporal worlds'.[14] Here, in short, is one of the root causes of both our modern disenchantment and the artistic revolution of the twentieth century. At a critical moment, in the years leading up to the First World War, the sense of plight overwhelmed each of the traditional forms of artistic expression in turn: not just music but painting, sculpture, dance, drama, the novel, poetry and architecture, all experienced the process of disruption and renewal identified by the term modernism. The whole business was thrown into relief by the birth of a new aesthetic medium, film, itself a technological product of the process of modernization, which provided novel means for reconstructing the experience of time and space in terms of each other.

Modernism registered the progressive acceleration of the rhythms of social and individual experience, the fallout of technological innovation in both public and private domains. Artistic imagination vicariously sensed the disruption and immanent disintegration of the traditional cultural order which these innovations entailed, and set about creating new models for coping with it. Not by choice but because such is its vocation. But modernism now belongs to the past. It is said that we have entered a new aesthetic phase, the postmodern, in which the entire cultural process has been taken over by the globalization of media and communications, and the concomitant law of information.

Stylistically, postmodernism is even more diverse, contradictory and contrary than modernism. With all its confusions and conundrums, it is neither a style nor a movement in the traditional sense at all (except perhaps in architecture, where the term originated), nor even a concept, so much as a force-field which holds every form of cultural activity in its grip. The cultural process is overwhelmed by the endless and instantaneous electronic proliferation of images, signs and signals of every kind − a flood which renders all cultural symbols increasingly orphaned and rootless. Nothing is what it seems, for every image tends to becomes a simulation or simulacrum, for which there is no longer a unique and authentic original. From cradle unto grave the atomized consumer is subjected to continuous overload. Moreover, the unending flow is mediated by the practices, devices and theories of the advertisers, whose devious methods also increasingly invade the most traditional sectors of cultural production. Modernism, says the cultural theorist Fredric Jameson, was still the critique of the commodity; postmodernism is the consumption of sheer commodification as a process. Culture has become a supermarket. The result is 'the penetration of commodity fetishism into those realms of the imagination and the psyche which had . . . always been taken as the last impregnable stronghold against the instrumental logic of capital'.[15] Like music.

There is a profound contrast, to be sure, between the modern and the postmodern, but also a crucial continuity. If Jameson is right that the concept of modernism implicitly refers to 'the social and psychic damage' which was done to previous forms of human life and perception, now irrecoverable, then postmodernism is not the negation of modernism but its intensification. The difference is only the same as what separates the monopoly or imperialist stage of capitalism from its multinational or global stage: they are stages within the same mode of production.[16]

But there is still a real transformation in the conditions of cultural production, stemming from a contradiction in what Mark Poster calls *The Mode of Information*.[17] Capitalist economics assumes that resources are scarce and therefore their allocation is best determined by market mechanisms. It also assumes that you can't have your cake and eat it too, the product can only be consumed once. But information isn't like that — and neither is music.

First, the consumption of information is like the act of cultural consumption: nothing happens to destroy the commodity. Secondly, information is cheap and easy to amass, and becoming ever easier to copy. Until recently, the laws of copyright which regulate the market for cultural products functioned well enough, because commodities like books and records (not to mention films) were relatively difficult to reproduce, or at least required considerable investment in the appropriate apparatus to do so. The latest technologies have changed all that: photocopiers, sound and video recorders, digital scanners and computers make every consumer into a potential reproducer. Whatever becomes information, anyone can now store and reproduce, repackage and refashion to their own purposes without anyone's permission, without payment, and largely without detection. Hence the expanding domain of information threatens the principle of private property. As a result, the progressive 'informatization' of cultural production brings about what the French economist Jacques Attali calls a rupture in the laws of classical economics.[18]

The results can be heard in the cacophony and confusion of contemporary music, which the recent introduction of synthesizers and samplers has only increased. On the one hand, the technification of music has distorted the process of listening and damaged our hearing. On the other, it increasingly throws everything back into the arena, as the ease of reproduction allows the circulation of music to escape the control of the market and discover new forms. In short, the old hierarchies of aesthetic taste and judgement may have broken down, but music continues to breathe and to live according to its own immanent criteria.

The inspiration for this book goes back to the period I spent as a music critic in the late 1960s and early 1970s, and especially what I learned from personal dialogue with a number of composers — including Pierre Boulez, Peter Maxwell Davies, Harrison Birtwistle, Michael Nyman — and the philosopher Isaiah Berlin. The embryo of the present text is an essay with the title 'The Trajectory of Western Music' which appeared in *Media, Culture and Society* in 1981, and which I could not have written without the crucial help of Glyn Perrin, who was also generous with his time and help while these pages were being drafted. Thanks also to Fredric Jameson for his encouragement; to Katerina Wolpe and Olivia Harris, who read and commented valuably on different sections; and to Steve Stanton and Ken Hirschkop, who read the complete manuscript; Steve Stanton also helped with the preparation of the illustrations. Finally my special thanks to Pat Kahn for her ever cheerful sustenance, both intellectual and otherwise.

Notes

1. Thomas Mann, *Doctor Faustus*, Secker & Warburg, London 1949, p. 78.
2. Max Weber, *The Protestant Ethic and the Spirit of Capitalism*, Unwin University Books, London 1930, pp. 14−15.
3. Elie Siegmeister, *Music and Society*, Workers' Music Association, London 1943, p. 45.
4. Ibid., pp. 6−7.
5. Richard Leppert and Susan McLary, eds, *Music and Society: the Politics of Composition, Performance and Reception*, Cambridge University Press, Cambridge 1987.
6. Edward Said, *Musical Elaborations*, Chatto & Windus, London 1991, p. 16.
7. Ibid., pp. x−xi.
8. Max Weber, *The Rational and Social Foundations of Music*, Southern Illinois University Press/Feffer & Simons, London 1977.
9. Arnold Schoenberg, *Theory of Harmony*, Faber & Faber, London 1978.
10. Boulez interviewed in *The Politics of Music*, dir. M. Chanan, BBC2, 1972; Karl Marx, Preface to *A Contribution to the Critique of Political Economy*, Lawrence & Wishart, London 1971; Greenwalt quoted in Baran and Sweezy, *Monopoly Capital*, Penguin, London 1968, p. 58.
11. The formulation comes from Marx, 1971, p. 21.
12. Walter Benjamin, 'The Work of Art in the Age of Mechanical Reproduction', in *Illuminations*, ed. Hannah Arendt, Schocken, New York 1969.
13. Ibid., p. 235.
14. David Harvey, *The Condition of Postmodernity*, Blackwell, Oxford 1990, p. 240.
15. Fredric Jameson, Foreword to J.-F. Lyotard, *The Postmodern Condition: A Report on Knowledge*, Manchester University Press, Manchester 1984, p. xv.
16. See Fredric Jameson, *Postmodernism, or, The Cultural Logic of Late Capitalism*, Verso, London 1991.
17. Mark Poster, *The Mode of Information*, Polity Press, Cambridge 1990.
18. See Jacques Attali, *Noise*, Manchester University Press, Manchester 1989.

PART II

The Shaping Forces of Music

2

Musica Practica

Music and Community

Music is performance art. What does this mean apart from gate-money, deficits, impresarios, agents, copyright, trades unions, the financial (and emotional) insecurity of rank-and-file musicians? It means the break, the rupture, the abyss between the world of these social agents and the space of music itself, where the form of interaction is embodied differently: through a language of sonic gesture that begins and ends beyond words. Music is a form of social communication; musical performance is a site of social intercourse, and a form of social dialogue.

According to Claude Lévi-Strauss there is an embarrassing problem about this. There are senders of music, composers, and there are receivers, 'the whole of mankind'. This is very different, says the anthropologist, from the situation with natural language, where 'the senders and the receivers are exactly as numerous as each other . . . with music the number of senders is extremely restricted while the number of receivers is very large'. There is consequently the problem of 'a language which is not working as a language should'.[1] This gives rise to a second problem: 'this kind of language cannot be translated into anything else, except itself. You can translate music into music. You can shape the melody from major to minor. You can even devise a mathematical equation which will permit you to change according to a certain rule the interval between the notes of a melody and it will be a translation of the melody. But you cannot translate music into speech . . .'

There is something odd about this argument. It almost makes it sound as if you ought to be able to translate one composer into another — Beethoven into Schoenberg, perhaps? or Pergolesi into Stravinsky? — when the phenomenon Lévi-Strauss is describing is rather different, a matter of the inner fabric of music: techniques of various orders, like transposition or inversion, by which sequences of tones are manipulated and a composition built up — in short, a form of discourse, which Stravinsky called simply 'the game of notes', that is never absent in any kind of music but is particularly developed in the Western tradition which promotes the office of the composer. It is no accident that the idea of the composer is co-extensive with the development of European musical notation, which (as Weber argues) facilitates this type of music. Take this context away and Lévi-Strauss's embarrassing problem looks different. Where are the composers of 'primitive' societies?

In surviving oral cultures the relation between musical senders and receivers is much more fluid and symbiotic than in modern Western society. The anthropological evidence is unequivocal. There are no composers in such societies set apart from other musicians in a separate caste, and music is far from an exclusive activity of specialized performers. Specialization may exist, either because certain types of music, associated with special activities like rite and ritual, are the prerogative of particular groups like shamans and priests, or because exceptional musical talent makes itself felt even in the least developed musical conditions. But tribal community encourages and sustains a degree of musical ability in virtually all its members through the widespread use of informal music. Moreover, music enters into the widest range of activities. There are songs for all sorts of everyday matters: to help cure disease, to make magic, to stimulate erotic emotions, to put children to sleep. There are work songs, to regulate the pace and co-ordinate the efforts of a group of workers. And of course there is music for ceremonies and warfare, celebrations and funerals. As Elie Siegmeister comments, 'no more effective means of creating a sense of group solidarity has ever been found than joint participation in music of this character'.[2]

The communal functions of music did not disappear with the demise of tribal society; on the contrary, until now every type of human society has succoured them. But as the millennium draws to a close, the conditions of musical life are radically different. Music is with us all the time, but is made by relatively few, and most of it is not heard as live performance at all. Professional musicians are socially distinct; full-time performing musicians rarely play with rank amateurs. Perhaps the separation is not as great as often supposed. According to a survey of non-professional music making in an English town by the social anthropologist Ruth Finnegan, many amateur ensembles actually include semi-professionals — people who earn their living in some area of the music business or teaching, though not primarily from performance. An amateur musician herself, Finnegan reports her surprise on discovering how much musical activity went on in the southern English town of Milton Keynes, and calls her book *The Hidden Musicians*.[3] But she also reports on the rifts and schisms which characterize this activity, and the lack of common ground between its different factions.

On the other hand, there is evidence that among the younger generation this is changing: attending a performance recently by an East Anglian youth orchestra, I was told that every member of the large percussion section and several of the instrumentalists also played regularly in rock or jazz bands.[4]

Nevertheless the general situation is clear. Art music and popular music are not only separate camps, there are also different camps within each of them. The professional composer may still be found at the centre of the edifice (an Andrew Lloyd Webber no less than a Peter Maxwell Davies) but is somehow marginalized at the same time, remaining largely isolated from social intercourse with the wider audience. It is not the general public which attends premieres and first nights. Like the audience at the concerts of the avant-garde, it consists in a loose fraternity of people with professional reasons for being there: musicians, artistic collaborators, publishers and agents, critics, radio, television and record producers. In the theatre, the gods are occupied by camp followers, in the concert hall the back rows are mostly students, who debate the music and sometimes buy it.

The perception of a lack, a void in the relationship of the composer to the wider community, became the central preoccupation of a group of socially conscious composers in Germany in the 1920s, several of them collaborators of the playwright Bertolt Brecht, including Paul Hindemith, Hanns Eisler and Kurt Weill. This is what lies behind the idea of *Gebrauchsmusik*, which was formulated by Hindemith. It is often translated as 'social utility music', or sometimes 'functional music', but I would be tempted to call it simply 'useful music' if Lloyd Webber hadn't debased the connotations of the word by calling his company the Really Useful Group: the point is the contrast Hindemith meant to draw with both traditional concert music on the one hand, and on the other, *Verbrauchsmusik*, commercial music — what French music publishers call *musique-papier*, the 'paper music' which forms the bulk of the music publisher's trade. The composers involved in this debate argued about the terminology, but all of them attacked the traditional apparatus of professional musical culture, which left the audience in a passive condition and separated musicians into a confraternity on their own; at the same time they took the social responsibility of music more seriously than those who claimed that they were usefully serving popular taste but simply kept piling up paper music.

Complaints by composers against the sloth of the professional musical apparatus are hardly unusual today, but in the 1920s the sense of urgency about the problem was relatively new, the transformation of the patterns of musical consumption by mechanical reproduction being still in its early phase. The image of the time constructed today by the nostalgia industry omits its most salient characteristics. The swinging twenties' carefree pursuit of novelty followed the unprecedented devastation of a war that ended in revolutions both successful (in Russia) and defeated (in Germany and Hungary); and its underbelly was political agitation and inflation, leading to the Great Depression and to fascism. These were also years of crisis in the music industry, and by the end of the decade, professional live music had begun to decline, musicians were forced out of work, the composer's pattern of earnings were disrupted. The musical temperament was channelled through the novel and paradoxical effects of reproduction by gramophone and radio, the effects of each multiplied by the other. These conditions did not encourage a lot of risk-taking. With little exception, new commercial forces in the music industry quickly became fixated upon the masterpieces of the past. The classical canon was closed off against intrusion; everything unfamiliar, untried, and experimental was left out in the cold.

A quasi-religious attitude to 'serious' music had already been detected by the poet Heine the better part of a century earlier, but even nineteenth-century bourgeois culture had not entailed the passivity of the listener in anything like the same degree as the new culture industry. Indeed quite the opposite: the commercial spirit of nineteenth-century capitalism had expanded the exploitation of music by developing new amateur markets. Of course it is true that the nineteenth-century concert hall cultivated a more respectful listening attitude, an attitude of secular devotion towards the pose of heroic individualism in the Romantic artist. This was the ideological refraction of the contradictory social position of artistic creation in the new bourgeois society, for on the one hand the artist was encouraged to claim the individualism promoted by the dominant ideology, and on the other, derided and penalized for departing, as a result, from the decorum and bounds which society leaders deemed permissible and in accordance with polity. Yet at the same time, the burgeoning commercial culture reinforced the bourgeois ideal in strongly promoting the role of the amateur musician, not only in the home and family but in the public arena as well. By the middle of the century, it was this market which provided the music publisher with the backbone of his trade.

Naturally there were variations in the forms of musical activity in the different social classes, and each had its own characteristic repertoire, but there was also plenty of overlap: the upper classes cultivated the salon, the orchestral academy, and the singing clubs; the middle echelons went in for domestic music making and orchestral and choral societies; below stairs and among the working classes, parlour music, choral societies and brass bands all flourished, as well as the informality of the tavern and the music hall. This wealth of activity stimulated a huge expansion in musical education over the course of the century which has recently been chronicled by several social historians, together with the philosophy that went with it. Musical pursuits were encouraged within the family for basically the same reason as mill- and mine-owners later encouraged them among their workers: they provided a means of disciplined socialization. There was also the self-interest of the age of utilitarianism. Within the milieu of the salon, a young woman could use the display of musical accomplishment to attract a marriage partner, a man to seek employment.

The growth of the music industry during the course of the nineteenth century largely centred around the piano. The spread of the piano served to promote some of the most successful commercial ventures of the epoch, like salon music, or the stream of arrangements of operas and symphonies which fulfilled the same function as records did a century later, but actively rather than passively. As a result, alongside the use of music for non-musical ends, the spread of musical education also produced distinctly musical effects. As long as an audience is made up of listeners who themselves play and sing, their listening also becomes, in crucial respects, an active process. Such listeners are able to adopt an attitude which bases its musical judgement neither on subjective emotion, nor on detached intellect, but on a third matrix: the practical knowledge of the instrument, or the voice, which guides both intellect and emotion in the moment of performance. The powerful effect of this widespread amateur musical practice can be captured in a straightforward proposition and its consequences: that whether among the bourgeoisie itself, or within the independent musical life of the labouring classes, musical culture at the height of bourgeois society was still formed largely outside the direct control of the market.

Music according to Barthes

Roland Barthes employed a concept in a late essay of his which bears directly on these questions. Resuscitating a medieval term, he refers to amateur musical practice in the nineteenth century as *musica practica*. There are two types of music, he says: the music that is listened to and the music that is played, two different types of relationship between music and the listener. People who play and sing — a certain instrument, a certain kind of music — listen differently from those who don't, even if they are indifferent or bad performers. They have a knowledge of *musica practica*.

Anyone can confirm this faculty for themselves who, even if they don't now play an instrument, once learnt, and remembers something of that learning: they will know that when you try and play something, or even sing a song from childhood, the memory seems to be traced by the fingers themselves (or the vocal cords), which know what to do without being consciously directed. Barthes speaks of 'a muscular music in which the part taken by the sense of hearing is only one of ratification, as though the body were hearing'.[5] There is nowadays experimental evidence of this from scientists. Neuropsychologists are able to detect the tiny and normally imperceptible muscular twitches which, say, a trumpet player makes with the lips while listening to a piece of trumpet music, and which do not occur when the subject listens to a piece played on another instrument altogether. Musicians have always been aware of this knowledge of theirs buried in the — what: mind? psyche? central nervous system? — and have often spoken of it in almost mystical terms, which to non-initiates sometimes seems like mere mystique. Yet *musica practica* is nothing but the form that musical knowledge takes directly from musical practice. Theoretically filtered or not, fundamentally it has no need of theory or even notation. It is the musical equivalent of the way the baby learns to talk.

Barthes strangely fails in his essay to bring out the wider import of the concept of *musica practica*. He presents it as a phenomenon occurring in a certain social class at a particular moment in history, without quite letting on that it's an ever-present form of musical knowledge which takes on different historical and class aspects, appears in different periods in altered historical and social guises, but still remains the essential feature of the way music is transmitted from generation to generation. He simply declares that nineteenth-century *musica practica* has disappeared: 'initially the province of the idle (aristocratic) class, it lapsed into an insipid social rite with the coming of the democracy of the bourgeoisie (the piano, the young lady, the drawing room, the nocturne), and then faded out altogether (who plays the piano today?)'.[6]

This may be an effective characterization of certain aspects of bourgeois culture, but in other respects it's misleading, obscuring the broader dialectical character of the phenomenon, the way it takes on different historical and social guises in different periods. Also, Barthes is singularly unfair to the piano. The piano is a supremely adaptable instrument, becoming increasingly widespread with the improvement of the upright around the middle of the century, and the introduction soon after of hire-purchase in order to sell it. By 1900 it reached far beyond the salon, the concert hall and the conservatory, and the range of different musics played on its keyboard was unprecedented. It entered music halls and pubs, church halls and seaside tea-rooms, saloons and brothels, and soon became a cherished durable consumer object within the upper reaches of the working class. In 1873 a South Yorkshire miners' leader giving evidence to a parliamentary investigation into the coal industry told them, 'We have got more pianos and perambulators, but the piano is considered a cut above the perambulator.'[7] In the United States it was second to the kitchen range.

The piano's popularity is easy to explain: it was the easiest of instruments to learn. While most musical instruments respond to a novice with a discouraging noise or no sound at all, the piano sings at first touch, and doesn't even need tuning up, except occasionally. As for the growing number of piano players, a large proportion were not, properly speaking, taught. Many played it 'by ear'. But this, after all, is always the way that basic musical knowledge is acquired; necessarily, though Barthes disregards it, the way in which the lore of *musica practica* is always transmitted. Adapted in musically literate cultures to the method of notation, nonetheless, whether in literate or oral cultures, this learning by imitation is the natural ground of all musical ability and training.

On the other hand, Barthes is not mistaken in claiming that the particular way in which the idle classes of the nineteenth century listened to music in the salon is dead now. This is connected with another point he makes: that the role of the performer has changed. The grand Romantic interpreter, the great creative virtuoso who transcribed the music of others as brilliantly as he composed his own — this figure has passed. Showmen of this kind were able to dazzle salon and concert hall so easily precisely because to these audiences their virtuosity seemed so physically astonishing; in the case of Paganini, veritably devilish. Paganini was guyed in a working-class song from North-East England, about a group of drunken miners who go to hear him play and are more impressed by his diabolism than his musicianship (a song which incidentally confirms that the new commercial concerts of the era were not quite out of reach of the working-class pocket). This kind of virtuoso has been replaced, as Barthes says, with the technician, 'who relieves the listener of all activity'. It is here that passivity, or cold scrutiny, or an admixture of the two, takes over. And Barthes is also right that this kind of listening belongs in a special way to the modern age of concert, festival, record and radio. The historical aura of music has been progressively denuded, eroded away. The silent contemplation of the audience has become, in the words of Walter Benjamin, 'a school for asocial behaviour'.[8]

In driving out the amateur, the whole vast modern commercial apparatus of music conspires to reduce the listener to the condition of compliant consumer, and thus to induce passive reception instead of active listening. The concert becomes parasitic upon the fame and success cultivated in the festival; the festival is the showcase which the impresario needs to capture for the promotion of the artist; the artist, to catch the impresario's attention, must now win international music competitions. All are parasitical upon the recording industry, which bitterly complains about the loss of profits from home recording, but is in turn a parasite upon radio and television, its operations heavily subsidized by the almost free publicity provided by these media. The relationship, which applies to both classical and pop music, is of course symbiotic. Where would radio have been without records to fill up airtime, records without the aural showcase of radio? The rise of pop music in the 1950s and 1960s was intimately tied to the growth of commercial Top 40 radio, which today includes television. In the age of MTV, a great deal of risk capital is invested in the production of music videos, and in the classical market television is the major target of promotion. (You would think, for example, that the stardom of the young virtuoso would entail a high rate for his appearance in a TV documentary; in fact the press agent of the record company with whom he has an exclusive contract tells you that you can film his recording sessions for a sum that is purely nominal.)[9] There are also tie-ins between record companies, television stations, CDs and the video market. The Japanese are in on the act, with Yamaha, anxious to promote the sales of its pianos in North America, providing instruments for a recent international piano competition in Toronto, not to mention Sony's purchase of CBS Records. The end result of the predominance and ubiquity of radio, records and tapes, the whole gamut of electro-acoustic reproduction from a two-thousand-pound hi-fi to the cheapest 'walkman', is that music becomes literally disembodied — in a word, the negation of *musica practica*.

Yet *musica practica* cannot be put down. With all its unruliness, it is such a fundamental element — there could be no music without it — that even the highly organized mode of production of music under late capitalism cannot do without it. Barthes is aware of this. 'To find practical music in the West', he says, 'one has now to look to another public, another repertoire, another instrument (the young generation, vocal music, the guitar).'[10] There is more to it than that, of course. The phenomenon is highly contradictory. In spite of the Dionysian force of such music, the public for rock is still in one sense profoundly passive, and paradoxically never more so than in the teenage girls who screamed at the Beatles in the 1960s or in the bodies gyrating to Soft Machine at London's Roundhouse at the end of the same decade. The audience at the Concert for Bangla Desh may have listened in quiet contemplation to Ravi Shankar, but at the other extreme one is reluctant to say that they listened at all. They (and this includes all of us at least some of the time) hear bodily, but in a different sense: with exposed nerves and a raw skin. This is an extreme form of music which hammers in us, our nerves responding not as conductors along our body, the resonator, but as if they were merely the relays of conditioned reflex. Yet within this mass audience, *musica practica* repeatedly attempts to reinsert itself, and forces commercial music to keep changing.

Fashion is not entirely a fabrication of the market, the fashion market is a corruption of human desire. *Musica practica* is an authentic object of popular pleasure, an embodiment of the human need for community. Capitalist production preys upon the vanguards of popular music, destroys their creative autonomy, their own sense of judgement, captures their instincts — a band gets stuck into its groove and another arises to replace it. The business of commercial music promotion is to keep the system geared up to these periodic injections of vital musical juices, plugging into the latest trend in order to take it over and plug it.

The Quarrel between Lent and Carnival

Musica practica belongs in medieval terminology to *ars mecanica*, or technique. It consisted, in other words, in the practical aspects of music making, whether composing, tuning instruments or actually performing. In contrast, music considered under the rubric of *ars liberalis* consisted in the speculative knowledge of the numerical proportions which entered into the relations of intervals and rhythms — in short, the abstract music theory found in such ecclesiastical authorities as Boethius.

The Christian Church is the bridge between the music of Antiquity and that of modern times. In the centuries following the barbaric invasions and the break-up of the Roman Empire, the Church became the only institution capable of exercising responsibility for the tasks of education, and thus for the formal transmission of culture. By the end of this transitional period of internal disorder, the Church's predominance, which now extended from one end of Europe to the other, had laid the foundations for a new universal art music.

The Church, however, engaged in a continual feud with secular *musica practica*, passing edicts against its dangerous influence. The Council of Cavaillon in 650 expressed indignation over the use of obscene songs in various religious ceremonies. In 813, the Council of Tours concerned itself with the unseemly manner of secular singing, a subject of concern also to the Council of Glasgow in 747, which condemned the influence of the styles of 'soft singing' and 'tragic acting'. These attacks follow the first Pope Gregory's ban on secular learning, and the subsequent reorganization of liturgical music which gave us the Gregorian chant. In Christendom at large, since the Council of Laodicea in 364, the musical parts of the services were performed by the regular priests and deacons. At the Council of Rome in 595, Gregory censured them for spending too much time on the cultivation of their voices and neglecting their pastoral duties, and issued an edict which strictly limited their musical participation. To relieve them, he took immediate steps to ensure a supply of singers trained in the approved manner at the Schola Cantorum in Rome. In short, he took in hand the entire refurbishment of the *musica practica* of the Church. (One of his undertakings was to establish orphanages to train children for Church office and supply singers to the papal choir, a practice that extended itself over the centuries to monasteries, cathedrals and the royal courts, and helps to explain why so many early composers received their initial musical training as singers, and often distinguished themselves initially as child choristers.)

A work by Thomas Mann's fictional composer Adrian Leverkühn, 'Of the Birth of the Holy Pope Gregory', one of a set of puppet theatre pieces based on medieval Latin texts, reminds us that we are speaking of legendary times. This Gregory is said to be the offspring of an incestuous union between a brother and a sister, who ends up marrying his mother, and is called to the Vicarage of Rome after seventeen years of penance. (Mann subsequently made him the subject of another novel, *The Holy Sinner*.) At all events, Gregorian chant can hardly be regarded as Gregory's own creation. Beginning with the codification of the existing repertoire, it required the continued attention of his successors over three centuries. The feud with the music of the pagan vernacular was protracted, and victory elusive; musicology inevitably exaggerates this victory, because what survives in the musical texts which comprise the libraries of the academies are the written models, not the more anarchic practice of performing them. But in practical and administrative terms, to organize and systematize the musical liturgy entailed a continuing programme for the training of cadres, who, owing to both the scarcity of liturgical books and the undeveloped nature at the time of musical notation, were required to memorize the psalter along with its music. Not that this was then such a forbidding task. We have forgotten the power of memory in oral cultures.

By the time of the division of the Carolingian empire in 843, says the musicologist Paul Henry Láng, a new liturgical music, based on Gregorian chant, had penetrated with papal missions to Scandinavia in the north and the Slavic and Hungarian territories in the east, and had displaced Mozarabic ritual in Spain. It was a floating, detached kind of monody, arhythmic, without accented beats or rousing melodic leaps; in short, a form of spiritual singing which corresponded to the Christian denigration of the body by excluding the corporeal forms of popular song and dance.[11]

Popular *musica practica*, by contrast, was linked to the culture of carnival and folk humour, a tradition stretching back to the Roman Saturnalia, in which not only is the body present, but as the Russian scholar Bakhtin showed in his study of Rabelais, it has profoundly positive significance. According to the cultural historian Peter Burke, there were three major themes in Carnival: food, sex and violence.[12] Eating and drinking were heavy, people sang and danced in the streets, they dressed up in costume or the clothes of the opposite sex, and took sexual licence. Activities in which the world was temporarily turned upside down were led by the Kings or Abbots of Misrule. Carnivalesque, incorporating the art of mime and clowning, jesters and juggling, festive pageants, marketplace comedies and parody — all this represented a temporary utopian realm of community, freedom, equality and abundance entirely opposed to the official and serious tone of the feudal and ecclesiastical order. Nonetheless both Church and nobles participated; especially the young adult males of the upper classes. According to Bakhtin: 'It was precisely the one-sided character of official seriousness which led to the necessity of creating a vent for the second nature of man, for laughter.'[13] Since this second nature might be repressed but was indestructible, it was wisely tolerated and even legalized, but only outside canonized ritual or on specially appointed feast days and festivals.

Carnival proper did not have the same importance all over Europe — the weather in the north discouraged elaborate street festivals in February — but there were other festivals outside the Carnival season which acquired the same character.[14] The two main periods of permitted laughter were at Christmas and at Easter. The former, known as *risus natalis*, was given over especially to song. Serious church hymns were sung to the tunes of street ditties. Christmas carols were interwoven with folk motifs on the theme of the cheerful death of the old and the birth of the new. A dominant aspect of these songs, says Bakhtin, is the parodic and travestying ridicule of the old. The influence of this tradition is very long lived. In France, Bakhtin observes, 'the "Noël" . . . became one of the most popular generic sources for the revolutionary street song'.[15]

The carnival spirit not only signified the logic of laughter and the suspension of social rank, it was also largely concentrated in what Bakhtin calls the material bodily principle, with its images of the human body and its functions — food, drink, sex and defecation. It is no accident that these are the same functions which in psychoanalysis govern the deepest level of the psyche, where psyche meets soma, mind touches body. From these psychic depths comes the imagery of grotesque realism, which reaches its apogee in the early Renaissance in the figure of Rabelais. What Carnival expresses is not the isolated biological individual (a modern, post-Renaissance concept) but the collective and ancestral body social, not private but universal. Rather than being derisive and negative, carnival-esque laughter, like the depths of the psyche itself, is positive and assertive. The spirit of Carnival is therefore opposed to severance from the world, to the pretence of the renunciation of earthly life, in short, to Lent. The aesthetic attitude of grotesque realism promotes the degradation of the spiritual, and brings about instead a return to earth, a restoration of contact with the regenerative power of the earth and of the body. Music, of course, is one of its most powerful agents.

As psychoanalysis would lead us to expect, these traits intensified as official Christianity became more repressive, foisting on the collective psyche the split between the spirit and the body which it projected upon the figure of its founder. In Max Weber's view (according to the recollection of his disciple Paul Honigsheim) the Christian deprecation of the body was to become a crucial factor in the rationalization of European music and its increasing emphasis on instrumental forms and cerebral processes.[16]

The opposition between Carnival and Lent was portrayed by Bruegel in the sixteenth century in a famous painting, 'Carnival's Quarrel with Lent': a fat man sits astride a barrel jousting with a thin old woman seated on a chair. Mock battles between figures like these were a common part of Shrovetide festivities, but the painting obviously has an allegorical meaning, which both Peter Burke and Jacques Attali remark upon. Burke, interpreting the fat man image of Carnival who belongs to the tavern side of the painting as a symbol of traditional popular culture, and the other figure, on the side of the Church, as the clergy, observes that at the time the canvas was painted in 1559, the Church was involved in a widespread reform movement directed to the suppression of popular festivities.[17] Attali also sees in the painting a battle between two antagonistic cultural principles, adding that music, though it hardly figures pictorially, occupies a very special position here: 'While the rich observe Lent and flaunt their money by giving alms to the beggars arrayed outside the door to the church, in the Carnival parade, a musician, tragic and disquieting in the mask that disfigures him, stands beside men playing dice.'[18] The visible musician, he says, evokes one kind of music, but implicitly there is also another, which accompanies the religious ritual. If the painting is a symbolic confrontation between misfortune diverted into festival and wealth costumed in penitence, it is also about music, where this confrontation becomes audible.

The struggle between Carnival and Lent evokes the opposition in ancient Greek culture between the rival forces of Dionysus and Apollo which is described by the young Nietzsche. At the time he wrote *The Birth of Tragedy*, where these ideas are first announced, he believed that the old gods had risen again and lived in the work of Richard Wagner. In later years, older, wiser and sick of Wagner's megalomania and anti-Semitism, he retracted his early hero-worship, but the value of his insight into the forces at play in ancient Greece is independent of this question.

The Apollonian represents a love of order and proportion — Apollo is the founder of states and the god of rational thought — where the Dionysian is wild and glories in elation and intoxication — Dionysus is the god of drunken ecstasy and madness. The Apollonian tends towards what Bakhtin calls monological discourse. Apollo becomes the apotheosis of what Schopenhauer called the *principium individuationis*, the principle of individuation, which safeguards individual existence by moulding Dionysian chaos into order and beauty. 'As a moral deity', says Nietzsche, 'Apollo demands self-control from his people and, in order to observe such self-control, a knowledge of self.'[19] In Dionysian chaos, on the other hand, the spirit succumbs in ecstasy to self-oblivion, forgetting the limits of self and the precepts of Apollo. It embraces 'the whole outrageous gamut of nature' in the craving for mystic union with the Universe. Nietzsche speaks of the example of the singing and leaping crowds infected with St Vitus' Dance in the German Middle Ages, which whirled from place to place under this same Dionysian impulse. In them, he says, we rediscover the Bacchic choruses of the Greeks, with their early history in Asia Minor, as far back as Babylon and the orgiastic Sacaea:

> There are people who, from lack of experience or sheer obtuseness, and firm in their belief in their own 'healthy-mindedness', will label such phenomena, either mockingly or pityingly, as 'folk diseases'. Such poor wretches cannot imagine how anaemic and ghastly their own so-called 'healthy-mindedness' seems in contrast to the glowing life of the Dionysian revellers rushing past them.[20]

But in music, Nietzsche believed, the two forces may combine, in the same way they did in Greek tragedy, where at one and the same time the Apollonian love of proportion succumbs to Dionysian ecstasy, and Dionysian experience is subjected to Apollonian order. Tragedy thereby becomes the Apollonian embodiment of Dionysiac insights and powers, where terror and pity combine with the acceptance of the mythic forces which threaten us. It is the power of music that lends this aspect to tragedy because, to follow Schopenhauer (as Nietzsche did in this regard), music is able to by-pass the world of appearance and give direct access to the inchoate world of the will: 'first, music incites us to a symbolic intuition of the Dionysian universality; second, it endows that symbolic image with supreme significance'.[21] Furthermore, the release created by tragic myth, says Nietzsche, has the same origin as the delight created by dissonance in music. Dissonance 'makes us need to hear and at the same time to go beyond that hearing'. Through the forward propulsion imparted by dissonance (we shall see how it does this later on), music embodies the Dionysian spirit 'which playfully shatters and rebuilds the teeming world' in Heraclitean flux.[22]

In the language of modern psychology, the Apollonian impulse hungers for maximum Gestalt articulation, the Dionysian drives towards the exciting confusion, fluidity and ambiguity of the creative unconscious. In Bakhtin's terms, it is heteroglot — it speaks in many voices at the same time. The contrast is embodied in the opposition between two different schools of psychological aesthetics, the Gestalt and the psychoanalytic. The former is concerned with the work of stable shapes and forms in the process of perception. According to Rudolf Arnheim, doyen of Gestalt psychologists, 'the artist directly grasps the full meaning of nature's creations, and, by organising sensory facts according to the laws of *Prägnanz* [pregnant form], unity, segregation and balance, he reveals harmony and order, or stigmatises discord and disorder'.[23] In complete contrast, the psychoanalyst Anton Ehrenzweig believed that 'There seem to exist in the structure of a work of art complex relationships that refuse to be caught in the stable and neat grid of common-sense visualisation. Incompatible outlines and surfaces permeate and try to crowd themselves into the same point in time and space.'[24] Citing the subversion of rationality by the eruptions of the unconscious in modernist art, which causes the breakdown of representation and looks to the unaware like schizoid behaviour, Ehrenzweig calls this kind of perception dedifferentiated; for it is like a regression from the articulate condition of consciousness to a less integrated level of psychic reality, a level which consciousness, to protect itself, can only regard as incoherent and primitive, but which may in fact be richly endowed with symbolism and aesthetic ambiguity.

In short, Dionysus represents the instinctual reality which psychoanalysis discovers behind the veil of the Apollonian image, a little like the latent unconscious content behind the manifest image of the dream. Nietzsche was right, says Norman O. Brown, 'in saying that the Apollonian preserves, the Dionysian destroys, self-consciousness. As long as the structure of the ego is Apollonian, Dionysian experience can only be bought as the price of ego-dissolution.'[25] According to this point of view, the ultimate power of music is its promise to hold the ego in suspension in order to allow it to experience safely and temporarily this Dionysian release. The truth to be discovered in the unfolding trajectory of Western music is that the two forces always operate in tandem, but at different levels and in different strengths. Music waxes and wanes in its relationship and its form of access to the mythopoeic depths, depending largely on whether Apollonian or Dionysian forces are in the ascendant. It is partly the fluctuating relationship between these forces which makes music the acute but also perplexing measure of historical change we shall repeatedly find it to be.

As for contemporary *musica practica*, it is perfectly consistent with this view that the hysterical behaviour of pop music fans should be seen by the anthropologist Gilbert Rouget as a stereotyped form of musical emotion similar to trance, and that for him it is Beatlemania that reminds him of the Dionysian rituals of ancient Greece. Nor is it an accident, in his view, that rock music consciously strives for the most powerful physical impact, indeed that 'through the din of vast amplifiers, such music obtains effects of violence and acoustic turbulences never before achieved'.[26] He is impressed by a description of a rock concert on the Isle of Wight, which at 10,000 watts could be heard at a distance of three kilometres. At these levels of amplification, the sounds act directly upon the body; especially the throb of the bass, which sets up resonant vibrations within the abdomen. The repetitive tunes and perpetual thrumming induce a light hypnosis; this, he says, is very much the effect that certain forms of possession music aim for, such as that of *ndo'p* in Senegal.

The same physical symptoms of trance music were observed by the psychiatrist William Sargant, pioneer of electric shock therapy, a reductivist who sees outward behaviour as nothing more than the manifestation of chemical changes in the brain. For Rouget, however, the evidence is ambivalent. On the one hand, he says, since trance is clearly an emotional form of behaviour, it is not surprising that musical emotions, under the pressure of cultural factors, should be expressed in this semi-sanctioned, almost socialized way. 'This would mean that we are dealing here with a relation between music and trance that, although strongly influenced by culture, is nevertheless based on a natural — and thus universal — property of music, or at least a certain kind of music . . .'[27] On the other hand, it is not directly reducible to the unmediated somatic or kinaesthetic effects of music, for in neither Beatlemania nor possession cults do subjects fall into trance who are not disposed to do so. Nor is it conceivably a question of genetic predisposition: the phenomenon is clearly a social one, in which the effect of music depends on its insertion within a system, a social code, in which trance becomes an allowable form of behaviour. The music then acts as a psychological signal rather than a physiological cause, in other words, as a message or a sign.

However, since music is also a system in itself, its relations with the cult are determined equally by its own organization. Therefore what we have is an interplay between signifying systems both of which are submerged within the domain of unconscious and subjective meanings. Only this can explain the great variety of different types of music which, in the cults of different societies and cultures throughout the world, in some way trigger the trance or possession. This variety, argues Rouget, rules out those theories which only see music in terms of one-to-one relationships of cause and effect; in a word, mechanically instead of semiotically, as a complex system of signs and meanings.

This conclusion about the semiotic character of music applies not only to trance music but to all kinds of music — for is it not true that music universally displays the same ambiguities, and the same elusive allusiveness?

Music according to Bakhtin

The need for community is the same thing as the need for dialogue. Community is the meeting place of different voices talking together, exchanging and debating experience and knowledge. Music is one of the instruments of this process, a means of social intercourse, and like all art-forms a vehicle of expression both individual and social. Social dialogue, however, is an untidy business, inflected by arguments and persuasion of every sort, full of interruption, interjection, allusion, hyperbole, and littered with echoes and cross-echoes, intended and unintended, conscious and unconscious. In short, it is a process whose features are neglected and underestimated by the procedures of formal analysis.

The discipline of musicology derives both its efficacy and its closure from analysing the formal qualities of music inscribed in notation, which elicits a highly technical language to match the music's complicated internal properties. This language seems to foreclose and dissolve away the discussion of music in almost any other terms (except perhaps emotional); the effect is reinforced by the absence in music of the representational content by which other art-forms — the linguistic and pictorial — are more clearly related to the body social and historical. This is the difficulty semiologists refer to as the problem of a semiotic system without a semantic level, or content plane, as Umberto Eco puts it.[28] Semiology (or semiotics), the study of signs as the vehicles of communication, traces the relationships between the sign as a signifier (of which there are several types), and what is perceived as being signified. The problem with music — the reason why most semiologists have avoided it — is the difficulty in identifying the latter, what is commonly called the 'meaning' of music.

The subjective feelings of either composer or listener make a very poor candidate — too vague and difficult, according to the French philosopher Bergson, to pin down in the fixed forms of language; for the words concerned are much too slippery. It is true that there is a well-known book called *The Language of Music* by the English musicologist Deryck Cooke which argues the contrary — Cooke even provides a lexicon of the basic phrases which supposedly make up the vocabulary of music, where the emotional expression of a musical phrase is derived from the words attached to it in the form of title or text.[29] But this common-sense approach turns out, on examination, to be far too one-dimensional. It ignores, for example, the difference between denotation and connotation, the associations which a word, sign or signal acquires from the contexts in which it occurs. It is completely insensitive to poetic and dramatic ambiguity, and manifestly ignorant of the semiotic analysis of the relationship between the signifier and the signified. In short, the book is a prime example of the intellectual retardedness of positivistic musicology.[30] The true situation is much more complicated than Cooke seems to imagine. Even if music seems unable to express anything definite — because it has no vocabulary — the fluid mixture of different levels in the way music communicates produces great semiological complexity, for each level leaves traces of different kinds to produce a confusion of signs extremely complex to unravel.

By far the richest account of the confusing process of social dialogue is that of Mikhail Bakhtin, whose ideas have only belatedly begun to achieve wider circulation and discussion. It was Bakhtin's great contribution to have introduced what he called the 'dialogical principle', which articulates, concerning the basis of the social relations of artistic creation, what in Marx is only implicit; namely, that all cultural production is part of a social dialogue unfolding in a particular historical moment, and therefore it is shaped by and immersed in the social and historical context. The 'living utterance', says Bakhtin, 'having taken meaning and shape at a particular historical moment in a socially specific environment, cannot fail to brush up against thousands of living dialogical threads, woven by socio-ideological consciousness around the given object of the utterance; it cannot fail to become an active participant in social dialogue.'[31] But Bakhtin goes further than Marx. As a recent exponent puts it, he shares with Marx the premiss that cultural process is intimately connected to social relations and that culture is the site of social difference and contradiction. For Bakhtin, however, the cultural sign is more than a reflection, a double or a shadow of reality: 'it is also itself a material participant in that reality'.[32]

Bakhtin offers an affirmative concept of cultural production that encompasses every style, form and genre, and which posits language and artistic expression as 'shared territory', the site of social and psychic contradictions among competing voices and conflicting discourses and ideologies. Hence his predilection for what he calls the polyphonic novel, the anti-tradition of Rabelais, Swift and Dostoevsky, where the voice of the author is only one of the multiple voices that people the text — the musical metaphor here is no accident: music provides the very model of a discourse which is composed of simultaneous voices. There is also his celebration of parody and the carnivalesque; his pleasure in 'grotesque realism' and the Dionysian; the exhilaration he feels in the face of difference and multiplicity. And the obverse: his suspicion of forms that seem to employ a monological and authoritarian voice — like the Stalinist fictions of socialist realism — where the active role of the other person in the process of communication is reduced to a minimum.

The musical equivalent of this position is represented by Bakhtin's friend and member of the informal Bakhtin circle in the 1920s, the Russian musicologist Ivan Sollertinsky. Professor at the Leningrad Conservatory and artistic director of the Leningrad Philharmonic, Sollertinsky was known as a prominent polemicist in favour of modernist music — even when official Soviet doctrine began to find it suspect — and a champion of the young Shostakovich. The author of enthusiastic books on Schoenberg and Mahler published in the early 1930s, he became embroiled when Shostakovich was attacked by Stalin in 1936 through the pages of *Pravda* for his highly satiric opera *Lady Macbeth of*

Mtensk — an incident which clearly reveals the political implications at stake.

Sollertinsky's work constitutes the first attempt to carry Bakhtin's ideas over into music, with the symphony occupying the place of the novel. Situating Beethoven at the head of the symphonic tradition and linking his style to 'the heroic energies generated by the French Revolution', Sollertinsky calls the Beethovenian symphony a musical working through of the 'ecstatic knowledge of human brotherhood', a 'great collective idea' animated by 'immediate revolutionary enthusiasm', which rests on the broad appeal of a (supposedly) universal musical language. Because the forcefulness of Beethoven's symphonic development implies a sense of struggle and the clash of wills, Beethoven turns the symphony into a fully dialogical form.

The apex of symphonic achievement in Beethoven is followed, according to Sollertinsky, by a progressive descent from the Byronic heights of full-blown Romanticism towards the introversion of Brahms and Bruckner — a decline which corresponds to the political failure of the social project of the bourgeoisie over the course of the nineteenth century — until it reaches the point where Mahler's symphonies pose the very problem of the symphony as an ideological form. Because the musical language of the symphony, the dramatic treatment of harmonic tension and resolution, has become weakened, Mahler's idiom develops a kind of dualism between lyrical subjectivity and sarcastic parody, including self-parody, where the conventions of classical style are confronted by musical material derived from popular genres. Here too, then, the symphony is double-voiced and expressly dialogical (and perhaps it is no coincidence that Mahler expressed a predilection for the novels of Dostoevsky). A last-ditch attempt to resurrect the utopian symphony as a viable form, the endeavour, says Sollertinsky, inevitably fails, but it serves 'as a prototype for modern progressive musical practice precisely because of these dialogical elements'.[33]

The strength of the dialogical principle is that it is not merely an aesthetic theory but an epistemology, a theory of knowledge which applies to aesthetic production because it applies to the human situation within which art is produced. The forces at work in the process do not impinge on the utterance from outside like mechanical pressures, but enter into it dialectically — in Bakhtin's terminology, dialogically — as a necessary constitutive element of its semantic structure. To borrow a simple analogy from Bakhtin's biographer Michael Holquist, consider the example of hearing somebody talking on the telephone to someone whose identity is unknown to us: we are usually able to guess the relationship between them from the form of words and their intonation, in short, the genre of the speech employed.[34] In other words, the utterance is shaped as much by what is not said as by what is, and not only because what isn't said has been left out but also because it cannot be put into words — it is the necessary envelope of non-verbal communication in which all speech is, so to speak, wrapped up. Music may be considered in exactly the same light. There is a wealth of information in the intonation of the notes, which is closely related to the genre and cannot be put into words. In the case of the genres of chamber music and jazz, analogies with dialogue and conversation are especially strong.

Not surprisingly, the clearest musical examples of the dialogical process are found in opera. And not only in the form of duets and ensembles but the solo aria itself, as the Welsh baritone Geraint Evans vividly demonstrated in a master class on television some years ago. The subject of study was Zerlina's aria 'Batti, batti' from *Don Giovanni*, where Zerlina is trying to calm Masetto down after he has discovered her with the Don. Evans, a most gifted actor, insisted on rehearsing it with the students as a two-hander, explaining that it was not a solo aria at all, but a duet, a quarrel in which one of the pair remains silent. One saw the student Zerlinas, who all started by singing prettily but undramatically, learning how to act; in other words, to direct their vocal gestures not towards an invisible audience but to their dramatic partner.

Mozart was altogether a past master in rendering the dialogical quality of a dramatic situation — above all in the great ensembles in *The Marriage of Figaro*, *Don Giovanni* and *Così fan tutte*, the finales to the acts where he typically arranges his characters in overlapping groups in which they are linked and separated by their different degrees of co-operation and antagonism, both dramatically and musically. As the sociologist Alfred Schutz once put it:

> Mozart does not merely communicate to us . . . the objective meaning that the situation has within the context of the plot (and even a dramatist of the stature of Gluck does only this). He shows us, in addition, the different meanings that the same situation has to each of the characters involved in it. He makes us understand that to each of them the presence and behaviour of the others are elements in his own situation. And this is precisely the condition in which each of us finds himself in everyday life. Mozart's dramatic art is a representation of the basic structure of the social world.[35]

Bakhtin argues on similar lines about the underlying nature of every form of utterance, including the artistic. Since communication implies community and community entails communication, the presence and behaviour of the other is an integral element. An utterance is therefore a kind of relation: 'any utterance — the finished, written utterance not excepted — makes response to something and is calculated to be responded to in turn. It is but one link in a continuous chain of speech performances.'[36]

The genres of the complex cultural communications that we call art are intended for a particular type of active and responsive understanding, which operates at long distance and with delayed action.[37] In short, the very condition of artistic creation is that each work is the product of a tacit dialogue which lies embedded in the complex circumstances in which it occurs; and this is no less true of music. Moreover, Bakhtin's emphasis on the utterance and the word, as opposed to the language system and the structure of the sentence, is in many ways equivalent to an emphasis in music on *musica practica* as opposed to the score and musical analysis — this is the level of the musical speech act, which is the source of differences in interpretation of the same score.

This approach therefore has implications for music as crucial as those it has for literature. In neither case can meaning really be stabilized and foreclosed, because music, like the uttered word — as opposed to the word in the dictionary — leads a socially charged life, which always tastes of the concrete circumstances. Every actor knows that the same words can be uttered in an infinite number of ways. Bakhtin's compatriot, the linguist Roman Jakobson, cites an exercise reported by a former member of Stanislavsky's Moscow Theatre, in which the actors were asked to give the words 'This evening' forty different shades of meaning. Jakobson tested the actor himself, and discovered with the use of a tape-recorder that Muscovite listeners were able to decode as many as fifty different versions.[38] If this is the case with words, which have definite meanings, how much more so with music, where intonation is everything?

At the same time, some insist that the meanings of music are very precise. Mendelssohn, for example, held that it is impossible to explain a piece of music, not because the music is too vague but because words are too vague. Music being an emotional language, the meanings of music are far too subtle for words. Many musicians attest that even the simplest alteration in the notes may change the feeling of the music. Bergson observed that if you dwell unduly on a single note of a tune, a qualitative change begins to takes place in the whole musical phrase. Bakhtin, for his own part, although he said almost nothing about music, took the view that music possessed a real but elusive content: 'Music is denied referential specificity and cognitive differentiation, but is profound in content: its form leads us beyond the boundaries of acoustical sound but does not take us into an axiological void — content here is, at bottom, ethical.'[39] This means, among other things, that there are no 'neutral' forms of music, any more than there are in speech; in both cases the utterance is completely shot through with intentions, purposes and ideologies, which constitute both context and subtext.

*   *   *

Ironically, the same Deryck Cooke who thought that music has a vocabulary also gave an account of the symphonic use of the march which shows how the dialogical process occurs in music:

> The brass-band march was, of course, the central symbol of the humanistic attitude . . . The first great humanistic march was naturally the Marseillaise . . . March-music entered the classical symphony — bringing with it an unavoidable touch of vulgarity — when Beethoven used the march style for his three great humanistic statements: the ultimate march-like transformation of the graceful theme of the Eroica finale, the battering main theme of the finale of the Fifth Symphony, and, most significant of all, the unequivocal brass-band march, complete with drum and cymbals . . . in the choral finale of the Ninth. The funeral march also played its part, honouring the burial of humanistic heroes, in the Marcia Funebre of the Eroica Symphony, and in Wagner's mighty Funeral March for the death of his humanistic hero Siegfried . . . It was Mahler who brought this tradition to its head, by including in . . . all his symphonies either triumphal marches to celebrate humanistic aspirations, or funeral marches to lament the burial of humanistic hopes, or both.[40]

The march is able to behave this way because it functions as a type of musical icon, which signifies something non-musical. David Osmond-Smith refers to this as 'the socio-historical connotations associated with a certain style or piece'.[41] It is largely through this iconic discourse that musical dialogue takes place; in other words, through the intended and, perhaps even more so, the unintended evocation of these associations and connotations set off against each other. Virtually every piece of music, as a result, incorporates reference and allusion to other works which it absorbs and transforms. This animation and stimulation of one text by another is what the semiologist Julia Kristeva, evoking Bakhtin, calls intertextuality.

Musical icons come in different types. Umberto Eco speaks of two kinds: 'musical "signs" (or syntagms) with an explicit denotative value (trumpet signals in the army)', and 'syntagms or entire "texts" possessing pre-culturalized connotative value ("pastoral" or "thrilling" music, etc.').[42] The former include what Diderot in another context called *les petits détails vrais*, imitative details like bird-song in Jannequin and Beethoven, or for that matter, the locomotive in Honegger's *Pacific 231* or the traffic noises in Gershwin's *An American in Paris*. The second type comprises the trumpet-calls and carillons, chorales, marches, fugues, lullabies, waltzes and dances of different kinds, which all become, especially in opera and ballet, dramatic and symphonic music, the carriers of connotations derived not from any particular context or textual association but from their implicit social and cultural functions (military, religious, ceremonial, formal, domestic, erotic, etc.).

There is also a third and special form of literary and intellectual symbolism in devices like the *idée fixe* in Berlioz or the *leitmotiv* in Wagner;

this kind of musical iconography is the prerogative of the composer: it becomes a discourse of allusions which are part of the intended content, like the literary or philosophical programme of the *Symphonie Fantastique* by the former, or the latter's operatic cycle, *The Ring*.

Intentionally or not, all types of musical icon attract connotations which are social and cultural in character; and while the composer may seek to use them, they are also liable to manifest their presence independently of the composer's will. On one level or another the composer cannot fail to respond to this undertow of significance — or what Bakhtin at one point calls the 'dialogical overtones' of the utterance. This kind of iconic discourse can be found even in composers of 'pure' music like J.S. Bach, where it comes to the surface in the *Passions*: constructed around the contrast between the aria and the chorale, the arias, in the style of Italian madrigal or opera, are used for the dramatic expression of the individual protagonists, while the German chorale serves for the devotional commentary of the congregation. The result, whether Bach intended it or not, is a public social statement as much as a private religious one, a powerful apologia for popular communal belief. In this way, even in Bach, music becomes a prime form of ideological expression.

What Bakhtin means by ideology is a socially created system of ideas, more diffuse than a religious or political creed, and not necessarily false and illusory. All the same, because of his emphasis on the social basis of the utterance, his vision of cultural history is a political one. For Bakhtin, cultural history is a kind of running battle between the traditional 'high' genres (like epic or lyric poetry), which seek to impose the single, monological voice of authority, and 'low' forms (like the novel) which introduce a heterophony of social voices, a kind of open-ended dialogue which Bakhtin calls heteroglossia, with a powerful subversive effect upon the ruling ideology of the day.

Genres are the historical forms in which the artistic utterance is cast. Bakhtin sees them as clusters of habitual figures of expression rooted in the socio-cultural situation in which the work originates. The genre serves as a necessary matrix for the artist to work with, even in the attempt to produce original and possibly non-generic creations. The genres of music are what musicologists think of as the catalogue of musical forms (motet, fugue, partita, sonata, symphony and so on) but which, because the socio-historical dimensions fall beyond their ken, they analyse almost exclusively as products of internal musical logic. To treat these phenomena in the spirit of Bakhtin will correct this blinkered academicism.

The key to the historical form of the genre is what Bakhtin calls its chronotope, or the manner in which it combines the representation of time and space. The term, which means 'time-space', is borrowed from

Einstein's Theory of Relativity, he says, and adopted for literary criticism 'almost as a metaphor (almost, but not entirely). What counts for us is the fact that it expresses the inseparability of space and time (time as the fourth dimension of space).' It is used to characterize the distinctive ways in which the treatment of time and space are combined in the literary genre, the manner in which 'time, as it were, thickens, takes on flesh, becomes artistically visible' while 'space becomes charged and responsive to the movements of time, plot and history'.[43] Bakhtin wants to show how each genre possesses a typical chronotope, the organizing structure of the narrative where 'the knots of the narrative are tied and untied'.[44] However, he is not just speaking of various formal temporal and spatial devices which may be said to identify different genres, though this is part of it, but also of the relationship which these characteristics bear to the cultural conditions in which they arise.

He begins his investigation of literary genres in Antiquity, where he discovers the earliest examples of two contrasting types, adventure and biography. The time and space of the former is 'empty' and 'abstract', for here events have no causal sequence or necessary connection in geographical space; in the latter time-space is unified by the life of a protagonist who bears a degree of responsibility for the events which unfold. He then goes on to consider the chivalric romance and the bawdy of Rabelais; the novel picaresque, the Gothic and the sentimental novel; and thence to Dostoevsky. He describes how they each involve different concepts both of space — geographical, social and personal — and of time — individual, social and historical, and their interrelation. The ancient genres are often long-lived, but the changes they undergo reflect the altered susceptibilities of both author and reader in the face of the historical transformation of the world. As late as the seventeenth century, for example, the fates of nations, kingdoms and cultures may still be drawn in terms of an 'adventure time of chance, gods and villains'; here geography too is unreal. (There are even traces of this in Shakespeare, for alongside the dramatic realism of the history plays is an example like *The Tempest*, whose location and personae are contemporary but fantastical.) By contrast, in the idyll of provincial life that emerges in the eighteenth-century novel, the world is centred on the ancestral home, the real estate of capitalist property and the domain of the family, upon which historical events impinge from the outside like alien forces.

In this general form, the closest parallels to the literary chronotope to be found in music again obviously occur in opera. The birth of opera itself constitutes the creation of a new artistic chronotope corresponding to its age, at least according to the classic account by Nietzsche in *The Birth of Tragedy*. Modern scholarly opinion now considers Nietzsche's view of opera, as the brainchild of a small group of Florentine intellectuals who

thought they were re-creating ancient Greek drama, as only one among
several strands. These included the lavish forms of courtly entertainment
and the popular form of *commedia dell'arte*, the withdrawal from polyphony
and the new emphasis on solo singing.[45] However Nietzsche's account
suggests the unifying factor which brought these various elements together
into a new chronotope. Opera, said Nietzsche, spoke to the humanistic
conceptions of the Renaissance, a culture of the Alexandrian type, which
recognized its ideal in the activity of theory. The basic form of opera, he
says, the pairing of recitative and aria, was a theoretical invention.
'Recitative stood for the rediscovered language of that archetypal man,
opera for the rediscovered country of that idyllic and heroically pure species
. . . who when their emotions were . . . aroused burst into full song' — the
country that in their imagination was Ancient Greece. The belief of the
inventors of opera was that they had discovered the secret of ancient music;
the proper world for this discovery to represent was necessarily mythical;
nor is it an accident that among the privileged myths was that of Orpheus
and the birth of music. In short, the humanists used a distant imitation of
Greek tragedy to combat the ecclesiastical notion of man as corrupt and
damned, and to recapture the concord of nature and ideal in an idyllic
reality.[46]

The history of opera from 1600 to the present has produced an
impressive succession of variant chronotopes, from the original allegorical
world of *opera seria* to the social realism of mid-twentieth-century composers
like Benjamin Britten, by way of the social comedy of Mozart, the
Romantic fantasy world of Weber, the realist melodrama of Verdi, the
mythic symbolism of Wagner, and the *verismo* of Puccini. A parallel history
runs from ballad opera to *opéra comique* and the epic musical theatre of
Brecht and Weill. As dramatic forms, each of these variants reveals
characteristic peculiarities in both narrative structure and stage scenario,
which take their cue from the historical culture of their time. The basic
unrealism of the form ensures that a predilection for elaborate stage
machinery and a magical scenography is a recurrent trait. Today we get the
various postmodernisms of Luciano Berio (Joycean and structuralist),
Harrison Birtwistle (pastoral, antiquarian and atonal) and Philip Glass
(Hollywood seen through the prism of harmonic minimalism).

But the operatic form also involves a special dimension of its own — the
singing voice. The social space it creates, whether mythical or realist, is
organized through the range and contrasts of the characters' voices. Thus
the ethereal castrato, for example, signifies the chronotope of myth and the
world of ancient civilization favoured by absolutist rulers, peopled by gods
and superhumans. The castrato has been called the third sex: neither male
nor female, but a voice which shares the characteristics of both, and thus
displaces the natural eroticism between the sexes with an imaginary

idealization; this also created room for what John Rosselli calls the cult of sexual ambiguity entailed by transvestism.

Rosselli sees the rise of the castrato as a by-product of economic collapse in a culture as susceptible to Christian asceticism as to sensuality. Observing that the economic crisis which struck Italy around 1620 was marked by increasing numbers taking religious orders as gainful employment became scarcer, a castrato, he says, 'could be thought of as an enforced celibate with an unusual chance of securing for his family an income, perhaps a fortune'.[47] Encouraged by the Church ban on women's voices — and their absence from the stage until the later 1600s (much longer in Rome) — the castrato provided opera with a spectacular high voice, but played either sex. The unrealism of a soprano hero, as Rosselli puts it, singing opposite a contralto heroine, contributed to a spectacle in which men regularly dressed up as women and women as men. In some of Cavalli's operas, for instance, a tenor nurse sings opposite an impudent young valet sung by a woman. And in a tradition to which Shakespeare was also party, the plot might call for a further sex-reversal, such as 'a woman acting the part of a man disguised as a woman, such as Achilles dodging the Trojan war'.[48]

When the castrato disappeared from the stage in the second half of the eighteenth century, the typology of voices was recast in a more naturalistic mould. In *opera seria* tenors had been relegated to the parts of kings and old men. By the 1830s, observes Rosselli, 'they were the lovers; the contralto in breeches began to seem old-fashioned'. The mature works of Bellini and Donizetti establish the norms for other male singers in Romantic opera, the baritone in the part of villains or men of power, the bass as priest or noble father.[49] The result, according to the French writer Philippe-Joseph Salazar, was to orient nineteenth-century opera towards a new image of the family belonging to nineteenth-century bourgeois ideology, an imaginary image with deep sexual undertones: the oedipal family, where the soprano struggles against the paternal bass in order to pair off with the tenor.[50] As a third recent writer, Jeremy Tambling, puts it, Verdi's heroines typically reflect various aspects of subjugation to the father and can almost all be run together.[51] The shape of the typical operatic plot reflects the business of parcelling out the voices in standard combinations. Solos are favoured by heroines making their entry, heros and villains singing of intrigue, and for mad scenes and death throes. Duets are especially for lovers, for father and daughter commiserating with each other, and also for male bonding. Disputes often come in trios, and finales in big ensembles. Choruses usually echo the action but sometimes advance it.

Nevertheless these situations open out into a recognizable world. Some of Verdi's operas, like *Traviata* and *Don Carlos*, project a new sense of realism akin to that of the nineteenth-century novel, both contemporary and historical. Sometimes the surrounding world is one where historical reality is suffused with underlying ahistorical influences, as the very title *La forza del destino* suggests. Others, starting with *Nabucco*, point in a different direction. Here, from the moment the curtain goes up on the chorus of Jews lamenting their exile, history is not only a record of individual exploits and fates but also relates the flux of peoples and humanity. These are the operas in which Verdi becomes the dramatist of nineteenth-century nationalism. He remains a child of his age when he composes *Aida*, commissioned to open the Cairo opera house in celebration of the construction of the Suez Canal. Verdi not only returns here to a quasi-mythical subject but, as Edward Said has remarked, in fulfilling the commission so uncritically he celebrates European domination of the Near East in a manner which makes it the accomplice of that domination.[52]

The chronotope, then, is more than the simple addition of certain characteristics of the treatment of time and space: it is a culturally and historically specific amalgam. Nor is this quality limited to genres with an explicit narrative content: all music gives structure to time and creates its own sense of space and volume. Musical time is not to be measured by the clock, says the aesthetician Suzanne Langer. It is 'radically different from the time in which our public and practical life proceeds ... Musical duration is an image of what might be termed "lived" or "experienced" time ... Such passage is measurable only in terms of sensibilities, tensions, and emotions; and it has not merely a different measure, but an altogether different structure from practical or scientific time.'[53] Likewise it creates its own peculiar sense of space — what Langer calls volume, or virtual space; a space filled by its own characteristic forms, which expand and contract as it unfolds. Indeed this is widely recognized: what Langer calls virtual space another writer calls kinetic space; a third calls it plastic space, and someone else, the staggered planes of musical depth. In short, the virtual space of music is a property of the musical language and forms employed. The complex interweaving of only two parts, played by two instruments or even a single instrument, is denser than a whole orchestra if the first piece is by J.S. Bach and the second is Mantovani.

Both time and space in the musical chronotope are multidimensional, and function on different levels. The relationship, for example, between the virtual space of the music and the physical space of performance is not one of indifference, but is complementary. Some music directly exploits the acoustical space of performance in order to render the virtual space of the music in a particularly plastic form. Examples which spring readily to mind include the works for antiphonal brass by Giovanni Gabrieli written for St Mark's in Venice or the brass bands in Berlioz's Requiem, which he instructed to be placed at its first performance in the four corners of the

chapel of the Invalides in Paris. If this serves to remind us that music is
frequently composed not only for particular performers but also to fit
particular kinds of acoustic space, then the truth is that acoustic spaces have
their own history and create their own expectations. Polyphony was
composed for the cathedral, the madrigal and the masque for the palazzo,
the *lied* and the sonata for the salon, the symphony and the concerto for the
concert hall. Each type of space implies a twofold set of social relations —
on the one hand among the performers, on the other between the
performers and the listeners — which corresponds to the cultural and
ideological values that the space represents and which the very architecture
is designed to express. These relations run the gamut from the formal
and hierarchical to the informal and convivial. The values they imply
inform the particular combination of forces and the musical language
employed, and therefore also characterize the chronotopes of the different
genres.

For example, the social relations implied by a Beethoven symphony are
different from those of a string quartet. Beethoven turned the symphony
into a public utterance of great ideological force; his string quartets were
intended as private statements to be shared by educated amateurs playing
to each other in a domestic space: the language of the string quartets could
therefore afford to be more demanding. Chamber music, remarks Adorno,
practises courtesy: the first step in playing chamber music well is to learn
not to thrust oneself forward but to step back. What makes the group
function as a whole is not forwardness — that would only produce
barbarian chaos — but reflective self-containment:

> Chamber music was the refuge of a balance . . . which society denied else-
> where . . . What makes such a homogeneous model space possible is the state of
> relative security enjoyed by individual, economically independent citizens, by
> entrepreneurs and, in particular, by well-to-do members of the so-called free
> professions. Obviously there is a relation between the flowering of chamber
> music and the peak period of liberalism. Chamber music is specific to an epoch
> in which the private sphere, as one of leisure, has vigorously parted from the
> public—professional sphere. Yet neither are the two embarked on irreconcilably
> divergent courses nor is leisure commandeered, as in the modern concept of
> 'rest and recreation,' to become a parody of freedom. Great chamber music
> could come into being, could be played and understood, as long as the private
> sphere had a measure of substantiality, albeit one already fragile.[54]

It almost seems like a miracle, says Adorno, that its period lasted so long.

Adorno is speaking here of musical form as the inscription of the social
relations in the performing group, actual or ideal, and thus of a contrast
between string quartet and symphony. Taken together, however, they
represent different faces of the same chronotope, and employ broadly the

same harmonic language. This language creates a particular cultural space, unified and integrated in a manner quite different from either the modal system of medieval music, or the polytonal and plural spaces of music at the end of the second millennium — as we shall later see in some detail. These larger differences are homologous to those of the changing historical chronotope from feudalism to late capitalism, by way of the Renaissance and the Enlightenment, the age of bourgeois revolution and the rise and fall of communism. In this way, music displays what Adorno calls analogical affinities for the historical world.

The changing configurations of time and space have been studied by David Harvey in *The Condition of Postmodernity*. In the world-picture of European feudalism, he says, distance in both time and space was weakly grasped; it merged into a mysterious cosmology populated by external authority, heavenly hosts or the sinister figures of myth and imagination. Social space consisted in an intricate territory of interdependence, obligation and control, with different rules at different levels. Artistic space was tactile, plastic, permitting many different simultaneous points of view. The Renaissance reconstructed these different levels. The world-picture was transformed by the voyages of discovery, social space was unified by the growing domain of chronometrical time, and artistic space by the invention of perspective.

The laws of perspective, which were first elaborated in mid-fifteenth-century Florence by Brunelleschi and Alberti, came to govern the language of visual representation for over four centuries, until transcended by modernism. This language, by conceiving the world from the point of view of an individual eye, promoted the individualism also assumed by the rational subject of Descartes' famous *Cogito ergo sum*. The result was a new kind of individual artistic subjectivity, which radically re-educated the sensibilities of the new generations. It is obviously no coincidence that the trajectory of tonal harmony is very similar, and classical harmony performs much the same ideological function as perspective. Neither system, however, is static, a fixed framework incapable of adjusting to historical change. Indeed the harmonic system was particularly good at it. But if the scheme of tonal relations gave rise to new dynamic structures, then the process inevitably came to imply a sense of direction. A sense of direction produced a sense of development, and to the optimism of the nineteenth century, this was tantamount to the idea of progress itself. Harmonic language thus took on the appearance of a linear path with the feel of causal relations between successive moments. As Christopher Small puts it, 'The music does not exist purely in the present tense, taking each moment as it comes, but leads the listener forward to coming events, often through passages which are themselves of no great intrinsic interest.' The result is that large-scale harmonic forms — this reflects the composer's role as historical subject — become 'in essence psychodramas, the spiritual voyage of an individual'.[55] This then is the underlying chronotope of nineteenth-century symphonism, from Beethoven to Mahler, with its affinity to the novel at a parallel stage of its development.

In sum, to follow Bakhtin is to regard pure musicology with suspicion: any doctrine which sees the artwork primarily, often exclusively, as the spontaneous expression of the artist's internal world is quite simply mistaken — because it fails to perceive the relation between the creator's internal world and that of social and historical reality; and if in Bakhtin's view the artistic creation, like every utterance, is always shaped by social and historical presences, this is no less true of music. Not only is the performing group itself a social one, but the musical utterance is always addressed to the hearer, to an audience: addressed either to particular persons like a patron and retinue, or else to an ideal (and idealized) listener, the generalized other embodied by a more or less anonymous audience (or in certain situations, an alter ego). Moreover, however anonymous this audience may be, it does not assume a purely passive role but actively participates in the formation of meaning by accepting or rejecting the music, in the use it makes of it, and through the social and individual significance which is brought to it. In short, the audience forms a community to which the musician implicitly also belongs, whose activity — whether composing or performing — is therefore, as Bakhtin says of verbal utterance, a way of locating oneself in relation to the social setting, a socialization of the self.

Notes

1. George Steiner, 'A Conversation with Claude Lévi-Strauss', *Encounter* XXVI/4, 1966.

2. Elie Siegmeister, *Music and Society*, Workers' Music Association, London 1943, p. 16.

3. See Ruth Finnegan, *The Hidden Musicians, Music-Making in an English Town*, Cambridge University Press, Cambridge 1989.

4. Personal communication by Glyn Perrin, 1991.

5. Roland Barthes, 'Musica Practica' in *Image-Music-Text*, Fontana/Collins, London 1977, p. 149.

6. Ibid.

7. Cyril Ehrlich, *The Piano*, Dent, London 1976, p. 97.

8. Walter Benjamin, 'The Work of Art in the Age of Mechanical Reproduction', in *Illuminations*, ed. Hannah Arendt, Schocken, New York 1969.

9. Personal experience.

10. Barthes, 'Musica Practica' in *Image-Music-Text*.

11. Paul Henry Láng, *Music in Western Civilisation*, Dent, London 1978, pp. 63–4.

12. Peter Burke, *Popular Culture in Early Modern Europe*, Temple Smith, London 1978, p. 186.

13. Mikhail Bakhtin, *Rabelais and His World*, MIT, Cambridge, MA 1968, p. 75.

14. Some of them still survive, like the popular carnival traditions in Belgium filmed by Henri Storck in the 1960s.

15. Mikhail Bakhtin, *The Dialogical Imagination*, University of Texas, Austin, TX 1981, p. 72.

16. Paul Honigsheim, *Music and Society*, ed. Etzkorn, John Wiley, London 1973, p. 35. This hypothesis fills a curious gap between Weber's two studies, *The Social and Rational Foundations of Music* and *The Protestant Ethic and the Spirit of Capitalism*. The former is musicologically exhaustive but says very little about the Church. It merely includes the passing observation that the musical systems of Christendom had no magical significance. This recalls the importance Weber attaches in the latter work to the progressive elimination of magic in the Judaeo-Christian tradition, until it is finally completely banished in Puritanism. But while *The Protestant Ethic* proposes that religion played a crucial role in developing the 'economic spirit' of capitalism — the ethos of the economic system which is also according to Weber expressed in its music — it says no more about what the connection with music consists in. It only mentions in a footnote what Weber calls 'a fundamental postulate of my whole thesis: [that] the Reformation took rational Christian asceticism and its methodical habits out of the monasteries and placed them in the service of active life in the world', a process which of course carried music with it. (See Max Weber, *The Protestant Ethic and the Spirit of Capitalism*, Allen & Unwin, London 1930, p. 235.)

17. Burke, p. 207.

18. Jacques Attali, *Noise*, Manchester University Press, Manchester 1989, p. 21.

19. Nietzsche, *The Birth of Tragedy*, Doubleday Anchor, London 1956, p. 34.

20. Ibid., p. 23; translation amended, cf. Tillman and Cahn, eds, *Philosophy of Art and Aesthetics*, Harper & Row, New York 1969, p. 293.

21. Nietzsche, p. 101.

22. Ibid., p. 143.

23. Rudolf Arnheim, 'Gestalt and Art' in Hogg, ed., *Psychology and the Visual Arts*, Penguin, London 1969, p. 258.

24. Anton Ehrenzweig, 'A New Psychoanaltyic Approach to Aesthetics' in ibid., p. 114.

25. Norman O. Brown, *Life Against Death, The Psychoanalytic Meaning of History*, Sphere, London 1968, p. 158.

26. Gilbert Rouget, *Music and Trance*, University of Chicago Press, Chicago 1985, p. 121.

27. Ibid., p. 136.

28. Umberto Eco, *A Theory of Semiotics*, Macmillan, London 1977, p. 11.

29. Deryck Cooke, *The Language of Music*, Oxford 1959.

30. For a critique of Cooke see David Osmond-Smith, 'The Iconic Process in Musical Communication', *Versus* 3. Anthony Storr, in *Music and the Mind*, HarperCollins, London 1993, chapter 4, also finds Cooke wanting, for broadly similar reasons.

31. Mikhail Bakhtin, 'Discourse in the Novel' in *The Dialogic Imagination*, p. 276.

32. Robert Stam, *Subversive Pleasures — Bakhtin, Cultural Criticism, and Film*, Johns Hopkins University Press, Baltimore and London 1989, p. 32. The main body of Bakhtin's work, dating from the 1920s to the 1940s, included writings on the political and cultural role of the novel, Dostoevsky and the German *Bildungsroman*, Rabelais and popular carnival; he also collaborated in critical works on Freud, linguistics and Russian formalism. With sympathies like these, and despite the religious belief for which he suffered internal exile, Bakhtin was part of the intense debate which took place in the early years of the Russian Revolution over the role and function of culture. His distinctive mark, and the strength of his intellectual vision, is a deep suspicion of systems and orthodoxy of every type and on every level. But this is not as much of a contradiction as it sounds: Bakhtin's form of faith evidently belonged to a populist tradition which distrusted the religious hierarchy.

33. Ken Hirschkop, 'The Classical and the Popular: Musical Form and Social Context', in Christopher Norris, ed., *Music and the Politics of Culture*, Lawrence & Wishart, London 1989, pp. 294–5.

34. Ibid., p. 61.

35. Alfred Schutz, 'Mozart and the Philosophers' in *Collected Papers*, Vol. II, Martinus Nijhoff, The Hague 1964, p. 195.

36. Quoted in Michael Holquist, *Dialogism, Bakhtin and His World*, Routledge, London 1990, p. 59.

Musica Practica 53

37. Mikhail Bakhtin, 'The Problem of Speech Genres', in Bakhtin, *Speech Genres and Other Late Essays*, University of Texas Press, Austin, TX 1986, pp. 68—9.

38. Roman Jakobson, 'Closing Statement: Linguistics and Poetics', in R.E. Innis, ed., *Semiotics*, Hutchinson, London 1986, p. 151.

39. Mikhil Bakhtin, 'The Problem of Content, Material, and Form in Verbal Creative Art', quoted in Gary Saul Morson and Caryl Emerson, *Mikhail Bakhtin, Creation of a Prosaics*, Stanford University Press, Stanford, CA 1990, p. 81; translation amended.

40. Deryck Cooke, *Vindications*, Faber & Faber, London 1982, pp. 121—3.

41. Osmond-Smith, 'The Iconic Process in Musical Communication', *Versus* 3.

42. Ibid., p. 11.

43. Bakhtin, *The Dialogical Imagination*, p. 84.

44. Ibid., p. 250.

45. Cf. John Rosselli, *Singers of Italian Opera, the History of a Profession*, Cambridge University Press, Cambridge 1992, pp. 4—5.

46. Nietzsche, *Birth of Tragedy*, pp. 113ff.

47. Rosselli, *Singers of Italian Opera*, p. 36.

48. Ibid., p. 58. This, he adds, in a society where 'down to the early 1950s . . . men still hooted at women if they wore slacks in town or rode a moped astride'.

49. Ibid., p. 177.

50. See Philippe-Joseph Salazar, *Idéologies de l'opéra*, Presses Universitaires de France, Paris 1980; especially pp. 108—43.

51. Jeremy Tambling, *Opera, Ideology and Film*, Manchester University Press, Manchester 1987, p. 63.

52. Edward Said, *Musical Elaborations*, Chatto & Windus, London 1991, p. 65. It is striking that none of the writers on opera cited here, from Nietzsche to Tambling, is a professional musician or musicologist.

53. Suzanne Langer, *Feeling and Form*, Routledge & Kegan Paul, London 1953, p. 109.

54. T.W. Adorno, *Introduction to the Sociology of Music*, Seabury Press, New York 1976, p. 86.

55. Christopher Small, *Music, Society, Education*, John Calder, London 1980, pp. 88, 22.

3

The Powers of Notation

The Prehistory of Notation

Notation, at the time of the modes and the minstrels, was the intellectual property of the Church. In the earliest of European notations (not counting the ancient Greek) at the time of Pope Gregory I, there was as yet no indication of pitch. There were only accents used to indicate the melodic curve or cadences in the rise and fall of the voice, from which the neumes developed. This kind of notation is called chironomic, and was already in use — according to Philo of Alexandria — by Essene sects around the time of Jesus, from whom the Church probably inherited it. The earliest surviving example is a mutilated strip of third-century papyrus from Egypt, with markings similar to those in later Byzantine texts. The method is still employed in the Jewish *ta'amim* which are used in the synagogue. This is the system of 'ear-marks' that are included in pointed classical Hebrew script alongside the vowel sounds to indicate the biblical chant; each sign represents a specific pattern of notes which is learned by ear, and which varies according to the mode being sung. It is not that in chironomic notation the actual notes to be sung are vague, that different notes would do as long as they fitted the shape (as even some musicologists seem to imagine), but rather that the signs comprise a language of motifs, with an order and a structure which in the case of the *ta'amim* follows the syntax of the written text.

The limitations of chironomic notation are easy to perceive: the fact that the Hebrew accents are the same for all the biblical books irrespective of the mode in which they are to be sung indicates that they are little more than an *aide-mémoire*. They can accomplish this function without indicating scale or rhythm, tonality, tempo or intervals. They cannot be sung by someone who does not know the modes and the rules for interpreting the code of signs (which perfectly suited the rabbis). The system of neumes was no

54

more efficacious, at least to begin with. But then nor did the early church choir sing from notation; the manuscript was for the choir master or at most the solo singer. In the seventh century there is still no written musical script, in any form, of melisma, decorative groups of notes such as the 'jubilations' which were a common practice of soloists. The more definite notation of the ninth century represents the first proper attempt to describe the melisma in articulated written form. The improvement of the system, the introduction of a four-line stave, is attributed to Guido d'Arezzo in the first half of the eleventh century, who also devised a set of syllables to denote the relative pitch of the notes of the scale, the ancestor of the modern do-re-mi.

Max Weber argued that there was a profound tension between music's rationalization, its organization since the late Middle Ages according to more and more clearly articulate principles, and the free-ranging 'irrational' basis of 'sociologically primitive' music (a term which today might well be allowed to take in rock, a music that wells up inarticulately from the real human need for *musica practica* on which the commercial music industry depends for its constant renewal). At the root of the separation was the great fear on the part of the organized Church of the free expression of popular sensibility. The system of neumes, however, did not differentiate between whole and semitone steps, and this circumstance, says Weber, 'favoured flexibility of official musical patterns with respect to the musical needs of ordinary practice, and the penetration of popular tonal traditions into musical development'.[1] In other words, the *cantus firmus* served as a framework, not a constraint, and the parallel movement of the voices in organum — the practice of parallel unison singing — was free and unfettered, with individual singers introducing their own variants.

The effect produces a fusion of two elements. Firstly there is the combination of the different registers of the human voice, which naturally lie a fourth or a fifth apart. (This, when rationalized, produces the modern categories of soprano, alto, tenor and bass.) The effect was much appreciated in medieval times, as when Hucbald defines a consonance as the 'judicious and harmonious mixture' of a man's and a boy's voice singing in unison.[2] Secondly, there are the individual alterations of particular singers, who vary their lines and sometimes move in contrary motion, ascending or descending not with but against the direction of the main tune, introducing a variety of spontaneous harmonic effects. This kind of singing is still to be found among groups of untutored singers within the dominant Western culture, like church (or synagogue) congregations in communities with the minimum of formal musical education. It is a mark of inauthenticity in Hollywood cinema that scenes of communal singing in such settings are often dubbed by off-screen choirs with trained voices intoning written-out harmony.

Because of the very unorderliness of organum, not to mention other forms of heterophony, an effective form of notation became, as Weber put it, an object of eager speculation by monastic musical scholars. Organum is relatively easy to notate, because the voices move in parallel, for which a single line will suffice. The notation of full-blown heterophony, which consists in overlapping segments and variants of the same melody in different tempi or with different rhythm, is much more difficult and took longer to accomplish. The two decisive stages were the fixing of semitone steps by inserting the neumes into a system of staff lines (the stave) and then the invention of the methods of time-value indication. Pitch and rhythm thus become the two fundamental parameters of what Trevor Wishart, an electro-acoustic composer, calls Western music's 'analytic notation'.[3]

Early pitch notation facilitated experiments in solo part-singing; these experiments stimulated the development of mensural notation, to control the parallel movement of the different voices by precisely measuring the length of the individual notes. The necessary techniques were modelled on poetic metre, which is not only logical — the music we are talking about was vocal — but testifies to the close relation in medieval philosophy between music and poetics. But the new mensural music was subject to the sanction of ecclesiastical authority. At first only ternary rhythm (3/4 time) was officially acceptable since it could be rationalized as a symbol of the Holy Trinity, and hence it was called *tempus perfectum*, perfect time. Not till the *ars nova* in northern Italy in the fourteenth century was duple or binary time (2/4) admitted to the scheme — which means not that it had not been used but that it was not previously condoned.

If the downfall of Gregorian chant was inevitable, one of the weak links was language. Already by the eighth century no one any longer learnt Latin as a vernacular language. As the centres of musical life subsequently moved from the monasteries to the collegiate churches, the princely chapels and the household chambers, knowledge of Latin grew weaker. The medieval composer no longer reproduced the accent and intonation of actual Latin speech. In pieces like Perotin's extraordinary *Viderunt Omnes*, dating from the early thirteenth century, words and syllables are broken up by techniques such as the hocket, in which open vowels are reiterated over many notes in a way that destroys their verbal integrity but is rhythmically highly charged. This is the very opposite of the verbal domination in Gregorian chant. A remarkable aesthetic alteration has taken place. Music has discovered a new form of Dionysian expression.

If the multiple voices of heterophony, including organum, gave rise to dissonance, so too did the new method of written composition. With early notation, composition became additive. Starting with the original voice, normally the tenor, often derived from plainsong, a second line was added above it according to the simple harmonic rules of the time, and then a third, below or in between. Sometimes, in the course of this process, when a third part was added – by the same or another composer – its harmony again based on the tenor, this created a strange result: it produced harmonic clashes, or dissonances, when all three parts were played together.

Peter Maxwell Davies, one of a number of late-twentieth-century composers deeply fascinated by medieval music and its discoveries, has exploited this peculiarity of the early additive motet in a work called *Antechrist*. Using as his basis a thirteenth-century manuscript, *Deo confitemini Domino*, he treats the original to fragmentation by serial means, and then brings it back in a strident instrumentation that accentuates its dissonances, returning to us the sense of aesthetic shock the piece would have offered to its original listeners. Not least, by returning to us the sense of aesthetic shock the piece would have offered its original listeners, the work amounts to a strong argument in favour of the idea of structural listening. For in listening to such a work we still know, despite the dissolution of the harmonic system, what counts both as harmony and as dissonance, and which sections are non-harmonic, or neither. In short, we take our cue from the codes utilized by the music itself; our ear is not a passive receptor but an active organ which chooses the matrix within which our hearing takes place – at least, the kind of hearing which we call listening.

More than one writer sees an analogy between the medieval motet and the Gothic cathedral, for as Wilfrid Mellers puts it, the music is built 'on the rock of the plainsong cantus firmus, the other parts being added separately, each as an independent entity'.[4] At the same time, however, the procedure stimulated the delight of many a medieval composer in the phenomenon of dissonance, and they soon felt increasingly free to break with ancient restrictions. They no longer felt obliged, for example, to keep the *cantus firmus* in the tenor. The chant could now lie in any voice, or could travel from one part to another. It could be moulded into a more flexible rhythm. This process was decisively helped by improved techniques of notation. The very sight of the music laid out on the page tempted the composer into allowing the plainchant to migrate between the voices. The results were very different from anything intended by the monastic scholars with whom the new notation originated.

When the parts were temporally aligned, and no longer seen as separate voices which were calculated independently of each other, this could promote a euphonious sense of harmony and smooth texture, as in England in John Dunstable's generation in the first half of the fifteenth century. The effect was widely appreciated and Dunstable himself was regarded at home and abroad as perhaps the foremost composer of his time. But not all mensural music aimed for this Apollonian ideal. The individual parts were not always written out in temporal synchronization. Notation had not yet imposed its uniformity, and motets exist in which the parts are in different time signatures, four, three and two, as well as singing different texts. The result — to which again the twentieth century reveals a curious affinity — is an extraordinary complexity in which the rhythmical stresses of the different parts never come together.

These and other paradoxical effects of notation can be seen in the interweaving musical lines of the *Ars Nova* of the Italian trecento, where early polyphony begins to develop new secular forms — the *ballata*, the *caccia* and others antecedents of the madrigal. The period is that of the Avignon popes. In Italy the division in the Church has weakened its influence, and as Gallo observes, although the composers of fourteenth-century Florence were all in religious orders there is hardly any evidence of this in their surviving output, which is almost entirely secular. Their world is that of the young gentlemen of Boccaccio's *Decameron*, who have left Florence to flee the plague, and who perform their songs and dances before and after sitting down to eat.

Boccaccio shows no knowledge of polyphonic music, but two subsequent collections of tales from the early 1400s speak of the new music favoured by the educated amateur, and both of them mention the composer and organist Francesco Landini. In the first, by Giovanni Gherardi, which describes the meetings of a group of Florentine intellectuals in 1389 in a manner directly modelled on the *Decameron*, Landini is the narrator of the final story. Gherardi describes his playing of the portative organ as 'infinitely sweet'. He also figures as a composer almost twenty years after his death in a collection of sonnets by Simone Prudenzani from about 1415, describing an imaginary series of musical performances of the day. More information about Landini is supplied by the Florentine chronicler Filippo Villani, who tells us that although he had been blind since childhood, his musicianship was unsurpassed. As evidence of his popularity, a larger body of his work survives than of any other composer of the period; it reveals a master of early polyphony at the dawn of the Renaissance, and one of the most advanced composers of the day. But in that case, we must temper our idea of notation. If the kind of music it stimulated could be mastered by the practical intellect of a blind composer, its relationship to *musica practica* was obviously a subtle one. This paradox persists. It is hard to imagine a painter who goes blind being able to continue painting, but we know several composers who have gone deaf and continued to compose. (Today, even more remarkably, the solo percussionist Evelyn Glennie has proved that you can continue to perform and to play new works even after going deaf as a teenager.) It is not notation itself but the conceptual space it creates on which this paradox depends, for this conceptual space is internalized by the musician's inner ear.

With these developments of the late fourteenth century, the prehistory of modern Western music comes to an end. From now on, the development of

European musical art is inscribed in its evolving notation. It is this that divides music into two — composition and performance. It also has another effect: it divides it into the part that is notated and the part that isn't, or can't be, because notation cannot properly capture it.

Rise of the Triad

One of the nodal points of Max Weber's argument in *The Rational and Social Foundations of Music* is that a rational notation — a notation that gives musical creativity the form of a calculable procedure based on comprehensible principles — is a necessary component in the organization of the larger and more complex musical groups and forms which emerged over the course of Western musical history. He sees the summit of Western musical achievement in the various forms of mature polyphony, of which he distinguishes three main types: contrapuntal polyphony, in which all participating voices have equal rank; polysonority, or fullness of choral sound; and harmonic homophony, in which the parts are subordinated to a leading voice, which serves as the vehicle of the melody. The gist of his thesis is this: that the development of polyphonic music in Western culture is the result of the invention of an improved notation aimed initially at reducing ambiguity in the inscription of melody; that this soon stimulated further notational refinements; and this more refined notation in turn made possible new combinations of voicing. Early polyphony thus evolved into what Weber calls harmonic chord music, which first reaches full fruition around the year 1600 after several centuries of development (and is followed by several centuries more).

There are non-Western societies and idioms, such as the Balinese, which have developed along different lines, without notated music, that still allow for large 'orchestras' and various kinds of heterophony. There are other extremely sophisticated musical systems, like that of the Indian raga, which have developed large-scale forms without notation. There are also other systems of notation, such as the Chinese. Joseph Needham wrote: 'If Ssuma Chhien is to be believed, there was even a system of notation for stringed instruments as early as the -6th century, for in the famous story of Duke Ling and the dancing cranes, it is stated that he made his Music-Master Chuan write down the tune of the kingdom-destroying music composed by Music-Master Yen in an earlier age.'[5] Those were legendary times. According to modern scholarship, the earliest surviving Chinese musical notation dates from the Tang Dynasty (618−907) and was pictographic. The pitch notation called 'gongchepu' was introduced in the tenth century.

Weber, who was well acquainted with the work of the first generation of ethnomusicologists, was not merely aware of considerations like these, he devotes a large part of the early chapters of his essay to a comparison of the many different musical scales used in different cultures. Enormously varied, there are nevertheless certain basic elements common to nearly all of them. Both the octave and the unequal division of the octave by the interval of a fifth are virtually universal. Pentatonic scales, those consisting of five notes (like the black keys on the piano) are very widely found. Many cultures have scales that employ quarter-tones. What is unique to European music since the early Renaissance is its use of the diatonic scales as the basis for a system of harmony in which the fundamental structural unit is the triad: the common chord, the sound which everybody knows even if they cannot name it:

The development of notation and the emergence of the triad go hand-in-hand, but before tracing the historical effects of the process, we must consider something of the technical significance of the triad within Western harmony. This arises from the fact that each triad may belong to three different keys, but in each of these keys occurs in a different position. For example:

Thus, where C is the tonic, the C major triad also occurs in the keys of G and F, known as the dominant and subdominant respectively to indicate their close relationship with the tonic. Because of these three positions, the triad is potentially ambiguous. It is this ambiguity, which is also found in other harmonic relationships belonging to the same system, that enables modulation between the keys to take place, most easily between keys that are closely related through sharing the tones of the triad. This is one of the differences between tonal harmony and modal harmony. The alteration is registered by the very word 'modulation': modulation does not exist in modal harmony, because the modal system provides no link between the modes. The modes lie parallel to each other, the system is not unified in the manner of triadic harmony. The music moves between the modes not by sliding from one to the other but by switching.

That the triad is relational explains the ease with which we recognize it at whatever pitch level it occurs and no matter how it is laid out — it is the structural relations between the pitches rather than the pitches themselves that define it. Dissonance is similar. The distinction between consonance and dissonance in the classical harmonic system is a function not of the predominance of the tonic, which identifies the key to which the piece or the passage belongs, but of the triad.

The analysis of the structural functions of the triad begins in the Renaissance with Giuseppe Zarlino, who was elected the first *maestro di capella* at St Mark's in Venice in 1565, and was the first theorist to recognize the fundamental antithesis between the major and the minor scales. The new theoretical model only achieved full expression almost two centuries later, in the work of Jean Philippe Rameau, who published his first major work on musical theory in 1726. Between the two, Zarlino and Rameau, lies the scientific revolution of the seventeenth century and the discovery of the harmonic series, the result of investigations by Vincenzo Galilei (father of Galileo and pupil of Zarlino), Mersenne, Kepler, Bacon and Descartes. Finally, in the early 1700s, the all-but-deaf experimenter Joseph Sauveur reformulated the findings of more than a hundred years' work as the science of acoustics.

What these researchers found is that a string or a column of air vibrates simultaneously along its full length and also successive aliquot fractions of it — halves, thirds, quarters and so forth. This produces a set of partial vibrations superimposed on the basic tone. As these simultaneous sounding tones get higher and fainter, the underlying tone, which acoustics calls the fundamental and harmonic theory the tonic, recurs in the form of successive octaves, while in between come various harmonic tones. The most prominent of these are the third and the fifth in the harmonic series. These two tones correspond to the intervals of a fifth and a third respectively, the two notes which together with the fundamental (or tonic) form the triad.

Unfortunately, the harmonic series is not as simple and regular as it first appears, and in the divergencies which disrupt it — to be examined in detail in a later chapter — Max Weber discovered the anomalies which were suppressed by the rationalizations of the Western harmonic system. To the Enlightenment, however, the discovery of the series made musical theory a paradigm of calculable order. Observing the apparent correspondence between the arrangement of the overtone series and the consonances of post-Renaissance music, they immediately concluded that the overtones were the necessary and sufficient explanation for harmony. The daily exercise of musical art was to them the validation of the hypothesis. In particular, Rameau's contribution was the rationalization of this new-found knowledge in a form directly related to compositional practice. He not only showed how the triad was derived from the harmonic series, but advanced the notion that the chord was the basic element of musical discourse, and that melody was therefore based on harmony. Further, he introduced the term 'inversion' to describe the relation between chords built up using the same notes but in a different order, arguing that these were effectively all the same chord because they all performed the same structural function — they were the pivots, for example, of modulation from one key to another. Hence the concept of functional harmony (another term introduced by Rameau) which was to dominate the teaching of harmony for almost two hundred years.

Functional harmony introduces a dangerous new split between theory and practice, for the theoretical formulation suppresses the difference in the *sound* of the 'same' chord when the tones are distributed differently, not to mention differently voiced (a modulation may be attenuated by making it sound softer, or emboldened by foregrounding a particular component tone). Even leaving this objection aside, the theory fails to deal with the phenomenon of dissonance, and is far from watertight when it comes to the question of the minor keys, whose intervals — because they stem from the modal system — cannot be derived in the same way. The gaps in Rameau concerning these matters are not simply evidence of the provisional character of the new theory, they also mark the anomalies which Weber spoke of, but which theorists over the next few generations suffocated beneath a compulsion to rationalize — even in face of the contradictory intuitive practice of composers who kept breaking the rules.

The rebellion of the Romantic movement was in good measure directed against this dangerously ideologized version of the scientific ethos, and was musically expressed in the restoration of the supremacy of melody over harmony. As harmony was required to follow melody instead of vice versa, the rules of harmony became stretched, and how to stretch them became a new preoccupation for many composers. At the beginning of the twentieth century Schoenberg interrogated the whole process from a new historical juncture, with a perspective in which certain Enlightenment tenets have been undermined both by Darwin and evolution theory, and the revolution in psychology associated with Freud and the concept of the unconscious. Though Schoenberg is not exactly a Freudian, he brings both these new models to bear on the history of rule-breaking by composers down the centuries. The result is a new dynamic model. For Schoenberg the overtone series is not a passive fact of the musical universe; it is a field which itself gives rise to the phenomenon of dissonance. Dissonances begin as distant overtones, and are therefore initially less comprehensible to the ear, but the composer's unconscious learns to pick them out and render them articulate. The perceptual process which produces this effect has an evolutionary character, which leads from the medieval modes to triadic harmony to chromaticism and thence to atonality.

Schoenberg, like many theorists, saw the evolution of harmonic polyphony as a process beginning with organum — simple unison singing in which the parallel lines of the melody are distinguished by the contrast between the timbres of human voices in different registers. It is not difficult to imagine how the resulting parallel movement, to which each voice contributes its peculiar timbre, was instinctively pleasing to the ear — because it reinforced the shape of the melody through imitating the overtones closest to the fundamental. It was also extremely impressive inside a Gothic cathedral.

This theory is not without its problems. For one thing, taking Bakhtin's observations about the heteroglot nature of cultural dialogue into consideration, what evidence is there that the beginnings of harmony were limited to organum? There is also a crucial problem of harmonic theory to consider. Organum employed the ancient consonances of the octave, the fifth and the fourth, which arise from the natural separation between the registers of human voices produced by biological differences. But these are not the intervals that comprise the triad of the common chord which produces the classical harmonic system. The problem, for orthodox harmonic theory, is the presence of the fourth. Because this interval in the overtone series comes higher up than the third, one would therefore suppose it to be weaker, yet in organum the third is absent.

Structurally speaking, the presence of the fourth comes from the division of the scale by the third harmonic — the tone corresponding to the interval of a fifth. The fifth is often thought of as dividing the octave into two halves. Since the third harmonic stands to the fundamental in the ratio 3:2, if you count the frequency value then these halves are equal. For example, in the case of a fundamental which sounds at 440 cycles per second, the octave is 880, and the interval of a fifth, corresponding to the third harmonic, is 660. (These are in fact the values of modern concert pitch, established by international convention, where 440 has the value of A above middle C, and 660 is the E above that.) Counting the intervals, however, the division is unequal. The lower half (from 440 to 660) is larger, comprising five tones; the distance from the fifth to the octave (660 to 880) which comprises the interval of the fourth, is one tone smaller. This occurs because frequency progression is geometrical, not arithmetic.

The relationship between the fourth and the fifth is a structural relationship, also called inversion: the division of the octave by the one logically produces the other. But with the emergence of triads and the growing strength of harmonic consciousness, it became decidedly problematic. The classical harmonic discourse of the seventeenth century constitutes the rationalization of a situation which emerged in the fifteenth century, though it already begins to make itself felt in Landini and even Perotin. In due course, harmony at the fourth is banished, and the third, corresponding to the next overtone, is admitted to full citizenship as a consonance, confirming the triad as the basic structural unit. This crucial shift represents such a radical alteration in musical language that after Weber and Adorno succeeded in introducing sociological criteria into the study of music, it was only a matter of time before critical musicologists started to think of it as the musical embodiment of the transition from feudalism to capitalism.

The primary seed-bed for this transformation was vocal music, which predominated in both formal and informal musical culture in Europe until the rise of concert life in the eighteenth century. When polyphony of Weber's first type came into ecclesiastical use in northern Europe in the early thirteenth century, the principal voice, the voice which carried the *cantus firmus*, was the *tenor*, in register approximately that of the modern baritone. Above it moved the *motetus*, roughly the same as a modern tenor, and the *triplex*, or third voice, a high alto; hence the modern term treble. When a fourth voice was used it was generally a second treble. The resulting music was relatively high pitched, and moved in the form of freely intertwining voices around a hovering centre.

But then the emergence of tonality shifted the centre of gravity, moving it down to a new lower voice, where it started to organize the harmonic structure from the bottom up in a manner that has since come to be regarded in European culture as natural. In short, as the hold of the *cantus firmus* weakened, the tenor lost its organizing function and began to float upwards; the bass now began to take over the function of the organizing line and grew firmer.

The migration of the voices completely transmuted musical perception. It was the sensuous quality in this shift which *produced* harmonic hearing as a perceptual form: it audibly brings the harmonic components into a new alignment. The pivot of the process, the rational classification of the voices according to the new harmonic logic, first appears in the written score around the year 1500; we do not yet find it in Dufay, who died in 1474. In Jannequin, Tallis and Palestrina it goes from strength to strength.

Is it possible that such a major shift in musical consciousness could have been the product of accidental or contingent causes? Is it merely coincidence that this change spans the passage from feudalism to merchant capitalism? From the stagnation of European society to its economic revival? From the moneyless, tradeless early Middle Ages to the renewal of commerce and urban life which produced the first stirrings of a new social order? How could these tremendous changes not leave their traces?

Given its enormous implications, musical notation must be reckoned one of the great inventions of the Middle Ages. It belongs with the other major new techniques of the time – horseshoes, windmills, treadle looms, the spinning wheel, clocks, lens-grinding, gunpowder and the printing press – which all contributed powerfully to the social and economic dynamism in which feudalism was transcended. Of course, a complex and extended process like this is neither a straight line nor evenly spread.

To begin with (and in broad outline) the period from about 1150 to 1300 was one of expansion, both economic and demographic. Society thrived – and musical consciousness too. But economic growth is cyclical, and when the optimal point of expansion has been reached, contraction is almost bound to set in. In the event, from around 1300 to about 1450 came an epoch of decline and economic crisis, exacerbated by the effects of war and the plague of the Black Death. Musical culture did not simply retract, however. The social forms of music are possibilities created by economic relations but not determined by them. Too many mediating factors are involved, both mental and material (language and idiom, instruments, institutions, etc.). It is not difficult to see that high musical art is more dependent on favourable economic conditions than is true of popular *musica practica*, which in times of social adversity still holds its own and can even flourish.

What happens in the burgeoning centres of capital when economic adversity strikes is of particular significance. Any advantage offered by place and circumstances will be used to resist, to try and restructure the economy, if possible to buck the trend and expand. When small economic pockets transform themselves in this way, this is good for cultural growth and for art music, which are always dependent on a strong local base. Thus did Italian city-states like Venice, Florence, Milan and Genoa successfully exploit their position as intermediaries between Europe and the East. (They controlled the spice trade, they developed local manufacture, and even established sugar plantation in Cyprus, Crete and Palestine.) In these cities, music prospered.

Meanwhile a different economic process in Western Europe had equally positive effects on musical life. Feudal landlords, faced with an unprofitable market and labour scarcity, had already commuted the services of serfdom into payments in kind; now they commuted payments in kind to payments in money, whose circulation was increasingly concentrated in the cities. Art music, which in the north was still a dispersed and isolated activity, again began to prosper, as a new culture established itself under burgher patronage.

In short, profound changes of an economic character universally altered the balance of social forces; the relationship of social classes was transformed to create a new economic and political geography, symbolized in the resurgence of the city both north and south – though with different regional characteristics. Thereby were set in motion transformations in every dimension of human sensibility. A leading role was taken by the cities of the south, and in Italy the cultural transformation was linked to the new scientific humanism of the Renaissance. Aesthetic sensibility developed novel responses, a new architecture was born, and in painting, a new definition of pictorial space was introduced: geometrical perspective. In music, the transmigration of voices produced a comparable reorganization of the musical texture — a transformation of heard space. To follow Bakhtin, the experience and representation of space and time acquired new forms and took on new meanings as new social and aesthetic chronotopes emerged.

The new sense of perspective promoted ideological integration. By conceiving the world from the standpoint of the seeing eye it not only promoted individual consciousness, it also displayed the Cartesian principles of rationality which became incorporated into Enlightenment ideology: perspective is the form in which the subject of Descartes' *cogito* sees the world when he opens his eyes (the gender, in Descartes, is male). Harmony performs the same role in music. The transformation of music presents a homology, or analogical affinity, to the historical process. The altered structural relations of music are akin to the new social hierarchy, and above all, to the new sense of direction in historical experience. In the former condition, you have a musical system, the modes, consisting of parallel and complementary planes, analogous to the stable and complementary character of the social relations of feudalism. In the new model, corresponding to the emergence of merchant capitalism, the old ideal structure has disintegrated, and a new dynamic force is discovered in the development of harmonic attraction.

Within this field of attraction, there also begins to emerge a new sense of subjectivity in music. Or rather, a new musical subject, the composer with an individual sensibility, who becomes its historical agent: persons in history who have a biography and leave the world a little different from when they entered it. We first see the composer in late-medieval times as a kind of supremely gifted natural like Landini. This type of figure has exemplars in every age, but two centuries later another kind of consciousness has begun to appear. A paradigm of the new model is Monteverdi, who in 1616 declines to set a short dramatic scene suggested by a patron because, he tells him, 'I do not feel that it moves me at all . . . nor do I feel that it carries me in a natural manner.'[6]

The composer as historical subject is implicit in the evolution of harmony. Without the agency of a self-conscious sensibility driven to unify the new spacio-temporal discourse of music, we should not expect to find Weber's second and third types of polyphony developing — the choral polyphony of the high Renaissance where musical space is saturated by the richness of harmonically equal voices; and the harmonic homophony of the eighteenth-century baroque, where harmonic parts are rationally subordinated to a single-line melody (except for J.S. Bach). Nor is it accidental that these two idioms typify respectively the religious intensity of the Counter-Reformation, and the ordered restraint of the rational bourgeois gentleman. But the interpretation of these influences is at once collective and individual, or inter-subjective. The composer as a historical person with a biography is a site where different forces meet, cultural and economic, historical, aesthetic and political, large-scale and small-scale, social and psychological, conscious and unconscious. This is not to ascribe to the composer a particular form of individualism, still less the possessive type of the nineteenth century, but instead, rather than dissolving the subject into history, to place history inside the subject, because the very concept of history has no meaning apart from the experiences of subjects. This kind of subject is implicit in the music without the need for histrionics, and becomes the shaping force behind it.

According to Schoenberg, the engine for this process of stylistic evolution was a phenomenon so subtle it had almost escaped theoretical attention: the feature known as the 'passing note'. The passing note, says Schoenberg, leads to the occurrence of the 'accidental chord', which is found when the melodic line is moving forwards above a sustained harmony beneath it and forms a fleeting and apparently accidental chord combination. Because of the way harmonic hearing is prestructured it escapes conscious attention, and occupies a transitive position between articulate chords. These transitive chords are apparently unintended, and seem to have no influence on the harmonic progression in which they are embedded, but really, says Schoenberg, they are not accidental at all, because they are the product of the movement of the melodic lines that contain them. A kind of necessary accident.

Passing notes are sometimes called non-harmonic tones, that is, tones outside the harmonic scheme of the piece in question, but only, says Schoenberg, because the theorists couldn't fit them into their system. However, 'One's inability to regard it as a chord does not mean that it is not a chord, but rather that it is not like any of those that appear in the system.'[7] They are dissonant (otherwise no one would object to them) and as such contain the seeds of new harmonic possibilities. At first they impinge upon harmonically structured hearing only unconsciously, to be sensed by the composer's subconscious or 'intuition' (for Schoenberg, these are the same), which gradually picks them out and pushes them forward. And thus, he says, 'we see composers of all periods continually learning new secrets'.[8] At first these strange harmonies can only be admitted to the harmonic system when suitably prepared and resolved. The business of the preparation and resolution of dissonances, which at one point Schoenberg calls the application of 'protective wrappers in which the dissonance is carefully packed so that it neither suffers nor inflicts damage'[9] — this process forms a large part of the musical texture and of the composer's craft.

As Ehrenzweig explains:

> According to Schoenberg's profound theory of harmonic beauty, a new chord begins its life as an altogether hidden and inarticulate 'transitive' chord and as such remains outside the harmonic system; it seems fully explained as a melodic accident. Later the new chord is allowed to appear half-concealed and half-articulate as a 'dissonant' chord which needs still to be explained by the melodic device of preparing and resolving a dissonance. Without this melodic context the dissonance sounds jarring and unaesthetic . . .[10]

In short, the pull of dissonance intensified harmonic tension, but dissonances once admitted to the system were recuperated by the powers of harmonic integration. As a result, at no time was the system closed; on the contrary, like subjectivity itself it was forever expanding and contracting.

Schoenberg's concept of dissonance is not just evolutionary and psychological, but significantly, congruent with Nietzsche's: it bespeaks the fluctuating rhythm of Dionysian and Apollonian instincts in the composer's psyche. Whenever the system expanded with Dionysian energy the result was increased chromaticism (that is, the inclusion of sharps and flats beyond those that are present in the keys employed in a given piece). In the Apollonian phase it contracted, and harmonic stability increased; it was as if melody had been domesticated again. But in Ehrenzweig's view, Schoenberg's theory is more psychodynamic still. There is a third stage of harmonic articulation, when the new chord is accorded the rank of a consonance and can stand on its own without melodic disguise. In the long run, the process does not increase the number of consonant chords, which remains rather small, but instead expands the repertoire of acceptable dissonances, which becomes so great that it would be difficult, says Schoenberg, to systematize the relation of even the simplest ones to each other. This led by a kind of exponential logic to the point when chromaticism became acute and relentless around the end of the nineteenth century; at this point the key-system began to suffer from a loss of definition. The result was the demise of what is fondly called tonality, for whose destruction Schoenberg used to be held personally responsible.

And then, concludes Ehrenzweig, a fourth stage is reached, for with the demise of the classic harmonic system 'these distinctions seem out of date. Dissonances are freely applied just like consonances and we tend to enjoy their "bite" more than the all too polished smoothness of consonances.' What has happened is that 'overripe aesthetic form elements become neutral "counters" without emotional or aesthetic value' and are therefore discarded.[11]

This condition is not unidimensional and Schoenberg's method was only one of several options followed by the avant-garde prior to the Second World War. The influence of 'exotic' musics, the pull of noise, the technique of polytonality in which unrelated keys are overlaid, all gave rise to unprecedented stylistic diversity. Only after the war, when Stravinsky adopted serialism and Boulez, Stockhausen and John Cage emerged as leaders of the avant-garde, did composers still working in some kind of tonal language, like Milhaud or Copland, Walton, Britten or Shostakovich, get left behind, and come to be thought of as conservatives. The reasons are various and confusing, but the situation was clear: when the English musicologist Deryck Cooke defended such composers in *The Listener* in 1967, he defiantly called his article 'Reactionary'.

Since then, however, another shift has occurred. Post-Schoenbergian music, which began with the discovery of Webern's minimalism in the late 1940s, has witnessed the reintroduction of consonances by the back door, so to speak, in a second and very different phase of musical minimalism: the 'process music' of Steve Reich, Terry Riley, John Adams, Philip Glass and Michael Nyman. Not that this music is either the primary manifestation of postmodernism or the simple rediscovery of the triad it is sometimes taken to be. The pluralism of the postmodern condition consists in the coexistence of styles not only alongside each other but in composers like Berio or Maxwell Davies, within the same work, the strange competition of voices made up, it seems, of every musical idiom that has ever existed.

The Authority of the Score

The process by which notation becomes, as Weber sees it, the decisive catalyst in the trajectory of European music is a complex one, which passes through certain critical stages of development. In the beginning the written page is not intended for use in performance but to serve as a reference copy. To serve the former purpose it needed an appropriate layout, with the parts suitably aligned, which it began to acquire in the fifteenth century. The earliest surviving choir-books, for example, have a large format and are written in large notes, though at first they still lack bar-lines; pictures of the time often show a group of a dozen or so men and boys grouped around the choir-book which stands on a lectern in front of them. Gradually, the visual appearance of notation, increasingly designed to facilitate performance, becomes suggestive, and begins to take on an organizing role in the musical texture. When bar-lines are introduced in the sixteenth century, and the unity of the measures is clearly marked, ensemble playing becomes easier and more precise. At the same time, their effect is to increase the tendency to think vertically. Now the *basso continuo* appears.

The *basso continuo* originated as an aid to performance. Organists, who conducted singers and gave them cues from the keyboard, and whose duties often included substituting for missing parts, began to use the bass line for mnemonics, which they wrote on the score in the form of numbers to indicate harmonies, to help them fill the sound out and give the singers a firm foundation. In Italy, around the turn of the fifteenth century, the practice transferred to the harpsichord and was institutionalized, and the figured or thorough-bass became the organizing principle of the accompanying continuo. Anyone fulfilling the professional function of musical director was expected to be able to play fluently from a figured bass, which meant not only leading the ensemble but also extemporizing on the written notes.

The score thus becomes the skeleton of performance. A piece of chamber music, for example, might consist of only the solo and continuo parts, the latter a mixture of notes and numbers to be played on any appropriate instruments, which necessarily varied with the circumstances. The rest, including ornamentation and embellishment, was left to the occasion. Similar conditions applied in the case of choral music. According to Thurston Dart, in the performance of music like Palestrina's not only would the chorus be accompanied by an extemporary organ, but the leading singer of each part would extemporize what he calls roulades; these roulades were at their most elaborate in cadences (hence the word 'cadenza'), and their use dates back at least to the time of Josquin, if not earlier. Similar practices developed in instrumental music. With the increasing size of the ensemble, the band was directed from the continuo or maybe the first violin desk; the primary task of the leader or continuo player was not interpretation in the modern sense but holding the performance together, while the players dressed it in colour, expression and ornament.

In short, in music both instrumental and vocal, the schematicism of the score rested on living conventions of performance, in which freedom to embellish and extemporize was a recognition of individuality in different vocalists and players. Moreover, within this framework an art of improvisation flourished as well. As Dart informs us:

> As early as 1390, the 'Monk of Salzburg' expected his composition pupils to be able to extemporise a counterpoint to a well-known tune, and the whole of composition teaching of the fifteenth and sixteenth centuries was based on the same technique. Morley's *Plain and Easy Introduction*, for example, begins by teaching the pupil the rudiments of music and sight-reading; part II of the book is concerned with what Morley and his contemporaries called 'descant', that is to say, improvised vocal counterpoint, and finally the pupil is taught how to compose on paper.[12]

This order of exposition is not arbitrary. The priority of descant correctly reflects the demands of *musica practica*.

Obviously, as a set of instructions for performance, the score is never just a blueprint. It is destined to acquire the status of a text. The difference is this. The blueprint has a one-to-one correspondence with the object it is used to make. Its realization is a matter of craft, and every competent craftworker reading the blueprint produces work to all effects and purposes the same (maybe not identical: two different music engravers may well space the same manuscript differently). Not so with texts. With texts you have to learn to read between the lines; you have to interpret, not just translate.

If modern critical theory argues that the literary text is always open to multiple interpretation, the musical score is the very paradigm of this condition. A score cannot be read *without* interpretation, its very purpose is to *invite* interpretation, and no two interpretations are ever quite the same. One need only compare the different recordings of Stravinsky conducting his own works, say *The Rite of Spring*, to realize that this is even true in the case of the composer as his own interpreter. Moreover, since both instruments and customs of playing them change, it is inconceivable that the art of musical interpretation could ever remain fixed.

This question has become the central problematic in the early music movement, where because of the incomplete nature of early notation, as well as the changes of musical orthography over the centuries, it is generally necessary to provide performing editions of archaic scores, which thus require the intervention of an editor. Consequently the score represents, according to one writer on the subject, 'not what the composer wrote, but an editor's theory about what the composer meant to write'.[13] Thus the musical text itself inexorably enters the identical process of interpretation and reinterpretation. The editor's version necessarily remains open to the performer's interpretation, and is therefore even further removed from the very authenticity which the movement proclaims as its objective.

The authority acquired by the score evidently has a good deal to do with the role which it affords in musical intelligence to the process of vision. The basic vocabulary is largely derived from the sphere of optical phenomena: notes are high or low, they move up and down, they are separated by an interval, etc. In musicological parlance, melody is synonymous with 'line' (and harmony with 'colour'). Notation, through these visual qualities, becomes an aid in comprehension and even composition. In *Doctor Faustus*, the narrator, Serenus Zeitblom, attends a series of lectures with the young Leverkühn by the music teacher Kretschmar, one of which is called 'Music and the Eye'. The theme of the lecture is the visual appearance of musical notation. Kretschmar 'assured us that a knowledgeable person could get from one look at the notation a decisive impression of the spirit and value of a composition . . . he sketched for us the enchanting pleasure which . . . the visual picture of a score by Mozart afforded to the practised eye; the clarity of the texture, the beautiful disposition of the instrumental groups, the ingenious and varied writing of the melodic line'. Indeed the visual aspect of the score takes on a most paradoxical quality. Continues Zeitblom:

> 'To hear with eyes belongs to love's fine wit,' he quoted from a Shakespeare sonnet, and asserted that in all times composers had secretly nested in their writings things that were meant more for the reading eye than for the ear. When, for instance, the Dutch masters of polyphony in their endless devices for the crossing of parts had so arranged them contrapuntally that one part had been like another when read backwards; that could not be perceived by the way they actually sounded, and he would wager that very few people would have detected the trick by ear, for it was intended rather for the eye of the guild. Thus Orlando Lassus in the *Marriage at Cana* used six voices to represent the six water-jugs, which could be better perceived by seeing the music than by hearing it . . .

The visual appearance of the score thus lends it a certain mystique. At the same time, by commanding allegiance, so that proper compliance becomes a necessary requirement of legitimate performance, the score comes to embody the very idea of the work's identity. The result is that the corpus of musical works in Western culture becomes co-extensive with the scores on the library shelves.

This authoritative identification of the musical work with the text is a rationalization of fairly recent origins, which already shows signs of dissolution. It is only finally consolidated in the the nineteenth century with the rise of the authoritarian conductor as the figure to whom the interpretation of this text is entrusted, and with the conditions of musical life which require the presence of such a figure in the first place. These conditions, primarily commercial and capitalistic (as we shall later see in some detail), are the manifestation of an increasing division of labour in the production of music and its control. The authority of the score is a concomitant of the transformation of the social relations of the composer brought about by the ascendancy of the publisher. The publisher not only took over from the aristocratic patron as the composer's principal support but also intervened in the market place on both their behalfs, in a manner that composers, as mere individuals, were incapable of doing by themselves. Nowadays, with the displacement of the publisher and the economic primacy of the recording, the written text has become a more paradoxical object.

The authority of the score was first mooted theoretically by a German church cantor, Nicolaus Listenius, in his treatise *Musica* dating from 1537. Distinguishing *musica practica*, or performance, from *musica poetica*, or the work itself, Listenius defined it as the task of the composer to produce an *opus perfectum et absolutum*, the musical text which endures after the composer's death. By the end of the century, in accordance with this new conception of their function, composers began to give their works opus numbers. Nevertheless, it is not for another two centuries that, as Carl Dahlhaus observes, this attitude becomes generally suffused in the musical consciousness of connoisseur and amateur.[15] As late as the 1760s, German philosophers are arguing differently. When Herder calls music an 'energetic' (*energische*) art, he means that it is essentially activity (*energeia*), and not a product or piece of work (*ergon*). The argument echoes Humboldt's view of language (which turns out to be rather modern) as 'something continual and passing on in every moment' and therefore preserved only incompletely in written form. For the metaphysician Hegel music naturally remains process, but because of its impermanence, his dialectics are only able to grant it, in Dahlhaus's phrase, 'a slight, vanishing degree of objectivity'.[16]

With Hegel we are in the age of the suffering heroic composer, and music is all subjectivity, or as Schopenhauer has it, pure will: 'The composer reveals the inner nature of the world, and expresses the deepest wisdom in a language which his reason does not understand . . . music . . . is the direct copy of the will itself, and therefore exhibits itself as the metaphysical . . . .'[17] (As Goethe once observed, 'It is now about twenty years since the whole race of Germans began to "transcend". Should they ever wake up to this fact, they will look very odd to themselves.'[18]) The corollary of this point of view is that the score is merely the contingent appearance of a piece of music in the material world. But in the age of art-religion, as Heine called it, when the emancipation of art from religion allows art to become the object of quasi-religious devotion, music, like all types of art, is detached from its social function and takes on the appearance of isolated and self-contained cult-objects: this is the *opus perfectum et absolutum*, to a degree unsuspected by the provincial sixteenth-century cantor. From this it is only a small step to the concept of *ars gratia artis*, art for art's sake.

Listenius's argument might appear to prefigure the positivist attitudes of twentieth-century musicologists; it did not correspond to the musical reality of his own times. For one thing, throughout the period of the baroque, composer and conductor were generally the same person, directing the band from the harpsichord or the first violin, and the score remained subservient to his presence. These circumstances are reflected in the paucity of subsidiary markings in the score of the time, intended to indicate expression and interpretation. Moreover, the orchestra was not yet standardized. As late as 1780, Mozart writes to his father back in Salzburg while preparing his new opera *Idomeneo* in Munich, to send him urgently 'a trumpet mute — of the kind we had made in Vienna — and also one for the horn — which you can get from the watchmen'.[19] Back again in Salzburg he was frustrated not to have the new clarinets he had found on his travels. In these conditions, orchestration was not yet fixed and there was no concept of authenticity. When Bach performed the music of Palestrina he was quite prepared to add wind instruments, double bass and organ accompaniment, while Mozart accepted a commission to 'improve' the orchestration of several works of Handel's for performance in Vienna. It is still decades before tampering with the orchestration becomes unthinkable, not until the concert hall has institutionalized the symphony orchestra and a new generation of composer-conductors have established new norms. Here it is Berlioz who takes pride of place, with his *Principles of Orchestration* — Berlioz, says Adorno, who created the first compositional technique conscious of its command over instrumental realization.[20]

If the end result of the process was to fix the instruments as well as the notes, such respect only applied to 'modern' music, the Romantic repertoire itself. Until fairly recently it was common practice to re-orchestrate older stuff, including Bach and Handel, supposedly adding colour and brilliance to match the enlarged environment of the nineteenth-century concert hall — a practice especially beloved of twentieth-century conductors of the ilk of Henry Wood, Stokowski and Beecham. In too many cases the glitter is false, the music becomes too thick and schmaltzy. On the other hand, the sinewy orchestrations of Bach by Schoenberg and Webern are not just versions but creative transcriptions and theoretical investigations of the original. The word which Peter Maxwell Davies employs for his own arrangements of Bach and Purcell for chamber ensemble is 'realizations'. This is completely distinct, however, from the fetishistic search for authenticity in the performance of pre-classical music on period instruments (or their replicas), which has generated a growth industry of learned disputation about performance style and instrumental construction, so successful that it has now encroached upon classical and even early Romantic music (Haydn, Mozart, Beethoven and most recently Berlioz).

Perhaps it is true that early music is best performed on period instruments tuned appropriately, but there are other difficulties to be confronted; not least, the falsity of the formal concert hall performance of what was once popular dance music and bawdy. In two of his Purcell realizations, Peter Maxwell Davies satirizes the whole endeavour by turning Purcell's pavans into foxtrots. What indeed is to count as authentic performance in the case, for example, of the domestic music by the Elizabethan composer Campion, who explicitly invited the players to change anything in it they didn't like? In the end, the very idea of authenticity is unmasked, and instead you have the question of the notion of performance itself: when the *opus absolutum et perfectum* does not yet exist, nor do the modern concepts of performance and interpretation. There is only the old medieval distinction between the practice of music, and its theory.

The Logic of Notation

Arguing on a radically different basis from Weber, Ehrenzweig nonetheless agrees with him about the active suppression by the Church in the late Middle Ages of irrational musical urges, which could not easily find expression, he says, in the articulate, rational melodies of the official Gregorian chant: 'The Church . . . tried to preserve the Gregorian hymns intact just as it became the custodian of classical rationality in the seclusion of its monasteries.'[21] The newly-invented musical notation was used to try and prevent any deviation from the traditional melody. Wherever these irrational and essentially Dionysian urges come from — Ehrenzweig links them with the ecstasies of the Crusades and the Gothic age — the invention of an analytic notation exacerbated the problem by imposing a distinction between articulate and inarticulate elements of musical form. If the possibility of recording a melody by notation presupposes an already articulate scale, notation renders what goes on between the steps of the scale not just, in Weber's word, unorderly, but in Ehrenzweig's, inarticulate: what is not articulated by notation is reduced to fleeting transitions henceforth accessible only to 'intuition'. Depth psychology, says Ehrenzweig, presents us with a model to comprehend the tension this process sets up. Consciousness penalizes the unconscious, thinking of it all too easily as a regression to more 'primitive' levels of thought. However, depth psychology reveals a dynamic aspect in this supposedly passive regression, in which inarticulate form elements behave in an active and plastic manner.

This line of conception is not inconsistent with the results of logical analysis. The North American philosopher Nelson Goodman has shown, in his book *Languages of Art*, that a successful notation must comply with a series of logical requirements if it is to constitute proper instructions for performance.[22] These requirements are syntactic as well as semantic — the characters that make up the notation must be clearly differentiated and articulate, which means the manner of inscription must be discontinuous, discrete and unambiguous; otherwise there is confusion over what the characters denote and whether the performance indeed complies with what the score predicates. (Hence the problems confronting the performer of early music dating from a time when notation was still relatively undeveloped.)

However, the import of this demonstration — even if the logician does not appreciate its significance — is not only that the conventions of notation are based on certain logical requirements, but they cannot always be properly satisfied even in a sophisticated system. The truth is that there are elements of musical performance — of *musica practica* — for which an unambiguous notation cannot be devised. For example, the same sign is used for phrasing and legato, and there is no adequate way of showing the distinction between short notes and certain types of staccato, These limitations give rise to intractable problems of interpretation. As Schoenberg observed: 'In tempo and its modifications; in dynamics, in accents and phrasing, in colouration — in all these fields we are still far from able to indicate perfectly what it is we want.'[23] He speaks from the point of view of an experimental composer of the early twentieth century frustrated over the difficulty of getting the performer to understand the stylistic requirements of his own music, but the problem has become a universal one. Any system of notation requires additional but incomplete subsystems, made up of both signs and words to indicate the great variety of non-discrete continuous effects which in fact until the eighteenth century the notation didn't even attempt to include. Among them are tempo indications, and effects such as *crescendo* and *diminuendo*, *accelerando*, *ralentando* and *glissando* (instructions, that is, to get louder or softer, faster or slower, and to slide between the notes). Because of the fluid and unbroken nature of these effects, the symbols devised for them inevitably took on a chironomic character.

This is what happened with the various forms of ornamentation such as grace notes or *appoggiature*, trills, shakes and turns of the baroque. These, moreover, were subject to different stylistic traditions in which they were executed differently. Furthermore, there was also the *fioritura*, an eighteenth-century word for the form of melodic decoration whose application was left entirely to the prerogative of the performer. With the growing differentiation of styles during the course of the eighteenth century — a question of the social history of music — difficulties appear with all these devices, and a certain confusion arose. Already by the time of Johann Sebastian Bach, says Schoenberg, there were differences of opinion about how to interpret these markings. 'This is seen not only from the fact that J.S. Bach began, against his contemporaries' practice, to write out his fioriture in full, but also from the fact that [his son] C.P.E. Bach found it necessary to write an "Essay on the true art of playing keyboard instruments".' Indeed the whole tradition, says Schoenberg, was bound to be lost 'in proportion to the growth of notation, since the latter was forced to develop in a mathematically simple way, whereas performance could correspond to the most complicated numerical relationships'.[24] This is also why notation fails to capture the rhythmic intricacies of jazz, with its subtle syncopation of the shifted beat. In short, if these elements of performance become expressive devices that evade the logic of notation, then this implies that the development of notation has the effect of shaping musical materials to satisfy its own demands, thereby marginalizing and excluding from its syntax whatever it is unable to capture.

Think of all the things a singer or instrumentalist can do (depending on the instrument) for which a conventional score rarely contains even the vaguest suggestion, such as *vibrato*, *portamento* and *rubato*: the wobbles, the scoops and slides, and the subtle alterations in tempo, not to mention variations in tone colour, which are nevertheless regarded as necessary parts of creative interpretation. Nowadays taste requires that their application should be sparing, yet these inarticulate elements are indispensable. Without them the performance is liable to sound flat and inexpressive. However, not only do such effects lack notation, they are not even fully subject to the performer's conscious control, and are largely left to spontaneous execution. They contribute nonetheless to the emotional impact of the music by giving it a plastic feel. As Ehrenzweig has observed, an inspired performer like Pablo Casals, say, places a *vibrato* or *portamento* only in certain places and not in others, 'obeying the command of some rigorous discipline which he is unable to put into words'.[25] Indeed if the performer attempted to control their application by conscious effort, either the intention would be liable to falter and mislead, or else the result would be mere mannerism, like the thick and over-sweet vibrato of a commercial string orchestra such as Mantovani's.

Think further of the way these features sound in jazz, blues, folk singing, all varieties of ethnic musics, even, if you like, crooning and rock music. Think of the way jazz players play their instruments, almost singing into them to produce all kinds of 'forbidden' timbres the same way the vocalist 'plays' the microphone: timbres which never occur when the same instruments are played in the classical manner, or didn't until recently, but the avant-garde has been busy reintroducing them (which also means devising methods for their notation). In many cases, such music is not only beyond our traditional notational means but also (except in their fetishized commercial forms) outside the harmonic system, in which such inflections carry no structural significance. But in examples like these they do. It doesn't just happen between the notes, these *are* the notes — as Bartók and Kodály began to realize when they started collecting folk music in Hungary in 1906, which they recorded in the field phonographically. When it came to transcribing what they'd recorded, they discovered that conventional notation wasn't equal to the job. It required modification to capture the quarter-tones, for example, which the phonograph revealed directly to the ear as characteristic of this music but 'cultured' Western hearing all too easily failed to register.

The drift of this argument is inescapable. Notation erected a block in the Western ear against the inner complexities of non-Western musics. A strange kind of deafness appeared in the most sophisticated ears — Adorno himself (as we shall later see) suffered from it. Under the hegemony of notation, the Western psyche came to fear the embrace of what it repressed, and responded to any music which manifested this repressed material as if it were a threat to civilization.

In evidence, there is an extraordinary passage in the compilation of criticisms and reports which Berlioz — who is otherwise a progressive thinker — brought together under the title *Evenings in the Orchestra*, a series of anecdotes, reviews and sketches with which the players in an orchestra pit purportedly entertain each other during the performance of lousy operas. Describing his visit to London in 1851, when he served as a member of the Jury at the Great Exhibition, he reports on hearing music from China and India. These are high cultures, but their instruments, to Berlioz, were crude and badly tuned. A young woman scratching at the strings 'was like a child who . . . amuses itself by banging away at random on a piano without knowing how to play'; the Chinaman's voice, 'a succession of hideous notes, nasal, guttural, and moaning', comparable to 'the sounds which dogs make when they stretch themselves after a long sleep'. 'As for the blending of song and accompaniment, its nature was sufficient proof that the Chinaman, anyway, has not the faintest notion of harmony . . . in my opinion, to call "music" the sort of vocal and instrumental noise which they produce is to misuse the word most strangely.' And so on; there're six pages of this stuff.[26]

The roots of this selective and discriminatory deafness go right back to the gestation period of harmonic hearing. In the 1480s, Tinctoris tells how he once heard the songs of a group of Turkish prisoners in Naples, which he found 'so ugly and so dull that the only thing they succeeded in doing was showing how barbarous were those who sang them'. Gallo, who quotes this passage, comments merely that European composers have long been given to consider only what they themselves wrote, in accordance with whatever rules were current, to be 'music', thus excluding all non-European music, as well as all European music which did not fall within the ambit of the dominant culture.[27] But there is much more to it than this. In the first place, in an era in which the Turks were the enemies of Christianity, Tinctoris is expressing an attitude that has every appearance of ideological motivation. In the second place, the example pinpoints a mutation in the structure of musical perception which came about somewhere in the elusive space between the late Middle Ages and the Renaissance. Before that, the Church may have tried to purify its music by excluding the profane, but it didn't imagine that what it took steps to suppress wasn't also music. According to Ehrenzweig, notation raised the stakes, and the result was that vital expressive elements were repressed, only to become a kind of musical subconscious.

As if to prove the old adage about exceptions that prove the rule, there is one theorist, belonging to the eighteenth century, who escapes these strictures: Jean-Jacques Rousseau, a musical autodidact who contributed the majority of entries on music in the *Encyclopédie* edited by Diderot and d'Alembert, and engaged in musical polemics. Rousseau was gifted with ears as critical as his philosophical intelligence. He rejected the dominant view of his time, exemplified in the rationalism of Rameau, in which the language of music was deemed to be governed by the laws of harmony, to which melody was necessarily subservient. Instead he drew from the knowledge that harmony was a historical invention of the Middle Ages, and that instruments needed to be tuned accordingly, the conclusion that in the music of sophisticated society, a calculus of intervals had been substituted for subtlety of inflection. Harmony, he wrote, 'can bring about unification through binding the succession of sounds according to the laws of modulation . . . But in the process it also shackles melody . . . It eliminates many sounds or intervals which do not fit into its system.' Indeed, peoples who tune their instruments differently 'have inflections in their singing which we consider false because they do not fit into our system and we do not care to notate them'. This, he added, 'can be observed in the singing of American savages, and is bound to be observable in various periods of Greek music too, if it were studied without a prejudice in favour of our own'.[28] Historians of music and its theory have not been kind to Rousseau, whose incursions into their field, both as theorist and composer, are generally seen as the work of a dilettante. Yet today we can safely say that this was not a merely speculative conclusion designed to conform with his critique of the false values of sophisticated culture, even if it had to await the appearance of ethnomusicology 150 years later for his observations to receive their scientific confirmation.

Notes

1. Max Weber, *The Rational and Social Foundations of Music*, Southern Illinois University Press/Feffer & Simons, London 1977, p. 86 (translation slightly amended).
2. Quoted in Gustave Reese, *Music in the Middle Ages*, Dent, London 1941, p. 253.
3. Trevor Wishart in Shepherd, Virden, Vulliamy and Wishart, *Whose Music?*, Latimer, London 1977, chapter 4 passim.
4. Wilfrid Mellers, *Caliban Reborn*, Gollancz, London 1968, p. 15.
5. Joseph Needham, *Science and Civilisation in China*, Vol. IV:1, Cambridge University Press, Cambridge 1962, p. 161.
6. Quoted in Lorenzo Bianconi, *Music in the Seventeenth Century*, Cambridge University Press, Cambridge 1987, p. 39.
7. Arnold Schoenberg, *Theory of Harmony*, Faber & Faber, London 1978, p. 323.
8. Ibid., p. 313.
9. Ibid., p. 49.
10. Ehrenzweig, *The Psychoanalysis of Artistic Vision and Hearing*, Routledge & Kegan Paul, London 1953, p. 116.
11. Ibid.

12. Thurston Dart, *The Interpretation of Music*, Hutchinson, London 1967, p. 62.

13. Walter Emergy, quoted in Philip Brett, 'Text, Context, and the Early Music Editor', in Nicholas Kenyon, ed., *Authenticity and Early Music*, Oxford University Press, Oxford 1988, p. 90.

14. Mann, *Doctor Faustus*, Secker & Warburg, London 1949, p. 60.

15. Carl Dahlhaus, *Esthetics of Music*, Cambridge University Press, Cambridge 1982, p. 11.

16. See ibid., pp. 10, 11.

17. Schopenhauer, *The World as Will and Idea*, Book III, #52, in Tilman & Kahn, eds, *Philosophy of Art and Aesthetics*, Harper & Row, New York 1969, pp. 285–7.

18. Quoted in Erich Heller, *The Disinherited Mind*, Penguin, London 1961, p. 90.

19. Eric Blom, ed., *Mozart's Letters*, Penguin, London 1956, p. 151.

20. T.W. Adorno, 'Music and Technique', in *Telos* No. 32, 1977, p. 82.

21. Ehrenzweig, *Psychoanalysis*, p. 85.

22. Nelson Goodman, *Languages of Art*, Oxford University Press, Oxford 1969.

23. Schoenberg, *Style and Idea*, Faber & Faber, London 1975, p. 300.

24. Ibid., pp. 299, 304.

25. Anton Ehrenzweig, *The Hidden Order of Art*, Weidenfeld & Nicolson, London 1967, p. 30.

26. Hector Berlioz, *Evenings in the Orchestra*, Penguin, London 1963, pp. 218ff.

27. F. Alberto Gallo, *Music of the Middle Ages II*, Cambridge University Press, Cambridge 1985, pp. 81–2.

28. Rousseau, 'Essay on the Origin of Languages which Treats of Melody and Musical Imitation', in *On the Origin of Language*, Ungar, New York 1966, pp. 57–8, 66.

4

The Inner Fabric of Music

Chomsky according to Leonard Bernstein

Music, says Umberto Eco, presents the problem of a semiotic system apparently without a semantic plane, in other words, without articulate content.[1] Music, like natural language, clearly involves a certain grammar, but it is not immediately obvious that it has a vocabulary or comprises anything equivalent to words. The word is a definite unit of signification which denotes a stable and well-defined meaning of the kind that can be listed in a dictionary. Music is not like this.

Music is not of course devoid of meaning. On the contrary, it means all sorts of things to all sorts of people. We are constantly faced with different kinds of meaning ascribed to music by listeners of different inclinations, and these meanings are located in different conceptual spaces. From a dialogical perspective there is no problem here — this is simply a statement of the multiplicity which is always present in the social, cultural and ideological situation of music, the conscious and unconscious echoes of different voices. Musicology, on the other hand, has too often dealt with this condition by suppressing its recognition, attending exclusively to music's formal properties, its affinity to mathematics. However, if music raises questions of difference from natural language, it is also different from formal languages like mathematics, algebra, symbolic logic or whatever. To put it crudely, in the case of formal languages the utterance is meaningless unless the code is known; whereas music, albeit rule-bound, appears readily intelligible, almost as if there were no code to be deciphered. Painting, dance and film are very similar.

True, there may be all sorts of difficulties if the work belongs to a culture alien to the listener, who may then not be equipped to understand its terms of reference, will be ignorant of the connotations which the music carries, and may even attribute to it qualities and properties it does not express. Yet a piece of music, like any work of art, may also provide an entry point, serve as a bridge between different cultures. This is only possible because, as we have remarked before, listening is structural, and the evidence of the structure is carried in the work itself. Indeed, according to information theory, the rules and elements of this structure can be mathematically defined and their distribution measured. It is precisely this regularity and the Gestalts which they form that the process of perception actively comprehends, and in doing so rewards the listener with enjoyment.

Eco observes that the whole of musical science since the Pythagoreans has been a protracted attempt to describe the field of musical communication as a rigorously structured system, which until very recently remained uninfluenced by contemporary structuralist studies — perhaps, he says, because these are concerned with methods that in its own way musicology absorbed long ago. Now that this line of inquiry has been opened up, however, what we find is a very uncertain set of relations between music and language.

Structural linguistics proposes the theory of double articulation to explain how natural language is made up of secondary units, called phonemes, which carry no signification in themselves but combine to form words which do. Words are made up of the primary units, known as morphemes. Morphemes are not quite the same as syllables, but in the same way as syllables, a word may consist of one or more morphemes. (The word 'morpheme' consists of two: morph-eme.) Morphemes, in turn, are composed of phonemes, which comprise a secondary level of articulation. Phonemes are not the same as letters of alphabet: a hard 't' is a different phoneme from a soft 't'. For theorists of the old school, phonemes are defined as the minimal speech units that arise naturally from the physiological structure of our mouths, throats and noses. In modern thinking, the essential property of the phoneme is its difference from other phonemes: Saussure, the founder of structural linguistics, calls them 'oppositive, relative and negative entities'.[2] In themselves, then, phonemes are meaningless. They form a non-signifying code which is the means and condition of signification on the primary level of articulation, in other words, on the level of the actual speech utterance.

Is there a similar form of double articulation in music? Henri Lefebvre notes that certain theoreticians have wanted to distinguish 'melemes': molecules or vehicles of musical signification which, like morphemes, are minimal units of signification made up of secondary elements which are themselves without meaning. According to this argument, the tone or beat by itself is musically meaningless; what counts is the difference from other tones and beats, and the combinations entered into. This approach is clearly promising, but it cannot, says Lefebvre, answer the questions which necessarily follow. What exactly is to count as the musical equivalent of the morpheme? Should the signifying unit be the interval? Or the chord? Or the group of notes? Even more crucially, what is the equivalent of the phonemes of which morphemes are made up? 'Where can you find the atom, the elementary sign, the musical unit? . . . is it the sound? The "note"? The pure sound produced by the tuning fork or the sound with its harmonics?' To these questions, the hypothesis of 'melemes' or melismata cannot provide an answer. In fact we should abandon the assumption of 'a single global definition of the relation "signifier—signified" in both verbal and non-verbal systems'.[3]

Despite such problems, Nicolas Ruwet asserts that music and language are perfectly comparable if you take language in the sense in which Chomsky and Miller use the term, following their definition that 'a language . . . is a set (finite or infinite) of sentences, each finite in length and constructed by concatenation out of a finite set of elements'. This, he says, applies also to music, 'given only that the musical equivalent of the sentence is the whole piece or movement, and the notion of concatenation includes both simultaneous relations (harmony) and oblique relations (counterpoint)'.[4] But this, as Leonard Bernstein pointed out in his televised Norton lectures of 1973, is hardly convincing. Although the German word *Satz* means both 'sentence' and 'symphonic movement', he remarked, it doesn't work well to compare a sentence with a whole piece of music; if you start at the other end and take the note to equal a phoneme, then a motif or a motto would equal a morpheme, and 'in that case, a phrase of music would have to correspond to a word (uh-o, we are getting into trouble here); a musical section would then equal a clause, and a whole movement would be a sentence . . .' — only there are no sentences in music, the fit is a bad one, so that if you define a full stop as a full cadence (at least in tonal music), which becomes the equivalent of a period at the end of a prose sentence, then you can easily find dozens of them in, say, a movement by Mozart, but in every case the cadence coincides with the beginning of the next passage, there is no full stop, no period, no pause, it is in the nature of music to be ongoing, 'it seems as if music is made up of relative clauses, all interdependently linked by conjunctions and relative pronouns'.[5]

Objections of this sort have not prevented people trying to discover Chomskian principles at work in music, and indeed this was the very project that Bernstein, unusually for such a conductor-composer, rehearsed in his lectures. Inspired by these lectures, the linguist Ray Jackendoff and the composer Fred Lerdahl teamed up to produce 'A Generative Theory of Tonal Music'. Convinced that music gave evidence of cognitive organization with a logic of its own, they found themselves forced to admit that the application of linguistics to music tends to mislead. It attempts too literal a translation of some aspect or other of linguistic theory into musical terms, if not by looking for musical 'parts of speech' then by applying the ideas of deep structure, grammatical transformation or semantics. One should not, they say, approach music with any preconceptions that the substance of a musical theory will look at all like linguistic theory.[6]

Bernstein himself proposed in his lectures that music possesses a rhythmical deep structure that is essentially symmetrical — periodic would be a better word — which transformations of various kinds mould into a complex aesthetic surface, full of ambiguities. (Some of these ambiguities are calculated and deliberate, some are accidental and involuntary.) Interacting with these rhythmic events, the harmonic texture is also produced by the transformation of a deep structure and equally rich in ambiguities, but governed by a different principle: the nature of the harmonic series.

Within this framework and following the tripartite division of the study of language between phonology, syntax and semantics, Bernstein examines the same three dimensions in music. He is prepared to draw the most exact analogies between linguistic categories and music because his purchase on the parallels is tempered by a keen sense of ambiguity, and of different types of ambiguity. For example, if verbal ambiguity is an utterance with more than one possible meaning, harmonic ambiguity is a chord which belongs to more than one key. The triad itself is ambiguous. But this analysis, while based on Chomsky, inevitably involves a critique of Chomsky, whose positivist approach renders him peculiarly insensitive to questions of semantics and ambiguity. The excuse he offers is that the phenomenon of poetry is not the concern of the linguist, not within the purview of an inquiry into 'normal' human speech.[7] As if poetry and ambiguity were somehow abnormal. Not everyone agrees. Linguists like Jakobson, language theorists like Bakhtin, see them not merely as perfectly normal behaviour but as necessary predicates of the very condition of language.

Bernstein is perfectly aware of this limitation of Chomskian theory. Ironically, he says, we can discover the logic in poetry — poetic logic — by using Chomsky's own transformational principles to reveal the deletions, antitheses, metaphors and other devices by which poetry is structured; and the same things happen in music. A linguistic instance first. Chomsky uses an example of a sentence which is phonologically perfect and syntactically impeccable, but semantically meaningless: 'Colourless green dreams sleep furiously.' Bernstein remarks that this sounds like a line of poetry, and proceeds to suggest a deep structure in prose form that might make sense of it. The same critique is even more graphically demonstrated by the English poet D.J. Enright in a poem called 'A Line and a Theme from Chomsky'. The line is the same. The theme is that of a US airman dropping napalm over the Vietnamese countryside, returning to base and having nightmares. Hence, colourless green dreams sleep furiously.[8] Perhaps it is not dissimilar when a composer like Stravinsky in *Petrouchka* takes a highly dissonant chord and makes sense of it by using it to establish two unrelated keys simultaneously.

A modern concept of ambiguity is central to Bernstein's musical semiotics, yet at the same time what he does is no more than revive the approach of medieval music theory. It was Guido d'Arezzo who first suggested that the structures of poetry could serve as a model for the organization of musical form. As Guido's work circulated throughout Europe the idea was widely taken up, and the authors of several subsequent treatises extended the list of correspondences; this became the basis for the system of composition known as *musica mensurata*, which involved a notation directly modelled on poetic metre. For Bernstein, music and poetry are both the result of the interplay of phonological and syntactical transformations. In the case of poetry the process of transformation interacts with semantic content to generate new meanings. In the case of music, with its lack of explicit denotation or direct referential content, a similar process has the effect of creating its own kind of meaning: the meaning is generated by the transformations themselves, acting on the generative cells of the music and on each other. In technical language (we shall come to the definition of the terms presently), 'a piece of music is a constant metamorphosis of given material, involving such transformational operations as inversion, augmentation, retrograde, diminution, modulation, the opposition of consonance and dissonance, the various forms of imitation (such as canon and fugue), the varieties of rhythm and metre, harmonic progressions, colouristic and dynamic changes, plus the infinite interrelations of all these with one another'.[9] These, says Bernstein, *are* the meanings of music. In Stravinsky's phrase, the game of notes.

Music and the Brain

Language and music possess different schemes of sonic articulation. Language uses vocal timbre as its primary dimension, concentrated in a narrow band of frequencies fitted to the differentiation of vowels and consonants. Other parameters, like intonation, are discounted (with certain exceptions: the role of pitch in Chinese or clicks in certain African languages). They return later, as the carriers of non-verbal expression (which may nevertheless considerably modify meaning). Music, on the other hand, extends from the bottom to the top of the range of hearing and uses all available acoustic parameters, though not in equal degrees of organization – timbre and dynamics are secondary to pitch and pulse.

This is a quite different kind of double articulation, involving interaction between two pairs of parameters. Pitch and pulse determine the primary qualities of melody and rhythm; timbre and dynamic intensity function as integral but secondary qualities, which refine the values of the primary qualities. (Until you get to electro-acoustic music: here the technological means of production produce a kind of reversal or annulment, in which timbre and dynamics, pitch and duration all become equal.) The result of this scheme is that while music still produces the clearest of shapes or Gestalts, their method of combination is not like that of phonemes; phonemic combination, as Saussure demonstrated, is a matter of simple binary opposition. Music, by contrast, is polyvalent, the geometry of musical tones is not Euclidean. Hence, the elements which in Chomsky's terminology are concatenated, are no longer finite; and they do not take the form of discrete syntactical entities. They permeate each other in ways that do not happen in language. Besides, the musical ear deals in much finer graduations than those involved in talking.

There is strong evidence from both the neurosciences and psycholinguistics that the musical faculty is separate from the speech faculty. Consider first the simple and decisive case, reported by the Soviet neuropsychologist A.R. Luria, of the composer Shebalin who, after a haemorrhage in the left temporal region of the brain, was unable to distinguish between the sounds of speech or to understand words spoken to him, yet continued to compose perfectly effectively. Here is evidence, says Luria, that while musical hearing and speech hearing may at first appear to be two versions of the same psychological process, in fact they are quite distinct.[10] Another case is that of Ravel, whose death in 1937 followed an unsuccessful operation on a brain tumour. Five years earlier, Ravel had been involved in a car accident which precipitated serious brain trouble. He lost the ability to undertand written words, and was unable to name or recognize written musical notes. Yet for about a year he could still play the piano and compose, and could still play scales and appreciate musical performance until his death. Various studies have now been carried out which demonstrate the lateralization of the musical faculty in the right hemisphere of the brain, on the opposite side to the language faculty. The latest, using brain scans to map the areas of the brain engaged while a pianist plays the piano, suggest that music calls on different areas of the brain linked by particular pathways: it involves a distributed neural network connecting several areas devoted to different aspects of musical activity. This picture is fully conformable with Gerald Edelman's Darwinian theory of brain development involving loops between different levels and areas of brain activity.[11]

These findings broadly conform with more complex evidence concerning the nature of phonemic hearing and its difference from music. It is well established that different languages employ different combinations of phonemes. In the late 1940s the sounds concerned became susceptible to frequency analysis through the sound spectograph; the resulting frequency patterns could be fed into a speech synthesizer, where the electronics made it possible to produce intermediate sounds between given phonemes. The results showed that the process of perception operates differently in speech and music.

One experiment took the spectographs of /b/, /d/ and /g/, and generated a series of thirteen intermediate sounds between them, equally spaced along a continuum. It was found that subjects did not detect these step-by-step differences; instead they registered abrupt perceptual discontinuities. The sounds were grouped together and perceived either as one or the other of the three given phonemes. Sounds at the boundaries were felt to be ambiguous, but within each group, subjects could detect no difference. This phenomenon is called categorical perception, and occurs only with the phonemes present in the mother tongue of the adult subject.[12]

This fits with experimental observation of babies during the critical period for the development of phonemic categories, which has shown that the brain becomes attuned to the categories active in the mother tongue, and that the categorical perception of other phonemes atrophies. After a certain age it becomes more or less impossible to learn the pronunciation of a new language without an accent. However, singers with highly developed musical ears are able to do so. Meanwhile, tests with other types of sound reveal that the brain does not attempt to apply categorical perception to sounds that do not normally occur in natural language: non-linguistic sound is perceived continuously, and often the smallest perceptual changes can be easily discriminated. This is the world of music.

Indeed other experimental data show that the human ear can detect well over 1,300 'just noticeable differences' between tones within the possible reservoir of pitches. Carl Seashore, in his classic study on the psychology of music, reported tests carried out on members of the Vienna Opera in which the keenest could discriminate 1/540th of a whole tone, and the poorest 1/49th (this was the orchestra which Mahler called the most musical he ever worked with). This is so much in excess of practical needs that Seashore suggests it is probably not attributable to training so much as self-selection and that people with exceptionally fine ears make exceptionally fine musicians, which slightly begs the question.[13] He also remarks that the scores achieved in the tests depended on a number of variables: the sonic region of the tones, their intensity, the capacities of both the hearer and the tester, and 'tonal fatigue', or the state of the hearer's ears. In short, pitch discrimination may be acute, but it's highly dependent on context. In Bakhtinian terms, the mathematical value of the note is an abstraction, like the phonemic value of a word, or even its dictionary definition. Its real, living and dialogical value is a function of the situation of the utterance which contains it.

Can any of this tell us anything sensible about the origins of music? Is the question even possible? Or is the condition of music the same as Herder argued in his prize-winning essay of 1769 about the origins of language, that without it the human being is not yet human, and with it they are already human, and that is all you can say? In that case, the question comes down to what another German philosopher described in his *1844 Manuscripts* as 'perceptibly existing human psychology'.[14]

This psychology is rooted in certain biological conditions. First the voice, produced by the larynx, which music shares with speech, and the spectrum of sounds that lie within the vocal range. Then the genetic instinct of the baby to babble and its inclination to vocal imitation, also shared by music and speech; and a world of sound to imitate: not just other human beings but also animal cries, bird-song, various noises big and little. Also the body which houses the voice and lends its natural rhythms, its forms of tension and relaxation, and which also produces sound by slapping and clapping. Music makes much more of this than speech, for which the body is more like a carrier, a vessel, than the sea in which it swims. Finally, there is the psyche, with both its Dionysian lower depths and its Apollonian intelligence, which each have their own typical forms of tension and relaxation.

But the psyche is the gateway between nature and nurture, the biological and the cultural. Thus, according to Lévi-Strauss, music operates according to two grids:

> One is physiological — that is, natural: its existence arises from the fact that music exploits organic rhythms, and thus gives relevance to phenomena of discontinuity that would otherwise remain latent and submerged . . . The other grid is cultural: it consists of a scale of musical tones, of which the number and the intervals vary from one culture to another . . .[15]

This explains, he believes, where musical emotion comes from. It springs from the fact that at each moment the composer, working within this double grid, withholds or adds more or less than the listener anticipates. In the former case, we might experience a delicious falling sensation; we feel we have been torn from a stable point on the musical ladder and thrust into the void. When the composer withholds less, the opposite occurs: 'he forces us to perform gymnastic exercises more skilful than our own'. Enjoyment 'is made up of this multiplicity of excitements and moments of respite, or expectations disappointed or fulfilled beyond anticipation . . .'

This is all very general, of course. On the question of music's relationship to language, he is more pithy. Music, says Lévi-Strauss, retains the negative imprint of its formal structures and semiotic functions: 'there would be no music if language had not preceded it and if music did not continue to depend on it'. If music speaks, 'this can only be because of its negative relation to language'. Music is like language without meaning. (Echoes of Eco.) It is understandable if the listener, 'who is first and foremost a subject with the gift of speech', should feel irresistibly compelled to make up for the absence, 'just as someone who has lost a limb imagines that he still possesses it through the sensations present in the stump'.[17]

The psychoanalyst Lacan holds a somewhat similar view. For Lacan, the unconscious itself is structured like language, and there is no articulate reality prior to language; beneath words there only lies concealed a formless plasticity which subsists in the gaps and interstices of the discourse of speech. According to the Freudian model of development, the reality principle is imposed on the infant from without, and this is what makes us social beings. Lacan argues that it is not reality that is imposed from without, but language, and it is the system of linguistic signifiers that turns us into social beings. Either way, music appears able to escape the reality principle and thus becomes utopian. For Lacanians, however, this utopian realm cannot be experienced except in terms of effects, which are always organized for us by the field of linguistic signifiers. There is a certain similarity between these ideas and Ehrenzweig's concept of the dedifferentiated level of perception inhabited by inarticulate Dionysian impulses.

Symbol and Psyche

Naturally there are several ways to think through the question of music in psychoanalysis. Ehrenzweig (a Viennese-trained psychologist and art historian whose approach could also be called structural) mentions that Freud suspected music to be 'an undifferentiated projection of an anal significance', observing how in that case 'our most sublime experiences would thus come from what is basest in the human mind'.[18] But this is no more than may be true for every form of artistic expression in so far as all of it consists in a similar process of sublimation.

Freud, by his own admission, was limited in his experience of music, though like a good Viennese he loved the opera. On one occasion, according to an account he gives in *The Interpretation of Dreams*, he found himself whistling an aria from *The Marriage of Figaro* to express an unconscious wish. He was waiting for a train at Vienna's Westbahnhof terminus, and spotted Count Thun, the aristocratic head of government, stalking on to the platform on his way to see the Emperor at his summer retreat. At the sight of the Count's imperious behaviour, Freud's resentment against the aristocracy escaped through his lips in the shape of Figaro's aria, *Se vuol ballare*, 'If the count wants to dance, I'll call the tune'. That night he dreamt what he called his 'Revolutionary Dream'.[19]

As always, what Freud noticed in his own mental processes became a model for his observation of others, and in the *Introductory Lectures on Psycho-Analysis* he gives an example of the way that tunes which suddenly enter our heads are conditioned by a subconsious train of thought. A young male patient was 'absolutely haunted by the tune (a charming one, I admit) of the song of Paris from [Offenbach's] *La Belle Hélène*, until his attention was drawn in analysis to the fact that at that time an "Ida" and a "Helen" were rivals in his interest'. In cases like these, the connection 'is to be sought either in the words which belong to [the tune] or in the source from which it comes'. He adds a reservation, however, an admission of ignorance: 'I do not maintain this in the case of really musical people of whom I happen to have had no experience.' In these cases, he thought, the emergence of a tune into consciousness could well be determined by its 'musical value'; in other words, not by virtue of extra-musical connotation at all.[20]

Freud's examples represent a type of musical icon: a musical entity like the fragment of a tune, a rhythm or even a chord, to which a certain symbolic meaning seems to adhere. They are instances, direct or indirect, of what the musicologist Richard Norton calls semantic domination, where words attached to the music in the form of vocal settings or even just the title of the piece condition the import of the music. This is not at all the same as Deryck Cooke in *The Language of Music*. Cooke reads the meaning he derives from the verbal text directly into the musical phrase, like a would-be denotation. Norton's concept of semantic domination is a form of connotation, which stems from a correspondence between different elements. Bakhtin would call it dialogical.

Freud himself discovered an example of the process at work in the case of his contemporary Gustav Mahler, when Mahler, distressed over the state of his relationship with his wife Alma, consulted him in 1910. According to Freud's biographer Ernest Jones, they met in a hotel in Leyden and 'spent four hours strolling through the town and conducting a sort of psychoanalysis. Although Mahler had had no previous contact with psychoanalysis, Freud said he had never met anyone who seemed to understand it so swiftly.'[21] In the course of the conversation Mahler suddenly realized why he constantly interrupted the flow of his music with

> the intrusion of some common-place melody. His father, apparently a brutal person, treated his wife very badly, and when Mahler was a young boy there was a specially painful scene between them. It became quite unbearable to the boy, who rushed away from the house. At that moment, however, a hurdy-gurdy in the street was grinding out the popular Viennese air 'Ach, Du lieber Augustin'. In Mahler's opinion the conjunction of high tragedy and light amusement was from then on inextricably fixed in his mind, and the one mood inevitably brought the other with it.

And this is exactly the character of Mahler's music, the unsettling juxtapositions of sadness and gaiety, like the jaunty tunes which so often interrupt the funeral marches in almost every one of his symphonies.

By an odd coincidence, while Mahler never used this particular tune, Schoenberg did, in his Second String Quartet, and for anyone who knows the story about Mahler and Freud, the Schoenberg quartet, written just a couple of years earlier, acquires an added poignancy. An ironic example of what Bakhtin calls intertextual reference: the evocation, accidental as well as planted, of one text by another.

A different type of psychoanalytic approach can be found in certain post-Freudians who consider the musical process as a means by which the lost maternal object is restored. General intimations of this kind can be found in Melanie Klein, for whom it is the desire for the restoration, internally and externally, of the good maternal breast which becomes the basis not only of the ego's capacity for love but also creativity. Creative activity is rooted in the infant's wish to re-create its lost happiness and the harmony of its internal world. The role of anxiety about attacks on the mother's body and the urge to make reparation are important factors in the creative impulse.[22] Again this is very general.

D.W. Winnicott, however, is explicit in locating the infant's earliest musical activity in the potential space of its earliest, and pre-articulate, fantasy life. Winnicott observed that the baby's first vocalizations occur at the same stage of development as that in which many infants adopt a special possession and invest it with peculiar autoerotic importance. These first 'not-me' possessions, which might begin with sucking a thumb or the corner of a sheet or blanket, he termed transitional objects. They are really part-objects, which are neither entirely internal nor entirely external but belong to a potential space between self and environment. This is an intermediate area to which the inner psychic life and external reality both contribute and where they are united in fantasy; a kind of half-way house, hence transitional. In this stage of development, there are various activities the infant may engage in which become transitional phenomena of the same quality. They include mouthing sounds, babbling, and 'the first musical notes'. Since these activities are found in every normal infant, it may be difficult to detect any special predilections among them until a later stage (though a review of transitional objects by one of Winnicott's followers found that their use is culturally conditioned by external factors like nationality and social class).[23]

Conceptually, however, there is a direct line of development from transitional phenomena to playing, from individual playing to shared playing, and thence to cultural and artistic phenomena. It is not difficult to see how this may happen in the case of music. The child inclined to do so

will move from the transitional arousal of musical instincts to singing and/
or an instrument. All it needs, apart from inclination and ability, is that the
characteristics of the transitional object are fulfilled: the object or activity
must never change until and unless it is changed by the infant, and the
rights which the infant assumes over it are not to be challenged (better still,
as soon as they are recognized they should be encouraged). We do not ask
of the transitional object, says Winnicott, 'did you conceive of this or was it
presented to you from without?' for it belongs to the potential space which
is neither but encompasses the contribution of both.

Conformable with this picture is the case of the child prodigy, whose
musical talent is already evident by the age of four or five, and who then
enjoys an uninterrupted musical education. Perhaps the most famous
twentieth-century instance is Yehudi Menuhin, who at the age of seven,
when he made his first public appearance, was already able to play works
like Mendelssohn's *Violin Concerto* and Lalo's *Symphonie Espagnole*. Menuhin
relates in his autobiography that as a toddler he would sing himself to sleep
with lullabies he made up himself. Overhearing one such cradle chant, a
friend of his parents, a synagogue cantor, thought it evidence of musical
talent, and a couple of years later encouraged them to take the little boy's
ambitions seriously when he declared, aged four, his desire to play the
violin.[24] As Menuhin himself puts it, 'music can be possessed without
knowledge; being an expression largely of the subconscious, it has its direct
routes from whatever is in our guts, minds and spirits, without need of a
detour through the classroom'.[25]

Winnicott's potential space is the very place where symbols are created
and meaning is discovered through the process of creative apperception.
The use of symbols provides a means of keeping in touch with the inner
psychic reality which is fed by instinctual life. This is similar in Melanie
Klein, for whom projective identification provides the basis of the earliest
forms of symbol-formation. 'By projecting parts of itself into the object and
identifying parts of the object with parts of the self, the ego forms its first
primitive symbols.'[26] This also describes the musician's relationship to his
or her instrument.

Inner psychic reality is essentially unconscious, though of course the
feelings to which it gives rise are not. Since it is related to the space from
which dreams emanate, we know that it not only leads forward to the
sublimation of instinctual life, but also back, to its earliest manifestations,
before the infant has achieved the integration of its ego, when the psyche is
still learning to dwell within the soma, the body. Indeed some psychoana-
lysts have argued that the force of music derives from the experience of the
foetus in the womb, whose acoustic dimensions they call the first psychic
space. Didier Anzieu speaks of a 'sonorous envelope' in which the unborn
infant exists 'bathed in sounds' — the mother's heartbeat, respiration,

digestion, and above all, her voice.[27] Moreover, these sounds may also come from outside the mother's body, communicating with the infant through the body's sympathetic vibration. Imagine, then, the musicality which may be nurtured in the womb by a mother who is herself a musician. This is not only plausible — we know that the baby is born with its ears already active, while the eyes take a little time to come into focus. It is also confirmed by the subjective reports of the sensitive mother. One friend of mine, the mother of three musical daughters, spoke of feeling her babies moving inside her whenever, as she did frequently, she attended a concert. If this is so, it may help to explain why musical gifts are so often seen in several members of one family.

If music provides direct access to these early states of being, it is through the process which by analogy with electricity Freud called cathexis, the concentration of mental energy in a certain object, its infusion into a particular channel of activity. It thus expresses not only the organic rhythms of the physiological grid described by Lévi-Strauss, but also the rhythms typical of the experience of the id, its intense and orgiastic experiences of frustration, tension and satisfaction, and what Winnicott calls the 'primitive' or 'unthinkable' anxieties of losing relationship with the body, becoming disoriented, falling into a void, going to pieces. These fantasies may later turn up as 'the stuff of psychotic anxieties', but at the same time, the imaginative elaboration of these experiences in the potential space of fantasy is the psyche's means of integration, and this too is translated, without further mediation, into the experience of music.

This quality of access to the deepest psychosomatic levels was evoked by Schopenhauer: 'The unutterable depth of all music by virtue of which it floats through our consciousness as the vision of a paradise firmly believed in yet ever distant from us, and by which also it is so fully understood and yet so inexplicable, rests on the fact that it restores to us all the emotions of our inmost nature, but entirely without reality and far removed from their pain.'[28] Music is therefore unlike the other arts, which are based on the realm of ideas, for it is the 'objectification and copy of the will itself'. It is all of a piece that Schopenhauer is the first philosopher of the psyche in modern European culture.

Something of this quality is revealed in a particularly poignant case of brain damage, that of a former BBC music producer and chorus master of the London Sinfonietta, Clive Wearing, reported by Jonathan Miller in a television documentary, *Prisoner of Consciousness*.[29] Struck down by a rare form of viral encephalitis, Clive Wearing suffered severe brain damage producing almost total amnesia, which extended to events taking place only a few minutes previously; so that in his own experience, and as he constantly repeats with a mixture of surprise and desperation (in front of a camera which he seems to take for granted), every other moment of his waking life is as if he had only just been given back to the use of his senses, has only just woken up from total sensory deprivation that has been caused by his illness, as if he had been dead and had just come alive again.

His wife, through her own observation, distinguishes between his semantic memory, which has remained intact, and his episodic memory, which has been destroyed: 'He knows I'm his wife, but cannot remember when we got married.' Clearly, she says, he remains the same person, and she always sees in him 'the Cliveness of Clive'. Indeed, other long-term memory traces are also present, or at least can be prompted back: he knows his telephone number, which has been the same for many years; he recognizes faces, though he cannot put names to them; he knows he was a student at Cambridge, and even what the acoustics of King's College Chapel are like, though he sometimes invents a fanciful past for himself in the attempt to make sense of these disconnected and partial remembrances. Miller explains that memory traces are laid down in different ways, and perhaps may also be accessed in different ways.

In the midst of this chaos, which Wearing in the film calls 'this hell on earth', it is extraordinary to discover the remarkable command he retains over his musical skills: although denying his ability, when brought in front of his old chorus, or seated at the chapel organ, he is able to conduct or to play a work he once knew intimately. That this is not just a reflex activity is revealed in another observation of his wife's, who says that when at first, after his illness had struck, he sat down at the piano, he would endlessly repeat any section that had repeat marks at the end of it, unable to remember that he had already repeated it; gradually, however, his ability to manoeuvre a musical structure improved, and he was able to get to the end.

The clinical facts of the case conform with what is known about the dominant role in the musical faculty of the right hemisphere of the brain, but from the perspective of depth psychology the data suggest much more. Miller himself sees an indication here that music is a way of organizing the flow of the present, of extending the present into a continuous structure, in a manner evidently independent of language. We know that music structures time. Here in this documentary, what we see in the musical sequences is that music carries the stricken subject beyond the disintegration of his self-identity and the severe limits of his present world. For us, who are in full possession of our faculties, music at its most intense and concentrated has the power to take us out of ourselves. For Clive Wearing, its blessedness is that it gives him back to himself.

The Grammar of Music

Saussure established a crucial operative distinction between two modes of analysis, the synchronic and the diachronic: the formal analysis of a given system as it exists in the present moment (synchronic), and analysis across time, or historical explanation (diachronic). He directed his own attention to the former, to the domain of what he called *langue*, language as a fixed and stable system of grammatical rules, which he distinguished from *parole*, the act of speech. Bakhtin was severe in the criticism he directed at the abstractions which result from synchronic analysis. As David Lodge puts it (quoting from one of the books Bakhtin published under the name of a colleague), 'To Saussure the word was a two-sided sign, signifier and signified. To Bakhtin it was a "two-sided act . . . determined equally by whose word it is and for whom it is meant . . . A word is territory *shared* by both addresser and addressee, by the speaker and his interlocuter." '[30] The character of this territory cannot be reduced to the synchronic dimension. The very structure of the utterance lies in its orientation towards both past and future. On the one hand, the words we use come to us already imprinted with meanings, intentions and accents of previous users, on the other a word is 'directly, blatantly, oriented toward a future answer word: it provokes an answer, anticipates it and structures itself in the answer's direction'.[31] For Bakhtin, therefore, the living utterance only exists within the diachronic dimension. The same is true of music. Moreover, diachronic analysis of the language of occidental music quickly reveals its trajectory to be the evolution of an inconstant grammar, whose rules are continually mutating.

Practically the only grammatical universal in music is the octave, which defines the range of the scale, and thus serves as the framework of the formal system within which the music is generated. But at different times in history, there have been different scales of various types; and each type produces its own grammar, depending on how many tones the scale contains and how these tones are arranged. Since the same is true of different cultures, synchronic analysis of the global state of music at any particular time always produces diverse results. Indeed, because of this great variety of scales there are theorists who deny the claim that music is a universal language. At best, they think, it can only be relatively so, or as Adorno put it, international without being Esperanto. Of course, as the Japanese facility for European music amply demonstrates, this is sufficient for its idioms to cross linguistic barriers with ease.

Notions of musical grammar are most persuasive when the music under consideration is harmonic, for then it appears that in any given historical period — except, it seems, our own — only certain harmonic combinations are lawful. This is not what could be called a strong proposition, however.

A complete and closed account of this grammar is never possible, because the system is inherently irrational (Weber) or psychodynamic (Schoenberg). But this casts a certain doubt on theories which identify the laws of harmony with a deep structure of some kind, like that of Heinrich Schenker, who continues more than fifty years after his death to dominate a large part of post-war musicology (especially in the USA).

Because of this vaguely similar emphasis on underlying structural levels, Schenker's theories bear a family resemblance to Chomsky's linguistics, but a very weak one. Musical structure is the property for Schenker of a single factor — harmonic tonality. You have to penetrate through the musical foreground, pass the middle ground and penetrate the background, to discover the distilled essence of the work's tonality, which Schenker called the *Ursatz*, the fundamental shape. This *Ursatz* has very little relation to the music that the listener actually hears; it is even more abstract than the kind of masterly technical analyses practised by musicologists like Tovey, whose perception of musical form was far more subtle. As Richard Norton, one of his critics, puts it: 'In page after page, there surfaces in Schenker the demand for a disembodied "ear" . . . which perceives and understands the subtleties that his system asserts.'[32]

According to Joseph Kerman, Schenker was ready in the service of his idealistic vision to strip away not only salient details of individual compositions, but also distinctions between compositions, composers and periods, with the result that the form of a Bach prelude is for Schenker in principle the same as that of a Brahms sonata movement.[33] Indeed he stripped away most of musical history, leaving hardly more than a dozen composers almost exclusively German and Austrian; the canonized composers of the Classical—Romantic tradition, with whom Schenker parts company as soon as the phenomenon known as progressive tonality appears (the symphony by Mahler or Nielsen which begins in one key and ends in another). As Norton puts it, both Ockeghem's popular virelay *Ma Maîtresse* and Mahler's Ninth Symphony are from Schenker's point of view unwanted aliens, because both begin with clear loyalties to one tonic but disavow this allegiance and take up residence elsewhere; Schenker did not allow that such a relocation of tonal citizenship was even feasible.[34] One is reminded of Schoenberg's acerbic comment about how his early string sextet *Verklärte Nacht* ('Transfigured Night') was rejected for performance on the grounds that it contained an inverted ninth chord with the ninth in the bass. Never mind what this is, it is enough that the orthodox music theory of the day didn't recognize its existence. 'It is self-evident; there is no such thing as an inversion of a ninth chord; therefore there is no such thing as a performance of it; for one cannot perform something which does not exist. So I had to wait for several years.'[35]

If scales are grammatical entities, then the permutations in the notes employed are a matter of syntax. Here, perhaps paradoxically, we discover something close to a universal grammar after all, for it turns out that music using different scales will nonetheless employ the same basic syntagmatic devices: many of the syntactical procedures which generate the strings of notes are fundamentally identical whatever the scale system. Music new and old unfolds by a process of structural permutation of groups of tones, consisting of repetitions and contrasts, parallels and antitheses, which constitute in music of any kind — a folk-song, a fugue by Bach or a raga, a jazz combo, a gypsy band, a symphony or a gamelan orchestra — what Stravinsky called the game of notes. In Bernstein's words, music is a continuing play of anagrams upon the notes of the scale.

The constant rearrangement and transformation becomes all the richer in harmonic music for the combined possibilities of succession and simultaneity, of horizontal and vertical structures. The possibilities along the horizontal plane alone are enormous. As well as the simple note-for-note repetition of a motif, reiteration may be varied in several ways: the figure may be expanded or contracted, it may be played backwards or even upside down (augmentation, diminution, retrograde, inversion).

All these variants may be answered by contrasting figures or counter-statements to which the same processes are applied. And not only answered successively, but simultaneously in the form of counterpoint and polyphony.

Although Bernstein borrows the term transformation from Chomskian linguistics to apply in a general way to the manipulation of the notes of a motif, the word is already present in contemporary musicology, where it is used to refer to a rather more specific phenomenon. It indicates the underlying technique of the thematic process of sonata form as practised over several generations, from the Classical composers proper (Haydn, Mozart, Beethoven) to the late Romantics (Tchaikovsky, Mahler, Sibelius), in which a motley of quite different-sounding themes may be derived from a single motif. In contrast, the unity of the preceding contrapuntal style of which J.S. Bach is the summation is based on the technique known as imitation. Imitation and transformation are phenomena of a different order: imitation implies recognition of similarity, transformation implies the appearance of difference. The rise of transformation is seen by many authorities as a momentous process in Western musical culture, which leads to the elevation of sonata form as the highest expression of pure musical art. The essential difference between the two is that imitation, whatever form it takes, is always recognizable, and intended as such; whereas the thematic metamorphoses of sonata form are not generally audible at a conscious level at all, in fact they are usually not meant to be (although they can also be designed in order to be so). This is not unlike the difference between the Classical form of theme-and-variation already perfected by Haydn and Mozart, in which the contours of the theme remain entirely recognizable in each of the variations that follow; and late-Romantic works like Brahms's *Variations on the St Anthony Chorale* or the *Enigma Variations* by Elgar, where this is no longer true (the Elgar *feels* unified but is famously lacking an identifiable theme). The key work in the evolution of the form is Beethoven's *Diabelli Variations*, which incorporates both these types set off against each other. (A third technique, favoured by jazz, is to base the variations on the theme's harmonic form.)

Thematic transformation and imitation both depend on principles already present in much earlier music. The theorist Josef Rufer, a pupil of Schoenberg's, holds that the seed-bed of formal coherence in musical art in its simplest form is repetition, reiteration; it appears in the earliest music, and indeed music is inconceivable without it. This is where the musicality of poetry comes from, and Bernstein is impressed by a remark of Roman Jakobson's to the effect that it is by means of the 'regular reiteration of equivalent units' that poetry provides an experience of time comparable to that of music.[36] Exact repetition, symmetrical like the ticking of a clock, or mathematical like the rhythm circuits on synthesizers, is of course monotonous and inexpressive, and is therefore subsumed already in the earliest *musica practica* to the principle of variation and alteration.

There are a determinate number of basic ways in which a musical figure can be altered without annihilating its elementary shape, or Gestalt. The fundamental options are a question of simple musical logic. The figure may be repeated in notes of either longer or shorter duration (known as augmentation and diminution). Notes may be added (Bernstein likens this to the figure of speech called auxesis) or taken away (deletion); a phrase may be telescoped with another, or embedded. The figure may be reversed, that is, played backwards, called retrograde. Simple alterations of pitch may be introduced, like one of the notes changing direction, or the whole figure may be inverted, that is, repeated note for note in contrary motion, the same interval going up instead of down and vice versa. (Notice that in this case the tone changes: a fifth above C is G, a fifth below it is F.) The variants may also be combined, to produce, for instance, augmented inversion or retrograde diminution and other more complex possibilities. Finally the notes may be transposed on to another pitch, and repeated exactly or otherwise.

These procedures might sound rather complex, but in their basic forms, and when only simple groups of notes are involved, the effect is easy enough to hear even without any formal knowledge of music, although in that case it leaves an inarticulate impression without name. This is also to say that these are elementary forms of *musica practica*, which can be found in the most archaic music, built up of the most minimal units of musical form.

A telescoped and embedded retrograde can be seen in an example given by Curt Sachs of a one-step Eskimo melody, in which *y* is *x* backwards with a slight rhythmic alteration:

The common use of these procedures in dance music and popular song — tunes of the kind you can whistle — makes it hardly necessary to offer examples by name; almost any will do that comes to the reader's mind. And for every simple variant, there are others more difficult to recognize because of more complex pitch alterations.

Monodic music, single-line melody such as Gregorian chant, consists in large measure of the varied reiteration of a certain repertoire of phrases. With the development of polyphony, however, a new means of repetition evolves which is literally unthinkable in monodic music, namely, the imitation by one voice of another. In the most elementary forms of *musica practica* this produces children's rounds like *Three Blind Mice* or *Frère Jacques* (the tune which in its minor version comprises the funeral march of Mahler's First Symphony). As long as the basic figure is sufficiently strongly shaped, these imitations are easily recognizable. But the same techniques of imitation provide the basis not only for counterpoint, like that of Mahler, but also the most elaborate mass by Palestrina or the most complex fugue by Bach. By constant permutation of the different combinations, a myriad of echoes may be set up between voices moving simultaneously alongside each other, and the most intricate flow of music created. Josquin composed an entire mass on the five-note figure *La sol fa re mi*.

Music of this type induces a special kind of hearing, commensurate with the inner play of voices. 'In order to enjoy polyphonic music', says Ehrenzweig, 'a change of attitude is necessary.' The listener must not attempt to follow the fugue theme, for example, as a linear melody — impossible because it loses itself in the polyphonic fabric — but as the germ-cell from which the intricate structure will grow; one should 'follow the unfolding of this structure with a diffuse [kind of] attention not concentrated on a single voice but on the structure as a whole; to feel how it gains in transparency and expands into infinite space'.[37] (Perhaps a comparable state of perception exists in the contemplation of painting when the eye takes in the display of colours, shapes and lines rather than the subject matter, which in the case of abstract painting disappears entirely.)

The decline of high polyphony and fugue brings the birth of sonata form. The same fundamental means are deployed in the thematic transformations of sonata style, but in a manner that after Mozart and Haydn becomes less detectable by the ear. The process is open to inspection in certain key works by Beethoven and Schubert. There is E.T.A. Hoffmann's contemporary demonstration of the thematic unity of Beethoven's Fifth Symphony, for example. Or Schubert's piano fantasia on his song *The Wanderer*, where he uses motifs derived from the song to construct a driving and compelling continuous four-movement structure. In works like these the composer's purpose is clearly to achieve the greatest possible contrast out of the metamorphosis of the chosen motifs. They are thus transformed in ways that change their surface morphology, the rhythm altered, accents shifted, the notes repeated and others interspersed. With the evolution of the symphony, this process becomes a highly sophisticated art. It is amazing, Rudolph Reti remarks, how even a slight shift of accent and rhythm can induce a total transformation of the motif, so that its Gestalt completely changes. He offers some striking examples from Tchaikovsky's Fourth Symphony.[38]

Nowadays there is a multitude of analyses of symphonies, concertos, sonatas, string quartets etc., by a school of theorists to rival the followers of Schenker, which amply demonstrate the activity of motivic transformation over the last two centuries. The authorities include two Viennese-born music critics, Reti and Hans Keller, and the English musicologist Alan Walker. These gentlemen are no less normative than Schenkerians in believing that only the works that confirm their thesis can be called masterpieces. The main claim is that motivic variation and thematic transformation is the cat's whiskers of musical thought; in Reti's words, '*one common underlying idea of structural thinking*, which spreads through the ages and became the backbone of our musical evolution'.[39] But the net they cast is wider and more flexible, though it has also been said that thematic relationships can be found in anything if you look hard enough. In this respect, Keller is probably the most sophisticated of these theorists, for he realized how the demonstration of thematic unity is similar to psychoanalytic explanation: logical criteria are beside the point, it only works if the patient feels convinced.

The Musical Unconscious

The roots of thematic transformation as a conscious mode of musical thinking can be found, according to Reti, in the fifteenth century. The music of Dufay may be taken as the representative example of this new kind of structural composition. Clearly the skill involved was generated by the same developments in notation that also produced polyphony. This is not just speculation. According to neuropsychologists like Luria, it is a characteristic of the human brain — and one of the features to distinguish it from the animal brain — that higher forms of conscious activity involve external mechanisms. Like the proverbial knot in the handkerchief, the writing we use to record our ideas, the multiplication table we use for arithmetical calculation — these 'external aids or historically formed devices are essential elements in the establishment of functional connections between individual parts of the brain'.[40] By such means, independent areas of the brain become 'components of a single functional system' — in short, 'historically formed measures for the organization of human behaviour tie new knots' in the activity of the brain. The musical instrument is an obvious example of this phenomenon; so is notation. It is only necessary to add that once learned, a large part of the brain activity involved in such functional systems necessarily remains subconscious, or what is often called intuitive.

Imagine the effect which notation must have on the trained composer, who learns intuitively to link the sound and the sight of notes, and in this way becomes aware of relationships between them that are not necessarily present to the ear. The result? As Reti puts it, 'whenever a theme rises in the ear of a structurally trained composer, all kinds of possible trans-formations will at once automatically flash across his mind'.[41] This is like Poincaré's famous description of the activity of the mathematician, who directly apprehends equations and their transformations in an instinctive manner, and whose facility is also the result of a highly developed notation, which becomes, through training, second nature.

Unlike harmonic structures, thematic transformation seems to have remained subliminal and largely untheorized. It was not exactly a secret art like alchemy, but Charles Rosen is only partly correct when he remarks in his study of the classical style that such suggestions are ludicrous.[42] What is ludicrous is the idea of an esoteric technique which composers disguised in the shape of easily understandable forms like sonatas so that a dim-witted public could grasp their music without too much difficulty. This is indeed, as Rosen says, psychologically implausible. On the other hand, there is clear enough evidence that at telling moments the thematic process is subconscious.

Whenever thematic transformation is at work, it quickly becomes responsible for the sense of unity and totality which the work projects. It does not necessarily matter if the listener cannot audibly discern these kernels of unity in a conscious and articulate manner. They will still operate — through their influence on the way the performer interprets the music. The musician is always aware of patterns in the music which escape the listener's ear; some of them make a highly conscious effort to become so. Yehudi Menuhin, for example, has written about the thematic analysis he undertakes of every work he plays: 'like a biochemist discovering that every human cell bears the imprint of the body it belongs to', he tries to establish why these notes and not others belong to the piece in question.[43] The results have an effect on the way he phrases the notes, and this communicates a certain nuance to the listener, something which the listener *hears*, even if the hearing is untutored, inarticulate and unaware.

But of course these qualities are felt by different types of listener in different ways. Adorno has described a number of different types of listener,[44] ranging from the 'expert', who listens structurally, 'tends to miss nothing and at the same time, at each moment, accounts to himself for what he has heard', to the 'entertainment listener', who is completely passive and can hardly be said to listen at all, but uses music merely as a background to cut off silence and kill time. Between them come the 'good listener', those (like Proust's Baron Charlus) whose cultural training has given them an unconscious understanding of music's 'immanent logic'; and the 'culture consumer', who makes up the bulk of concert and opera audiences — voracious listeners, well-informed, enthusiastic record-collectors — for whom 'the structure of hearing is atomistic: the type lies in wait for specific elements, for supposedly beautiful melodies, for grandiose moments'. Then comes the 'emotional listener', for whom music triggers 'instinctual stirrings otherwise tamed or repressed by the norms of civilization'; and the 'sensuous' listener, in whom music stimulates visual images and vague reveries (readers who feel belittled by finding themselves in this category may take consolation from the company of the poet Heine, who wrote that 'Berlioz's music reminds me of extinct species of animals, of fabulous kingdoms and fabulous sins, of sky-storming impossibilities, of the hanging gardens of Semiramis, of Nineveh, of the wonderful constructions of Mizraim').[45]

The most curious of Adorno's categories is what he calls the 'resentment listener', a stark anti-type to the emotional kind. These are listeners whose musical preferences are the expression of emotional repression rather than indulgence, like the stern Bach purist and the ancient music lover, who scorn the established repertoire which nourishes emotional listening. The category extends to militant devotees of the contemporary avant-garde who also despise easy emotionalism; and populist opponents of the avant-garde who militate in favour of the established repertoire; what these resent is intellectualism. Here too he locates the typical jazz listener, whose resentment, he says, is equally directed against the classic—Romantic ideal on the one hand, and unadulterated commercialism on the other. Adorno is particularly fascinated by this category, which he discusses at greater length than the others, and more speculatively, possibly because, without realizing, he belongs to it himself, in dismissing jazz and disallowing the untutored any creative musical contribution.

No one, of course, is purely one kind of listener or another; we oscillate between different positions according to the type of music and the circumstance. In the past it was perhaps primarily the different demands of different types of music which prompted different habits of listening. In the modern acousmatic age, when music has been torn free from the locus of its social origins, our listening habits have become unanchored, and we easily apply different types of attention to all kinds of music.

Rudolph Reti finds authority for his analysis of thematicism in the writings of Schumann, to which he gives a symptomatic reading. He shows how Schumann deplored the lack among many composers of a true understanding of symphonic form. Frequently, said Schumann, 'the slow movements are there only because they are not supposed to be missing; the scherzos are scherzos in name only; and *the last movements no longer know what the preceding ones contained*'.[46] What does this suggest, asks Reti, if not that awareness of thematic unity was firmly established, but not exactly common knowledge?

When Schumann analyses Berlioz's *Symphonie Fantastique*, he doesn't appear to find the thematic unity of the five movements either unexpected or exceptional, and when speaking of the thematic unity of Mendelssohn's *Scottish Symphony*, Schumann says that 'the melodic courses of the principal themes in the four different movements are akin; this will be detected even upon cursory comparison'. Here, says Reti, the wording implies that there must also be instances where thematic identity is less easy to detect. Then Reti shows that in the same *Symphonie Fantastique* there are two layers through which thematic unity is expressed, of which Schumann and Berlioz himself accounted only for one, the 'outer' layer: that of the various appearances of the famous *idée fixe*, reiterations which are almost literal, like variations. But beneath these obvious variations, says Reti (and takes seven pages in demonstrating it), 'there is a second structural layer, brought about through the thematic homogeneity of all the other themes in all the movements'. Was Berlioz just not telling, or didn't he realize it himself?

Schoenberg argued, with great psychological acuity, that the faculty of music has its own subconscious. He once reported how he worried for years over the apparent lack of relationship between the two principal themes in his First Chamber Symphony, a work which compresses an entire symphonic structure into one densely-worked extended movement, like Schubert's *Wanderer Fantasia* only much more fluid. Twenty years later he discovered the relationship: the second theme was a complex inversion of the first, 'of such a complicated nature that I doubt whether any composer would have cared deliberately to construct a theme in this way; but our subconscious does it involuntarily'. This subconscious domain, where musical time and space interpenetrate each other, possesses peculiarly elastic dimensions, which nurture superior powers of scanning. Mozart left the most striking testimony of these capacities, when he described the way he composed in his head before setting pen to paper, usually when he was alone, perhaps travelling in a carriage, or lying in bed awake at night — a description which again recalls Poincaré on mathematics: fragments of musical ideas would come to him in abundance and gradually join together in his mind, until 'at last it gets almost finished in my head, so that I can see it as a whole, even when it's a long piece, at a single glance, like a fine painting or a beautiful statue'. Remarkably, he heard it in his imagination not as a succession of sounds 'but all at once, as it were. A rare delight! All this making and inventing is like a vivid dream. But best of all is hearing it all at once.' Then all he had to do was write it down, which he could easily do with any amount of bustle and noise around him.[47]

It is no accident that in contrast to the positivism of the Schenkerians, the proponents of thematicism are all amateur psychologists, with a penchant for theories about the relationship between the conscious and the subconscious and their relative contributions to the activity of composition. For one thing, the activity of the subconscious is documented. As Alan Walker says, composers who dream music are not at all uncommon. Tartini's *Devil's Trill Sonata* came to him, like Coleridge's *Kubla Khan*, in a dream. Mahler on one occasion dreamt of a voice ('That of Beethoven, or perhaps Wagner') saying to him 'Why not bring the horns in three bars later?' only to discover, next morning, that this was indeed the best way to overcome the problem he had.[48] Stravinsky recounts the most extra-ordinary dream of all (which suggests an unexpected affinity in him for surrealism), which came to him while he was composing *Threni*:

> After working late one night I retired to bed still troubled by an interval. I dreamed about this interval. It had become an elastic substance stretching exactly between the two notes I had composed, but underneath these notes at either end was an egg, a large testicular egg. The eggs were gelatinous to the touch (I touched them), and warm, and they were protected by nests. I woke up knowing that my interval was right . . . Also, I was so surprised to see the eggs I immediately understood them to be symbols. Still in the dream I went to my library of dictionaries and looked up 'interval', but found only a confusing explanation which I checked the next morning in reality and found to be the same.[49]

(One could be forgiven for thinking that Stravinsky's dream eggs, lying in their nests, are symbols of his mother's good breasts.)

The evidence, then, suggests that the musical subconscious has remarkable properties which go far beyond the power of attracting Freudian associations. Not only can it perform on musical material the same operations as the primary process performs in dream language (namely to integrate opposites, displace the significant to the insignificant, condense incompatibles and ignore the rational order of time and space). In addition, the musical subconscious is continuous with musical consciousness, it *doesn't need to disguise itself*. In other words, utterances by the musical subconscious are not nonsensical.

According to the Freudian model, the work of the primary process is inaccessible to the logic of consciousness, and the subconscious operates as a filter which by means of censorship renders unconscious 'content' suitable for apprehension. In contrast, conscious and subconscious in music map directly on to each other: the symbols they use — intervals, modes, harmonies, keys, rhythms, timbres — are the same. Which is not to say, of course, that they cannot also carry other unconscious charges, which remain disguised, whereby hang other tales.

It is probably this continuity of mental functions that explains the famous stories about feats of composition which Walker trots out: how Schubert wrote the first movement of a string quartet, all 264 bars of it, in four and a half hours, a speed which even an expert copyist would find hard to match; how Mozart composed an overture and Berlioz a symphonic movement in a single night, and Handel the whole of *Messiah* at such speed that he averaged seventeen pages of the score per day. What happens in such moments is that normal conscious attention is suspended, and the musical subconscious takes over. Wagner reported composing the Prelude to *Rheingold* in a 'cataleptic state'. Even Brahms spoke of the semi-trance of the rare inspired moods when a composition is simply revealed, already clothed in harmony, form and orchestration. Stravinsky said of *The Rite of Spring*, 'I heard and I wrote what I heard. I am the vessel through which *Le Sacre* passed.'[50] (There was also a section of which he said that while he could play it on the piano, he did not at first know how to write it down.) Aaron Copland has described this state of mind with great sensitivity:

> The inspired moment may sometimes be described as a kind of hallucinatory state of mind: one half of the personality emotes and dictates while the other half listens and notates. The half that listens had better look the other way, had better simulate a half attention only, for the half that dictates is easily disgruntled and avenges itself for too close inspection by fading entirely away.[51]

Ehrenzweig sums up: music is a symbolic language of the unconscious whose symbolism we cannot fathom.[52] Yet something of its structure is revealed by the psychoanalysis of perception. We can imagine musical expression, he says, as a conversation between artist and public conducted on two levels simultaneously. On the surface it uses an articulate language of form, an aesthetic superstructure that employs various more or less traditional elements open to rational analysis. Underneath, a secret conversation takes place using inarticulate symbols which are available only to subjective interpretation. Louis Gottschalk, who toured the United States as a composer-pianist during the Civil War, described this secret conversation felicitously when he wrote in his diary: 'Play a melancholy passage to an exile thinking of his distant country, to an abandoned lover, to a mother mourning for her child, to a conquered warrior, and be assured that each one of these various griefs will appropriate these plaintive harmonies to itself and will recognise in them the voice of its own suffering.'[53]

But the ground of this conversation has an ineluctable tendency to shift, largely because of the tension between depth perception and recognition. The inexorable process of articulation repeatedly draws new Gestalts to the surface and turns them into clichés, forcing the composer to find new depth symbols to replace them; in this way the musical language is constantly recharged. The situation, says Ehrenzweig, is curious. A language which constantly has to invent new symbols in order not to be robbed of meaning would hardly appear to be able to make sense. We would be reduced to mere guessing as to what the speaker means, who might as well not speak at all but merely indicate that what they want to convey is inexpressible. That is exactly what seems to happen in the secret conversation of composer and audience (more acutely in certain periods than others) and it gives the impression of some kind of extra-sensory communication like telepathy, rather than what is understood by language.[54]

In pursuit of the elusive meaning of music, both psychoanalysis and the dialogical principle lead to the conclusion that music is process more than meaning. There is a different emphasis, however, in the accounts they give. For psychoanalysis, meaning is a kind of deposit which coagulates in corners and interstices. For the dialogical approach, on the other hand, meaning is elusive because the living conditions of *musica practica* are rich, complex and confusing. They have the quality Bakhtin calls heteroglossia, and in this respect music is entirely like language: 'At any given moment of its historical existence, language . . . is the embodied coexistence of socio-ideological contradictions between the present and the past, between different epochs of the past, between different socio-ideological groups in the present, between tendencies, schools, circles and so on.'[55] There is no universal musical language because the musical universe is completely heteroglot. It consists in the proliferation of competing and intersecting voices which coexist within any given historical space: divergent dialects, each with its own repertoire of genres, the idioms of different generations, classes, genders, races and localities asserting their presence, and each contributing their own utterances to the cultural heterophony of the times.

Notes

1. Umberto Eco, *A Theory of Semiotics*, Macmillan, London 1977, p. 11.
2. See Roman Jakobson, tr. John Mepham, *Six Lectures on Sound and Meaning*, Harvester, Brighton 1978, p. 41.
3. Henri Lefebvre, 'Musique et sémiologie', *Musique en jeu* No. 4.
4. Nicolas Ruwet, 'Musicology and Linguistics', *International Social Sciences Journal*, Vol. XIX, No. 1, 1967.
5. Leonard Bernstein, *The Unanswered Question*, Harvard University Press, Cambridge, MA and London 1976, pp. 59–61.
6. Fred Lerdahl and Ray Jackendoff, *A Generative Theory of Tonal Music*, MIT, Cambridge, MA 1985, pp. 5–6. Unfortunately they fail to follow their own advice.
7. Conversation with Chomsky in Oxford in 1969.
8. Another version appeared recently on the letters page of the *Guardian*: 'The best known of Noam Chomsky's "sentences" which are grammatically correct but otherwise meaningless is: "Colourless green ideas sleep furiously" ' wrote a Professor in Bristol. 'Has not meaning now overtaken this sentence? Does it now describe the environmental policy of the present government as set out in Chris Patten's White Paper?'
9. Bernstein, p. 153.
10. A.R. Luria, *The Working Brain*, Penguin, London 1973, p. 41.
11. Reported by Robert Temple, 'Songs without words', *Guardian*, 24 July 1992.
12. See Jonathan Winson, *Brain and Psyche*, Anchor Press, New York 1985, pp. 163–7.
13. Carl E. Seashore, *Psychology of Music*, p. 57. McGraw-Hill, London and New York 1938.
14. Karl Marx, *Economic and Philosophical Manuscripts of 1844*, in Marx and Engels, *Collected Works*, Vol. 3, Moscow 1975, p. 302.
15. Lévi-Strauss, *The Raw and the Cooked*, Harper Colophon, London 1975, p. 16.
16. Ibid., p. 17.
17. Lévi-Strauss, *The Naked Man*, Harper & Row, New York 1981, p. 647.
18. Anton Ehrenzweig, *The Psychoanalysis of Aristic Vision and Hearing*, Routledge & Kegan Paul, London 1953, p. 165.
19. Freud, *The Interpretation of Dreams*, Standard Edition of the Complete Psychological Works of Sigmund Freud, Vol. 4, pp. 121ff.
20. Freud, *Introductory Lectures on Psycho-Analysis*, Allen & Unwin, London 1922, pp. 89–90.
21. Ernest Jones, *Freud*, Penguin, London 1964, pp. 358–9.
22. Cf. Hanna Segal, *Introduction to the Work of Melanie Klein*, Hogarth Press and Institute of Psychoanalysis, London 1978, pp. 9, 92.
23. Davis and Wallbridge, *Boundary and Space, an Introduction to the Work of D.W. Winnicott*, Penguin, London 1983, p. 71.
24. See Yehudi Menuhin, *Unfinished Journey*, Macdonald & Jane's, London 1976.
25. Ibid., p. 88.
26. Segal, p. 36.
27. Quoted in Claudia Gorbman, *Unheard Melodies, Narrative Film Music*, BFI/Indiana University Press, London 1987, p. 62.
28. Schopenhauer, 'The World as Will and Idea', in F. Tillman and S. Cahn, eds, *Philosophy of Art and Aesthetics*, Harper & Row, London 1969, p. 288.
29. Transmitted on Channel Four, 14.8.86, dir. John Dollar.
30. David Lodge, *After Bakhtin*, Routledge, London 1990, pp. 89–90; quoting from V.N. Volosinov (M.M. Bakhtin), *Marxism and the Philosophy of Language*, New York, 1973, pp. 85–6.
31. M.M. Bakhtin, *The Dialogical Imagination*, p. 280. University of Texas, Austin, TX 1981, p. 280.
32. Richard Norton, *Tonality in Western Culture*, Pennsylvania State University Press, Pennsylvania and London 1984, p. 44.
33. Joseph Kerman, *Musicology*, Fontana, London 1985, p. 85.
34. Norton, p. 77.

35. Quoted in ibid., p. 233.

36. Bernstein, p. 147.

37. Ehrenzweig, *Psychoanalysis*, p. 42.

38. See Rudolf Reti, *The Thematic Process in Music*, Faber & Faber, London 1961.

39. Ibid. p. 247, original emphasis.

40. Luria, p. 31.

41. Reti, p. 70.

42. Charles Rosen, *The Classical Style*, Faber & Faber, London 1971, p. 41.

43. Menuhin, pp. 136ff.

44. See T.W. Adorno, *Introduction to the Sociology of Music*, Seabury Press, New York 1976, chapter 1 ('Types of Music Conduct').

45. Max Graf, *Composer and Critic*, Kennikat Press, Port Washington 1969, p. 212.

46. Reti, pp. 286ff.

47. See E. Holmes, *The Life of Mozart Including his Correspondence*, Chapman & Hall, London 1878, pp. 211—13.

48. Alan Walker, *An Anatomy of Musical Criticism*, Barrie & Rockliff, London 1966; see also Natalie Bauer-Lechner, *Recollections of Gustav Mahler*, Faber Music, London 1980, p. 78.

49. Stravinsky, *Conversations*, Faber & Faber, London 1959, pp. 17—18.

50. Igor Stravinsky and Robert Craft, *Expositions and Developments*, Faber & Faber, London 1981, pp. 147—8.

51. Aaron Copland, *Music and Imagination*, Harvard, 1961, p. 43.

52. Ehrenzweig, *Psychoanalysis*, p. 164.

53. Louis Gottschalk, *Notes of a Pianist*, Knopf, London 1964, p. 107.

54. Ehrenzweig, *Psychoanalysis*, pp. 73—4.

55. M. Bakhtin, *The Dialogical Imagination*, p. 291 (translation altered following Hirschkop, in Norris, ed., *Music and the Politics of Culture*, Lawrence & Wishart, London 1989, p. 286).

PART III

The Political Economy
of Music

5

Music Becomes a Commodity

Print, Publisher, Composer

The rise of polyphony during the Renaissance was dominated by vocal music, yet to modern eyes, early manuscripts not only look archaic, they also seem to treat the placement of the text beneath the notes in cavalier fashion. The reason is that while the new idiom would seem to call for a new and clearer arrangement of the words to be sung, as long as polyphony remained the preserve of trained singers there was no special need to be at all precise in this regard; the singers could work it out for themselves, according to stylistic convention and often under the personal guidance of the composer. The dissemination of music through printing altered these conditions, by placing music in the hands of new kinds of performers who were largely amateur, with less extensive knowledge of the learned conventions. Hence the growth in the seventeenth and eighteenth centuries of music manuals and instruction books. But from the start, music printers concerned themselves with clarity of presentation. In the 1470s, a Burgundian choir-book had set a new standard: the words are carefully placed beneath the notes to which they belong. This was the script that became the model for the most accomplished of early music typefaces, that of Ottaviano dei Petrucci in Venice thirty years later.

With the advent of printing come a variety of formats and layouts. Partbooks make their appearance, so called because each book contains only one set of parts (and the different partbooks that belong together have not always survived intact). There is also the kind of publication known in German as *Tafel-Musik* ('Table Music'), in which the parts are arranged upside-down and sideways to each other, to enable a small number of players and singers seated round a table each to read the appropriate part the right way up.

It is far from coincidence that this is also the period when the character of secular music begins to change, when the old fixed forms of the medieval chanson disappear, and with the generation of Josquin and Jannequin around the turn of the fifteenth century, new, more plastic shapes develop. Around 1450 the European economy had begun to re-expand and markets to grow. Printing marked the entry of music into commodity relations. Thereafter the evolution of European music and the improvement of its notation is powerfully affected by what is printed, for whom, who prints it and how it is paid for.

Music as a commodity is younger than literature, and it was printing that made it an object of commerce. Literature had already achieved this status with the scribes of ancient Rome, and throughout the Middle Ages manuscripts were copied and sold by dealers in considerable numbers — more than 300 copies of Dante's *Commedia Divina* have survived from the fourteenth and fifteenth centuries. Indeed it was precisely the growth of this market which stimulated the invention of printing. There is no trace, however, according to the twentieth-century music publisher Ernest Roth, of a similar trade in music.[1] Composers were first and foremost performing musicians employed in jobs which they owed to their aptitude for providing the right type of music for the right occasion. When copies of their music circulated, it enhanced their reputations more than their income. Before the advent of printing only the fewest copies were made of even renowned pieces, not enough to create a commercial trade. Nor did the conditions of formal and professional music making provide sufficient business for the music printer. When Petrucci became the first person to offer printed sheet music for sale in Venice in the early 1500s, the market which he tapped consisted primarily in non-professional music lovers: the principal customer was the educated amateur performer. The growth of music publishing thereupon followed the growth of this domestic *musica practica* and becomes its barometer — it is obviously related to the spread of musical literacy — until market conditions and improved technology in the late eighteenth century promoted the music publisher to a new prominence, with corresponding effects on the composer's sources of income. (Berio once joked that Beethoven was the first truly modern composer because he was the first to sell the same work twice over to two different publishers. Actually, so did Haydn.)

Because the inscription of music is radically different from the inscription of language, music printing was not so much a sideline of general printing as a specialized branch of it, with its own technological problems to solve. The earliest music printing consisted in woodblocks (or occasionally metal) for short musical examples in books of theory or instruction. The disadvantage of the woodblock was that each musical passage required its own block; it was laborious and costly, and the work was crude and imperfect because from wood it was difficult to obtain sharp outlines. The need for books of liturgical music therefore stimulated the first musical typefaces, which employed at least double printing of the notes upon the staves; there were several methods but all required careful registration. Petrucci himself employed triple impression, printing first the staves, second the text, initial letters and signatures, and lastly the notes.

Petrucci's method, though highly accomplished, was still slow and costly. Simple economic pressures demanded a cheaper process, even at the expense of clarity and elegance; in short, a music type incorporating both notes and stave lines which could be printed in a single impression. I have found no comprehensive work on the history of music printing, and different writers give credit to different figures for the various innovations towards this end. One source names Erhard Oeglin in Augsburg in 1507 – one of the printers employed by the leading Augsburg bookseller Rynman – as the first to use a single impression movable type, another says it was in 1512, a third gives the credit to Pierre Haultin in France in 1525. (Haultin, a member of the family that held the leading position among French Protestant printers, is also named by one writer as the first to employ punches in order to engrave a metal plate.) In the long run, however, music was of little concern to general printers, and as a specialized trade was often organized by musicians themselves. In England in the late sixteenth century, it was the composers Thomas Tallis and William Byrd who held the royal patent for printing and importing music; two hundred years later, Diabelli and Clementi are among the leading music publishers in Vienna and London respectively.

Broadly speaking, the long-term effects of music publishing were not dissimilar to those of general publishing. The growth of the general publishing market did not just serve to disseminate established forms of writing but created the space for new ones, and a technique that began as a support for an existing system of power ended up shattering it instead. In the beginning, as Lucien Febvre has chronicled, the Church was strongly in favour of printing. It was thought that it would strengthen and extend its reach, and there was a large demand for liturgy, scripture, theological works, works of classical antiquity and student primers. Indeed, the fact that Latin was an international language (albeit a dead one) was a powerful stimulus to the rapid spread of books and printing. But this factor was not enough to withstand the growing force of new religious currents, which on the contrary, printing equally fuelled. Finally the Counter-Reformation took its toll on the printers. The prosperity of the specialists in religious books came to an end, and with the growth of the vernacular, not only did the major part of the book trade cease to be quite such an international affair, but it inclined instead to the emergence of the nation state.

Music publishing conforms with this process in a general way, but there are also significant differences. When music printing made its first

appearance, European art music had a universal character which also derived
from the Church. But it remained universal even with the development of the
national styles, for as Adorno put it, music is a universal language without
being Esperanto: it does not crush peculiarities. The process was gradual. In
the early stages, he observed, in late-medieval times, wherever national traits
become recognizable — as in the Florentine *ars nova* — they crystallized in
bourgeois milieux, while 'the late medieval Dutch schools that extend down to
the Reformation would probably be difficult to conceive without the fully
developed urban economy of the Low Countries'. In a word, the
'nationalization' of music paralleled its bourgeoisification.[2] In the course of
this process, the fall of Latin was no problem: it was replaced by Italian as the
language that provides the terms and terminology of musical nomenclature.
The universal acceptance of Italian — due less to the predominance of the
early Italian music printers than to the subsequent rise of opera, which took
Italian singers, musicians and teachers to every corner of the continent —
helped to ensure that even with the rise of national styles, the market for
printed music remained international.

The evolution of musical language in the course of this process placed
increasing demands on both notation and music printing. At the start, the
basic elements of the script were fairly few and simple. On the one hand,
therefore, the problem of designing a music type was relatively straightforward, on the other, because of the technical difficulties involved — above
all, the problem of combining notes and stave lines — it was of limited
application and slow to improve. An alternative for certain instruments was
the use of tablatures, like the little illustrations in modern guitar manuals
which show learners which frets to place their fingers on, and here the
development of a market for music printing stimulated experiment. For
stave notation, designed for the voice, is not by any means the most
appropriate for instrumental playing, especially when the instrument has a
fingerboard or a keyboard; in these cases a more diagrammatic representation of the notes may make things easier. The proliferation of tablatures
went hand in hand with regional traditions of performance, and in that
sense belong to the vernacular. But here the effects of music publishing
were the opposite of general publishing: because the music printer is
already more specialized, vernacular traditions were penalized by the
demands of the international market, and in print form, gradually
declined.

At the same time, unlike booksellers who could build up backlists to live
off, music publishers had no handy stock of scores of earlier music to
exploit. The public they catered for was a new one, and its tastes were
constantly evolving. Music publishers therefore quickly learnt to bring out
new music and in this way helped to foster innovation, if only to keep up
with the market. The result was that despite the considerable technical

problems entailed by musical notation and the costliness of the enterprise, printing gave scope to the advent of both polyphony and diatonic harmony. Moreover, it not only produced growing standardization in the appearance of the musical script but also nurtured the growth of the composer — in much the same way that the evolution of general publishing nurtured the author — and the composer became the principal agent not only in the growing complexity of musical language but also in its deepening subjectivity.

Whatever the rival claims over technical innovation, one thing is clear: the capacity of music printing soon began to lag behind the rapid development of musical form and style which printing itself helped to stimulate. According to the account of the British Museum music librarian A. Hyatt King, tablature was obsolescent by the second half of the sixteenth century.[3] The rise of the madrigal, followed by the birth of opera and the development of other large-scale vocal forms, made the printing of music in score a general necessity. A score initially comprised four staves; as operatic resources increased the number grew. By the time of Lully in the mid-seventeenth century, there were ten or eleven.

According to the data presented by Bianconi in his study of seventeenth-century music, the madrigal formed a growing part of the output of printed music in Italy over the course of the sixteenth century, peaking between 1580 and 1590, only to disappear abruptly after 1620.[4] Its novelty lay first of all in its relationship to the literary text and the way the setting centred on the portrayal of poetic images. But the influence of the text worked on two levels. It provided not only the sequence of images, but also a field of overtly rhetorical dimensions, and the madrigal was conceived in terms of concepts such as oratory, declamation and eloquence. It was originally intended as a form of *musica practica* for the amusement of the singers themselves, both courtiers and citizens, amateur and professional, but there was also a tendency to isolate the individual voice and exploit the professional's vocal artistry, and one of the sub-genres of the madrigal was thus the dramatic scene. The outcome of this tendency was opera.

The polyphonic madrigal reaches its peak with Gesualdo, the dramatic scene with Monteverdi. In Gesualdo, poetic and musical images are linked through analogy and antiphrasis, similarity and contradiction: all this is provided for by the text. The resulting musical texture displays the most subtle combinations of polyphonic devices, alternating between slow, twisting progressions, chromatic and dissonant, full of swooning cadences, and headlong florid passages, melismatic and declamatory. Duke Carlo Gesualdo, Prince of Venosa, an infamous figure — an aristocratic double murderer who did away with his wife and her lover — was endowed with the most acutely melancholic sensibility; his undisciplined counterpoint, his pervading chromaticism and stylistic contrivances, continued to exert a kind of secret influence throughout the seventeenth century. Behind the façade of a public style that was now very different, a kind of secret brotherhood grew up through the circulation of handwritten manuscripts. As late as 1706, we find Scarlatti writing to a correspondent of the pleasure he took in singing and studying the madrigals of Gesualdo.

If this is the sophisticated music of a cultivated prince, the development of the madrigal in the hands of Monteverdi bears an ambivalent relation to his social position as a member of the professional classes. The son of a physician of Cremona, he was employed at the court of Mantua first as a string player and then as *maestro di capella*, in other words, as supplier of music for the private delectation of the court and the academies. His subsequent rise to the even more prestigious rank of *maestro* at the Venetian Ducal Chapel affected his relationship with the public. The position was not only influential and well-paid; Venice had a musical public beyond the court, and Monteverdi could afford the luxury of printing his Sixth Book of Madrigals without dedication − without, that is, either patronage or subsidy save the outlay of the publisher, who could be certain of excellent financial returns.

The innovations Monteverdi began to introduce in his Fourth Book when he was still at Mantua − not so much their harmonic or contrapuntal audacity, but the development of a declamatory musical speech − had provoked the ire of the Bolognese theorist and cleric Giovan Maria Atusi, 'guardian of public decency in matters polyphonic' according to Bianconi.[5] To which Monteverdi replied in the preface to his Fifth Book of Madrigals, where instead of the *prima pratica*, or primary practice defined by the theorist Zarlino, in which the harmony is 'mistress of the words', he advocated a new *seconda pratica*, where 'the words are the mistress of the harmony'. When he reaches the Sixth Book, the change in style, says Bianconi, is indicative of a cultural milieu that was decidedly more modern in outlook than that of the Mantuan court; he describes it as 'a breach in the monopoly of the polyphonic madrigal and its esoteric destination'.[6] But the theatrical pieces of books seven and eight were written for the Mantuan court, with which he never severed contact. If this is the manifestation, as Bianconi suggests, of a certain ambiguity in Monteverdi's personality, it is also symptomatic of the cultural temper of his age, which cannot yet shake off the courtly mantle while underneath it is changing its spots.

Although contrapuntal writing subsequently became less elaborate, the growth in the century following the madrigal of a florid style in music for solo keyboard and stringed instruments led to the introduction of quicker tempi and altered rhythms, for which printing, says Hyatt King, was ill-equipped. Such music required an ever increasing variety of sorts to make up a font, far in excess of the requirements of the printed word. (By the mid-nineteenth century the number of sorts in a single font of musical type reached more than 450.) Even so, single-impression movable type was able to meet the needs only of relatively simple music; complicated chords and rapid passages were impossible or too cumbrous. More complex music required the more costly process of engraving.

Copper engraving was invented early in the fifteenth century and rapidly developed in the service of map-making. The earliest known application of the process to music occurred in Italy in the 1580s, but a hundred years later the centres of production were found in northern Europe. This shift encapsulates the effect upon music of a century of international crises consisting of economic depression, wars, and political upheaval. To begin with, there was the economic collapse of 1619–22, which severely affected every sphere of financial activity: as Bianconi observes, nor did music and the music publishing business escape. An increase in production costs and retail prices produced a general pattern of market contraction, particularly severe in Italy, and the demise of the polyphonic madrigal coincides with the collapse of Italian music printing in the 1620s. Afterwards, says Bianconi, this music is no longer of the same use: in the social and political strife sparked off by the economic crisis, the ideals of courtesy and politeness embodied in the madrigal disappear. Moreover the whole Italian economy suffered in the course of the seventeenth century a definitive loss of advantage in the face of northern ascendancy; new methods and centres of production in the publication of music are a symptom of this wider alteration. Since movable type was still expensive and imperfect, Holland and England, as the leading maritime nations with the most developed map-making industry, were the countries best placed to respond to the new conditions, and they quickly conquered the market for the publication of engraved instrumental music throughout Europe.

The crisis in Italian music printing especially affected the production of anthologies, which required the greatest investment on the part of the printer, while the printing costs of works by individual composers were often defrayed by their patrons, or the pre-purchase by subscription of a not inconsiderable number of copies. Simultaneously the rise of opera created a new kind of composer, for whom participation in an essentially entrepreneurial structure (however rudimentary and embryonic) 'brings a hitherto unknown degree of exposure to the risks of economic failure and artistic success, the inconstancy of public taste and competition with rivals'.[7] Here the composer works under contract in the same way as the singer or costume designer. His position of subordination is underlined by the fact that on termination of his contract, he surrenders the score and all his rights over it to the impresario. Glory and riches are the prerogative of singers; which only symbolizes the pre-eminence in the seventeenth-century musical world of performance over composition.

In France, the socio-economic crisis produced the rebellion of the Fronde, which ended with the consolidation of royal supremacy. Musical life in Paris was now regulated by a corporation of musicians under royal patronage. This corporate management of music was a highly centralizing influence, which privileged the forms of public regal musical represen-tation, above all opera. The concession of a royal monopoly to the printer Ballard ensured the maximum prestige for official editions of royally patronized music such as the *tragédies lyriques* of Lully: the 'Lully operation', as Bianconi calls it, may be seen as both the tool and the result of the absolutist policies of Louis XIV and his Prime Minister Colbert. The career of Lully, who as a thirteen-year-old dancer exchanged his humble Florentine origins for Paris, where he became the favourite of the young *Roi Soleil*, is the perfect example of the way a composer's 'destiny' is often forged less out of personal initiative than through contact with particular artistic institutions and social structures. The monumental productions which Lully served up for his royal master belong to a musical economy from which market competition has been pretty well eliminated.

In Germany, devastated by the Thirty Years War of 1618–48, music publishing remained relatively undeveloped; printers restricted themselves to the reissue of earlier Venetian editions and the production of sacred and secular anthologies for a safe market. In England, the upheavals had a radically different effect. In sweeping the old feudal order away, the Civil War and the Restoration which followed favoured the expansion of the economy and strengthened the country against its principal rivals, France and Holland, both of whom it defeated in war. Music was a beneficiary; already in the midst of these events, in the 1650s, a new breed of music printers began to set up shop. The most famous was John Playford.

In England, even before the royal monopoly was swept aside, the public regulation of music was more diverse than in France, with universities offering degrees in music by the early sixteenth century, and a parallel musical life developing among the nobility. One of the graduates towards the end of the century was John Dowland, little appreciated at court but highly acclaimed both at home in noble dilettante circles and abroad, whose published music ran to several editions. Thomas Morley took advantage of the new market with his tutor, the *Plaine and easie introduction to practicall musicke*, dating from 1597. In the 1650s came Playford's *Introduction to the skill of musick*. Forty years later, when this volume reaches its twelfth edition, one of the collaborators was Henry Purcell.

Dowland was a composer of songs and instrumental works for solo and consort who shares the melancholy ethos of Gesualdo; Morley was the leading composer of the English madrigal school; Playford laid the basis for the relaunch of the English musical press in the aftermath of the Civil War; Purcell, the leading musical functionary at court, was also until his early death the arbiter of public taste — where he led, the market followed. In 1683, he invited subscriptions in the *London Gazette* for an edition of his own trio sonatas of which he himself was both editor and distributor. The same journal carried announcements of a new series of musical concerts. The growing market was fertile ground for a variety of entrepreneurial forms, which clearly prefigure more modern patterns of musical consumption but in embryonic shape.

Thus, with the growing centralization of civil and political life throughout Europe, a new public emerges, and there are corresponding changes in the forms of musical consumption. Music printing is hard pressed in the face of the proliferation of styles and forms which this process brings with it. Moreover, as Bianconi observes, 'public' in this context (and from now on) means different things. To begin with, it is not homogeneous; it consists, for example, in both private gatherings and paying audiences, activities which involve different patterns of expenditure and entail different relationships with composer and publisher. The former are dispersed, but include both patrons and purchasers of scores; the latter gather in one place to listen to professional musicians *en masse*, without purchasing the score themselves.

The different publics encourage different forms of music; each is subdivided by different habits and tastes, though of course the different groups and sub-groups tend to overlap. The courts and cities of the seventeenth century, says Bianconi, saw the abundant use of music for demonstrative purposes on a scale hitherto unknown. On the other hand, 'no less "public"', though quite different in kind, is the late seventeenth century market — particularly expansive in the northern capitals of London, Paris and Amsterdam — for instrumental chamber music' — music for private consumption sustained by socially conditioned collective taste.[8] Right across Europe, the universality of the polyphonic style, propagated through the printed editions of the sixteenth century, gives way to the diversity of national styles with their individual mentors and models:

> The relatively subordinate social position of the seventeenth century musician is a consequence of his new found role as supplier of musical 'services' to a 'modern' consumer audience. His overall relationship to society and authority . . . is now more functional . . . his art is potentially more varied, 'articulated' and effective. Indeed, behind the somewhat deceptive façade of apparent ideological homogeneity, the vastly more 'articulated' and many-sided nature of seventeenth century music betrays analogous tendencies in the civic structure of seventeenth century European society as a whole.[9]

Music publishing developed accordingly. Engraving became predominant for high art, but the diversity of the market meant that it never came near to replacing movable type. This remained the process whereby thousands of instrumental and vocal partbooks, large quantities of church music, and even stage works poured from the presses. The two methods were not in competition with each other; although they overlapped, each was suited to particular kinds of music, and there was pressure for the improvement of production techniques in both. However, engraving developed faster. The engraver's productivity was increased by the use of punches, first employed for certain in the 1660s for note heads, later for accidentals, clefs and time-signatures. Then copper plate was replaced with pewter (an innovation credited to Handel's English publisher John Walsh around 1710), which was not only cheaper but softer. It was therefore both easier to work and it became easier to correct mistakes: the plate could be readily beaten flat again and re-engraved.

Then came the development of a new method of printing by stereotype, patented by William Ged of Edinburgh in 1725 and soon employed by printers in London and Leipzig, by which a page of music-type is turned into a metallic plate by means of a mould (or later by means of electrotyping, introduced in the 1840s). This process offered the advantages of the durability of the plate, while the type could be distributed and the size of the font kept small. But in the 1750s movable type began to catch up, when the Leipzig printer Johann Gottlob Breitkopf introduced a new font based on radical principles. Breitkopf broke the individual sort down into separate pieces for head and stem, attached to stave-segments of varying length, with another piece attaching to the end of the stem with one, two or three flags to indicate the time-value. (A similar typeface designed by the leading French typographer Fournier was less successful only because the monopoly of music printing in France held by the firm of Ballard prevented its diffusion.) This method proved particularly suitable for the growing market, with the rise of the piano, in keyboard music of every kind, solo and accompaniment, instrumental and vocal, which soon came to account for well over half the music publishers' collective output. The leading position which the firm thus acquired was consolidated after Breitkopf's death in 1794, when it was taken over by Gottfried Christoph Härtel to become Breitkopf & Härtel, and began to publish a series of complete editions of Mozart, Haydn, Clementi and Dussek. Although they were not in fact complete and fell short of modern scholarly standards, they were the forerunners of the definitive editions which the same firm began to publish in the 1850s of Bach, Handel, Palestrina and Beethoven, followed by Mendelssohn, Mozart, Chopin, Schumann, Schubert and Schütz, for which the editors included Brahms, Liszt and Clara Schumann. The firm in this way played a major role in the canonization of the German tradition to which these composers belonged by birth or adoption.

*   *   *

Hyatt King mentions in passing that in the eighteenth century the profession of music engraver in France boasted a notable succession of highly skilled women unparalleled elsewhere. He offers no explanation; one would like to know more. He also mentions what he calls the curious fact that the first engravers active in Vienna in the 1770s — there was little music printed there before then — were all foreigners. Here the explanation is not difficult to find, and is also another reason why engraving, for all its advantages, only spread slowly and always left room for movable type, with all its disadvantages. The skill of the engraver was always at a premium and accomplished engravers a scarce commodity. It was not a traditional skill in Vienna, a relatively insignificant city until the mid-eighteenth century, so when the music market suddenly expanded there, it was foreigners who came and opened it up. The same was true of singers and instrumentalists, librettists and composers. Until Schubert, none of the great 'Viennese' composers was born there.

Engraving is a slow, high-cost, labour-intensive process which resists mechanization. Every head, stem and tail, every dot and line, must be punched into the plate separately, every tie and slur drawn with a sharp stylo. A good engraver, who must calculate the spacing of the notes to achieve the most convenient layout, needs about four hours, says Roth, for a quarto page of piano music of medium difficulty, and the best worker cannot complete more than three pages of a difficult orchestral score in a week's work. On top of this, the engraver has to know more about music than the compositor about literature. Music has to be engraved from manuscript and the variable standards of musical handwriting set greater problems than in literary manuscripts. The 'correct spelling' of music has remained rather more flexible than it became in language, because there is always more than one way for a composer to notate what is intended. In later times, no musical typewriter came to the assistance of the composer or copyist; attempts to design one foundered on the problem that only the simplest music submits to regular spacing, a problem, we can add, that also affects the design of computer 'music processors'.

In short, despite the improvements, there always remained a number of practical restraints which continued to distinguish the business of music publishing from the printed word. The format of printed music is dictated by practical needs and conventions. Printed music is meant not for reading but for playing, it is generally not held as close to the eyes as a book, and the size of the sheet and the notes must be chosen so that the player need not turn the pages too often. The turns must occur at a suitable rest or sustained note, which often disturbs the even distribution of the engraving. The typography needs to be designed for quick legibility and not on aesthetic grounds. For a short time the spirit of baroque art tried to reform the design of printed music, says Roth: 'A canzona by Frescobaldi, engraved freehand on to the copperplate, with ledger lines drawn across its whole width, the stems and tails embellished with flourishes, is a true ornamental pattern,' he observes.[10] But the danger of illegibility was apparently too great. Music must be read at a glance. Frescobaldi's engraver had no successor, and no Bodoni arose among the designers of musical typefaces.

Around the turn of the eighteenth century, however, there appeared a new alternative to both engraving and movable type in the form of lithography, the only process for music printing (says Hyatt King) whose inventor, Alois Senenfelder, is undisputed. Senenfelder developed a process based on his own discoveries, employing special stone, special ink and special washes, which quickly became known as 'chemical printing'. Indeed this term is the more accurate since stone was replaced within a few years by metal plates, to make the process easier and quicker. Lithography served the production of graphic art as much as music. The direct nature of the process, says Walter Benjamin, 'permitted graphic art for the first time to put its products on the market, not only in large numbers . . . but also in daily changing forms'. It enabled artists to illustrate everyday life, and 'virtually implied the illustrated newspaper'.[11] It offered comparable advantages to music in the attempt not just to keep up with changes of taste but to exploit passing fashions as well. The lithographic process was rapidly adopted by leading music publishers like Breitkopf in Leipzig, Schott in Mainz, and Ricordi in Milan. It especially proved its usefulness in the innumerable editions combining music and illustration which became increasingly popular with the continuing expansion of the music market during the course of the nineteenth century.[12]

Yet once again, lithography only added another method to the available technologies, rather than displacing any of them. Until modern rotary presses superseded lithography for printing music in the late nineteenth century, the great nineteenth-century music publishers, in the age when they first acquired financial prominence in musical life, relied on no single method of printing exclusively, but employed each in accordance with its suitability for a particular sector of the market. They could hardly do otherwise and remain in business. Though susceptible to influence in various ways, musical taste was highly volatile, and the publisher was still a long way from the ability to manipulate it easily. As the practice of commercial concerts expanded, as opera flourished and operetta became increasingly popular, the publisher could only create a supply of music to exploit a demand which followed its own laws of progression. The only viable method was to provide a large and varied diet of music for popular consumption − the largest part of it domestic and for the piano − and it emerges from Ernest Roth's account that chance still played a very large element in a publisher's success.

Musica Practica in the Print Age

The spread of printed music had a variety of effects on popular *musica practica* and its relations with art music. Naturally considerable changes occur, but only gradually. They became more profound after the great religious reforms of the sixteenth and early seventeenth centuries, which addressed themselves to the suppression of the Carnival tradition. The severity of the condemnation and the length of time this confrontation lasted suggest that the popular traditions were remarkably resilient, as innumerable references in contemporary literary sources testify. In Shakespeare alone, more than twenty different ballad tunes are indicated either by name or by allusion.

Peter Burke, the historian who examined the great and little traditions in early modern Europe, maintains that while the upper classes used to participate in popular culture and shared many of its values, there was also two-way traffic. As a result, in the first phase following the advent of music printing, musical style was dominated more by a contrast between the sacred and the profane than between upper- and lower-class taste. Both Catholics and Protestants agreed that music had an important part to play in worship, though they differed in their notion of its proper use. The dominant idiom of Latin church music evolved under circumstances that did not favour voluntary expression on the part of the congregation. It became extremely refined, whether in the Italian Orlando di Lassus or the Englishman Thomas Tallis (who also contributed to the simpler style required by the new Protestant Church in England). But this was music which when it circulated did so mainly in manuscript form, since not only was there was no commercial market for it, but printing techniques were not up to its inscription. The music that got published, being mainly secular, was still close in style to the popular manner and to popular sources. Moreover, as gifted popular musicians increasingly learned to read music, a growth of talent occurred. In England in 1589, for example, the town waits in Norwich were of such ability that Drake asked to take them with him on his next voyage. Ten years later the composer Thomas Morley dedicated his Consort Lessons to the 'excellent and expert musicians' who made up the waits in London.

Naturally printing favoured the music for which there was a market, and the market was to be found primarily in the growth of secular music among the emerging middle classes. We see these conditions in Shakespeare's England, during the so-called golden age which stretches from before the defeat of the Spanish Armada to the Civil Wars. It is the time of Byrd, Morley, Dowland, Wilbye, Weelkes, Gibbons, Campion, Tomkins and a good many more, and of the development of a tradition of domestic music among the educated. The growing strength of the money economy gave townspeople, merchants, and even the upper yeomanry that Shakespeare himself came from, the resources for increasing domestic expenditure. Part of it went on musical instruments — virginals, citterns, viols and lutes — and the music to play on them. This was mainly vocal and instrumental chamber music, including airs for individual voices and madrigals for several, designed to be played by small parties of friends. Singing was usually accompanied. The instruments appropriate to such music have a tone that is quiet and subdued, making it possible for players and singers to hear each other easily. This gave special qualities to instrumental consorts and appropriate instrumental arrangements became popular, which in the hands of a Byrd and a Dowland developed into the purest secular art music of the day.

The market evolved in stages. In the early years of the sixteenth century, when Petrucci began publishing music in Venice, it would have been hard to find a market in England sufficient to absorb the costs. Its development reveals the growing influence in England of the humanistic values of the Italian Renaissance. By the 1560s, manuscript copies of Italian madrigals circulated widely among the nobility and country gentry, a musical vogue which had its counterpart in the Italianate style of the 'new poetry' of Sidney and Spenser. But in 1575, when Byrd and the ageing Tallis were awarded an exclusive licence by the throne to publish music, they miscalculated. They immediately produced a joint collection of motets, under the title *Cantiones Sacrae*, and this religious music proved a financial failure. Tallis is said to have withdrawn his co-operation and nothing more was printed in England till after his death in 1585, when Byrd assigned the licence to another printer, and it eventually passed to Thomas Morley.

Between 1587 and 1630, over eighty collections of vocal music were published in England, and although composers, like poets and playwrights, naturally sought aristocratic patronage for their work, it is clear simply from the title pages of these publications that they were not intended exclusively for the aristocratic audience. One of the earliest, a collection of Italian madrigals brought out by Nicholas Yonge in the 1580s, is inscribed 'for merchants and gentlemen'. Other inscriptions, like 'apt for voyces or viols' further reveal their domestic usage, where the number of voices and the instrumentation varied according to the circumstances, and instruments were used either to double voices or to replace them.

The published music of John Dowland reveals the full range of popular sources called upon by fashionable composers. Dowland is a critical example because his extensive travels made him the most European of English composers. Back in England, the latest ideas developing in Florence were still unknown. Dowland's visit in 1595 (he was then aged thirty-two and had first gone abroad at the age of seventeen) placed him in an exceptional position. He would have come into contact with the experiments in extreme chromaticism being carried out there, particularly by composers at the court of Ferrara. He would doubtless have heard the madrigals of Gesualdo, who was living there at the time of Dowland's visit. At all events, his own masterpiece, the seven *Lachrimae* for a consort of viols (or violins) and lute published in 1604, is the most remarkable music: like Gesualdo, a fabric that continually exploits momentary dissonance, suspensions, false relations, and the clash of parts moving against each other combining to produce a musical texture of extraordinary emotional intensity. Indeed one of his biographers, Diana Poulton, has observed how Dowland, in arranging concordant lute solos for consort, would purposefully introduce dissonance and discords.[13]

Such was the temper of the time that the composer who wrote in this manner was no more distant from popular taste than his contemporary Shakespeare. Like all composers of the day, educated or not, Dowland regularly based new pieces on popular melodies. His songs include settings of ballads and other popular tunes; his instrumental music uses dance styles in different metres, including the pavan, galliard, almain, gigue and courant. Songs become dances and vice versa. Often these sources carried connotations of coarse Rabelaisian humour and bawdy. The tune which is known in Dowland as *Lord Willoughby* was also set by Byrd, where the name Rowland is attached to it. The melody is associated with a comedy jig almost certainly written by Will Kemp, one of the most famous clowns of his day and a member of Shakespeare's company. Texts of the jig have survived not in English but in German − Kemp travelled to the Low Countries with the Earl of Leicester in the 1580s. The story is an old favourite from the *Decameron*.

There is also significant evidence of Dowland's popularity from literary sources. Theatres were a major focus for popular culture for both dramatic and musical reasons till 1642, when the Puritans closed them down. In a capital city like London, all classes of people except the very poor could and did attend the theatre, and made corresponding demands upon the playwright both dramatically and musically. It seems that Dowland's *Lachrimae* were much to the taste of this audience, and their renown spread beyond purely musical circles. Poulton has a long list of references to them that crop up in dramatic works of the day by Middleton, Massinger, Webster, Jonson and Nabbes, as well as a number of non-dramatic sources. In Beaumont and Fletcher's *Knight of the Burning Pestle*, when a common Londoner calls for music in a tavern, his wife demands 'Let's have Lachrimae'.

The Puritans closed the theatres, but except for extremists, the beneficent aspects of music were not a target. Their disapproval of music is a myth. Their animosity was directed on the one hand towards the King's servants, church musicians and church organs; the latter they saw as symbols of popish luxury and superstition. On the other, some also railed against 'fiddlers and minstrels', who corrupted the manners of the people and inflamed their debauchery by lewd and obscene songs, and in many places town waits were also dismissed. One school of thought holds that once the offending musicians were turned out and some of the offending organs destroyed, music was simply left to get on with its ordinary business; another, that although high-handed, the Puritans had an active love of music — of the right kind, that is. At any rate Cromwell himself was a great music lover and maintained a small body of domestic players. And in 1657, Parliament listened sympathetically to a petition and appointed a committee for the Advancement of Musick.

Most significant of all, the years of the Commonwealth saw the appearance (150 years after Petrucci in Venice) of the first specialist music publisher in England. *The English Dancing Master*, issued in 1651 by John Playford, hardly supports the notion that the Puritans suppressed all music indiscriminately. In fact this collection constitutes a principal source of popular music. Clearly the tunes have been fashioned to the susceptibilities of the market, and many of the arrangements cast them straightforwardly in the major key. But some of them betray their origins by their modal character, and the introduction of accidentals which give the tune a minor twist; the effect is much exploited by the English folk-song revivalists of the early twentieth century like Vaughan Williams. Playford followed this volume with a number of other collections, both vocal and instrumental, including books of rounds and catches and other light-hearted stuff, as well as music by the leading composers of the day, Orlando Gibbons and Matthew Locke. Music clubs flourished in Oxford, musical life in London was prosperous, and throughout the country, as one writer has put it, 'Music, driven out of palaces by the Civil Wars, descended into the home and took root there most strongly.'[14]

A different pattern of development is to be found in Germany, where the golden age was yet to come. At the end of the Thirty Years War the country was split down the middle religiously, and politically fragmented into 300 dukedoms and principalities, owing theoretical allegiance to the Holy Roman Emperor in Vienna. Paradoxically this backward condition was not at all bad for music: in spite of the devastation of the war, the public sphere provided a lively ambience for it. Music was encouraged through the often over-ambitious displays of magnificence by the courts, the more economical civic pride of the towns, and the post-Reformation zeal of the Church — the latter especially in Central Germany, the home country of Lutheranism, where the Bach family lived and worked.

The Bachs constitute only the most outstanding example of a widespread phenomenon, both before and since but especially then. In France, for example, the Couperins flourished from the seventeenth to the nineteenth century, and there are many other musical families throughout Europe whose names were less prominent or shorter-lived. Indeed with the growth of the music profession, according to a German music historian who has studied the period closely, by far the greatest number of orchestral musicians appear to have come from families of musicians.

Even if musical genius remains one of the mysteries of genetics, the subject of musical families belongs less to genealogy and heredity than to *musica practica* and historical sociology. The phenomenon reflects a social trait in music which stems directly from the characteristics of *musica practica*: the affinity we have already noted between music and the crafts, with which it shares a predisposition towards training through apprenticeship. This affinity is also reflected in the way musicians became organized. The milieu in which the Bach family worked and propagated was governed by guild thinking and professional regulations, which treated of practices in the court orchestras, the town bands and the church choirs. By thus promoting group solidarity, it decidedly advanced the art of professional music.

The special solidarity of the Bach family, however, is due to something more: the fact that musicality is always most favoured when encouraged from the earliest childhood within the bosom of the family, which means rather earlier than in the ordinary development of craft talent. It is almost a *sine qua non* in the case of prodigies, where talent may be manifest as early as the age of three or four. At such an age, it is generally either nurtured at once or else its growth will very likely be stunted. And though it often survives adversity, the fact remains that the overwhelming majority of musicians to achieve distinction are indeed the children of musicians. This is the way of *musica practica*.

The great Bach, Johann Sebastian — his own childhood was chequered: he lost his parents as a boy and his education was entrusted to an older brother — was intensely conscious of the meaning of family solidarity. He himself compiled the document which provides the most reliable evidence of Bach family history, an annotated family genealogy known as the *Ursprung*. The family itself regarded this as an important document, and copied it several times, adding details. It has provided musicologists with the richest pickings. It traces the Bach family back to the mid-sixteenth century, naming its head as Veit, by trade a baker, who had been driven from Moravia or Slovakia around 1545 in the expulsion of Protestants by the Counter-Reformation.

The family story reveals the transition from one musical world to another. Veit played the cittern as a hobby; his son gained employment as a musician, though not exclusively. This happened in the third generation, which by accepting salaried positions became sedentary, and improved the family's fortunes. Socially this represented a break with the popular cultural tradition of the *Spielmann*, the itinerant musical jobber. A kind of latterday minstrel, the *Spielmann* was unorganized, outside the guilds, a member of the lower ranks who were not normally permitted citizenship. (In Elizabethan England, where secular musicians had begun to form guilds for their self-protection a hundred years before, itinerant musicians were lumped together by Parliament along with vagabonds and thieves.)

The Bachs now formed a dynasty. The New Grove's Dictionary of Music (1980) records six generations between Veit's grandchildren, the eldest born around 1580, and Wilhelm Friedrich Ernst, number 84, who died in 1845. Seventy of them were musicians, and the author comments that by the turn of the seventeenth century they were so widespread in Thuringia that the name 'Bach' and the word 'musician' were regarded as synonymous. In 1730 Johann Sebastian proudly wrote to a friend that all his children 'are born *Musici* and I can assure you that I am already able to form a concert *vocaliter* and *instrumentaliter* from my own family, as my present wife sings a very pretty soprano and my eldest daughter too joins in not badly . . .'.[15] It was typical that the successor to a position vacated by a Bach would be another Bach. It was also rumoured that the Bachs had a secret family formula for writing fugues.

The break with non-craft music should still not be thought of as sharp, however, either in Germany or in England, where a generation before J.S. Bach, Henry Purcell, fondly known as the Orpheus Britannicus, is a case in point. Authenticated biographical details are scanty — not even the name of his father is certain — but he came from a musical family and both his father and his uncle (whichever was which) were musicians of the Chapel Royal where he himself was a chorister. Indeed the whole of his short life — he was thirty-seven when he died in 1695 — revolved around the Chapel Royal, to which he was appointed as composer when only eighteen. (In addition, two years later he became organist of Westminster Abbey.) Official duties required him to produce a large amount of church music, but stupendously gifted, he composed, with equal ease, in every genre of the day: anthems and odes for sacred and ceremonial use; for domestic use, keyboard music, and sonatas and fantasias for strings; a huge amount of incidental music for the theatre, and in *Dido and Aeneas*, the greatest of early English operas. Some of this music is among the most advanced of the day anywhere in Europe, yet Purcell, says one of his biographers, 'would as soon make a song to be sung about the streets as . . . an anthem'. He is indeed the composer of a large number of popular catches, some of them among the bawdiest examples of the genre, and 'his sense of humour in these works seems to have been frankly Rabelaisian'.[16]

Throughout Europe, popular dances formed a constant element in music both courtly and domestic; in England fiddlers of the artisan classes, like James Oswald and Niel Gow (the latter the son of a village weaver), were taken up by polite society. As for Germany, Johann Sebastian's biographer Forkel (writing half a century after his death, at the very beginning of the nineteenth-century Bach revival, and relying as his main source of information on his son C.P.E.) describes a typical Bach family gathering:

> Since the company consisted of none but [Church] Kantors, organists and town musicians . . . first of all . . . a chorale was sung. From this devotional opening they proceeded to jesting, often in strong contrast to it . . . they would sing folksongs, the contents of which were partly comic and partly indelicate, all together and extempore . . . They called this kind of extempore harmonising a quodlibet . . . and enjoyed a hearty laugh at it.[17]

(I am reminded of the musical parties which once ended the Aldeburgh Festival, when Benjamin Britten, Peter Pears, George Malcolm and others would let their hair down with cabaret and jazz hits of the 1930s; here there was the added element of a camp sense of humour.)

The fact is that music in Johann Sebastian's time was not yet segregated along class lines as rigidly and exclusively as it later became. It is also wrong to assume that the popular audience were not acquainted with art music and advanced idioms. High genres were disseminated first through the Church, second through the theatre and the rise of opera. In England, for example, fine music had been cultivated by the theatre since Shakespeare's day; art music was open to the participation of gifted players both amateur and popular; and operatic excerpts were disseminated by the Restoration stage, which reached beyond the confines of the licensed playhouses to embrace the popular audience at the great fairs. The ballad operas of the 1720s, directly modelled on Italian opera, achieved their greatest success in this way. A recent biographer of Handel observes how Hogarth's painting of the Gaol Scene from *The Beggar's Opera* evokes the model of Italian opera quite clearly, 'Macheath as the Senesino figure between Polly and Lucy as Cuzzoni and Faustina . . . against a backdrop which could easily pass for one of the prison scenes in the King's Theatre stock' — the King's was where the operas of Handel were then presented, the Italian names are those of the singers.[18] The ballad operas were pastiche, for which professional composers arranged popular tunes as arias, and mixed them with numbers taken from current operatic successes. *The Beggar's Opera* itself includes music by Handel as well as Purcell, which Johann Pepusch, another German expatriate composer engaged by John Gay to provide his words with tunes, freely borrowed.

The popular parody of upper-class music was a predilection which still survived from the carnivalesque tradition. The result was that everywhere, a strain of opera flourished which closely followed popular values. The *comédie à vaudeville* appeared in France, ancestor of *opéra comique*, while

German culture produced the *Singspiel*, which Mozart turned back into high art in *Die Entführung aus dem Serail* and *Die Zauberflöte*, and which subsequently descended into Viennese operetta. In Italy, where *opera seria* included a popular audience, since the civic opera houses originally gave free admission to the pit and the galleries to the servants of the patrons, the *commedia dell' arte* of the itinerant players influenced the development of *opera buffa*, out of which Mozart created works like *Don Giovanni*. The history of opera is thus a prime example of the dialogue between genres through which the different social classes talked to each other. Or sometimes shouted at each other: in nineteenth-century Italy, in the time of Verdi and the Risorgimento, when the cheaper parts of the auditorium were enlarged and the popular audience became a larger economic element in the development of the opera industry, the Italian opera house became a scene of popular political agitation.

We must not imagine that during the course of these developments the population in the countryside was much affected. The interface between the musics of different classes was the city and the town. Rural music, preserving the most ancient traditions, was marginalized. With the growth of urban society, however, the process came to include the urban popular classes within its reach, or at least most of them at any rate occasionally. In London and leading English cities, the pleasure gardens that grew up in the eighteenth century — Vauxhall, Sadler's Wells, Marylebone, Ranelagh, Lambeth Wells — with their tree-lined walks, refreshment booths and bandstands, provided relaxing open urban spaces where social distinctions tended to be disregarded at least enough for the ranks to mingle. James Boswell spoke of Vauxhall as 'that excellent place of public amusement . . . peculiarly adapted to the taste of the English nation; there being a mixture of curious show, gay exhibition, musick, vocal and instrumental, not too refined for the general ear; for all of which only a shilling is paid; and though last, not least, good eating and drinking . . .'. Pepys noted that 'a man may go to spend what he will, or nothing' and the shilling admission was low enough for throngs of thousands at a time when concert audience numbered at best only a few hundred at a time.[19] For the final open rehearsal of Handel's *Music for the Royal Fireworks* at Vauxhall in 1749, twelve thousand people paid 2/6d each. The English were proud of these pleasure gardens. Burney regarded an imitation he visited in Paris as decidedly inferior.

In Germany, the criss-cross influences of music in the city were lubricated by a growing class of professional musicians, who mainly belonged to the upper echelons of the lower ranks (as they largely still do today). The flautist Quantz, who became *Kapellmeister* to Frederick the Great, was the son of a blacksmith who learnt his trade as an apprentice in a town band. The increasing numbers were due to the institutionalization of the town players and the development of the court ensemble. In the latter, sedentary musicians advanced to the status of middle-ranking servants. In the former, they acquired a certain status as representatives of independent municipal government, though they always had to confront burgher prejudice against their profession, and one of the duties of the town music director was the prosecution of unlicensed performers like the *Spielmann*.

The *Spielmann*'s greatest enemy, however, was the clergy, who still saw the popular musician as a dangerous source of pagan influence. Indeed, the persistence of heathen religious practices in northern Germany up to and beyond the end of the fourteenth century in some degree preserved the association of the medieval *Spielmann* with ancient soothsaying, sorcery and magic. From the sixteenth century on, these 'demonic' powers become increasingly a subject of legend and fairy-tale, issuing in the Romantic movement in stories like those of Tieck and Hoffmann; the theme resurfaces in the twentieth century in Thomas Mann's *Doctor Faustus*.

Meanwhile the designation *Spielmann* gave way to the appellation *Musikant*, or dance-musician, while at the other end of the scale, *Musiker*, a term corresponding to the Latin *Musicus*, was now more generally applied to the composers and solo performers of art music. Every institutionalized musician sought to be differentiated from the *Spielmann* — until Romanticism was in bloom and Schubert was able, in the final and deeply pathetic song of *Die Winterreise*, to identify himself with the dejected hurdy-gurdy man. In earlier days, however, the vehemence of the town musicians' protestations of moral righteousness bespeak the *Spielmann*'s daily proximity, and the itinerant was under constant suspicion; especially when the peasant wars brought an increase in the numbers of the robber class, and pipers, bagpipers and fiddlers were repeatedly reported to be partisans and even peasant leaders. (On the other hand, there was tolerance for the mountain people of the border regions of Saxony and Bohemia, popularly known as *Präger Studenten*, who became itinerant musicians out of material need and travelled round northern Germany in costume, like the Tyrolean singers of a later period.)

In short, the acute ideological division between high and low culture, art music and popular music, which the twentieth century inherited from the nineteenth, is a phenomenon erected on what was still in the eighteenth century a fairly functional distinction between the formal and the informal, the genteel and the rude. No doubt many informal musicians lacked either sufficient skill or the musical literacy to advance to careers in the formal sphere, while others would have been lacking not skill so much as practice and opportunity. The division was there; Quantz said in his autobiography, 'although I otherwise enjoyed the way of life of the town musician, the tiresome playing of dances, which is so harmful to more refined

performance, made me yearn for a release from it'.[20] But the formal
musician often still sang and played informal music, even if not in public. It
was not until later that social pressures of various kinds, including shifts in
the stratification of the social classes, interceded to break such practices,
and the division became more absolute.

Of the Origins of Concert Life

The process we have been describing has many ramifications. One of the
most significant is the way it explains the marginalization of rural music,
and as a consequence, the idealization it then underwent at the hands of
urban intellectuals of later generations. Indeed the origins of Romanticism
can be partly traced in changing attitudes towards folk art in the late
eighteenth century on the part of the philosopher Herder and the young
Goethe. (Later there followed, in waves, the nationalist revivals of the
nineteenth and early twentieth centuries, which culminated in a return of
the repressed, and its recovery for the modernist movement in the seminal
work of composers like Bartók and Stravinsky.)

The key feature is the development of the concert as the central
institution of bourgeois musical life. At root, the concert is born of the
musica practica of the educated classes at leisure. In England, the antecedents
of public performance by professionals before a paying audience can be
found in the musical clubs of Oxford and Cambridge in the 1650s and the
gatherings of gentlemen amateurs in the London taverns that are
chronicled by Anthony Wood, Roger North and, of course, Pepys. North
described how these consorts of amateurs attracted numerous listeners, and
when the amateurs withdrew into private gatherings, the 'masters of music
entered and filled the consort, which they carried on directly for mony
collected as at other publik enterteinements'.[21] These activities belong to a
growth in the exploitation of leisure which occurred on several fronts and
encouraged each other. The first coffee-houses were opened in London in
1652. Fifty years later there were one thousand of them, offering the
pleasures not only of the new beverage but also of tobacco. A few years later
the physician and satirist Bernard Mandeville remarked on the great
impact the new luxury commodities — he also mentions tea and purple
cloth — were having on the national economy. Consider, he says, what vast
traffic is done, and how many thousands of families depend 'on two silly if
not odious customs; the taking of snuff and smoking of tobacco; both which
it is certain do infinitely more hurt than good to those that are addicted to
them!'[22] There were those who thought much the same of music. Tea and
coffee, meanwhile, were regularly celebrated in poems, songs and cantatas,
the latter composed amongst others by J.S. Bach.

The credit for the first regular series of public commercial concerts is usually given to the London violinist John Banister. They were held in his own house in Whitefriars in 1672 and advertised in the *London Gazette*, thus drawing on the same coffee-house audience that provided the readership of the early newspapers. The ensemble at these meetings was the same as the consort favoured by amateurs; some of the players also sang and much of the music was vocal. When Banister died at the end of the decade, the mantle fell on a music-loving coal merchant: Thomas Britton, known as 'the musical small-coal man', had started a similar weekly music meeting in a room above his shop in 1678, where Banister's son was one of the players. Initially Britton's meetings were free, but after Banister's death his son began to charge a yearly subscription; cash, however, was not yet exchanged at the door. Those who played at Britton's concerts over the years included Thomas Arne, Pepusch (musical arranger of John Gay's *The Beggar's Opera*), the painter Woolaston, the poet John Hughes, and in Britton's last years, Handel. For composers these meetings were a most welcome alternative site of activity, not initially for their earning power but for their unassuming character: their informality and conviviality held a promise not to be found in the decorum of the aristocratic houses, and encouraged a new style which in due course led to new forms.

These early concerts also corresponded to the susceptibilities of social rivalry and indicate certain political undercurrents. Banister was not an amateur but a musician ascending the ladder of his profession. He was the son of a city waits player; his father taught him to fiddle as a child, and his talent took him to the French court for training, and thus to his appointment as leader of the restored King's band. He had not, however, returned 'an absolute monsieur', and he launched his concerts when he was dismissed for saying in the King's hearing that he thought English violinists better than French. This patriotism earned him the approval of persons like Pepys.

As for the musical small-coal man, Britton was a precocious member of the tradesman class. An acknowledged connoisseur, he was praised by such leading patrons as the Earls of Pembroke, Sunderland, Winchelsea and Oxford (who engaged him to assist in collecting the great Harleian Library), his concerts were accused by some of being a cover for seditious purposes, and he was variously called a magician, an atheist, a Presbyterian and a Jesuit. If this kind of suspicion often surrounds members of a lower social class as they attempt to claim a more privileged status, the body politic has long regarded such musical activities as a cover for something more sinister, like the chamber music society in one of the Boulting Brothers' Cold War thrillers, where Shostakovich, whose music is weird and atonal to the ears of the police, provides the cover for Russian spies.

One could scarcely wish for more striking evidence of the intimate link between music and social history than the tales of Banister and Britton, in whom the origins of the paying concert as the characteristic form of bourgeois music are so clearly symbolized: a professional musician booted from the court and a coal merchant. On the continent, the new institutions of bourgeois cultural life took slightly longer to appear. The first regular concert series were mounted in Hamburg in 1722 and in Paris in 1725. In England, by this time, the ensemble was growing and new concerted forms were developing, and London musical gatherings of the tavern type had been replaced by concerts for the nobility and upper middle classes; by the mid-century concert-going became a central part of the aristocracy's high social season, like opera in Italy. The concert, in short, had been expropriated. As William Weber recounts, one important series, the Concerts of Ancient Music, was directed and to some extent performed by the highest noblemen, and became so prestigious that the King often attended. 'Wealthy members of the middle class went . . . but had no leadership role within them. Middle-class performing clubs which appeared had little prominence in the city's social life.'[23]

Similar music clubs in Italy, where they were called Academies, were widespread, and they soon grew up in Germany too, where they were often called Collegia Musicae. In Paris, the first concerts were nominally religious, presented like Handel's oratorios on the thirty-five holy days during the year when operatic performances were forbidden; the repertoire gradually became more secular. But the development of Paris concert life was hemmed in by restrictions intended to protect the opera and royal leadership. The musical life of London and Paris thus reveals contrasting relationships, says William Weber, between the nobility and the state in the two countries. The English nobility, following the Restoration, was closely and extensively involved in the central authority of the state, within which they took control of cultural life away from the monarchy. In France, the weakness of the nobility allowed the Royal House to maintain tight controls over artistic institutions as a means of hemming the aristocracy in. While state controls over publishing and the opera weakened considerably during the second half of the century, control over concert life remained strict, and even though noblemen supported domestic musicians, Parisian concert life remained less developed than that of London.

Vienna, on the other hand, was a special case. As a commercial activity early concert life was undeveloped, but music was everywhere, with salons and concerts at every level from the highest aristrocacy to the popular pleasure gardens — the Augarten, the Belvedere park, the Liechtenstein palace gardens, and the Bastei 'by the refreshment stands'. Indoors these activities, in which professionals and amateurs often played together, took place in a wide range of venues, from the theatres on days free from opera, where visiting virtuosi would perform, to private houses. It is not for nothing that Vienna earned its reputation as Europe's musical capital. The decisive factor in Viennese musical life, says one of Mozart's recent biographers, was that domestic music making took place on all social levels, and many amateur musicians — dilettanti as they were then called — deserved to be heard in public; many of them were equal in skill to the professionals. The nobility were often musical amateurs and keen patrons of chamber music — Beethoven's pursuit of them and theirs of Beethoven helps to explain why he wrote more chamber music than symphonies and concertos, and it was often written to be played by the patrons who commissioned it. But every self-respecting bourgeois home had a piano, and the relative ease of finding good musicians meant that the middle class were also active in organizing musical events. The result was that most public concerts were also *Dilettantenkonzerte*, while professional musicians were invited to perform at 'private' concerts, where private only refers to the setting. Consequently the Viennese salon was a very different kind of social institution from the Parisian version. In Vienna the salon was neither an attempt to defend nor to ape aristocratic culture, it was a gathering for the purpose of music making in the more intimate setting of any house that was big enough, aristocratic or bourgeois. The event was actually open to anyone interested, 'people of all social levels mingled freely, and nowhere else were class differences so little in evidence'.[24]

Vienna was a port of call for every famous virtuoso of the day, but paradoxically, compared to London, it was less conducive to the professionalization of the commercial concert. Accordingly London also attracted large numbers of continental musicians, who either stayed for extended periods, like Haydn, or who settled there, like Salomon who brought him over. London succoured a specialized labour market for the freelance musician, like opera in Italy. But elsewhere during this period, beyond the leading metropolitan centres, most professional musicians were still either retained servants or civic or church employees with scant control over their professional opportunities.

London saw the most intensive development of the commercial concert, but contributed little to the initiation of the symphony, the most important new musical form of the age and the highest aspiration of the nineteenth-century concert composer. As every standard musicological study records, the symphony was born in Mannheim. Why this should have been is not sufficiently explained by knowing that the Elector Palatine, Duke Carl Theodor, was himself a trained musician and therefore a good patron. Mozart points us in the right direction when he complains to his father of the dissolute court musicians in Salzburg: 'Ah, if only the orchestra were organized as they are at Mannheim. Indeed I would like you to see the discipline which prevails there and the authority which Cannabich wields. There everything is done seriously. Cannabich, who is the best conductor I have ever seen, is both beloved and feared by his subordinates.'[25] The orchestra's achievements under this kind of regime were crucial. Special emphasis was placed on the blend of instrumental colour. Because the orchestra was made up of a number of equally gifted instrumentalists who were also competent composers, great strides were made in forging a style both unified and unifying. The Mannheim orchestra not only helped to give the symphony a paradigmatic form in the works of Cannabich and his predecessor, Stamitz, it also adopted a whole armoury of ways of playing such music: new conventions of phrasing, uniform bowing by the different string sections, the introduction of controlled crescendo and diminuendo. These were not just questions of local style: their incorporation into the score reveals their structural significance in the creation of symphonic form.

These developments did not take place in London precisely because the London concert was commercial, and the orchestra, however enthusiastic, was not a permanent body but an *ad hoc* band employed on piece-rates. Even though, as in New York a century later, a high proportion of the players were German, these conditions did not lend themselves to the creation of a style that was more than a style. This required more rehearsal time and the greater cohesion of a regular band, in short, greater discipline, which was far more likely in the court of a beneficent German prince. Above all, what made it possible for the symphony to emerge in the German court orchestra were the given patterns of social decorum and deference to be found in court life itself. Just as musicians had a clearly delineated social position within the court hierarchy, so it was second nature to them to keep proper musical order. Once the style was taken up into the form, however, which began to make its own demands, the same conditions became more and more restrictive. By Mozart's time, composers and musicians generally had grown pretty dissatisfied with their position at court. Haydn found a new relationship with the audience in the concert rooms of Paris, London and Oxford which stimulated the most mature and accomplished of his symphonies. Mozart struggled to free himself from the oppression he felt in the Salzburg court, and piano concertos and opera gave him a considerable measure of success. But if this new relationship and this release from bondage are musically expressed with almost immediate consequences for symphonic form, it wasn't until well into the nineteenth century that the corresponding social changes turned into new forms of economic exploitation and new relations of production. The process must be seen in its proper context: the break-up of the traditional social hierarchy, the political impact of the French Revolution, the advance of the Industrial Revolution. These forces served to develop the interests of new audiences, not just through the economic progress of the bourgeoisie, but by altering the balance of cultural power to allow them to assume the cultural rights of their erstwhile social superiors. Composers welcomed the changes not only because they offered economic independence from the aristocratic patrons under whom they chafed; at least to begin with they had reason enough to identify with the new audience. The contradictions only appeared later.

Notes

1. Ernst Roth, *The Business of Music*, Cassell, London 1969, p. 61.
2. T.W. Adorno, *Introduction to the Sociology of Music*, Seabury Press, New York 1976, pp. 157−8.
3. A. Hyatt King, *Four Hundred Years of Music Printing*, British Library, London 1979, p. 10.
4. Lorenzo Bianconi, *Music in the Seventeenth Century*, Cambridge University Press, Cambridge 1987, p. 2.
5. Ibid., p. 25.
6. Ibid., p. 21.
7. Ibid., p. 83.
8. Ibid., p. 65.
9. Ibid., p. 90.
10. Roth, p. 61.
11. Walter Benjamin, 'The Work of Art in the Age of Mechanical Reproduction', in *Illuminations*, ed. Hannah Arendt, Schocken, New York 1969.
12. For a detailed account, see the present author's *The Dream That Kicks*, Routledge & Kegan Paul, London 1980.
13. Diana Poulson, *Dowland*, Faber & Faber, London 1972, p. 347.
14. Michael Foss, *The Age of Patronage, the Arts in Society 1660−1750*, Hamish Hamilton, London 1971, p. 7.
15. M. Gal, ed., *The Musician's World, Letters of the Great Composers*, Thames & Hudson, London 1965, p. 42.
16. A.K. Holland, *Henry Purcell*, Penguin, London 1948, p. 57.
17. Quoted in Christian Wolff et al., *The New Grove Bach Family*, Macmillan Papermac, London 1983, p. 20.
18. Jonathan Keates, *Handel*, Hamish Hamilton, London 1986, p. 137.
19. Arthur Loesser, *Men, Women and Pianos*, Simon & Schuster, New York 1954, p. 206.
20. Quoted in Edward Reilly, Introduction to J.J. Quantz, *On Playing the Flute*, Faber & Faber, London 1966, p. xiv.
21. Quoted in Foss, p. 77.
22. Quoted in W.F. Haug, *Critique of Commodity Aesthetics*, Polity Press, Cambridge 1986, p. 21.
23. William Weber, *Music and the Middle Classes*, Croom Helm, London 1975, p. 4.
24. Volkmar Braunbehrens, *Mozart in Vienna*, Oxford University Press, Oxford 1991, p. 148.
25. Eric Blom, ed., *Mozart's Letters*, Penguin, London 1956, p. 114.

6

Market Forces

Growth of Concert Life

Nineteenth-century concert life, says the social historian William Weber, exhibited the intense social energies of the middle classes in the period of their ascendency. As concerts proliferated throughout Europe and their customs and design took on characteristically modern forms, they were accompanied by a giddying social atmosphere in the expanding audience, with eager trips to concert halls and passionate support of performers and musical styles. Not only that, but this passionate involvement became a means of social advancement on the part of both individuals and groups.[1] In the following century, as modern musicology became established in the academy, it tried to ignore all this, as if it demeaned the discipline to speak of such mundane realities. But how could anyone seriously imagine that this was not transmuted into the brilliant seductive surface of nineteenth-century music?

Weber distinguishes five periods in the history of the concert in London, Paris and Vienna before 1870. First, the scattered appearance of commercial concerts from about 1680 to around 1750, the year that J.S. Bach died. This is followed by their growing frequency in the period 1750–1790, in which the Haydn orchestra became the standard ensemble. A hiatus between 1790 and 1813 is due to war, more serious in some places than others. Then from the end of the Napoleonic Wars to the revolutions of 1848 there is a rapid explosion of concert life, with a growing calendar of events catering to different class interests. This is followed by the institutionalization of the concert world in the period to 1870, in which aristocrats and upper middle class merge into a single élite audience, while orchestral management is undertaken by social élites or conductor-impresarios. After 1870, where Weber's survey ends, there are two more periods. The first begins with the rebellion of the professional musician against the authoritarianism of the conductor and sees the establishment of the major full-time symphony orchestras; this continues well into the twentieth century. And then the present period, beginning in the 1930s but flowering after 1945, in which the orchestral economy becomes fully dependent on electro-acoustic reproduction. The former period sees the transformation of the rank-and-file orchestral players into a kind of aristocracy of labour, and their unionization; the latter we can call the age of the concert hall as museum, in which contemporary composers write less and less for the full symphony orchestra because it is less and less responsive to them.

The middle classes began to take on new roles in cultural life at the end of the Napoleonic Wars. The fundamental factor underlying the growth of concert life in the nineteenth century was the relative health and stability of the capitalist economies and the rise in the middle-class standard of living. These conditions also stimulated a boom in the sale of instruments and publications, both of which had been growing steadily since the middle of the eighteenth century. Three principal types of concert developed. Most commonly, the 'benefit' concert: not the charity event which the term implies today but concerts promoted by individual musicians for their own benefit. The musicians concerned were mostly local residents with a reputation to maintain, some were travelling virtuosi. It was as a virtuoso pianist playing his own works that Mozart gave the benefit concerts in Strasbourg which he discusses in his letters to his father. Secondly came events promoted by permanent organizations of professional musicians, regulated by a board drawn from their members and with admission by subscription, prime among them the philharmonic societies which were the forerunners of symphony orchestras. The third type was the 'low-status' concert promoted by amateur musical organizations, and with a social base lower than the others, among the lower middle and artisan classes.

As the different types of concerts developed, different audiences manifested distinct tastes. On the basis of careful examination of membership records of musical societies in England, William Weber discerns a strong preference for German classical style among the professional classes, while the commercial classes preferred the operatic and virtuoso styles. But even if divisions of taste corresponded to social distinctions, conditions as a whole were highly volatile and significant changes of preference were registered.

The display of musical taste resounded with political overtones, and changes in preference were often symptomatic of quite unmusical considerations. In the earlier part of the century, England offers some very clear illustrations of the ways in which concert life reflected political issues. As Europe emerged from the Napoleonic Wars, and the upper echelons of the bourgeoisie found themselves engaged in competition with the aristocracy for social prestige, struggles over control of the élite concerts paralleled the broader conflict in which they were engaged over the issue of political reform, for art and music are battlegrounds of symbolic power. When the Reform Act of 1832 failed to solve the deeper political problems but merely divided the upper and middle classes from the masses, the lower middle classes entered the musical arena: the 1830s saw the emergence, especially in London, of new choral organizations with strong roots among religious dissenters. When the Crown mounted a Handel Festival in Westminster Abbey in 1834, says William Weber, 'it had the obvious purpose of dramatising royal leadership after the bitter dispute of electoral reform. Its administrators not only restricted admission to a carefully chosen list, but also excluded local church choirs from the chorus, inviting only singers from Anglican churches and predominantly upper-middle class provincial choruses.' This discrimination caused a bitter outcry among the new choirs in London, who responded by promoting their own Handel performances, which led to the formation of the important Sacred Harmonic Society. Symbolically, this society in due course became the proud owner of the bust of Handel which used to stand in the Vauxhall Gardens. Ironically, and as if to demonstrate the ultimate victory of commercialism and the culture industry over political assertion and social pride, this bust now adorns the offices of the music publisher Novello's — which a few years ago became part of the Granada television group.

Shortly after the Handel affair, in the 1840s, there emerged the first of a new kind of public musical form, the promenade concert. This was to prove for a period the most important means by which the heritage of informal musical entertainment belonging to the London pleasure gardens was turned into large-scale commercial enterprise among a broad public, and it was here that individual professional musicians first took command and a new kind of musical entrepreneur appeared. To put it bluntly, many musicians felt increasingly fed up with the élite concerts, where they were restricted in the music they could play, and frustrated by employment designed to provide a backing for the diversion of wealthy amateurs. As one reviewer of the time put it: 'Lords spiritual and temporal are useful in their proper places, but they are sorry managers of a concert.'[2] Such musicians were more than willing to work for one of their own instead. This period sees the ascendancy of composer-conductors like Mendelssohn and Berlioz, but commercially speaking the most successful concert series, at any rate in London, came under the baton of the French musical showman Louis Antoine Jullien (who subsequently took himself off for a period to New York, which European opera stars and instrumental soloists had started visiting in the 1820s).

In the capitals of Europe, at the same time as the rise of the bourgeois composer-conductors — some of whom, like Berlioz, were known for their radical political sympathies — the nobility retreated into their salons. However, the richer members of the bourgeoisie, wishing to extend their political victories into the social sphere, competed with them. Heine complained that 'bands of youthful dilettanti, of whom one has learned by experience to expect the very worst, perform in every key and on all the instruments that have ever been invented'.[3] The salon nevertheless became an important site of activity for professionals. This was where budding virtuosi made the contacts that brought them pupils; it was also a step on the ladder towards the concert platform and fame, and in the most prestigious salons, only musicians of real distinction were heard. But in those salons where amateurs performed, the event also took on other functions. Because it belonged to the domain of family and society, the event became the primary site for the musicality of bourgeois women. Here they could exert vigorous leadership, and those with real musical gifts might even launch professional careers. Beyond the salon the world was far less favourable and they suffered intolerable tensions between their private and professional lives. Most were were forced to give up their careers when they married.

In the bourgeois salon, the interests of the hosts were to cash in on the social exchange. The salon was the locus where music became a commodity which could be exchanged for social status. Indeed, here the daughter of the house went on display with the purpose of attracting suitors. As one woman wrote to a London music magazine, she had taken up singing on the advice of her friends for the sole purpose of marrying into a wealthy family, and had accomplished her goal in a short time. At the same time, a correspondent of a Leipzig music magazine wrote that in Vienna young men took up chamber music in order to gain access to the salons of highly-placed families through whom they might get good jobs. Unmusical parents would therefore indulge in these activities for social reasons, but there was also a strong belief that musical pursuits provided a valuable means for the socialization of children. 'The watchword of middle class values', says William Weber, 'was discipline, and musical training helped instil it in young people. For girls especially, learning the piano was virtually a puberty rite, since it was conceived not as a hobby but rather as a social obligation integral to their upbringing.'[4] The same idea of the benefits of music subsequently becomes the rationale for the activities of philanthropic mill and mine owners who promoted brass bands and choruses among their workers, though probably many would not have made the financial sacrifice if not for the radical activities of the mechanics institutes which first demonstrated the hunger of workers for making music.

The origin of the bourgeois salon lay in the domestic musical life of the aristocracy in their town houses, but there, as Mozart had complained, the habit was to give the musician a gift — a watch, an initialled snuff-box — not money. It nevertheless rewarded the effort because musicians who rendered service gratis could also freely display their accomplishments: a kind of social contract operated. The composer Flotow described in his memoirs how the system worked during the heyday of the salons in Paris in the 1840s:

> . . . one makes several appearances in the course of the winter, and then, at the beginning of Lent, one announces a concert and sends a dozen high-priced tickets . . . to the hostess of every salon at which one has played. That is the usual practice . . . The cost of such a concert is negligible. It is given on a profit-sharing basis, takes place in daylight, which saves the expense of lighting, and no heating is necessary, because the audience turn up in their outdoor clothes. Placards at street-corners are unnecessary, and in any case would serve no purpose. Nor is there any need for a box-office, and there is hardly even any need to have an attendant on duty at the door to collect the tickets . . . The audience consist of habitués of the various salons and always give the virtuosos, whom they have already met, and the music they play, most of which they already know, the warmest possible reception. Any artist who is ambitious can easily maintain himself in Paris in this agreeable fashion, without wasting much time or trouble over it.[5]

In a word, salon life provided a network of social obligations lying ready to be exploited. It diversified patronage and constituted an up-market focus for commercial activity. The related growth industries of concert-giving, music publishing and journalism all fed off the social prestige of the salon, which continued to provide a focus down to the last great salons of Paris and London in the 1920s, where Russian émigrés like Stravinsky or *enfants terribles* like William Walton were popular.

Production and Consumption

From the point of view of political economy, music in the nineteenth century is a huge success story, a greatly expanding field of profitable activity. For the individual musician, however, it was somewhat risky. According to the social historian Cyril Ehrlich, 'the most basic fact about professional musicians in nineteenth century Britain is the huge increase in their numbers . . . which far outstripped the rapid growth of the country's population: the latter almost doubled during this period, while the number of musicians increased sevenfold'.[6] This had its problems. 'The musical profession', said a gentleman by the name of Henry Fisher in 1888, 'is perilously easy to enter, for the simple reason that it does not require the investment of large capital.' 'Except among the richer classes,' said another, 'almost everyone who studies music ends up teaching music to someone else. Such is his fate whatever may have been his ambition.'[7] In short, the industry was over-supplied.

Ehrlich is impressed by the effects upon music in the nineteenth century of the laws of supply and demand. Some of the relevant social patterns, he says, were already perceptible by the late eighteenth century, but by the middle of the nineteenth 'they were far more powerful, met less resistance, and were augmented by potent new influences'.[8] In plain language, commercialism had got the upper hand. But the demand for music, he continues, 'is not autonomous and therefore cannot in reality be separated from supply. In the simplest sense supply creates a demand: the taste for music is both slaked and stimulated by its availability.' Or as Marx put it, not only does production create consumption, but consumption creates production by providing a motive for it. And although Marxist economists hardly registered it, the work of art was for Marx the very paradigm of this process, which is central to his whole system of economic analysis: 'The need which consumption feels for the object is created by the perception of it. The object of art — like every other product — creates a public which is sensitive to art and enjoys beauty. Production thus not only creates an object for the subject, but also a subject for the object.'[9]

The increasing demand for music was thus immediately translated into an increasing demand for musicians. There was no other means by which 'productivity' could be increased. That is, apart from capital investment in new and larger halls and theatres, which indeed went on at intervals throughout the century; but this is only a partial solution, subject to physical limitations. Meanwhile, for individual musicians in need of work, there were opportunities in both teaching and playing, as well as the useful drudgery (as Ehrlich puts it) of tuning and repairing instruments, of copying music and of selling it. Income, however, was partly seasonal, and subject to fluctuations in the economy, changes in fashion, and political events. Of all the professions, wrote a certain Bryerly Thomson in 1857 — a lawyer who compiled a book of advice on choosing a career — music was the 'most undefined and vague'. The reason was that it was 'altogether unprotected. Its portals are open to all who choose to enter.'[10]

Why? Because despite increasing demands for its services and the widely acclaimed skills of its leading practitioners, the music profession lacked sufficient coherence to form protective associations. Musicians worked in a cut-throat market place open to anyone with a minimum of talent, and without enforceable contracts, experienced and reliable agents, or in many cases, accepted codes of conduct. However, a successful career inevitably brought social mobility, and few occupations offered so many opportunities for the individual to cross the frontiers of wealth and class which were closed to the majority, by 'entering rich households to play and teach, sometimes mingling with the company or even achieving a certain degree of intimacy with one's betters'. But the need, says Ehrlich, to piece together an income from diverse sources imposed a sense of vulnerability which tended to encourage mercenary behaviour, and the increasing influence of market forces required attitudes and skills more common among tradesmen than artists.[11]

Still, music was one of the few occupations that were open to women, mostly as singers but also as instrumentalists; the latter mostly earned their living by teaching, a few as soloists. The barest handful composed — Fanny Mendelssohn and Clara Schumann, for example — but failed to make a living that way. In the case of Clara Schumann, in order to support her large family after Robert's death she had to sacrifice her composing to a concert career — for which she became her own manager. Even before that, finding time to devote to composition was a severe problem, as Robert perfectly realized, though his attitude to Clara's ability was a little ambivalent. By all accounts he fell in love with her partly on account of it, and though he would have preferred her to give up concerts, Clara, he writes in the second year of their marriage, 'has written a number of small pieces which are more imaginative and tender than ever before. But children, a husband who is always dreaming, and composing do not go together. She lacks constant practice and this often saddens me, for many a deep thought is lost because she cannot develop it.'[12] Her music, it should be said, though naturally very Schumannesque, shows a marked originality of nuance distinct from her husband's.

The imbalance Ehrlich describes between supply and demand in the music profession is not the only reason for its problems and weaknesses. Music, as we have seen, is a peculiar kind of commodity. Let us look more closely at why. First, as with all art-forms, the act of consumption is not a physical one, but rather the reception of a symbolic content. This is a process which has had its own dedicated branch of philosophy going back to Aristotle's *Poetics*; since the eighteenth-century German Baumgarten, the field has been known as aesthetics. The aesthetic nature of art enables it to escape direct determination by the economic domain, and for each art-form to fulfil its own immanent laws. In modern times, roughly since the latter part of the eighteenth century, philosophers have recognized these laws in the special quality of artistic production, which, as Schiller asserted in his *Letters on the Aesthetic Education of Mankind* of 1795, makes it closer to play than to work.

Economists, too, began to distinguish certain peculiarities in the character of aesthetic labour. According to Adam Smith in a famous passage from *The Wealth of Nations*, musical performance fell into the category of 'perishable services', the type of activity which 'does not fix or realize itself in any permanent subject, or vendible commodity, which endures after the labour is past'.[13] Perishable services, he explained, like those of the 'menial servant', do not regenerate the funds which purchase them. The maintenance and employment of servants is altogether at the expense of their masters, the work they perform is not of a nature to repay expense. The labour of some of the most respectable orders in society, says Smith, as well as some of the most frivolous, is in this respect the same: churchmen, lawyers, physicians and men of letters on the one hand, and on the other, buffoons, musicians, opera singers, opera dancers, etc.

Marx commented wryly in *Theories of Surplus-Value* on the 'polemical effect' of these arguments. Great numbers of 'so-called "higher grade" workers — such as state officials, military people, artists, doctors, priests, judges, lawyers, etc. — . . . found it not at all pleasant to be relegated *economically* to the same class as clowns and menial servants and to appear merely as . . . parasites on the actual producers (or rather agents of production)'.[14] Musicians, however, were used to it. They, of all professions, were at the bottom of the pile. As the French economist Attali puts it, the court musician, who is not a productive worker, 'is paid a wage by someone who employs him for his personal pleasure . . . His labour is exchanged for a wage or paid in kind; it is a simple exchange of two use-values': material sustenance for spiritual sustenance.[15]

Marx was quite aware of what this means. There is a certain truth, he says, in the comment of 'the learned Garnier' that 'there is *necessarily* a direct and immediate relation between the person who uses the experience of the physician, the skill of the surgeon, the knowledge of the lawyer, the talent of the musician or actor, or finally the services of the domestic servant'.[16] This face-to-face appreciation of the musicians' activity was an important factor in sustaining their sense of dignity and identity — it always has been and always will be — and explains why musical art advanced by strides in courts where the patron was a real one, a music lover and amateur musician. On the other hand, Mozart has told us what would happen in a court where music was not esteemed: musicians lost their self-respect, and in Salzburg under Archbishop Colloredo ended up drunk and indisciplined.

According to Marx, however, Adam Smith's argument is problematic. On the one hand he posits correctly that in order to be economically productive, labour has to reproduce its own value and more: it has to be capable of returning a profit; when it is performed only as a service, it is unproductive. But what this comes down to, says Marx, is that only wage-labour that reproduces capital is economically productive: therefore 'an actor . . . or even a clown . . . is a productive labourer if he works in the service of a capitalist (an entrepreneur) to whom he returns more labour than he receives from him in the form of wages'.[17]

Smith, however, identifies the production of economic value with the production of material commodities, and is consequently misled. There are certain types of services, says Marx, which can be easily rendered into commodity form and subordinated to the capitalist mode of production; for example, those of the tailor, the shirtmaker or the instrument-maker. Others cannot: they persist in retaining their character as services. The labour of the actor in the theatre, for example, cannot be sold to the public in the form of a take-away commodity but only in the form of admission to the activity itself; it therefore has to 'be consumed while it is being performed'.[18] The same is true of musical performance: until the arrival of the record, it could only realize exchange value, and hence yield profits, through the box-office. One need only add that the box-office is fickle.

In thinking about the puzzles involved, Marx appears to have been keenly struck by the idiosyncrasies of music, for he keeps going to music for examples; sometimes rather odd ones. Assume, he says in *Theories of Surplus-Value*, that instead of buying a piano in a shop, 'I buy all the materials required for a piano . . . and . . . I have it made up for me in my house'. In this case the workman who makes the piano, instead of being a productive worker employed by a piano-maker, 'is now an unproductive worker, because his labour is exchanged directly against my revenue'.[19] Perhaps this is not such an odd example after all; it is only what princes and dukes had done for centuries. Again, it is not a contradiction, says Marx, if the violin-maker, the organ-builder, or the music-dealer are productive, but the professionals for whom they produce are unproductive:

> It may seem strange that the doctor who prescribes pills is not a productive worker, but the apothecary who makes them up is. Similarly the instrument maker who makes a fiddle, but not the musician who plays it. But that would show that 'productive workers' produce products which have no purpose except to serve as a means of production for unproductive workers.[20]

In short, the particular form of labour, and the nature of its product, is irrelevant to whether it is productive or unproductive economically. The question concerns the relations of production within which the activity takes place. The uncertainties of the musician's career correspond to the economic fragility of these relations. The crux is whether the musician is employed directly to create a profit for an impresario. The same is true in other fields of aesthetic and intellectual production. 'A writer is a productive worker not in so far as he produces ideas, but in so far as he enriches the publisher who publishes his works, or if he is a wage labourer for a capitalist.'[21] Hence also, 'A singer who sings like a bird [in other words, freely] is an unproductive worker. When she sells her song, she is a wage earner or merchant. But the same singer, employed by someone else to give concerts and bring in money, is a productive worker because she directly produces capital.'[22] And if Italian opera stars commanded fees large enough for them to become investors in their own right, Marx observes another consequence of this state of affairs when he mentions 'theatre directors who buy singers for a season not in order to have them sing, but so that they do not sing in a competitor's theatre'.[23]

This is still only part of the story. According to our earlier analysis, the opera star and the virtuoso are paid not a wage but a fee, the value of which is calculated not on the basis of labour-power expended in doing the job but in the form of artistic rent. As for the rank-and-file, the rule of the box-office determines the time available for rehearsal. The assumption is that of a standardized product. But like any form of aesthetic labour, the reduction of labour time in the rehearsal of music to a homogeneous standard makes no sense. Artistic work isn't standard and homogeneous but concrete and individual, subject moreover to psychological variation. There is no correlation between the quality of a painting and the amount of time taken to produce it. The same applies not only to the composition of music by the composer but also to preparation for performance: long works may sometimes be quicker to rehearse than short ones, difficult passages may take longer to rehearse than entire movements. The law of unequal rehearsal time confirms that the aesthetic commodity cannot be successfully measured by the number of hours expended on it. Aesthetic labour does not respect utilitarian functions. A kind of magic is also necessary. The threat that hangs over it in the capitalist mode of production is this: that for the purposes of making a profit it will be treated exclusively according to economic criteria, as wage-labour measured in the expenditure of time. This is why Marx spoke correctly when he spoke of the hostility of capitalist production to art.

Copyright and Royalties

The category of artistic rent also explains the effects of these developments on the composer. According to Attali, the labour of the composer is not in itself productive labour simply by virtue of the fact that it produces an object in the form of the written work. The composer is not positioned inside the system of exchange value within music, but at the origin of its growth. This is not merely a theoretical assertion. As the Musical Copyright Defence Association (MCDA) told a government inquiry of 1927 into the record industry, 'the composer is the source and origin of the success of these mechanical reproductions'.[24] Perhaps this is unjust to the performer. On the other hand, only a few composers are located within the business as wage-earners, like those engaged by Hollywood, whose employability is based on their reputation for productivity. For the rest, a lucky handful receive commissions; mostly, remuneration takes the form of a percentage of the profit obtainable from the product, through the sale of either the physical object (the score) or its use (the performance and the recording). The composer is 'reproduced' and economically sustained in the printed copy and its audition — which increasingly includes mechanical reproduction — by virtue of copyright and the royalty laws. Copyright is a form of property; the compensation provided by royalties is a kind of rent. Hence, while impresarios and publishers are the entrepreneurs of music, and musicians and employees in publishing are its casual or salaried labourers, the composer is a rentier.

This also means that nothing a composer writes has any economic value until it enters the market. Very occasionally the market grants huge success. The most outstanding example today is Andrew Lloyd Webber, who is said to earn £100,000 a day in royalties from his musicals (not counting recordings, of which 10 million had been sold by the end of 1991); *Cats* alone has made £587 million since opening in 1981, which is twice as much as Spielberg's blockbuster movie *ET*.[25] But Lloyd Webber is very much the exception. For the vast majority of composers royalties form by far the smaller part of their income, which must necessarily also be drawn from activities like performance and teaching. Nevertheless, entitlement to royalties positions the composer within economic relations in the same way as the author.

Copyright does not attach to physical ownership of the work, it grants the right to receive a share in the income from its exploitation; the form of exploitation depends on the sector of the market where it lodges. The form of copyright originally enjoyed by music applied to the printed score but did not automatically extend to performance rights. In the first place, performance rights were not yet legally constituted; the first such legislation was introduced during the French Revolution. In any case, in the eighteenth century, the composer was lucky to find a publisher prepared to pay an advance. The common practice was publication by subscription, by which the expenses could be cushioned; otherwise composers either relied on the generosity of patrons or had to share or even shoulder the costs themselves. Meanwhile, the composer's income derived principally from a salary or retainer, and secondly from personal participation in commercial performance (we find an excellent account of these conditions in the letters of Mozart).

These arrangements with the publisher were logical enough when the markets for printed music were principally amateur, domestic or religious, comprising mainly chamber music, songs with instrumental accompaniment, devotional pieces and so forth: once the music was sold it exited the market like an ordinary commodity, and no one made anything from it when it was played. But with the growth of commercial concert activity, and as published scores diffused beyond the composer's reach, such a state of affairs became increasingly anomalous, and far more complicated than the business of literary rights.

In the case of opera, composers often kept their own full scores and sold copies of the parts to the theatres (or the impresario) at an inclusive price in lieu of royalties. If the result was a more than average success, the system worked against the composer and in favour of the impresario, who took all the profits; but the composer could increase his rates as his track record improved. The composer could also lose out, when the opera was a hit, to unscrupulous publishers, who were quick off the mark in bringing out unauthorized arrangements. (Mozart was caught out this way by the huge popularity of *Figaro*.) The arrival of performance rights was therefore of particular help to operatic composers, and since theatrical performance, at least, was relatively easy to police, accepted by publishers. Verdi and Wagner earned considerable sums from copyright income from the performance of their works, especially Wagner, who made it practically impossible for them to be staged without him. But in other domains, a performance right was much more difficult to collect.

Relations between publisher and composer had begun to alter with the expansion of the trade in printed music in the latter part of the eighteenth century. This development, by capitalizing the publisher, allowed him to take the risks involved in exploiting the market and to bid for the composer's services. As publishers begin to provide a growing proportion of the composer's income, the growth of their business enables them to begin to support the composer, replacing the patronage of the aristocracy as the bedrock of his livelihood. However, according to Ernest Roth, only one practical method of paying the composer presented itself at the time: the publisher bought a work outright for a flat sum. And yet it was almost impossible to calculate that sum.

> It was a guess, based on the chances of the work's success as the publisher saw them. If he sold more copies than expected he had a good bargain and the composer lost; but the reverse was more frequently the case, because failures are always more numerous than successes, although history does not register them. There was no need to sign formal documents; an exchange of correspondence was sufficient. If, like Beethoven, the composer had the public behind him the publisher could not bargain. He probably did not even try because he had to outbid the five or six other competitors. If the composer was less well established the publisher secured for himself a premium for the risk that he took. The custom of the flat rate, *à fonds perdu*, as it was called with a hint of sarcasm, continued well into this century ... Richard Strauss still sold his publishing rights for lump sums, reserving for himself performing and mechanical rights.[26]

When commercial concerts flowered and gate-money became a potentially more significant form of earnings, the situation was further transformed, but this time not at all in the composer's favour. A musical economy based on performance fees depends on an effective means of collection. Because of the growing multiplicity of performance sites, composers could not effectively collect the dues without forming an alliance with the publishers. Since publication became the basis for the commercialization of music, for a composer not to find a publisher was a serious matter. Another way of putting this is to say that the publisher became a dominant force in determining the development of the music business until well into the age of mechanical reproduction. But not, as we have seen, entirely determinant: musical taste was still largely shaped beyond the publisher's reach, in the domains of *musica practica*, where the composer traditionally made his reputation as a performing musician − a circumstance which required the publisher's tact. The business involved risk but also luck; the relations between the multiple factors involved was neither mechanical nor predictable. Roth explains: 'Imagine seeing for the first time the first of Chopin's Preludes, Op. 28, in manuscript, a graphic image such as had never been put on paper before, and having to decide whether publication would be a sound investment.'[27] However, Chopin's first publisher − incidentally a swindler − gleaned the reward of the surprisingly fierce passion of Chopin's moneyed audience. In Britain, the publisher John Boosey pioneered a new relationship with the composer: percentage royalties on sheet-music sales, in the interest of spreading the risk. Composers came to accept the arrangement partly because publishing houses like these also took on the costs of promotion − both Boosey and Chappell, for example, opened their own concert halls. (But in those days, capitalism being a less sophisticated affair, they did not see the point of charging themselves performance dues.)

In fact, before the middle of the nineteenth century, musical copyright was either non-existent, or else a fragile and precarious affair. While payment by commission was a long-established practice − there are odd reports of payments to composers for individual works as early as the thirteenth century − there was no kind of legal protection for the written musical score (unless by common law) until well after the interests of writers had been looked after. Authors' rights − as opposed to copyright vested in the printer-cum-publisher − had first been asserted in England in the 1640s, when the Stationers Company, petitioning for the restoration of privileges after the abolition of the Star Chamber, added to their arguments the claim that 'there is no reason apparent why the production of the brains should not be as assignable as . . . the right of any goods or chattels whatsoever'.[28] The philosopher John Locke then proposed a theory of intellectual property rights in his *Two Treatises on Civil Government* of 1690, whose basis was the labour expended by the author in the creation of the work, or as the jurists who followed him argued, an author's right was based in natural law. Four years earlier, an ordinance adopted in Saxony, directed against piracy, had recognized an author's right which the

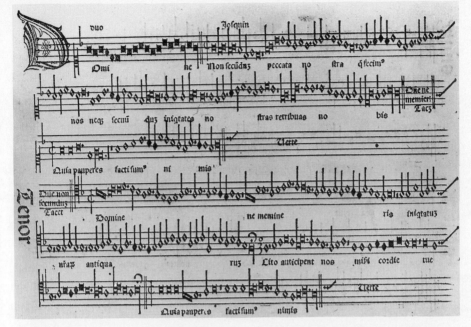

FIGURE 1   Among the first sheet music to go on sale in Venice in 1503. Motets printed by Ottaviano dei Petrucci, using type and triple impression. (British Museum)

FIGURE 2   A tablature for the lute by Joan Ambrosio Dalza, printed by Petrucci in 1508, using type and double impression. (British Museum)

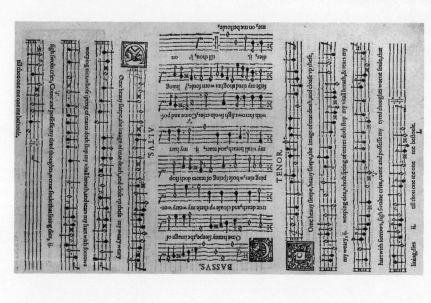

FIGURE 4 Dowland's first *Book of Songes*: table music, each part facing a different performer. Printed in London in 1597. (British Museum)

FIGURE 3 Canzonettas by Simone Verovio: among the earliest engraved music, printed in Rome in 1586. (British Museum)

FIGURE 5   Vocal score printed from type in one impression by J.G.I. Breitkopf in Leipzig in 1756. (British Museum)

FIGURE 6   A Haydn piano sonata printed by lithography, Munich 1797. (British Museum)

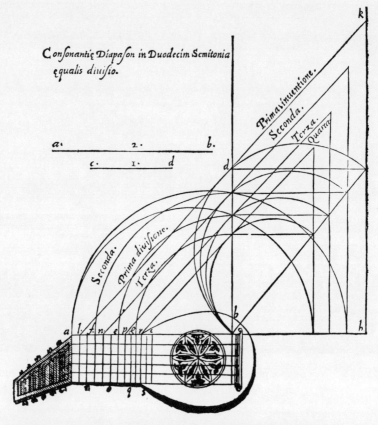

FIGURE 7   Zarlino's diagram of 1588, using Euclidean geometry to determine
the fretting of a lute according to equal temperament.
(Zarlino, *Institutione harmoniche*, Venice 1588)

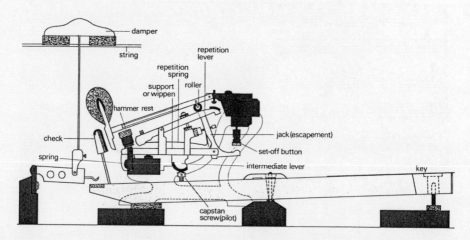

FIGURE 8   The action of a modern grand piano. The escapement sits above the key.
(From The New Grove Dictionary of Musical Instruments)

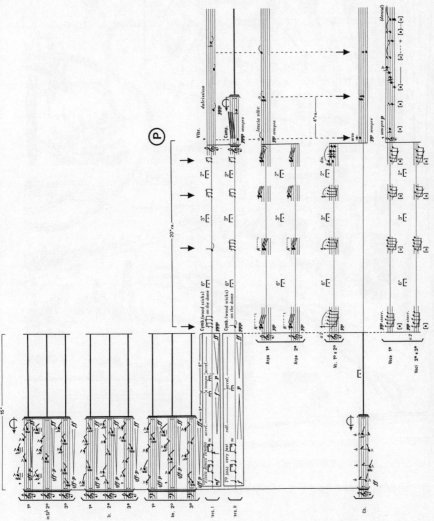

FIGURE 9   Twentieth-century notation: Luciano Berio's *Laborintus II* (1965).
An example of the adaptation of traditional notation.

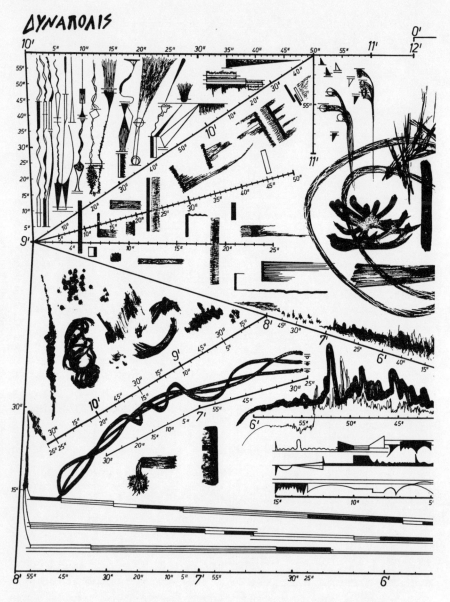

FIGURE 10   Twentieth-century notation: *Dynapolis* by Anestis Logothetis (1963). An example of full-scale graphic notation.

publisher acquired from the author. The new English legislation of 1709 (Statute of Queen Anne), however, did not refer to such matters; principally concerned with resolving similar problems and abuses which were plaguing the book trade, it did not touch upon the niceties of an author's creative or moral rights. As for music, it was not until a judgment of 1777, which ruled that printed compositions were books within the meaning of the Act, that the printed score was properly included.

Similar developments began to follow in other countries, but there remained no protection of performance anywhere until the French Revolution, which with its ideology of natural justice, instigated not only an author's right but also a theatrical performance right. Here the argument for an author's right were used in support of struggles not only against piracy but also between publishers in Paris and the provinces, and in the name of this right authors fought against the actors of the Comédie Française; in the 1760s, Beaumarchais became their leader, declaring that 'however powerful the attraction of fame, if we are to enjoy it even for a year, nature condemns us to dine three hundred and sixty times'.[29] The Revolution took power and began to enact the abolition of privileges; a performance right was decreed in 1791, copy and reproduction rights two years later.

Performance rights were gradually adopted by various other countries during the course of the nineteenth century; in Britain a theatrical performance right, which included opera, was first recognized by Parliament in the Dramatic Copyright Act ('Bulwer-Lytton's Act') of 1833. The grant of a right, however, is not the same thing as exercising it. A performance right has to be *collected*; agencies to collect it were needed, and legal judgments to make people pay up. This was not to be achieved without strategic alliances between composers and publishers, for which the conditions varied from country to country.

The first performing rights collection agencies were French: the Société des Auteurs Dramatiques, founded in 1791 by the musician Framery, well known in his day as a writer on music, and the Société des Auteurs, Compositeurs et Editeurs de Musique, or SACEM, dating from 1851. Both find their antecedence in the Société des Auteurs et Compositeurs Dramatiques, founded by Beaumarchais in 1777, to agitate against the unfair treatment meted out to authors by the Comédie Française and other French theatres. Framery's initiative followed a revolutionary edict of the same year which declared that: 'The works of living authors may not be presented in any public theatre . . . without the formal and written consent of the authors, on pain of confiscation of the total income of the performances to the benefit of the author.'[30] These associations had only limited clout, however. The former did not even admit the publishers to its membership; the latter concerned itself with a specific field of activity, the lyric theatre, which was progressively overtaken by the growth of new markets for other genres like *chanson* and the *café-concert*. SACEM owes its birth to the initiative of an author of *chansons*, Ernest Bourget, who in 1847 started taking his claims for authors' rights against *café-concerts* and similar establishments to the courts and winning. SACEM was set up four years later by 'a group of creators and publishers' mainly involved, according to the sociologist Pierre-Michel Menger, 'in the genres of light music'. 'Serious composers very soon affiliated, but the administration of the society, responsible to the members, was always largely controlled by creators and publishers of the undemanding music which was consumed most.'[31] Gradually similar author-and-publisher agencies appeared else-where, depending on the state of the business and the law in different countries. Italy's SIAE dates from 1882, the German GEMA from 1903.

The juridical framework for the moral and intellectual rights of the author begins as a national and domestic matter. The economic pressures in the industry in which the author is the primary producer, however, grew more and more international. In the countries which led the production of the written word, publishers became increasingly concerned with the problem of foreign protection — for both their own authors abroad and the foreign works which they published at home. Here, music publishers and composers were worse off than authors and publishers of the word: music does not need translation; artists too, since lithography and other advances in graphic reproduction, were also in trouble. France was again the country which took the lead on the international stage, first by seeking bilateral copyright treaties, and then in 1852 by declaring piracy of foreign works in France illegal. The measure was not entirely altruistic: the problem of piracy is most acutely felt where a language is shared by neighbouring countries. Belgian printers sold their pirated editions in France (so did the Dutch, whose typographers have always worked in different languages). Six years later, the first international congress of authors and artists met in Brussels, and called for uniform worldwide copyright legislation. It was a non-government organization, the International Literary and Artistic Association, founded in 1878, which prepared the draft text for the meetings at government level which Switzerland agreed to convene in Berne.

When the Berne Convention was established in 1886, with Britain as one of the founder countries, the signatories agreed to extend the same protection to works by authors belonging to the member countries as to works by its own nationals, though the dues would still have to be collected; also the provisions did not at this stage extend to mechanical reproduction. SACEM proceeded to employ an agent in the UK for protection of performing rights in French music and the collection of royalties; British publishers failed to follow their lead even in their own territory until the

Performing Rights Society was established in 1914. The main reason for
this delay, according to the economists Peacock and Weir, was that in
Britain the exploitation of performance rights was regarded by both
publishers and composers as inimical to the main business of selling
copies.[32] The more a piece of music was played in public, it was thought,
the more people would buy it — a perfectly natural argument — and the
payment of publisher's royalties was a more important part of a composer's
income in Britain than some other European countries where the payment
of performance rights was already in practice. Indeed the performance
right instigated in Britain in 1833, and extended to cover musical
composition in general in the Copyright Act of 1842, had earned itself a
bad name through 'unscrupulous' operators who bought up copyrights in
successful music 'for the sole purpose of enforcing penalties against . . .
unwitting performers'.[33] The practice led to new legislation in the 1880s
(the Copyright Acts of 1882 and 1888), which suspended performance
rights unless they were specifically claimed by a notice on the title page. In
fact many British publishers encouraged sale by printing a *dis*claimer, such
as 'This song may be sung in public without fee or licence.' The ease of
piracy led to two further musical copyright Acts in 1902 and 1906, but it
was the rise of the gramophone which led to changes in international
copyright law and altered attitudes in the British music business.

Piracy in such a system as this was endemic; legislation was never
sufficient to prevent it, any more than nowadays in the audio-visual media.
In the case of commercial successes, the sums involved could be very
considerable — especially across the Atlantic. The first American copyright
laws were statutes passed by the newly independent colonies in the 1780s,
most of which viewed copyright as an author's right. But when the first
Federal copyright law was passed by Congress in 1790, it left out any
protection for foreign works. Indeed the USA was totally recalcitrant about
protecting anyone except its own, and only in the 1990s has it joined the
Berne Convention. As a result, a European success could be introduced
without paying a penny for book or music. It happened to Gilbert and
Sullivan, and the huge popularity of transatlantic pirate productions
induced their manager, Richard D'Oyly Carte, to take on the expense of
mounting simultaneous premieres of new operettas on both sides of the
ocean himself, in order to beat the pirates.

The multiplication of the salons and a growing middle-class pianistic public
together encouraged, through the medium of the publisher, the development of the genres of the piano repertoire. The young Wagner, on the
other hand, was unable to find a publisher for his grandiose operas — first
Schott refused him, then Breitkopf & Härtel — and was left no choice but
to finance publication himself; it took him thirty years to overcome the

resulting debts, in spite of a growing income from the performance of his works. Mahler too, with his enormous symphonies, had to pay the costs of publishing them himself; for him the price was the constant battle of sustaining a career as a supremo conductor, in order to finance his work as a composer, but leaving him only his summers to compose in.

Music was becoming divided against itself. As the music critic Bayan Northcott has put it, once composers 'emerged as free professionals in competition with one another, the search for novelty was bound to assume new urgency, and [they] could no longer allow themselves to fall back upon the kind of prefabricated materials that had enabled their Baroque and Classical predecessors to turn out music for the moment with such facility'. Herein lies a crucial clue to the development of musical style over the century which begins with Beethoven, in whom the split first appears. Novelty brought difficulty, both in terms of execution and the demands it made on the audience's concentration and goodwill. Up to the time of Brahms, says Northcott, 'it did not necessarily matter if a composer got a bit too far ahead of the public since . . . he could always attempt to subsidise himself by publishing sets of popular Hungarian dances for the parlour piano trade'.[34] According to Roth, however, among the avant-garde at the turn of the century 'only Debussy seems to have had no difficulty in finding a proper publisher'.[35]

Schoenberg learned from experience to drive a hard bargain with his publishers. Stravinsky's case was somewhat different. Because Russia, like the USA, was not a signatory to the Berne Convention, leading Russian music publishers had opened branches in various European capitals; in theory, international copyright protection was ensured as long as a work was first issued by one of these branches. Unfortunately, in the case of *The Firebird*, Stravinsky's publisher Jurgenson slipped up, and he was so resentful at the loss of income from this lack of protection in the case of what proved his most successful ballet that it induced him to produce a new version for a smaller orchestra, and sell it to another publisher, Chester's of London. This only got him into further trouble: Jurgenson's firm was nationalized by the Soviet government but his Leipzig branch was sold to a German, who promptly sued Chester's and won. Such problems embittered Stravinsky, and tempered his attitude to publishers ever after.

As for the likes of Berg and Webern, they could only fund the publication of their scores themselves, an undertaking they could scarcely afford. Only rarely was a publisher seen to be generous. When Kurt Weill made his original contract with Emil Hertzka of Universal Edition, it entitled him to no advances or retainers, only royalties — Hertzka was known not only for his excellent judgement about contemporary music, but also, not to mince words, for a certain meanness. However, the story is told that two days after the premiere of *The Threepenny Opera* he 'did something that nobody would ever have expected': he took the contract with Weill, which still had four years to run, tore it up and made a new one very much to Weill's advantage.[36] (EMI likewise showed uncharacteristic generosity to the Beatles when their sales rocketed by 80 per cent between 1963 and 1964, doubling the penny royalty they received on a single.)

The reason for the composer's vulnerability isn't hard to find: it is not a question of jurisprudence but the natural law of *musica practica*, by which music circulates freely. In this way, the growth of the music business over the nineteenth century rested on the efficacy with which publishers and composers responded to the demand of the domestic market, including the salon. Even the success of an opera was measured by the quantity of sheet-music sales of selections and arrangements for domestic consumption, where the object is the provision of music for playing where performance is free.

The publisher didn't have it all his own way, by any means. Even before mechanical reproduction there were the effects of new markets, and the competition of new rivals. A new breed of impresario begins to appear in response to the growing audience, who becomes set upon turning aesthetic and technical prowess into spectacle and showmanship. Paganini and Liszt had revealed the susceptibilities of the modern public, but the publisher had nothing to fear and everything to gain from such charisma. He only felt threatened when fresh capital stepped in to manage it, driving a wedge between publisher, composer and performer.

While the model for the traditional impresario was provided by the Italian opera industry, it is no accident that the paradigm of the new variety was found in the United States, where a huge untapped market was forming and old conventions had little meaning. Here, there was a new kind of business to be made, by promoting the reputation of the musical artist as a freak. In 1851, when the circus showman P.T. Barnum enticed the 'Swedish Nightingale' Jenny Lind (it was he who invented the sobriquet) across the Atlantic, to undertake a tour of a hundred concerts in the space of nine months, she earned for herself more than $200,000, and for him, more than half a million.

If the methods by which Barnum raised this audience — a barrage of publicity handouts, bogus claims and leaks to the press, topped by organized street processions to fête the celebrity — epitomize what the New York music critic Joseph Horowitz calls the ballyhoo tradition in American music — nowadays known as hype — then the timing of this development is also no accident.[37] Barnum was the acknowledged master of every trick of the huckster's trade, but the moment is also a significant one in the evolution of modern advertising: ten years after Volney Palmer set up his pioneering agency in Philadelphia, thirteen years

before J. Walter Thompson started running the agency which quickly
became the doyen of the industry. The new agencies, in order to establish
their respectability, would give up the lucrative but widely dishonest patent
medicines business as soon as they could afford to, but the modern
advertising industry may still if it wishes discover its origins in both
Barnum's ballyhoo and hucksters selling snake oil from the back of horse-
drawn wagons. The purpose of advertising is intervention in the market
place in order to capture and if possible create demand; Barnum was one of
the first to show how it was done. As Sol Hurok, a prominent post-Barnum
impresario, once put it, 'an impresario doesn't make an artist, he makes an
audience'. If previously it was the personage of the artist, preferably
charismatic, who made the audience, then in the new business a gullible
press is co-opted into a monster publicity campaign, using procedures
already familiar to the playwright Sheridan: 'the puff preliminary, the puff
direct, the puff collateral, the puff collusive, and the puff oblique, or puff by
implication'. But in a constituency of millions who have had no means to
formulate their own opinions, the product is a new relationship between
the performer and the audience, in which the performer attracts a fetish
value.

What the New World lacked in indigenous resources, says Horowitz, it
was prepared to entice with dollars and applause. There was no shortage of
candidates. In 1825, Mozart's librettist Lorenzo da Ponte, who ended up in
New York because he had always been an adventurist ready to try his luck,
had the pleasure before he died of hearing the first transatlantic
performance of 'his' *Don Giovanni* mounted by one of the great tenors of the
day, the Spaniard Manuel Garcia — who, as his own impresario setting out
to present seasons of Italian opera in New York and Mexico, was as much
an adventurist as the aged poet. By mid-century, New York had a
Philharmonic increasingly staffed by expatriate Germans. As for soloists,
from Jenny Lind to Paderewski the fortunes made in the United States by a
succession of famous artists and their less well-known agents were out of all
proportion to the composers', and economically more important than the
publishers' share too. As the Viennese critic Hanslick quipped, America
was 'truly the promised land, if not of music, at least of the musician'.[38]

Concert Halls, Audiences, Orchestras, Conductors

In the days when concerts were held in assorted venues — taverns,
theatres, entertainment gardens and homes — they did not differ greatly in
their social manners from the other kinds of socializing and entertainment
which took place in those locales. As the superior heroine of Fanny
Burney's late-eighteenth-century novel *Evelina* remarked, 'indeed I am

quite astonished to find how little music is attended to in silence; for though everybody seems to admire, hardly anybody listens'.[39] The altered demeanour of the audience, first detected by Heine, belongs with the construction of purpose-built concert halls and their new professional management. In other words, the subjective individualism associated with the appreciation of art music is a historical product of the imposition of decorum in the concert hall in the century following Mozart, in which musical life began to develop the stable, tightly organized institutions and customs described by William Weber; until, as Walter Benjamin observed, in the decline of middle-class society, contemplation had become a school for asocial behaviour.[40]

The first purpose-built concert halls sometimes imitated the theatrical form of the opera house, which has, of course, its own architectural history. The opera house horseshoe had a triple function: to project the musical sound forwards; to allow the members of the audience themselves to be on visual display; and to minimize the diffusion of their chatter. The concert hall is more bourgeois. First, the spatial-acoustic arrangement was intended to create a balanced sound. Second came a new seating arrangement, with more of the audience now facing the orchestra directly; this suppresses individual display in the auditorium, and displaces it to corridors, bars and salons. Here too we find important clues to the history of style, especially the evolution of the Romantic symphony, for the result is a more attentive relationship to the music, which begins to develop a more and more complex idiom, culminating in vast Late Romantic symphonic canvases of Gustav Mahler, whom many regarded as the greatest of the composer-conductors.

The process gains from refinements in the arrangement of the band which help to focus the sound acoustically, to create what one writer calls 'the unity of a single, corporate source'.[41] This is the sound exemplified to this day by the orchestras which belong to the great nineteenth-century concert halls of Vienna or Amsterdam. One of the reasons that the Boston Symphony had the reputation of being the most European-sounding of America's great orchestras is that their hall is a replica of Leipzig's bombed Gewandhaus and thus encouraged the same kind of sound. Architecturally, these halls are masterpieces of acoustic engineering. Built of stone, they have been found to have the optimum construction for enhancing resonance throughout the frequency range, from bottom to top. They seat an audience between two and two and a half thousand. Any larger and the acoustic balance is lost — the acoustics of London's gigantic oval-shaped Royal Albert Hall were disastrous. But the size and shape of a hall like the Amsterdam Concertgebouw produces a pattern of sound reflection and gives the resonance a delay and a duration such that the sounds are fused without being muddied. Above all, they are halls to embody the ideals of bourgeois democracy. It is true that the size of the audience is limited, but inside they share a uniformly warm and responsive acoustical state of being. These qualities are reduced in large modern auditoria like the Royal Festival Hall in London, where the acoustic tends to be clearer and more exciting, but also more exposed and not so warm (though some compensation can nowadays be achieved by using subliminal amplification of the missing frequencies).

At the same time that these halls were being erected by national and civic authorities, the professionalization of the bourgeois concert and the spirit of commercialism combined to change the attitude of the audience, which now grew less differentiated. In a word, control of concert life ceased to be a scene of political self-assertion on the part of a certain social echelon or faction, and a new homogeneity appeared. Here are further pointers to the development of the musical idiom. After the failure of the 1848 revolutions, the altered political conjucture introduced new ideological tendencies, for which the concert hall provided a unifying space. The 'principle of nationality' established by the Peace of Vienna turned into nationalism, and music began answering to the task of what the Victorian political theorist Walter Bagehot called 'nation making'. Especially in Eastern Europe, where folkish elements, real or imagined, now began to acquire political significance, and the concert hall became the very symbol of national musical life.

The concert hall had promoted a new arrangement of the band and its relation to the conductor. Instead of grouping around the harpsichord or squeezing into the pit, the instruments came to be placed in blocks in a semi-circle around a podium. The symphony orchestra thus acquired an ideal balance. (Not quite the same as today, when first and second violins are usually placed next to each other; a hundred years ago they faced each other on either side of the conductor. Today's arrangement enhances projection and brilliance of sound; that of last century places more value on contrapuntal separation between first and second violins.) The new arrangement required a conductor as an anchor. The introduction of the baton, often ascribed to Louis Spohr in the 1820s, brought a new gestural rhetoric of direction, and the art of interpretation now began to evolve. Since the conductor had his back to the audience, however, the first to gain a new identity were composer-soloists like Paganini and Liszt. The visual attention of the audience enhanced their predilection for individual display and bolstered the cult of the virtuoso. Dussek is said to have been the first pianist to sit with his profile to the audience. Thus a new kind of virtuoso celebrity appeared — and also a new kind of solo recital, on the model established by Liszt in the 1840s.

But conductors had to wait for stardom only a little longer. The first generation of modern conductors were primarily composers going about their business. As Horowitz puts it, the composers responsible for making orchestras harder to co-ordinate had of necessity to demonstrate how to do it themselves.[42] Spohr and Mendelssohn instilled new standards of ensemble, Berlioz a new charisma, Wagner a new interpretive style. The process quickly acquired a dynamic of its own, with a special affinity to the fate of the Romantic ego: the exalted individuality, the lack of restraint, the radical isolation, the opposition to prosaic and banal reality. Wagner, in his essay 'On Conducting' of 1869, impugned the 'elegant' Mendelssohn and other 'time beaters' for mistakenly idealizing their own discreet aesthetic as 'Beethovenian Classicism'. In Wagner's opinion, Beethoven's symphonies demanded conductors of greater 'energy, self-confidence, and personal power'. These declarations Wagner supported by demonstration. Hanslick, reviewing a performance by Wagner of Beethoven's *Eroica* in 1872, which he calls 'a kind of illustrative appendix to his essay', points to continual modification of tempo as the novel element.[43] In a word, expressive exaggeration. Wagner thus became the founder of a style which was handed down through Hans von Bülow to Richard Strauss, Mahler, Nikisch and Furtwängler, only to be impugned in turn by the new objectivity of the 1920s and after as arbitrary, distorted, full of mannerism and excess.

It is no simple matter, however, to get a hundred different musicians all to exaggerate expressively in precisely the same way, and thus the conductor, drunk on his inflated ego, became a martinet. Ironically, the most infamous of podium tyrants was an Italian outsider. Horowitz chronicles 'one of Toscanini's most publicised tirades', which occurred in 1919 during a rehearsal of Beethoven's Ninth in Turin. 'Enraged by the seeming nonchalance of a member of the second violins, he struck the man's bow with his baton — whereupon the bow, according to most accounts, rebounded into the player's eye.' A lawsuit followed, in which the conductor was absolved through the intervention of one Annibale Pastore, a professor of 'theoretical philosophy', who explained that Toscanini was prey to fits of 'sublime frenzy' which pre-empted his 'normal personality'.[44]

Most conductors had to rest content for their authority on their function as agents of more mundane forces. If the box-office determines the available rehearsal time, it is the conductor who controls it, and he owes the success he has to the effective use of it. The similarity of these conditions to the professional supervision of production at large — the analogy between the orchestra and capitalist production methods which was noted by both Boulez and the American corporate executive — first occurred to an old German communist quietly working things out in the British Museum, when he wrote: 'The capitalist mode of production has brought matters to a point where the work of supervision, entirely divorced from the ownership of capital, is always readily obtainable . . . An orchestra conductor need not own the instruments of his orchestra, nor is it within the scope of his duties as conductor to have anything to do with the "wages" of the other musicians.'[45]

It may not have been part of his duties, but it sometimes happened nonetheless. There is the case, for example, of Mahler, normally regarded as one of the most tyrannical of the breed. In Hamburg in 1894, where the impresario of the opera house where he was employed stopped paying the musicians during the summer months when the theatre was closed, Mahler wrote in protest to the Burgomaster. Three years later, as the newly-appointed director of the Vienna opera, he was appalled when he discovered how little some of the players earned and immediately took steps to raise their salaries, compensating for the expense by economies in other areas.

Marx went on to contrast the orchestra with a factory co-operative, in which the capitalist and his agent become redundant as functionaries within production. 'In a co-operative factory the antagonistic nature of the labour of supervision disappears, because the manager is paid by the labourers instead of representing capital counterposed to them.'[46] There is a curious element of prophecy here. As orchestral musicians became increasingly professional, and their professionalization gave them an increasing sense of collective identity, they indeed became increasingly impatient with the conductor lording it over them at the same time, and less inclined meekly to accept his authority, especially when they didn't share in the material benefits. In 1882 in Berlin, a remarkable event occurred when fifty members of an orchestra owned, run and conducted since 1868 by Benjamin Bilse, resigned *en masse*, complaining of low wages and other indignities; and then re-formed themselves into a new orchestra and proceeded to hire their own conductor. Thus the Berlin Philharmonic was born.

From now on, orchestras new and old increasingly became self-governing bodies, which sometimes took the form of co-operatives. The Czech Philharmonic originated as an *ad hoc* body in 1896 as the result of a strike for improved conditions by members of the National Theatre Orchestra; they were out on strike again in 1901 but this time they were dismissed, so they turned the Philharmonic into a proper independent orchestra. Two years later players in the Damrosch orchestra in New York, founded by Leopold and inherited by his son Walter, created their own short-lived co-operative. The next year the London Symphony was founded by a small group of players in defiance of the refusal by Henry Wood to tolerate the deputy system in the orchestra of his Queen's Hall Promenade Concerts. The best he could offer his players was a retainer for the exclusive use of their services during the season. Without any guarantee of work during the rest of the year, they decided to leave him and set up a new orchestra of their own.

The logical conclusion of these democratic co-operative tendencies was the Persimfans — a Russian acronym for 'First Symphonic Ensemble' — a conductor-less orchestra which flourished in the Soviet Union in the early years of the Bolshevik Revolution. The theory was that the orchestra should be run on the same principles as a chamber ensemble. All players studied the full score, and rehearsals were abundant and prolonged (this is essential). In fact the members of the Persimfans were all experienced musicians who had played the classics repeatedly under many conductors; they were thus even capable of handling difficult new music, and were responsible, for example, for the Soviet premiere of Prokofiev's fiendish *Scythian Suite*. Otto Klemperer, who heard them on a visit to the Soviet Union in 1929, spoke of the impression they made in Beethoven and Tchaikovsky, which forced him to ask himself 'a serious question: is a conductor really necessary?' Nevertheless, after careful consideration, he said, he felt not only that there were works 'of such complexity that an assured performance without a conductor is scarcely possible', but also that however well prepared in rehearsal, the concert itself always needs 'an improvised "something"' [that] can only derive from a conductor, 'otherwise a performance is machine-like'.[47]

Unfortunately it has turned out that in the age of mechanical reproduction a performance may also become machine-like under a conductor. Not that this happened with Klemperer himself. It was Toscanini who came to exemplify the streamlined and machine-like orchestral style of the age of the LP record. With Toscanini, says Adorno, there is 'iron discipline. But precisely iron. The new fetish is the flawlessly functioning, metallically brilliant apparatus as such, in which all the cogwheels mesh so perfectly that not the slightest hole remains open for the meaning of the whole . . . The performance sounds like its own phonograph record.'[48]

Notes

1. William Weber, *Music and the Middle Classes*, Croom Helm, London 1975.
2. Ibid., p. 98.
3. Quoted in Siegfried Kracauer, *Orpheus in Paris, Offenbach and the Paris of His Time*, Vienna House, New York 1972, p. 47.
4. Ibid., p. 30.
5. Quoted in ibid., pp. 47–8.
6. Cyril Ehrlich, *The Music Profession in Britain Since the Eighteenth Century*, Oxford 1985, p. 51.
7. Quoted in ibid., p. 100.
8. Ibid., p. 54.

9. Marx, *Grundrisse*, Penguin, London 1973, p. 92.

10. Quoted in Ehrlich, p. 43.

11. Ibid., p. 31.

12. Quoted in Eva Rieger, 'Dolce semplice? On the Changing Role of Women in Music', in Gisela Ecker, ed., *Feminist Aesthetics*, The Women's Press, London 1985, pp. 146—7.

13. Adam Smith, *The Wealth of Nations*, Everyman edition, Vol. 1, p. 295.

14. Marx, *Theories of Surplus-Value*, Progress Publishers, Moscow 1963, Part 1, pp. 174—5.

15. Jacques Attali, *Noise*, Manchester University Press, Manchester 1989, p. 38.

16. Marx, *Theories of Surplus-Value*, p. 186.

17. Ibid., p. 157.

18. Ibid., p. 173.

19. Ibid., p. 160.

20. Ibid., p. 173.

21. Ibid., pp. 157—8.

22. Quoted by Attali, p. 39.

23. Marx, *Grundrisse*, p. 282.

24. Cited in Alan Peacock and Ronald Weir, *The Composer in the Market Place*, Faber Music, London 1975, p. 88.

25. Profile of Andrew Lloyd Webber, *The Independent*, 25 January 1992.

26. Roth, *The Business of Music*, Cassell, London 1969, p. 63.

27. Ibid., p. 55.

28. Quoted in Edward W. Ploman and L. Clark Hamilton, *Copyright, Intellectual Property in the Information Age*, Routledge & Kegan Paul, London 1980, p. 11.

29. Ibid., p. 17.

30. Quoted in Pierre-Michel Menger, *Le Paradoxe du musicien, le compositeur, le mélomane et l'état dans las société contemporain*, Flammarion, 1983, p. 179.

31. Ibid., p. 179.

32. See Alan Peacock and Ronald Weir, *The Composer in the Market Place*, Faber Music, London 1975.

33. Ibid., p. 35.

34. Bayan Northcott, 'He who pays the piper . . .', *The Independent*, 18 August 1990.

35. Roth, *The Business of Music*, p. 55.

36. Hans Heinsheimer, who worked for Universal Edition at that time, quoted in Douglas Jarman, *Kurt Weill*, Orbis, London 1982, p. 48.

37. Joseph Horowitz, *Understanding Toscanini*, Knopf, New York 1987, pp. 18ff.

38. Ibid., p. 24.

39. Quoted in Weber, p. 3.

40. Walter Benjamin, 'The Work of Art in the Age of Mechanical Reproduction', in *Illuminations*, ed. Hannah Arendt, Schocken, New York 1969, p. 238.

41. Alan Durant, *Conditions of Music*, Macmillan, London 1984, p. 34.

42. Horowitz, p. 334.

43. Hanslick, *Music Criticisms, 1846—99*, Penguin, London 1963, pp. 104—5.

44. Horowitz, p. 83.

45. Marx, *Capital* III, Lawrence & Wishart, London 1972, pp. 386—7.

46. Ibid., p. 387.

47. Heyworth, *Otto Klemperer, His Life and Times, Vol. 1 1885—1933*, Cambridge University Press, Cambridge 1983, p. 318.

48. Adorno, 'On the Fetish-Character in Music and the Regression of Listening', in *The Essential Frankfurt School Reader*, p. 284.

PART IV

Musical Engineering

7

Instruments, Technology, Tuning

Genotypes

Our survey thus far, albeit sketchy and often schematic, confirms the importance which Max Weber attaches to notation. We have seen that the spread of notation — above all by means of printing — brought about the transformation of *musica practica*. We have also seen that the history of musical form and language, mainly treated by musicology as an internal affair, is in reality dialogical, a history of responses to changes in the social and ideological circumstances of music. Clearly these changes are broadly related to the development of the forces of production in society at large. Are the conceptions of nature and social relations that underlie Greek imagination and art, asks Marx in a famous passage, still possible when there are railways, locomotives and electric telegraphs? 'What is a Vulcan compared with Roberts and Co., Jupiter compared with a lightning conductor, and Hermes compared with Crédit mobilier?'[1] Or, one may add, the Bacchae compared with Beatlemania?

But how are we to understand this relationship in concrete and material terms? It seems to be in the nature of music to cut itself off from the realm of the mundane. As Fredric Jameson puts it, music becomes a self-contained and autonomous sphere at a distance from everyday social life and, as it were, parallel to it. This of course is our clue, for it means that not only does music thereby acquire an internal history of its own, but it also begins to duplicate on a smaller scale all the structures and levels of the social and economic macrocosm. It develops its own internal dialectic, its own producers and consumers, its own infrastructure. It contains, for example, its own history of inventions, what might be called the engineering dimension of musical history: that of the instruments themselves.

Here a curious circumstance emerges. In the image of musical history

165

constructed by musicology, this engineering dimension is recognized only, if at all, in the most abstract form. Even the scholars whose very subject is instruments all but omit it, or at best skirt round it with the occasional mention of the secret techniques of instrument-makers. As a point of contact with the social and economic macrocosm it is strangely absent, even in Marxist writings. There are two lessons in this. It reminds us first of a bias buried deep in modern cultural susceptibilities: a split between radically different styles of explanation of the world which we have suffered ever since the scientific revolution of the sixteenth and seventeenth centuries divided everything up dualistically, into mind and body, subject and object, fantasy and reality, art and technology. Second, it implies that this history is highly problematic, for musical instruments stand in the same ambiguous relationship of cause and effect to the development of works, forms and movements as their technological equivalents in the wider world; like the steam engine, for example, in relation to transport systems and the industrial revolution. In each case, the technology is both agent and symptom of change.

In both worlds, says Jameson, the microcosmic and the macrocosmic, inventions arrive on the scene with a kind of symbolic fitness. In the view of Adorno, whose arguments Jameson brilliantly synthesizes, 'it is not for nothing that the newly soulful tone of the violin counts among the great innovations of the age of Descartes'. Indeed, throughout its long ascendancy, Jameson continues,

> the violin preserves this close identification with the emergence of individual subjectivity on the stage of philosophical thought. It remains a privileged medium for the expression of the emotions and demands of the lyrical subject, and the violin concerto, much like the *Bildungsroman*, stands as the vehicle for individual lyric heroics, while in other forms the massed orchestral strings conventionally represent the welling up of subjective feeling and of protest against the necessities of the objective universe. By the same token, when composers begin to suppress the singing violin tone and . . . transform the stringed instrument into a plucked, almost percussive device (as in the 'ugly' pizzicati, the strummings and 'weird' falsetto effects of Schoenberg), what happens to the violin is to be taken as a sign of the determination to express what crushes the individual, to pass from the sentimentalization of individual distress to a new, post-individualistic framework.[2]

Throughout the period known by historians as 'early modern Europe', until at least the seventeenth century, most musical instruments were used — apart from music for dancing and military purposes — in order to accompany singing, by doubling or supporting the vocal parts. Gradually, however, with the changing functions of music and the emergence of a great variety of new genres and forms, the individuality of instruments themselves began to impress itself, and they started to combine first into consorts and then into orchestras. The increasing complexity of musical language, the growth of new instrumental idioms, changes in the location of performance to domestic and then specialized indoor settings — all this inevitably created pressure for changes in the instruments employed. Histories of musical instruments show that makers sought to meet new demands by improving the mechanisms of their instruments; by refining their sound; by extending their compass and dynamic range; and by inventing new ones.

The typical instrument-maker was often a musically gifted artisan, such as a turner or a metalsmith. The register book of the Company of Turners in London records a good number of wind instrument-makers between the end of the seventeenth century and the middle of the nineteenth who all learnt their trade as bound apprentices to master turners. There were also instrument-makers who were professional musicians, including virtuosi who worked with favourite craftsmen consciously looking for improvements. There were a good many families. In Paris, for example, the Hotteterres, who flourished in the seventeenth century, were responsible for decisive alterations in both the flute and the oboe. In some places, like Germany, a specialist trade appears among organ-builders. Another type emerges with the evolution of furniture and the perfection of the craft of the cabinet-maker. The best craftsmen in the Italian courts, for example, not only turned out luxury furniture using the tools and skills of advanced carpentry but also instruments which were part of the sumptuary expenditure of their high-placed patrons. The growing splendour of keyboard instruments was one of the results.

With the instrument-maker's trade being based in traditional craft skills, innovation and invention mostly proceeded by practical intuition rather than the application of theoretical or scientific knowledge. The same holds true, outside music, for the majority of inventors as late as the nineteenth century — figures like James Hargreaves, Richard Arkwright and James Watt, whose inventions made the industrial revolution. According to the economic historian Maurice Dobb, it is remarkable how many of the key inventions of the industrial revolution 'were the products of practical men, groping empirically and keenly aware of the industrial needs of the time'.[3] Music produced its own inventors of this type, entirely practical men like Adolphe Sax, the musically gifted son of Belgian master craftsman; the inventor of the saxophone, hailed by Berlioz in 1842 for the rare quality of its sound, he learnt his trade at his father's benches where instruments were made on contract for Belgian military bands, and then moved to Paris where he became an international supplier.

The inventions of the early industrial revolution were often practical solutions to problems which had not yet been solved in theory, and which helped to set the agenda for science as a result. Music and acoustics had stood in similar relationship ever since early-medieval thinkers divided the speculative science of music from *musica practica*. When acoustics emerged in the scientific study of the seventeenth century as a branch of physics, the scientists often went to the instrument-makers to learn from them, and thereupon discovered precisely how speculative the ancient scientific knowledge of music was. The product of their researches was the theoretical solution to the problems of tuning, which the instruments then had to incorporate. By the end of the eighteenth century, instrument-makers began to lean on the work of scientists in refining their products. In the 1780s, the piano-maker John Broadwood, who started as an apprentice cabinet-maker, consulted a couple of physicists over the best point along the length of the string for the hammer to strike it. Theobald Boehm, who developed the modern flute in the 1830s, was especially assiduous in this respect, interrupting his career as a performing musician in order to go to college and study acoustics properly. For the most part, however, it is trial and error, rule of thumb and traditions handed down from generation to generation of instrument-makers which account for the characteristic quality of sound that each instrument generates, as well as their peculiarly individual appearance and design. As Fontanelle, secretary of the French Academy of Sciences at the turn of the seventeenth century, remarked: 'Nature had the strength to make musicians fall into the system of harmonic sounds, but they fell into it without knowing it, led only by their ear and their experience.'[4] In other words, not only the performance of music but also the construction of instruments fell within the traditional domain of *musica practica*.

In brief, the different instruments assumed their modern forms by a process akin to biological evolution. This has long been recognized. For one thing, the biological metaphor is useful for their classification, since instruments seem to give the same appearance of order, genus and species as plants or animals. The ethnomusicologists von Hornbostel and Sachs proposed four principal orders: chordophones, in which the vibrating agency is a string; aerophones, in which it is a column of air; membranophones, where it consists in a stretched skin; and idiophones, consisting of instruments such as bells, gongs and xylophones, in which a solid body vibrates as a whole. To these a fifth order must now be added, which only appears in the twentieth century: electrophones, in which the sound is produced, or at least amplified, by electrical or electronic means. Notice that from this point of view the human voice is an aerophone. Indeed, as we shall soon see, it was already thought of as an instrument long before anyone classified it this way.

Within each order there are different species, corresponding to the different methods by which the vibrating agency is set in motion; strings, for example, may be plucked, bowed or hammered. Each species, in other words, is made up of a family of instruments. However, it quickly becomes apparent that these categories are idealized abstractions, and that there are strong similarities between species or sub-species belonging to different orders. Instruments sounded by striking, for example, may be either idiophones, like the xylophone, or membranophones, in other words drums, and both are found in the percussion family. Or take the dulcimer and the piano, both of them string instruments — chordophones — sounded by means of hammers; in the former the hammers are hand-held, in the latter, they are operated by a complex mechanism. Yet the dulcimer is considered a percussion instrument and we think of the piano as one of the keyboards, and thus a member of the same family as the organ, which is an aerophone. To complicate things further, the concepts themselves change. In the Middle Ages, according to Grouchy, people thought of the action of the bow on the string of the fiddle as hitting, and classed the fiddle as a percussion instrument, though he himself finds this unsatisfactory.

In other words, to extend the biological metaphor, musical instruments give every evidence of mutation and cross-fertilization. Indeed they are liable, as one old-fashioned writer puts it, to almost unlimited miscegenation.[5] One need only add that they also appear to obey the laws of natural selection, which means not only that those which survive and develop are the ones most adaptable to the changing environment, but also that there are others that become extinct. This must not be pushed too far. The twentieth century has shown that in the world of music, or at least in the early music movement, resurrection is also possible.

It occurs to very few musicologists, however, that since musical instruments are not actually living creatures but artefacts, there are significant connections between instruments and technology. In a word, if the Bronze Age was able to produce simple trumpets made of metal, then only industrial Europe was capable of making them with valves and pistons able to sound every note in the tempered chromatic scale in tune with a whole orchestra. In this way too, therefore, music becomes an expression of the society that produces it, for the idiosyncrasies and complexities of its languages and idioms are indirect reflections of the means of production. To be sure, the technological connection is generally oblique and subtle, but as I intend to show, it is far from trivial. To investigate the technology of musical instruments is to understand, as we shall see, the way that pitches are determined and scales are constructed; and if instruments are the means of production of music, the indispensable match of the voice, then pitches and scales are the basic elements of its grammar and syntax; in that case, the question of musical engineering and the technological development of instruments is integral to an understanding of the development of musical languages.

Prototypes

Perhaps this is a line of inquiry that has hardly been explored — except by ethnomusicologists — because most of the fundamental discoveries are prehistoric. To grasp the sound-generating property of a reed, for example, entails no more than pinching the end of a ripe straw and squeaking on it, like children do. Similarly, the audible character of a vibrating string would be obvious to anyone handling a hunting bow. In this way, the Stone Age acquired a pragmatic acquaintance with the acoustic behaviour of a variety of natural objects, including conch shells and animal tusks, ancestors of the trumpet and the horn. They also made drums and flutes not only from found objects like animal bones but from clay as well. Indeed palaeolithic humanity discovered not only the principles of the flute, but also two different ways of assembling pipes to make instruments capable of sounding a series of different notes: on the one hand by boring finger-holes into a single tube; on the other, by combining tubes of different lengths. The latter, of course, is the principle of both the panpipes or syrinx, and — a subsequent development — the organ. Applied to strings, the result is the lyre, ancestor of the harp.

Many instruments are made of wood. The basic skills of woodworking were practised from the time when copper tools were introduced in Egypt, about four thousand years ago. The double pipes of the ancient Near East, generally known by the Greek name aulos, were not complicated in structure, but the fashioning of the reeds, whether single or double, represents musical techniques in definite advance of neolithic instruments. It implies much more control over the notes produced, as well as the use of specialized materials. The ancient Greeks found the best reeds growing on the shores of lakes in Boeotia and Phrygia. (In nineteenth-century France there were farms which had specialized in growing the special grasses for centuries.)

Less sophisticated as musical instruments, but distinctly advanced in metal technology, are the two trumpets found in the tomb of Tutankhamen, dating from about 1350 BC, one made of silver, the other of sheet bronze partly clad with gold. According to Sachs there is evidence to suggest that instruments seen in ancient Egypt were most probably known in Mesopotamia as much as two millennia earlier. What is certain is that the civilizations of Sumeria and Babylon made music with both vibrating strings and reeds. The lyres of Ur, dating from about 2500 BC, with their gold and silver casings, are elaborately assembled artefacts, with as many as eight to eleven strings supported by arms and fixed over a bridge connected to a resonance chamber or soundbox. Moreover, the oldest surviving texts in which mathematics are applied to music are tuning manuals from ancient Mesopotamia.

Even the earliest wind instruments must have led to the discovery, again pragmatic, of the effect we know as harmonics. The term is a loose one, not to be confused with the harmonic series discovered by the seventeenth-century scientists, though it is indeed the harmonic series that determines which notes can be produced as harmonics. Harmonics, when speaking of wind instruments, refers to the phenomenon that different notes can be produced by varying the pressure of the breath and the lips (also loosely known as overblowing); not just any note, of course, but a certain possible number of notes regulated not only by the harmonic series but also by the physical properties of the pipe in question. The difference between the horn and the trumpet is due to the latter; it derives from the difference between the horn of an animal, with a conical shape, and the tube of a cane or hollow branch, which is cylindrical: these are two different kinds of bore which give different acoustical properties. How easily harmonics can be produced will be familiar to anyone who has even only started to learn the recorder; the art lies not in producing harmonics, but in controlling them. That some of the early instruments based on these principles were capable of sounding a number of harmonics is no indication that their full capabilities were used, though there is every likelihood that many of them were — judging by contemporary examples of archaic music. A comparable problem exists in the case of the earliest finger-hole flutes: we can get a rough idea from the arrangement of the holes of the probable scales employed, but it's a long way from a scale to a tune, and there is also no way of telling whether the players of these flutes modified the notes by partially closing the holes, by overblowing, or by varying lip tension, though again all of these seem likely.

In any event, the great variety of sizes and variation in arrangement that are found in the earliest instruments is a consequence of the rough and ready nature of the technologies which produced them, which did not make easily for standardization or precision. The fixing of pitches and the creation of scales was not a simple process, but the result of interaction between technology and practice. Max Weber is doubtless correct when he suggests that sociologically primitive music was largely dependent on the lore of magic, which forbade any deviation from established magical formulae on pain of attracting the wrath of the gods: '. . . the instruments which helped in the fixing of the intervals were often differentiated according to the particular god or demon to whom the magical tone formulae were addressed. The Hellenic aulos was originally the instrument of the mother of the gods, later of Dionysus. The oldest keys of the Greek music system also were typical differentiations of tone formulae used in the service of certain gods or at specific festive occasions.'[6]

It is nevertheless this mythological world of ancient Greece which produced the decisive developments for the future of European music;

discoveries that belong with the very birth of abstract science, or with what the modern scientist J.D. Bernal calls the radical capacity to separate factual and verifiable knowledge from emotional attitudes and traditional beliefs.[7] If this meant, in music, the separation of calculation from magic, it is instruments which show the consequences. The evidence may be slim, but historical logic urges that Greek civilization was based not only on its distinctive economic organization but also, in spite of its philosophers' disparagement of technical expertise, on important technological advances. Probably the most relevant to the present inquiry, dating back some time before the emergence of the new science, were the draughtsman's compass and the pole lathe, both of which greatly advanced the flexibility and precision of craftsmanship which the instruments show.

Pythagoras, the crucial figure for our present concerns, saw in numbers the key to the understanding of the universe, manifest on the one hand in geometry, on the other in the discovery that strings divided by simple ratios emitted regular musical intervals; we shall come back to these discoveries later. Bernal explains that subsequently the Pythagoreans ran too much beyond the facts, and substituted number mysticism for experimental knowledge. Music was not immune to this tendency, but it didn't break the connection with technological experiment. Bertrand Gille, the author of a monumental study of the history of technology, is quite explicit about this. Geometry, he says, which quickly took the lead over other disciplines because it lent itself so well to intellectual thought, to ratiocination, was indisputably born of practical problems and remained closely linked to technology (especially because of its role in architecture). But the most concrete link between science and technology, he says, was undoubtedly music. The translation of a range of notes into a range of numbers came about by constant confrontation between art and hypothesis.[8]

The evolution of Greek musical instruments was hardly rapid by modern standards; nevertheless it fits this picture well. We know from the *Iliad* that the lyre, kithara and aulos were in use by the ninth century BC. The kithara was a smaller version of the lyre, equipped in Homeric times with three or four strings, increasing to nine or twelve by the fifth century BC, the period when Pythagoras made the first important discoveries in the science of sounding strings and his findings provided a rational basis for the construction of diatonic scales. The aulos similarly increased the number of its finger-holes, and since a greater number could no longer be covered with the performer's fingers, rotating rings were devised by which the holes could be opened or closed at will. Kurt Geiringer comments that this was a most remarkable development, for it anticipates improvements in wood-wind instruments which only came about in the early nineteenth century.[9] In sum, as Weber argues, by the end of the classical period several instruments were capable of producing the full chromatic scale. These advances were not restricted to the Greeks but became generalized throughout the Middle East, and in Arabic music too the common scales represented only a selection of the available instrumental tones. (I ignore developments in India and China, though these too would have to be considered in a more complete study.)

Some authorities hold that it was the attempt to mechanize the syrinx that led to the invention of the organ, which first appeared in the form of the water organ, or hydraulis. The hydraulis was a combination of the principle of the syrinx with that of the bagpipes, an instrument which seems to have originated only a little earlier, but which remains, in comparison with the hydraulis, quite unsophisticated. The hydraulis was invented in the third century BC in Alexandria, the most advanced centre of science and engineering of its day, by one of its leading engineers, Ctesibios, a contemporary of Archimedes. None of Ctesibios' own writings has survived, but the instrument, and the pressure-pump it employed, were described during the following centuries by Philo of Byzantium, Hero and Vitruvius. Air was pumped by bellows which operated pistons, which forced it into a cylinder part-filled with water; the water kept the air in it under pressure, in this way changing an intermittent air flow into the even air pressure required to sustain the sound from the pipes. Gille comments that the pressure-pump is so well known that its importance hardly needs to be emphasized; we shall later discover that this is not the only occasion when the invention of a musical instrument embodied a mechanical principle with a far wider application. He adds: 'According to Vitruvius, the pistons were polished with a lathe, rubbed down and oiled. We know nothing about how the cylinders were made, but this was certainly a more complex operation. The difficulties involved in constructing these machines meant that only relatively few were built.'[10]

The hydraulis provided a compass of one and a half octaves. Obviously impractical in northern climes where water freezes, it was played by actuating slides. It seems that in due course a method was devised to operate the slides by means of some sort of keyboard, which Hero describes in his *Pneumatics* in the first century AD; this involved the use of springs to return the keys to their initial position after their release. At any rate, the fourth-century Roman poet Claudian speaks of the organist's 'light touch' and 'nimble fingers . . . rousing to song the waters stirred to their depths by the massive lever'.[11] By this time the pipes were made of copper or bronze.

There is ample evidence of the increasing use of metal in the instruments depicted in Etruscan art. Roman 'brass' instruments (they too were, in fact, made from bronze) were based on these prototypes, and were used for military and ceremonial purposes. The finest of Roman trumpets, called the tuba, was a thin cylindrical instrument four or five feet long, made from sheet bronze in detachable sections. This allowed for the separate casting of the mouthpiece, which helps to determine the instrument's tone, and the shaping of the bell, which strengthens and radiates the sound. But what could these trumpets play? According to one authority, acousticians of the ancient world who were interested in instruments that could demonstrate the behaviour of intervals pass over the horns and trumpets in silence.[12] Obviously a range of harmonics was possible, so the reason is probably that the simple shapes employed at the two ends of the instrument hardly make for accurate tuning. This would suggest that in spite of the sophistication of their technology, the Romans lacked the technique to make the fine adjustments necessary.

It seems it was also in the fourth century that the hydraulis gave way to the pneumatic organ. Here the connection with the bagpipes is more apparent. In the bagpipes, the player blows down a tube into a leather bag, using his arm to maintain the pressure of the air which is thereby forced from the bag to the sounding pipes. In the pneumatic organ the air is blown by bellows into a bag or wind-chest which is compressed by weights. Technically there seems to be no reason why such an instrument could not have been invented quite independently of the hydraulis. However, it probably required the technological splendour of the hydraulis to create the demand for such an instrument in the first place, and to provide the impulse for the development of the techniques for making the necessary pipes, which apart from the fact that they came to be made of metal are in certain respects different in design from those of early mouth-blown instruments. The hydraulis would then have been displaced by the pneumatic organ because the latter was technically easier to build.

At this stage in its history, the organ, as a relative newcomer, had no association with ritual and religion. In Rome it became an instrument of the theatre, the gladiatorial stadium, and the rich amateur — a particular favourite of Nero's, for instance. As a result it acquired connotations anathema to the early Christians, at least in the imperial capital. The attitude of the early Christians to musical instruments in general was so strongly antithetical that they were excluded from the ritual. Indeed any instrument associated with pagan cults and the Roman theatre was banned, which in effect meant practically all of them. After the fall of the Empire secular musicians took to a wandering life, and inevitably most of the musical knowledge of classical culture, together with many of its instruments, was lost to Europe. Classical learning survived, however, in the Arab world, from which many musical instruments were later reincorporated. These included fingerboard string instruments, already common in ancient Egypt, for which the word lute is the generic term as well as the name of a particular species. Meanwhile the dominant instruments in Europe during the Dark Ages were ethnic adaptations of ancient models.

The history of the organ, however, was a little different. It seems that after the Roman débâcle, the tradition of organ-building continued unbroken in Byzantium. From here it was then introduced into the Western liturgy in the eighth century, along with tuned handbells. There was a need for instruments to teach the correct intervals, and to guide and accompany singing and keep it in tune; handbells can do some of this but an organ did it better, and moreover produced an extremely impressive sound, especially inside a resonant building like a basilica.

Greek Music Theory

The discovery of the musical ratios is first ascribed to Pythagoras by Xenocrates, a pupil of Plato who became head of the Academy around 339 BC, though it is very likely that the knowledge came from Mesopotamia. According to the standard account, Pythagoras calculated the numerical ratios of the principal consonances by stopping a taut string along different fractions of its length. He found that a division halfway raises the pitch an octave; division by a third (conventionally expressed as the ratio 3:2) raises it by a fifth; and three-quarters (4:3) by a fourth; in the scale of C this produces the octave of C, plus G and F respectively. As the musicologist Richard Norton observes, the Greek term *harmonia*, which expresses these relations, has several meanings. In the first place, Harmonia was the daughter of Aphrodite and Ares. Second, as a non-musical term the word meant joining or fitting things together. Even musically it has several meanings, not always distinguishable from the context: octave, tuning, scale and mode.[13] Notwithstanding these ambiguities, and despite his belief in the mystical property of numbers, the achievement of Pythagoras was to demonstrate that music was not tied to the human world by mythic decree but emerged by virtue of its physical qualities.

Recent scholarship has observed a significant difference between the two figures of Pythagoras and Aristoxenus. Pythagoreans considered *harmonia* as a physical property; Aristoxenus was concerned with its implications for musical composition. Second, according to Norman Cazden, 'Pythagoras correctly generalises that standards for identifying harmonious agreement among musical tones are susceptible of numerical formulation. Aristoxenus correctly observes that this '. . . recognition of tones and their differences does not constitute the art of music, for music begins only when there is a musical system . . . and such a system is not given by external measurements but only by the ear of the musician nurtured in that system'.[14] In other words, if Pythagoras was impressed by the properties of certain intervals, then it must be because these intervals were already regarded as harmonious; they belonged, in other words, to a musical system which already existed.

Nevertheless, it is evident that the Pythagorean discoveries served to institutionalize particular musical relations; specifically, those we call diatonic. We are told that Pythagoras also observed the division of the octave by a fifth, which produces the measure of the diatonic interval. This division has a special property: it divides the octave into unequal halves. Two different intervals are produced, above and below the divide; these are the fifth below and the fourth above, the fifth being the larger of the two. The difference between them is critical: Pythagoras calculated it as the ratio 9:8, and it is this interval which constitutes the whole tone.

This interval imposed itself as a standard measure through the discovery of what happens if it is divided into the octave, and the implications this has for tuning. First, it emerged that the octave comprises a fourth, plus a whole tone, plus another fourth. Second, that the fourth comprises two whole tones with a half tone (or semitone) left over. This lent itself admirably to the stringing arrangement known as the tetrachord (from *tetrachordon*, 'four strings'): two tetrachords, arranged so that the lower string of the top pair sounds a tone higher than the top string of the lower two, produce a scale with the pattern tone-tone-semitone, tone, tone-tone-semitone. This is the equivalent of the scale of C major.

Observe, however, that the arrangement of intervals within the tetrachord is variable: it may also consist of tone-semitone-tone, or semitone-tone-tone; moreover the two tetrachords need not be the same. There are also different ways of joining the two tetrachords, either by inserting a tone between them, or by adding a tone to complete the octave. This is enough to produce not only a diatonic scale in C, but a series of scales, each beginning on the successive notes of the scale of C, and each with a different shape; these are the modes of Greek music, and if you try them out on the piano you'll discover that none of them requires any except the white keys; they do not, in other words, require the chromatic intervals which are represented by the black keys. But beware: because of the way the piano is tuned, they sound distinctly odd, and are not a true and accurate representation of the modes at all.

The tuning of instruments according to these intervals gives rise to anomalies. The trouble is that intervals are ratios, and ratios behave in idiosyncratic ways, so that the precise values of the pitches differ by a tiny amount — which is nonetheless perceptible to the trained ear — depending on exactly how they are produced. The mathematics are quite straightforward. Next in the set of Pythagorean ratios comes 5:4, which gives the interval of a third — in the scale of C, the distance from C to E. Now a third is two tones, which gives another way of calculating its value, but the results are different. The frequency of C multiplied by 5/4 is not the same as multiplying C by 9/8 to get D and then D by 9/8 again to get E. If C is 512, D is 576; then E, moving from D, is 648. Calculated the other way it is 640. The Greeks knew nothing of frequencies, of course, but they identified this discrepancy (because it can be heard). Known as the 'syntonic comma', the discovery is credited to Didymus and dates from around the beginning of the Christian era. In a word, and *pace* Max Weber, pitch is irrational. The initial simplicity of the prime integers known to the ancient Greeks did not quite match the acoustical facts.

The concrete effects of this irrationality, however, were swallowed up in a musical system which was organized not in the form we know today as tonality, but rather of modes. Modes are not like keys, in which the arrangement of tones and semitones is structurally identical from one to another, either major or minor. On the contrary, because there are variations in the order of their constituent tones and semitones, each has its own characteristic shape. This is in fact the origin of the difference between major and minor, which is all that is left of the modes within the system of tonality.

The principal distinction between the modal system and that of tonal harmony is that in the former, the modes lie alongside each other, and you are either in one or another. This doesn't mean you cannot move from one to another — you can switch between them because they lie parallel to each other — but the system is not unified and integrated. In the tonal system, when you move between keys by the means known as modulation, an implicit relation to other keys remains present in the background, and at certain moments you can be in two keys at the same time. But the possibilities of modulation remained limited until a method of tuning was devised in which the theoretical potential of the system could be fully realized — a development which only took place by stages during the second half of the eighteenth century.

This now universal method is called equal temperament, a form of tuning where the distance between each of the semitones of the chromatic scale is rendered equal and unvarying. Simple to state, but the mathematics are relatively complex; hence the delay between the first examples of equal temperament during the Renaissance and its eventual universal adoption. Not only that, but as we shall later see, the conversion to equal temperament has critical implications, because it is a system which falsifies every interval except the octave itself.

From Fiddle to Concerto

The standard medieval method of showing the connection between musical intervals and mathematical ratios was the monochord, a single string stretched over a wooden soundbox with a moveable bridge. It is described in the first half of the tenth century by Odo of Cluny, who also wrote instructions for setting the 'keys' on the hurdy-gurdy. This is an instrument in which the strings are rubbed by a rotating wheel, in short, a kind of mechanical monochord. It required a certain mechanical skill in its manufacture, thus confirming the role of the early-medieval monastery as the guardian of technical knowledge.

In theory, the Aristotelian classification of métier, where technical skill was low on the list, still held sway in medieval times, but the drive for technical progress in the growing cities reveals a different order of things in practice. Historians have recently revised the old image of medieval times as a period of stagnation. In fact the economic dynamism of the late Middle Ages produced a period of crucial technical innovation, which reached its peak around the middle of the twelfth century. New techniques with the most profound effects adopted around this time include windmills, the first clocks (incorporating the verge and foliot escapement), the spinning wheel, treadle weaving looms, gunpowder and horseshoes. Music thoroughly shared in this ethos of innovation. Notation itself was a great invention. In medieval Flanders, a place where new technology made the burghers rich — a prosperity reflected in the rise of a school of Flemish composers — the same techniques that powered their machines found uses in music: the famous carillon of Mechelen, the most complex peal to be heard in Europe, was operated by the same type of cam that worked the trip hammers of the fulling mill. Musically the most significant mechanical innovation of the period, however, was the balanced keyboard — the arrangement whereby the notes are engaged by a row of levers resting on a pivot, so that when the fingers depress them they operate what is called the action of the instrument. This device not only made possible the portative organ played by Landini. It also led within a short time to the earliest stringed keyboard instruments.

The written music of the time neither distinguishes vocal from instrumental parts, nor does it specify the instruments to be used, still less how they should be played. However, a host of illustrations and paintings, as well as innumerable references in non-musical manuscripts, inform us of the typical instruments of minstrel and troubadour, such as flutes and drums, pipe and tabor, transverse flute, various reed instruments, bagpipes, lyres, lutes, and fiddles. Unfortunately this is a limited source of information when it comes to what they sounded like. Nevertheless, the Middle Ages show an evident delight in the variety of instrumental colours. Indeed, as Christopher Small has observed, medieval music 'made much use of non-harmonic sounds — not only percussion, such as bells, drums, rattles, tambourines and triangles, but also pitched instruments which produce sounds with a high proportion of non-harmonic noise — the crumhorn, racket, bagpipes, shawm and sackbut'. Probably the sound of medieval singing was also, as it is today in blues and rock and generally outside the Western art tradition, much harsher, rougher and more nasal than in art music since the Renaissance; not, however, to the exclusion of beauty of tone, which is also found in styles like the blues, and 'not, it must be emphasised, because they did not know how to produce "smooth" sounds, but because they liked "rough" sounds'.[15]

Many of these instruments are of extra-European provenance, like the shawms, trumpets and drums of the Saracens. It is these that are the ancestors of the equivalent modern orchestral instruments. The ancestry of the violin, on the other hand, is unknown. The earliest indication is a three-stringed lira depicted in eleventh-century manuscript illustrations in conjunction with a bow. *Vielle* or fiddle is the generic term for this instrument. Did the fiddle come to Europe from the Middle East, or even further afield (the bow was already known in China)? The monochord and the hurdy-gurdy suggest another provenance, for the fiddle is like a hurdy-gurdy in which the mechanical contrivance has been replaced by another, technologically simpler, means of sounding the instrument. Whichever, by the time of Grouchy it had become a highly adaptable instrument. Other instruments, he says, 'may move the minds of men more powerfully by their sound — for example the drum and trumpet when played at banquets, jousts and tournaments', but the fiddle is more sensitive. It is also the most versatile, and 'a good performer on the fiddle uses normally every kind of *cantus* and *cantilena* and every musical form'. Strings in general — psaltery, harp, lyre, and lute as well as fiddle — are regarded by the Parisian theorist as the foremost category of instruments. Why? Because on these instruments, 'distinctions of pitch are finer and more subtle because they have strings which can be shortened and lengthened at will'.[16]

The fourteenth century divided instruments into two groups, designated by the terms *haut* (loud) and *bas* (soft). The former comprised trumpets, drums, cymbals, bagpipes, shawm, hunting horn; the latter consisted in strings, flutes and soft reed instruments, and the portative organ. The portative organ was played sideways. The left hand operated the bellows, while the right ran up and down a small keyboard. When the keyboard was adopted to work with horizontal strings instead of vertical pipes, the position of the hands changed accordingly, and in due course, the resulting instruments played a decisive role in the development of musical language. These instruments consist in two families, clavichord and harpsichord, both of which are documented by the 1430s.

The difference between them is in the method employed to sound the string. The action of the clavichord is so simple it hardly seems to deserve the term 'mechanism' at all. When the key is depressed, a metal tangent at the other end rises and strikes the string; it remains in contact with it until the key is released. The instrument is so arranged (betraying its ancestry in the monochord) that a single string may be struck at different points; it is conceived, in other words, as a melody instrument, which is not well adapted either for contrapuntal or harmonic music. The fact that the tone is produced by a direct stroke upon a string makes it responsive to the player's touch, but at the same time, because the tangent remains in contact with the string until the key is released, the sound is damped. Hence the clavichord is a very quiet instrument, totally unsuited to ensemble or public playing.

The mechanism of the harpsichord is more ingenious. The key raises a jack with a quill on it, which plucks the string as it goes up. The quill is mounted on a flexible tongue, which on the way down allows it to slide past the string silently. Because the notes are produced by plucking, its tone is not sustained, but the mechanism produces a sound that is stronger and brighter than an instrument plucked by hand. It is thus ideal for accompaniment, especially because with two hands you can play harmonies and counterpoints. The harpsichord family therefore lends itself to two types of use, as an instrument which may be used to hold a performance together, especially of vocal music, and as an instrument which enables the individual, playing alone, to produce a fuller musical texture.

In public and ceremonial music making, the range of instruments was large and varied. They were used in combinations which partly depended on what was available, and partly on the appropriateness of their sonorities to the character of the music and the place of performance. In this situation, the emergence of a new musical public towards the end of the fifteenth century has several effects. In particular, it calls for instruments appropriate for domestic use by amateurs with limited skills but keen sensibilities, partisans of the secular music encouraged by the new harmonic discoveries. One way their needs are met is by the rise of fretted string instruments (ancestors of the modern guitar), where the frets on the fingerboard guide the player in pitching the notes. Over the following century, the sonority of vocal polyphony, with its ensemble of balanced voices, sought its counterpart in the instrumental grouping and produced the idea of the consort, a group of instruments of the same kind, like recorders, but of different sizes, corresponding to the different voices of the vocal ensemble. With the strings this trend produced consorts of viols, an instrument which was equivalent to adding frets to the fingerboard of a fiddle and holding it vertically on or between the knees.

*   *   *

The consort calls for the standardization of tuning. At the same time, the emergence of diatonic tonality creates a new problem of temperament. Tempering means tuning in order to get rid of the anomalies in the intervals of the scale which interfere with the functioning of harmonic relations. The mathematics of tuning known to the ancient Greeks produced the 'just' intervals that were still used in European music, in some cases until as late as the seventeenth century. But as we have seen, the initial simplicity of the overtone series is deceptive: the prime integers known to the Greeks did not quite match the acoustical facts, which instead produce the anomaly called the syntonic comma. Because of this anomaly and the way it accumulates within the system a problem emerges in the business of tuning the instrument.

The difficulty with just temperament is that octaves and fifths are true and perfect, but it needs two types of semitone (one larger, one smaller), and leaves perceptible differences in other intervals. These differences become acutely problematic with the emergence of diatonic harmony, which is constructed on the principle of the equivalence of the keys erected on each of the semitones which make up the chromatic scale. The same chord in a different key has the same structural value because the internal relations are identical. This equivalence did not exist in the modes based on just intonation which proceeded chordal harmonic music, since each mode had its own characteristic shape. Instruments tuned accordingly were unsuitable for diatonic harmony, in which it becomes theoretically possible to move by modulation from one key to another by changing the component notes of a chord (including the chords which are merely implied by the successive notes of a melody) so that a different tonic exerts a stronger pull. Just intonation was therefore replaced by mean-tone temperament, in which thirds were adjusted to enable the system to function for related keys.

The problem was most acute in the case of keyboard instruments, because here the notes had fixed values. The crucial difficulty was that of enharmonics. These are accidentals which are notated differently in different keys, like D# in the key of E, which in the key of B♭ is E♭. Indeed, because of the irrationality of pitch, these notes have different values in different keys, and are therefore inflected differently. When modulation takes place, there is a microtonal alteration in the value of the semitone at the point of overlap when the one dissolves into the other and the key changes. Wind players could modify the intonation of their notes (within certain limits depending on the kind of instrument), and string players could not only inflect their notes but could even retune to match the tuning of other instruments. But this alteration is physically suppressed on keyed instruments with pitches of fixed value. When mean-tone temperament was adopted for keyboard instruments and it became easier to get

certain keys in tune together than others, the difficult ones showed up in the
enharmonics; especially on the organ, where the howling effect was
graphically known as a wolf.

In the end, to allow the use of any and every key, it turns out to be
necessary to make an adjustment to *every* interval, except the octave itself.
This is equal temperament, where adjustments are made which, as the
term implies, render every semitone exactly the same. The idea was simple
enough, but difficult to accomplish because of the fairly complex
mathematics required. As far as keyboard instruments are concerned, it
was not until the introduction of logarithms at the start of the seventeenth
century that the solution became relatively easy. Joseph Needham
mentions that equal temperament was calculated in China a little earlier
than in Europe, and suggests that the solution may have been brought to
Europe by the Jesuits. (He adds that the Chinese rejected it, on the grounds
that it interfered with the moral order of the universe).[17] However, there
was also another solution, applicable to stringed instruments, which
Europe discovered independently, as a result of the publication in 1482 of a
Latin translation (by a thirteenth-century scholar) of Euclid's *Elements*.
Theorists immediately set about showing how geometry could be applied to
the monochord. By drawing rectangular frames and dividing them by arcs,
the correct position of an interval could be marked on the fingerboard. A
geometrical method for spacing the frets of the lute for equal temperament
was published in the 1580s by the Italian theorist Zarlino.

Around the same period we find a learned Italian amateur at the court of
Ferrara, by the name of Ercole Bottrigari, pointing out the problems of
matching different systems of temperament, and classifying instruments
according to their tuning as stable (organ, harpsichord, harp), stable but
alterable (viol, lute, recorder, flute, cornett), and entirely alterable
(trombone and bowed strings without frets). A lute or viol fretted in equal
temperament, he observes, will not sound particularly well with a
keyboard, while violinists normally play in a Pythagorean temperament
which needs to be modified if it is to blend with either a keyboard or a lute.
Therefore, in forming a broken consort, in other words a consort of
instruments of different types, any two of these classes of instruments may
easily be mixed; players of either type of alterable instrument can adjust
their intonation to that of stable instruments. But he advises against mixing
all three, since the problem of matching the intonation is then insuperable.
His description of the effect which would then ensue, however, is distinctly
odd: it would be a *concerto*, he says, instead of a *concento*, a 'battle' of
instruments instead of the union and concord of voices and sounds.[18]

The strange way in which Bottrigari uses the word *concerto* reveals the
pedantic thinking of a conservative. The advice appears logical, but
progressive composers like Monteverdi were experimenting with forms of

tuning which allowed them to mingle instruments, precisely so as to exploit their contrasts, and the emergence of a new instrumental sensibility is recorded precisely in the word *concerto*. Its original Latin sense of *con-certare*, 'to compete or struggle together', is transformed to mean co-operation, 'bringing together', and finally 'agreement': concerto and concert, a musical form and the act of performance. The modern everyday meaning of the word, says the Italian musicologist Bianconi, presupposes an initial heterogeneity, a dissimilarity between the different elements to be 'concerted': 'Elements . . . which would never themselves have been capable of natural or spontaneous harmonisation . . . are made to "concert" with each other: voices with instruments, soloists with *ripieno* ensembles, one choir with another . . . one style of song with another . . . and so on.'[19] The union, concord and co-operation of disparate yet concerted elements is brought about by an agreed compromise in tuning, an engineered convergence of divergent forces. It is a humanist principle deeply characteristic of the Renaissance. A philosophical and ideological imperative adds its pressure to the problem of temperament.

The instrument which more than any other symbolizes the new sensibility, and which also comes to lead the evolving orchestra, is the violin. When it first appeared in what is more or less its modern form around 1550, it mainly served for dance music, which was avidly consumed by all ranks of society from peasants to princes. It was played by professional dance musicians relatively low in the social scale, especially as compared with the players of viols, who were more likely to be gentlemen amateurs. The violin, more delicate in construction than the older fiddle but of stronger and sweeter tone than the viol, presents to us the very image of the natural ornamental beauty of the product of skilled craftsmanship, yet here too the artefact is the product of engineering. In fact every part of it, every twirl in the woodwork, is highly functional, and the rapid perfection of the instrument by makers like Stradivarius is revealed by his famous patterns to be the result of the geometrical calculation of the very fine tolerances to which the wood needed to be worked. The instrument would not have been possible without the improved precision tools, including the calliper ruler, developed in the sixteenth century.

The early manner of playing inherited from the fiddle was quickly superseded by the lengthening of the bow in response to the needs of sonata and concerto. New kinds of bowing stroke were developed, as well as special effects like *pizzicato* (plucking), *sul ponticello* (bowing on the bridge) and the mute, partly, says one historian of the instrument, for expression and partly 'for imitative effects ranging from tempests at sea to farmyard noises and bird calls'.[20] Violinist-composers emerged like Vivaldi and Tartini who began to exploit the instrument in solo concertos, making technical demands that induced further alterations in both the instrument and the bow, which further expanded the player's technical scope, especially through the elaboration of left-hand technique. Tenor (viola) and baritone (cello) versions of the instrument are developed, and the family is completed by the double bass. In the middle of the eighteenth century come the first important violin manuals — Geminiani's in 1751, and in 1756, the *Violinschule* by Mozart's father, Leopold. The improvement of the bow to give more tautness to the hair also gives it more elasticity. Where earlier music made elaborate use of short phrases, the new style calls for long crescendos and decrescendos, the hallmark of the orchestra at the court of Mannheim which so impressed the Englishman Burney on his musical travels through Europe.

In the case of woodwind instruments, the benefits of improving tools of trade accrued more slowly. We first learn of machines for boring wooden pipes from the Italian engineer Taccola in the early fifteenth century, though without any indication of when such machines were first introduced. We know, however, that at the end of the fourteenth century, the bit in boring or drilling tools became detachable, and cutting edges began to improve. But decisive improvements in the workings of the lathe did not take place until later in the seventeenth century; only then did it become capable of really accurate work, and refinements begin to appear in flutes and reed instruments. Improvements came from dividing instruments into jointed sections, to allow more accurate boring and positioning of sideholes, and the addition of one or two keys to operate holes beyond the reach of the fingers. Writing in the 1750s, the German flautist J.J. Quantz informs us that the time and place of the improvements cannot be given with certainty 'although I have spared no pains to discover reliable answers', but in all probability they were less than a century old, and 'no doubt undertaken in France at the same time that the shawm was developed into the oboe, and the bombard into the bassoon'.[21] In their new forms, these instruments found a place alongside the violin family and the continuo as more or less permanent members of the emerging orchestra.

Discoveries of Acoustics

The major acoustical discovery of the seventeenth century was the harmonic series, the set of overtones which accompany the sounding of a musical note. What happens (as we noted earlier) is that the string or column of air that is set in motion to create a musical sound, produces not a single frequency but a simultaneously sounding series. It vibrates simultaneously along its full length and also successive aliquot fractions of it — halves, thirds, quarters and so forth. This produces partial vibrations in which, as the sounds get higher and fainter, the basic note, or fundamental, recurs, an octave higher each time, geometrically spaced along the series (positions 1, 2, 4, 8, etc.). In between come various intermediary intervals which behave in the same way (3, 6, 12 . . .; 5, 10 . . . etc.). However, because the successive intervals in the series become progressively smaller as you go higher, the series is different from a musical scale — in which, by definition, identical intervals repeat themselves in each octave. With the evolution of diatonic harmony, trouble began to break out where the two conflict.

It's like this. The intervals of the scale enshrined in Greek music theory were based on measurements produced by stopping a string, raising the pitch, and comparing the result. The effect this has is to compare a smaller division with a larger measurement which remains constant. The harmonic series, on the other hand, compares a larger variable with a smaller constant. Obviously the two sets of ratios diverge. This is the source of what Max Weber called the intractable irrationality of the facts of acoustical physics.

If this irrationality was theoretically undetectable before the seventeenth century, its effects were present from the beginning, shaping the creation of scales. Sounds vibrate; to produce a scale, the vibrations must be aligned appropriately. This is the work of tuning. Tuning is the art, or science, of organizing these vibrations, creating order out of entropy, by aligning the overtones. The lower overtones are within the range of human hearing and they play a crucial role in aural perception. In certain untuned instruments they can be heard distinctly — in the ringing of bells, for instance. Aligning them by means of tuning focuses the pitch.

With the first few intervals in the harmonic series, any difference between the two types of series is tiny and easily accommodated. These are the intervals which anchor diatonic harmony: tonic — octave — fifth — second octave — third — another fifth. At the seventh overtone, however, a distinct deviation appears in the harmonic series compared with the diatonic scale. It happens that an interval produced by a harmonic with a prime number from seven up (or its multiple) is distinctly smaller (or in some cases larger) than the nearest corresponding diatonic semitone. By fateful coincidence, the first diatonic interval affected by this deviation is also the seventh member of the set (e.g. the note B in the scale of C). This interval is two whole tones higher than the fifth (in the given example, G). This, however, raises it considerably above the value of the seventh harmonic on the fundamental of C, for which the corresponding note would actually be lower than B♭ by a third of a semitone. The result is that the note becomes harmonically unstable.

It is no accident that this is the principal blue note. The blue notes are a sign of the African origins of jazz, of a different scale system, different methods of tuning, a different sense of timbre and rhythm, a different sense of harmony. According to the ethnomusicologist Ernest Borneman, the basic West African scale is pentatonic and without semitones.[22] When this scale, in which the intervals correspond very closely to the natural overtone series, encounters the equal tempered diatonic scale, the third and seventh steps of the latter become ambiguous, for the peculiar temperament of the latter tries to sharpen or flatten them. The result of the ambiguous third is that it hovers between the major and the minor; the errant seventh is more elusive. Moreover, the effect of the blue note is augmented by the predilection of African musical traditions for effects of timbre which inflect the pitch: vibrato, tremolo, and the rhythmic alterations of syncopation and polyrhythm, which strengthen the natural tendency to sharpen accented beats and flatten unaccented ones, so that strong beats shifted to weak ones by syncopation become flattened in the process. Jazz pianists, to invoke the blue note, often hit adjacent semitones like B and B♭ together in order to re-create the ambiguity. Bartók does something similar to represent the non-diatonic scales of East European folk music.

Medieval music, which knew no more about the ratios of intervals than the Greeks, and nothing yet about vibrations either, dealt with the problem of harmonic instability by the device of *musica ficta*. When voices were moving in parallel and one of these unstable notes occurred, it offended their ears (because the interval, to be harmonic, needed to be either a fifth or a fourth). They therefore either flattened or sharpened one of the notes in order to round the sound, a procedure which they didn't bother to notate (hence *musica ficta*); the result is a minefield of problems for musicologists. With the development of diatonic tonality and the introduction of new scales, the practice necessarily disappeared, and a new difficulty arose: the problem of enharmonics — sharps and flats with slightly different values in different keys.

The discovery of adequate principles to govern the production of the new scales became increasingly imperative, but the arithmetic never quite came out right. The new experimental science tracked the problem down to the alignment of the partial vibrations in the harmonic series. By the 1690s the English mathematician Francis Robartes has identified the 'imperfect' overtones, and asks 'What is the reason that the 7th, 11th, 13th and 14th notes are out of tune, and the others exactly in tune?' He explains that the fractions of a seventh, eleventh, thirteenth and fourteenth do not represent the ratios of any diatonic or chromatic interval.

In an age when physics was not yet parcelled up into sub-disciplines, the problems of music had already intrigued several generations of scientists before this question was formulated. An interest in what later came to be called acoustics first appeared in the work of Vincenzo Galilei around 1590; closely followed, in the early 1600s, by Kepler, Bacon and

Descartes himself, the foremost philosopher among natural philosophers. All of them question Pythagorean ideas about simple arithmetical ratios. Descartes commented in his *Compendium musicae* of 1618, 'The basis of music is sound; its aim is to please and to arouse the affections. The means to this end, i.e., the attributes of sound, are principally two: namely, its differences of duration or time, and its differences of tension from high to low. The quality of tone itself (from what body and by what means it emanates in the most pleasing manner) is in the domain of the physicist.'[23]

Galileo and Mersenne both published the laws of the vibration of strings at about the same time in the 1630s. Both authors established independently of each other that the frequency of vibrations of a string depends on its length, its mass and its tension. Mersenne, a Minorite friar who ran a kind of scientific salon in Paris and corresponded with contacts throughout Europe, may be credited with more, for it was he who realized the musical importance of the overtones and urged his numerous correspondents to seek an explanation for them. In the case of open strings he identified at least four harmonics, but he still found it paradoxical that a string should vibrate at different frequencies simultaneously — he couldn't *see* it. Early the following century, Joseph Sauveur, who devised a method to make the vibrations visible, proposed the term acoustics for the science of sound, and established the concept of the fundamental. The work of Sauveur leads straight to the celebrated theorem of Fourier, which treated the principle of superposition that explained the paradox that worried Mersenne. Another result of these developments was the invention of the tuning fork in 1711.

The findings of Sauveur, like Mersenne before him, were partly based on collaboration with instrument-makers. In this way he learned that organ-builders had intuitively discovered the properties of harmonic pitches when they mixed together different sets of pipes by means of stops to obtain various timbres. The portative organ of medieval times had long been superseded. To cope with all the notes, the instrument had grown in size and ceased to be portative. The organ now became the most thoroughly mechanical instrument of the times. The player's hands are quite removed from the source of the sound: the action of the fingers merely releases valves, opening the pipes to air that is blown mechanically and menially by a bellows operator. Changes of volume and tone colour were brought about by throwing in and out the different stops, which were introduced gradually over the fifteenth and sixteenth centuries as the manufacture of pipes grew more sophisticated. Separate sets of pipes were designed with their own characteristic timbre and loudness, but neither the volume nor the quality of the tone could be affected by the degree of the player's muscular effort. In a word, neither *crescendo*, *diminuendo* nor accentuation were possible. German organs of the seventeenth century were not even provided with a swell-box. As Arthur Loesser has explained, clear and even articulation were the desired qualities in both instrument and executant. The player, 'his right hand on one manual, his left on another, his feet busy on the pedal keys . . . would often play a so-called "trio": three clearly drawn melodic lines, independent, congruous, and rigorously separated; and if we wish to borrow the vocabulary of Leibniz . . . we could call them three windowless monads building the best of all possible worlds by pre-established harmony'.[24] On account of this, perhaps, the organ was one of the last instruments to make the adaptation to equal temperament; by the time it did so, the shape of the musical world had been redrawn, with a completely new instrument at its centre. The pianoforte.

Nevertheless the organ remained a fruitful field for developments in musical engineering, and its automation produced — like its very invention — a technological innovation whose influence was felt far beyond the world of music. The Renaissance had produced a craze for automata powered by water. In the water gardens of the Villa d'Este at Tivoli near Rome, built in 1550, there were fountains and grottos where water-powered figures moved and played and spouted. In the eighteenth century, automatic music was produced in the same way by water organs which became popular enough for Mozart and Haydn to compose for them. The air was released into pipes by valves opened selectively according to a pattern of cams or pegs rotating on a cylinder. The music merely had to be translated into the pattern of pegs. This principle, basically the same as the Mechelen carillon, was used by the son of an organ-builder, Basile Bouchon, in an attempt to solve the problems of productivity in the silk industry in Lyons by means of automation. To guide the placing of the pegs on the cylinder of the automatic organ, a pattern of holes was cut into a sheet of paper. Bouchon applied the idea to the silk loom; his method was then improved by Jacques de Vaucanson, who was appointed head of the silk enterprise after the Cardinal de Fleury had been impressed by one of his mechanical ducks. The cylinder was set in a frame with a ratchet, which responded to the pattern of holes in the paper as it revolved. The silk-weavers responded to the threat of automation with riots, and Vaucanson's mechanism was abandoned, until in 1800 a silk-weaver called Jacquard put it together again with minor improvements, which included replacing paper with punched cards. Again the workers threatened with automation rioted, and like the English Luddites smashed the new machines. But before the century was out, the idea of punched cards was applied again, this time by Herman Hollerith in the 1880s, who added electrical sensors in order to tabulate the results of the American census. This, in the twentieth century, became the favoured method for the insertion of data in mechanical calculators and early electronic computers.

The Voice as Instrument

The scarcity of phrasing marks in early music is no indication of a lack of awareness about phrasing. Phrasing and expression always follow the laws of *musica practica*. This applies equally to vocal and instrumental performance, and at a time when instruments were primarily used to accompany singing, vocal artistry provided the paradigmatic style of delivery. The model is found in old textbooks like *De modo bene cantandi*, which dates from the 1470s, where one Conrad von Zabern explains such matters as where singers should take their breaths. Following these principles, the choir could become an ensemble of finely tuned instruments, with uniform attack and rhythmic precision, controlled dynamics and a smooth and even body of tone — the choir of Lassus and Palestrina, Byrd and Tallis.

In the course of time, concerted instrumental music naturally began to imitate techniques that were first developed *a capella*, like the contrasts of tone colour and dialogue-and-echo effects that were favoured by the choral music of the early Baroque. Simultaneously, a different and opposite development takes place, as instruments begin to acquire a more individual voice, each with its own characteristic phrasing which varied from the reigning vocal model. This individuality is brought out in the Baroque concerto, in the contrast between the concerted instruments and the solo parts. The effect of these trends on vocal music was a change in the model of vocal delivery over the course of the seventeenth century, co-extensive with the appearance of opera. The voice now began to be thought of as a special type of instrument, and a new kind of singing emerged which eventually came to be known as *bel canto*.

One dictionary says that 'so far as can be ascertained, the intention of the founders of the *bel canto* seems to have been to discover an answer to the technical problems set by the polyphonists . . . the strong emphasis laid . . . upon the instrumental side of vocalism was . . . their response to the instrumental nature of the demands of polyphonic music'.[25] It is not surprising if the origins of the term are obscure — the history of singing is inevitably elusive, even more so than instrumental performance. Indeed prior to the invention of the phonograph, quality of voice remained almost impermeable to objective study. Not only does the voice die upon the ear, but unlike instruments the technology of voice production is hidden from inspection; even control of pitch is achieved entirely by intuitive and unconscious effort. As another source puts it, 'By some mysterious means, a particular note being imagined, the [vocal] cords are immediately and subconsciously adjusted to the exact tension required; the breath is then expelled and the imagined note is produced. This is the equivalent of a violinist turning the pegs of his instrument without sounding the strings and finding the strings perfectly tuned.'[26]

As a simple description the term *bel canto* is next to useless. Nowadays it is
sometimes employed to distinguish a certain style of singing — the pure
pitches and nightingale trills of Joan Sutherland, say — and a certain
repertoire — Donizetti and Bellini rather than Moussorgsky and Wagner.
In this sense, Rossini lamented the loss of *bel canto* as long ago as the 1850s,
when ornamented coloratura began to give way to a more dramatic style of
expression in middle-period Verdi. But in the next breath Joan Sutherland
is compared to Maria Callas, the first modern singer to revive the classic *bel
canto* roles, and despite the fact that Callas's voice was far less sweet,
sometimes even ugly, Sutherland is found wanting. It is not just that Callas
knew how to act and Sutherland didn't, but that Callas could act with her
voice, and *that* is *bel canto*.

If the discourse of the art of singing is inevitably subjective and
relativistic, its vocabulary is Italian because the Church had turned Italy
into a power-house of vocal artistry, and the 'invention' of opera taught
the whole of Europe how to sing. Although Max Weber curiously
overlooks to mention it, *bel canto* is another of the apparently unique
features of Western musical culture. The vocal sound is not strictly
unique to European music, but nowhere else has it been artfully
cultivated to become a structural element in musical style and form. In
short, *bel canto* describes the paradigmatic operatic voice, the resonant
full-throated sound with an even tone throughout its range, capable on
the one hand of the effortless delivery of the most florid music, and on the
other, the colouring of the voice through the dramatic enunciation of the
words that are being sung.

The opinion among the professors of singing appears to be that the
essential character of *bel canto* is first of all a method of breathing with the
diaphragm which intensifies voice projection without necessarily increasing
volume. It is the controlled use of the same contraction of the abdominal
muscles which the adult employs when coughing or groaning. Obviously
this is a very useful technique for professional singers whose voices are no
longer taken up by the reverberant echo of the interior of a church, and
who don't want to have to strain to fill a palace banqueting hall or a theatre
with relatively soft acoustics. In the normal method of breathing, the
natural elasticity of the lungs supplies air to the glottis as if they were
inflated rubber balloons; it is called costal breathing. This is what happens
when we speak and call out. But singing needs more breath than speaking,
and although both methods of breathing can supply the air easily enough,
the natural elasticity of the lungs in costal breathing is not amenable to
direct control. On the other hand, the conscious deployment of diaphragmatic breathing transforms the singer's voice; its effect is to make the entire
bodily frame from chest to head more resonant (though for anatomical
reasons, this is less pronounced in women than in men).

There is more. Some singers make special use of the membranes known as the false vocal cords, which form the ventricle that lies immediately above the larynx. These can be constricted in order to control the attack and produce what is known as the *coup de glotte*. According to Lucie Manén, herself a singer trained in the tradition, this technique, which she calls the ventricular mechanism, is essential to true *bel canto*, and intimately connected with the ability to control the harmonics of the voice and thus to extend its range of timbres.[27]

Manén's conclusions are the product of a remarkable marriage of scientific investigation using advanced technologies with accurate introspection about her own sensations while singing. The scientific investigation of vocal production dates back only as far as the anatomical studies in the 1740s of Antoine Ferrein, who identified and named the vocal cords. Ferrein concluded from his anatomical analysis that speech and song are produced entirely by the vibration of the vocal cords, induced by air pressure from the lungs. Yet he also observed that 'street-singers in Paris and choral singers in the provinces produce their tone not only by means of the invisible vocal cords, but − as can be observed externally by their necks − also by use of the other parts of the larynx'.[28] Ninety years later the Italian surgeon, Francesco Bennati, a leading ear, nose and throat specialist who was also an accomplished *bel canto* singer, came to the conclusion that there were two different mechanisms for voice production in the larynx: the *voix ordinaire*, the ordinary speaking voice which can also be employed for singing, and the *voix orotunde*, the fuller, more rounded voice of the *bel canto* tradition. Yet the precise manner of the production of the *voix orotunde* eluded him. According to Manén it also eluded Bennati's contemporary, Manuel García, regarded as the leading *bel canto* teacher of his day.

The likelihood is that *bel canto* derives originally from a style of singing associated with a type of popular song called the *frottola*, which was current in Northern Italy at the end of the fifteenth century. Possibly it had descended to the plains around Mantua from the southern Alps, and for certain, it quickly spread the length and breadth of the country from Venice to Naples. The word probably comes from *frolta*, a gallimaufry; the form was a hotchpotch consisting of slick versification combined with deliberately artless music, composed to be sung at Carnival and therefore with an expected lifetime of a month of two, like the famous *sambas* of Carnaval in modern Rio de Janeiro. Sometimes sentimental, sometimes bawdy and Rabelaisian, the *frottola* was essentially no different from other types of street song, from which it sometimes borrowed, but it strongly appealed to the courtly and intellectual public in circumstances in which the modernizers favoured the vernacular, and it was taken up by professional composers. The paradigm of the composed *frottola* comes from the pen of

Heinrich Isaak, a Fleming who served Lorenzo de' Medici, and also wrote French *chansons* and German *lieder* with equal facility. The crucial factor in the dissemination of the *frottola* was printing: Isaak was one of the composers published by Petrucci, who issued eleven books of them by different composers between 1504 and 1514. It is the first case in musical history of a craze inspired by commercial opportunity.

The craze was over by the 1530s, but as fashion changed, the *frottola* left the influence of its vocal style in a number of new types of song. On the one hand it inspired a series of low genres across the country, like the melodious *napoletana*. On the other came the arrival of Netherlands polyphony, brought to Italy precisely by composers like Isaak. Polyphony like this made new demands on the voice, which were well served by the technique of diaphragmatic breathing. Moreover, such voice control also suited the increasing emphasis of Renaissance humanism upon literary refinement, for it encouraged the setting of more subtle texts, which is one of the decisive features of the madrigal. We are doubtless still a certain distance from full-throated *bel canto*, which is first suggested at the very beginning of the seventeenth century by Caccini, whose opera *Euridice* dates from 1600, followed two years later by a collection of madrigals entitled *Le nuove musiche* — 'The New Music'. It is here that we first find, if not the term *bel canto*, then the idea of singing with the larynx, *cantare con la gorga*. And Caccini, says Manén, stressed the importance of the 'start' of the sound in the manner of the *coup de glotte*.

In short, a process with a certain logic has begun to unfold. Encouraged by the Italian language itself, which is full of pure and sonorous vowels and very few diphthongs, a technique emerges which marries variety of timbre and vocal expression with smooth breath control, producing clarity of articulation combined with voice projection. Opera would hardly have been possible without it.

Historically speaking, the term *bel canto* was intended to mark a difference between the new style of singing and the traditional styles known as *canto declamato* and *canto parlando*. But what exactly do these terms refer to? There is a dearth of clues in the musicological literature, where the slipperiness of the topic means it is virtually ignored. *Declamato* seems to indicate a 'calling' voice, characteristic of outdoor singing. A few commentators identify this with a 'peasant' singing style, others with troubadour music; the two styles were probably close to each other, and the troubador voice probably much less pure and mellifluous than the present-day manner of singing this music cultivated by the ancient music movement. *Parlando*, or 'speech-like', suggests a form of delivery more like an extension of the speaking voice. Some commentators identify it with 'natural' singing in the vernacular, as opposed to the trained singing of the church.

I am tempted to think of *declamato* and *parlando* in terms of the modern-day intonations of blues and folk singers, popular singers and singing actors, even (within reason) of pop stars. Clearly, the strongly delivered *declamato* voice requires great breath control and produces a sustained sound. *Parlando*, by contrast, would have a greater variety of timbre and more grain, so to speak. One thinks of singers like Bessie Smith, Billie Holiday, Bing Crosby, Frank Sinatra, Elvis Presley; or of Lotte Lenya, Edith Piaf or Violeta Parra. The comparison is problematic, of course. The old terminology is probably not applicable today, when the determinants of vocal style are of quite a different order, and vocal production is conditioned as much by its relationship to the microphone as by what is owed to traditional idioms. A whole tradition of popular singing, from crooning to bossa nova, is unimaginable without the microphone, to which the closest thing without it is singing quietly to oneself — I am thinking here of the silky soft-throated intimacy of singers like Antonio Jobim, João Gilberto or Vinicius de Moraes and his partner Toquinho, who make Brazilian popular music so inimitable.

But whenever you mention names, a different problem intrudes. The names are invariably ciphers for voices which stand out from any attempt at classification, either on account of their exceptional quality or their personality, and sometimes both. What kind of voice should we really call Paul Robeson's, which leaves no one indifferent whatever he's singing — opera, spirituals or the political songs of the 1930s? What of the English contralto Kathleen Ferrier, the Argentinian maestro of the tango, Carlos Gardel, the Scottish folk singer Ewan McColl, Cuba's modern troubadour Pablo Milanes — what should we call their wonderful mellifluous purity of tone that thrills you in a manner you scarcely dare to admit but cannot resist? As Roland Barthes has put it, the human voice is a phenomenon which escapes the approaches of informed study — physiology, history, aesthetics, even psychoanalysis — because whatever they have to say, there will always be a remainder, something more, not spoken, a difference of the type that psychoanalysis at least identifies, and assigns to the objects of desire. In short, that our relation to a favourite voice is virtually erotic.[29]

If Barthes is right, it is no accident that *bel canto* is surrounded by mystique, which serves to disguise the truth about it: that this is a technique for the capture of the very essence of eroticism in the voice, the perfect sublimation of the repressed, and this is precisely why it becomes the very soul of opera.

Notes

1. Marx, *A Contribution to the Critique of Political Economy*, Lawrence & Wishart, London 1971, p. 216.

2. Fredric Jameson, *Marxism and Form*, Princeton University Press, Princeton, NJ 1974, pp. 14–15.

3. Maurice Dobb, *Studies in the Development of Capitalism*, Routledge, London 1963, p. 269.

4. Quoted in the *New Grove's Dictionary of Music and Musicians*, Macmillan, London 1980, Vol. 14, pp. 664ff.

5. See *Grove's Dictionary of Music and Musicians*, Fifth Edition, entry on Instruments.

6. Max Weber, *Rational and Social Foundations of Music*, Southern Illinois University Press/Feffer & Simons, London 1977, pp. 40–1.

7. J.D. Bernal, *Science in History*, MIT Press, Cambridge, MA 1965, Vol. 1, p. 161.

8. Bertrand Gille, *The History of Techniques*, Gordon and Breach, London 1986, Vol. 1, pp. 268–9.

9. Kurt Geiringer, *Instruments in the History of Western Music*, Allen & Unwin, London 1978, p. 36.

10. Gille, Vol. 1, p. 290.

11. Quoted in *Grove's*, Fifth Edn, Vol. VI, p. 284.

12. Anthony Baines, *Brass Instruments*, Faber & Faber, London 1976, p. 63.

13. Richard Norton, *Tonality in Western Culture*, Pennsylvania State University Press, Pennsylvania and London 1984, chapter 4, passim.

14. Quoted in ibid., p. 100.

15. Christopher Small, *Music, Society, Education*, John Calder, London 1980, p. 21.

16. Piero Weiss and Richard Taruskin, *Music in the Western World, A History in Documents*, Schirmer/Collier Macmillan, London 1984, p. 65.

17. Joseph Needham, *Science and Civilization in China*, Vol. IV:1, Cambridge University Press, Cambridge 1962, pp. 214ff.

18. Quoted in Frank Harrison and Joan Rimmer, *European Musical Instruments*, Studio Vista, London 1964, p. 26.

19. Lorenzo Bianconi, *Music in the Seventeenth Century*, Cambridge University Press, Cambridge 1987, p. 36.

20. David D. Boyden, 'The Violin', in Anthony Baines, ed., *Musical Instruments Through the Ages*, Penguin, London 1978, p. 118.

21. J.J. Quantz, *On Playing the Flute*, Faber & Faber, London 1966, p. 30.

22. See Ernest Borneman, 'The Roots of Jazz', in Hentoff and McCarthy, eds, *Jazz*, Cassell, London 1960.

23. Quoted in Weiss and Taruskin, p. 189.

24. Arthur Loesser, *Men, Women and Pianos*, Simon & Schuster, New York 1954, p. 9.

25. *Grove's*, Fifth Edn, Vol. IX, pp. 43ff.

26. Ibid.

27. Lucie Manén, *Bel Canto*, Oxford 1987.

28. Quoted in ibid., pp. 6–7.

29. Roland Barthes, 'The Grain of the Voice' in Barthes, *The Responsibility of Forms*, Hill and Wang, New York 1985.

8

The Age of the Piano

Invention of the Piano

Until the arrival of the synthesizer in the 1970s, the most remarkable of modern musical instruments was the piano, invented in Florence at the beginning of the eighteenth century by a Paduan instrument-maker, Bartolomeo Cristofori, in response to a request from his patron, a prince of the Medici, for an instrument to 'improve' on the harpsichord. It then took about seventy-five years for its gradual adoption throughout the main centres of European musical culture. Its rise corresponds to the transition from the pre-Classical Baroque to the ascendancy of the sonata, the symphony, and bourgeois culture. Indeed, it was one of the principal agents of this change.

What does it mean to say that an instrument, the piano, was invented? In the first place, if we argue that musical instruments evolve, it indicates a special and exceptional occurrence. But of what nature? Inventions don't just drop from the skies into a vacuum in the inventor's mind. They happen when there's a reason for them, a need or desire, plus the necessary knowledge and means. Very few inventions, at any rate of the practical kind, are the result of disinterested curiosity; some are motivated by the wish of a patron, but most by either economic necessity or economic opportunity. In short, they depend on a series of factors which are primarily social rather than individual in nature. It is therefore rare to find only a single inventor; usually there are different people involved in the same search at the same time, in different places, often unknown to each other. The piano is no exception. There was also someone called Schroeter in Germany, and a certain Marius in France; there even seems to have been an attempt a hundred years earlier, in Holland. But it was Cristofori who first successfully constructed such an instrument, in which the strings were struck from below by hammers activated by the keys, and the sound was damped when the key was released.

   The essential feature of the pianoforte, the feature inscribed in its name, is its dynamic range, soft—loud or loud—soft, pianoforte or fortepiano. This is what made it different from both harpsichords and clavichords, the two families of instruments which, within a hundred years, it completely replaced. Not surprisingly, it combines crucial features of both of them: the action of striking instead of plucking comes from the clavichord — though the method employed by the piano is far more ingenious — and the damping mechanism is taken from the harpsichord. In this way, the piano took the advantages of each in order to overcome the limitations of both. In doing so, it also took over their musical functions, which it not only combined but also enlarged upon. These functions corresponded to the nature of the instruments. The tone of the harpsichord was strong, penetrating and brilliant, well adapted to the accompaniment of singers and other instruments, for use in social gatherings and public performances. The clavichord, on the other hand, was soft and delicate, the perfect instrument for private and intimate solo playing. The piano, in satisfying both these functions, becomes through and through an instrument with a dual nature: both private and public, solo and ensemble, intimate and exhibitionist. It is this range of functions that makes it universal (the very name is the same in all the major languages except German). And as George Bernard Shaw once put it, the invention of the piano was to music what the invention of printing was to poetry.

   It is not that harpsichords and clavichords were in any way ill-conceived, but rather that developments in musical style came up against certain limits in them, as if, to satisfy new expressive needs, music was looking for a new kind of intonation, a new tone colour, a new sound. The same cultural impulses that nurtured the rationalism of the Enlightenment and the discoveries of acoustics also produced a predilection for conventionalized sentiment, which found its voice in what the Germans called *Empfindsamkeit*, the French *le style galant*. In contrast to the intricate counterpoint of the Early Renaissance and the polyphonic style of the High, the new idiom called for greater harmonic stability, the separation of melody from accompaniment, and the moulding of the phrase by nuance and dynamic inflexion, at all of which the piano excelled. The harpsichord, wrote Couperin in 1713, 'is perfect as to its compass, and brilliant in itself, but . . . it is impossible to swell out or diminish the volume of its sound'.[1] Because the notes are produced by plucking, its tone is not sustained, and it is thus incapable of the singing quality known as *cantabile* which becomes one of the piano's most outstanding characteristics. In fact the piano offered several advantages. It not only lent itself to dynamic inflexion, but the two hands could learn to accomplish different gradations of loud and soft at the same time. It could play solo to its own accompaniment. Its invention, in short, accomplished more than what was asked for, as of course all the best inventions do.

The nub of the instrument is what is called the action. Strings and bridges, soundboards, even cabinets are found in other instruments. What is unique about the piano is the way the hammer strikes the string. This is what gives the instrument the essential feature from which it takes its name, its dynamic range, and it was the action which was invented by Cristofori for his patron, Prince Ferdinand de' Medici. The date usually given is 1709, but recently uncovered evidence has pushed it back to 1700. The Prince was one of the great patrons in musical history, reportedly a gifted musician, an excellent harpsichordist and a singer of skill and charm; the theatre he built at the Villa Pratolino mounted productions of operas by Alessandro Scarlatti, Pasquini, Peri and Handel which became famous throughout Europe.

Cristofori's invention was extraordinarily ingenious, for in order to work, it needed the hammer striking the string from below immediately to fall back freely, leaving the string to resonate until it is damped by the action of releasing the key. The piano hammer must be detached from the key, but resting upon it in such a way that it can be tossed against the string when the key is depressed, with a force that corresponds to the pressure of the finger on the key. The device required to accomplish this is much more complicated than the harpsichord jack. It needed a relay mechanism. What Cristofori provided was an escapement, a device that allows the hammer to transmit to the string the impulse which sets it in motion. The sound, from the nature of the hammer action, is stronger and better sustained than that of the clavichord, and a damper is essential to prevent the results being negated by an offensive jangle of noise caused by the resonance of unwanted harmonics. In short, the escapement — several different types were developed subsequently — has the effect of converting the all-or-nothing action of the harpsichord into an analogue mechanism which is thereby more expressive.

The achievement is remarkable but historians of the instrument never seem to ask what made it possible, not musically but technologically. It is true that almost nothing is known about the man who accomplished it. We can only suppose, however, that he was very much of his age, and his age was scientific. Indeed, the invention of the piano comes at the end of the century which saw the solution of the central problems in the science of mechanics, a century moreover, in which music and the new science were on intimate terms. It is symptomatic that Galileo's father was a lutenist, composer, mathematician and musical theorist. Cristofori, who belonged to the very same environment, was clearly as well placed as anyone could be to make use of all this knowledge.

The clue is the escapement. Escapements belong to clocks, they are the very heart of the timekeeping mechanism, and it cannot be an accident that the piano appeared hardly more than a quarter-century after the publication in 1673 of the Dutchman Christiaan Huygens's *Horologium Oscillatorium*, which announced the birth of a pendulum timepiece with a new type of escapement that really worked. (Another 'coincidence': Huygens, scientist and inventor of the anchor escapement, was also the son of a musician and, like both Galileo and his father, also made contributions to acoustics.) Cristofori was bang in the middle of all this. Huygens's work was controversial in Florence: he was accused of plagiarizing Galileo, who had also designed a pendulum clock with a novel escapement, but without any real success. The Medici were Galileo's disciples — advocates of the new science, they saved him from the Inquisition; Leopoldo de' Medici, grand-uncle of Cristofori's patron Ferdinando, was an eager horologist and proud possessor of one of the earliest, as yet imperfect, pendulum clocks, constructed in 1658.

Clock-making was one of the first industries to put the new theoretical findings into practice. The advance of clock-making can be traced in the invention before and after Huygens of a succession of designs for escapements of different types. The same thing happened in the case of the piano. From England comes evidence not only to confirm the connection but to suggest that at the time it was obvious: here the piano escapement was also known as the hopper, short for grasshopper; the term was first used to describe a new type of escapement invented in the 1730s by John Harrison, who thus perfected the ship's chronometer and won the Great Prize offered by Parliament. The Harrison brothers were the sons of carpenters and this too is noteworthy. Clock-making and piano-making followed similar patterns of development, both combining traditional handicraft knowledge with the new rationalism; what the Germans called 'learned handicraft' (at first outside the guilds and only much later unionized). Both began as luxury items produced by versatile craftsmen among related trades (early clock-makers were often metalsmiths) who possessed between themselves the necessary practical knowledge to apply the new scientific principles — until later the market grew large enough to allow for the establishment of specialist manufacturers.

Business Expansion

In many ways, the piano is one of the eighteenth century's pioneering inventions, which leads, by the beginning of the nineteenth century, to a growing sector of industrial production; especially in the hands of the English firm of John Broadwood, the first to apply the methods of factory organization to its manufacture. Broadwood was also responsible for major improvements in the instrument which incorporated the results of scientific research and helped him achieve his industry lead — a fine example of the exploitation of what Ernest Mandel calls technological rent. This is only one aspect of the story. At the same time the growth of the piano comprises a series of related trades, from the piano-makers themselves to the publishers of piano music and the growing ranks of piano teachers and piano tuners. The centrepin of the industry is the virtuoso pianist-composer. In this regard, the piano is a different type of commodity from the clock; the clock has the most profound cultural effects because it universalizes the rational ordering of time, but as a commodity it remains unitary and self-contained. The piano, by contrast, has a multiplier effect, like the invention of photography, or computers.

An account of Cristofori's new instrument was translated from the Italian and published in a musical journal in Hamburg in 1725. At the end of the 1720s, the Saxon harpsichord-maker Gottfried Silbermann made his first pianos in Dresden. The first pieces written specifically for the piano are sonatas by Lodovico Giustini, published in Italy in 1732. Four years later, we discover J.S. Bach giving one of Silbermann's instruments a try. He was not much impressed. He found that it had a pleasant tone, but the treble was weak and the action too stiff. His sons, however, became adepts. Johann Christian, known as the English Bach, was the first to play one in public in London, in 1768. In Germany by the 1770s the piano is all the rage. The instrument's growing popularity bespeaks the growth of chamber music among the German burghers. Max Weber believes that the essentially bourgeois nature of the piano explains its initial neglect in the land of its invention, where the indoor culture of Nordic Europe remained undeveloped. The infant instrument needed a domestic environment.

It was an age much fascinated by mechanical toys like the automata of the French inventor Vaucanson, who was responsible not only for the mechanical duck already mentioned, which ate and shat, but also for a famous mechanical flute player, which was widely exhibited in several countries. It is not surprising that once the piano mechanism had been devised, improvements began to follow. Generally piecemeal until the 1770s, they were stimulated by the potential of a growing market: a progressive musical life was developing among the middle classes, centred as much on domestic music making as public gathering, and pianos were cheaper and simpler to manufacture than the harpsichord. The market was succoured by a comparable growth of music publishing following the introduction by Breitkopf in Leipzig in 1750s of his new music printing process, which quickly spread to the centres of musical life throughout Europe. As we saw earlier, Breitkopf's new musical type was particularly suited to keyboard music, and especially economical for printing fast-selling music. Keyboard music quickly came to account for the largest portion of the music publishers' output, along with a growing number of musical journals and tuition manuals.

The instrument played by Johann Christian in that first public recital in London was made by Johannes Zumpe. Zumpe was one of a group of craftsmen, apprentices and pupils of Silbermann's attracted by the English market in the difficult times of the Seven Years' War, who set up workshops in the English capital where they came to be known as the Twelve Apostles. Zumpe's early squares, with actions less efficient than Cristofori's, were still a novelty, and sold for £50 each, at a time when a single manual harpsichord by Broadwood's boss Shudi cost at least thirty-five guineas, a double manual about eighty. Within ten years, John Broadwood had begun to resolve this situation.

Broadwood took out his first patent for a grand piano in 1777, at the same time Sebastian Erard began making pianos in Paris. Both were the sons of cabinet-makers who came to the capital to be apprenticed to harpsichord-makers, Erard from Strasbourg, Broadwood from Scotland. Both of them made good — Broadwood even married the boss's daughter. These two, plus another Frenchman, Henri Pape, were variously responsible for nearly all the crucial improvements which transformed the piano into the modern instrument, with its even and homogeneous tone colour from bass to treble across six or seven octaves. Other improvements were still to follow, but it was Broadwood who first rationalized the method of stringing and housing the instrument; Erard improved the action, and Pape was the first to use felt instead of leather for the hammers themselves, which at one swoop gave them a much more rounded tone. There is a certain technical logic in this course of development, but if Broadwood's contributions came first this is because London offered the advantage of the fastest-growing middle class in Europe and quickly became the centre of manufacture. Broadwood was a smart operator and the market gave him a head start. He had good business sense, too: whenever a popular virtuoso came to London, he used to send along a piano for his concerts. A simple question of sales promotion.

In 1777, working with a craftsman from Holland and a young apprentice, Broadwood patented an improved action which included a check on the descending hammer, known thereafter as the English Grand Action. In 1783, he added a foot pedal that lifted the bank of dampers and held them until the pedal was released — the first sustaining pedal. He was also, as we noted earlier, the first piano-maker to undertake scientific research. As he imported steel wire from Berlin and soundboards from Leipzig, he consulted two scientists by the names of Toberius Cavallo and Edward Whitaker Gray, both customers of the firm, over how to get the best tone out of these components. They conducted experiments to determine the best point to strike the strings, and the vibrating length that would give the best tone. The result was the introduction of changes to the bridge and an adjustment in the position where the hammer strikes. These improvements gave better control over the notes at the top and the bottom of the keyboard, and Broadwood was thus able to extend the piano's range. The innovations were immediately successful, and within a short time were adopted by all piano-makers.

By the turn of the century the piano has completely replaced all other keyboard instruments in domestic, concert and theatre use. The result is changes in the piano-maker's business. Take the example of Johann Andreas Stein of Augsburg: aided by a small number of assistants, Stein turned out about 700 claviers in forty years, or about seventeen to eighteen a year. Two years after his death in 1792, his daughter Nanette set up her own enterprise; by 1809 she had made 800 instruments, an annual output more than double her father's. This could only be accomplished by enlarging the plant, increasing personnel, introducing a rigorous division of labour, and the purchase of certain ready-treated materials; in other words, more than just enlarging the workshop. Machinery is still absent — this is still the world of Adam Smith rather than Karl Marx — but no longer is it old-fashioned artisanal production. As Loesser comments, 'A piano maker who expands into a factory ceases to be a craftsman; he becomes a businessman.'[2] Or in this case, -woman.

Technically, the piano is an extremely intricate apparatus which employs an abundance of serially repeated parts: keys, jacks, hammer shanks, springs, strings and tuning pins. The corresponding division of labour required in its manufacture makes an elaborate list: there were sawyers, bracers, markers-off, roughers-up, turners, plinthers, scrapers, carvers, hammer leatherers, stringers, finishers, polishers, gilders, tuners and action regulators. It was Broadwood in London who took the next step in the process. The firm introduced steam-powered machinery after the Napoleonic Wars, although only for sawing and planing the heavy woodwork. The machines developed in the 1790s for more delicate operations were not yet capable of the precision required for piano parts. Nonetheless, the advantage which accrued to Broadwood by these methods was decisive. When he died in 1811 he left a personal estate of more than £100,000 — in modern terms, the fortune of a multi-millionaire.

Arthur Loesser, in *Men, Women and Pianos* (which remains the best work on the subject), compares the piano in the 1820s to 1840s, with the automobile in the United States in the 1900s: 'to own one, especially one of the latest models, was honorific: it was a badge of successful modernity . . . the instrument contained hundreds, perhaps thousands, of moving parts: it was full of "machinery" '.[3] Machinery, he says, was the 'brightly shining morning star' of the day, a symbol of progressive thought and enterprise in the quest for mastery over nature. The function of the automobile is rapid locomotion, that of the piano the performance of certain kinds of music. In either case, the individual who could triumphantly command the mechanism's full capacity became a special object of thrilled admiration. Virtuosity became a heady sport.

In its domestic setting, the piano proved particularly adept at accompanying singers, discreetly keeping them in tune and filling out the harmony. This had also been the function of the harpsichord in opera and the court orchestra (not to mention the organ in the church), but the piano required only minimal technical knowledge and not much technique. A new musical genre evolved, to satisfy the growth of domestic singing, the song form known by its German name of the *lied*. The form and the instrument appealed especially to young women − the keyboard, it was said, enabled women to maintain their decorum and modesty while entertaining themselves and their visitors. There she could sit (according to one account), 'her well-groomed hands striking the keys with no unseemly vehemence . . . gentle and genteel, a symbol of her family's ability to pay for her education and her decorativeness, of its striving for culture and the graces of life, of its pride in the fact that she did not have to work and nor did she "run after" men'.[4] Music here becomes an integral part of the process of valorization of the patriarchal nuclear family which runs deep through the development of capitalism.

In Germany, the élite of musical aficionados were known as *Kenner und Liebhaber*, 'connoisseurs and amateurs'. Arthur Loesser calls his chapter about them 'Connoisseurs and Amateurs are Influential. Concerts may be meetings or shows.' They involve themselves in musical clubs, each town with its own *collegium musicum* where burghers met to play and listen to music. For this constituency, *Kapellmeisters* had turned out treatises on piano technique, with advice on problems like fingering and ornamentation. Books like C.P.E. Bach's two-part *Essay on the True Art of Playing Keyboard Instruments* (1753 and 1762) become the models for later volumes by long-forgotten names. What is interesting, says Loesser, is not so much the development of new fingerings, but the erection of fingering into a technique, a method. One of these manuals was written by a Swabian clergyman who called himself Humanus. One is reminded of E.P. Thompson's description of methodical Methodist ministers in Britain, Bible in one hand, slide rule in the other, supplementing their meagre incomes by calculating nautical tables for the Royal Observatory.

The manuals and the methods they advanced tell us nonetheless of crucial shifts in style. These include the demise of the 'learned' figured bass and the dilution of the practice of decoration and embellishment. Older keyboard music − Bach and Handel − became more difficult to play.

Musical style becomes (in Loesser's words) 'lightened and simplified', as players learn to use more of their fingers (in organ and harpsichord playing, the thumb had been little used). Contrapuntal complexity gives way to homophony, the clean melodic line with a harmonic accompaniment, which typically takes the form of an easy rocking movement in the left hand, known as the Alberti bass — a bit like boogie-woogie. Scales, Alberti basses and arpeggios using the thumb, became the basic shapes of piano playing. Enter Mozart.

Mozart's well-known letter to his father in 1777 on his way to Paris, about his visit to Johann Stein's piano workshop in Augsburg, shows more than familiarity with the instrument, but real knowledge and intimacy. What he likes about Stein's pianos is that their tone is even, with clean damping, because they have an escapement which eliminates jangling and vibration. The knee pedal is sensitive (Broadwood introduced foot pedals six years later), and without the least reverberation. Stein's love of music leads him to finish each instrument with infinite patience 'until it can do anything'. Every soundboard is deliberately cracked by exposure to rain and sun, then wedged and glued so that it will never crack again.[5] From this and other letters we learn a good deal about how Mozart believed the piano should be played, including the way the pianist should sit and behave: with decorum. The same as the style of his music: with flowing melodic lines, uncluttered by over-embellishment; this is the style which will blend with the most lyrical of orchestral instruments, the woodwind, including the mellifluous clarinet, another new instrument which captured Mozart's imagination. Yet only a few years after his death, Mozart's playing was already considered old-fashioned. Beethoven said to Czerny that Mozart's touch was 'neat and clean, but rather empty, flat and antiquated'. He also talked about Mozart to Karl Holz. 'Was Mozart a good piano player?' Holz wrote in the deaf master's conversation book. His reply prompted Holz to add, 'Well, the piano was still in its cradle then.'[6]

At this time there were two distinct types of piano, the English and the Viennese. The difference, clearly described by expert witnesses like the virtuosi Hummel and Kalkbrenner, lay in the different mechanisms employed by the action, which clearly correspond to the more advanced techniques of production employed in England. The simpler action was the Viennese, which was light, had relatively little carrying power, and needed little pressure to depress the keys. The English version was more complex, the piano was bigger, more heavily strung, more brilliant in tone. Mozart's *cantabile* belonged to the more intimate Viennese instrument. It was the English piano, with its resonant sound and carrying power, that helped shape the style of his rival Clementi, the paradigm of a new breed of pianist—composer—entrepreneur well adapted to the world they moved in; Mrs Thatcher would have loved him. Until Beethoven arrived on the scene, Clementi surpassed his contemporaries in dash, boldness and vigour. He was even called the father of modern piano technique — but this is due, as much as anything else, to his accomplishments as a businessman, in which he also vividly contrasts with Mozart.

Clementi's story reads even more like a novel than most. Born in Rome in 1752, he was brought to England as a boy by the connoisseur and Member of Parliament Peter Beckford, with whom he lived in Wiltshire until, properly prepared, he descended on London in 1773. He never looked back. On a visit to Vienna in 1781, he fought a piano duel with Mozart; tradition has it that Clementi won. The piano duel, where performers would vie against each other in the art of improvisation, was a Viennese penchant; there was no doubt about the winner when the young Beethoven, a few years later, was pitted against both Cramer and Gelinek. By the 1790s Clementi had earned enough money to make a sizeable investment in the music publisher and piano manufacturers Longman and Broderip — whose name soon changed to Clementi & Co. He himself worked on improvements to the action of the instruments the company made. In 1802 he took some of them on tour to Europe, together with a young protégé of his own to demonstrate them: John Field, the composer of the first piano pieces with the title 'Nocturne'.

Pianist-composers like Mozart and Clementi played mostly in salons, not concert halls, and actually neither of them did much touring. The first of the great touring breed was Jan Ladislav Dussek. It was he who first placed the piano in the position now familiar on the concert platform, thereby accomplishing two things: first, to use the raised lid to throw the sound forward into the auditorium, and second, to show off his handsome profile. *Le beau* Dussek they called him, after his first appearance in Paris. But he was also the first composer to indicate the pedalling in his own music, and he contributed significantly to fingering technique, anticipating Chopin in his ideas about shifting fingers on the same key without actually striking it so as to get a pure *legato*.

Musical life in Paris had been disrupted by the revolution; the heyday of the Parisian salon and the Parisian piano was to come in the 1830s. Erard benefited from Broadwood's example when he came and set up shop in London during the French Revolution. Back in Paris, though he never challenges Broadwoods in the scale of production, he introduces crucial innovations in the action in the 1820s which establish new standards, with immediate consequences upon style, including a repetition lever for clear articulation at the fastest tempi. To gain publicity, the firm adopts the young Chopin as their protégé. Their Parisian rival Pleyel responds by capturing Liszt (who later defects to the Viennese firm of Bösendorfer). Broadwoods, however, who in 1817 had sent their latest model to Beethoven as a gift, is still bigger business than both of them put together.

Max Weber believes that the intense competition of the manufacturers played a crucial role in the development of the instrument, closely linked to that of the composer and the virtuoso whose sponsorship they sought. Pianist and manufacturer played off against each other to their mutual advantage, using the newest forms of spectacle and publicity, even borrowing the methods pioneered by Josiah Wedgwood for selling chinaware. These forces, says Weber, 'brought about that perfection of the instrument which alone could satisfy the ever increasing technical demands of the composers. The older instruments were already no match for Beethoven's later creations.' Characteristically Beethoven disdained the commission which the manufacturers granted their sponsors, demanding that it was passed on to his friends in the form of a discount.

Factory methods bring economic advantage, but the concert platform is where pianos make their reputations, which the manufacturers needed in order to sell their smaller and cheaper instruments in the domestic market. The cost of this reputation is the effort required to improve the concert instrument, which was not yet strong enough to withstand the full force of a muscular player. Beethoven was famous for broken piano strings. So was Liszt. A review of a concert by the latter in 1840 reports: 'his playing had such strength, clarity and smoothness that it borders on the marvellous. Rarely does an instrument stay in tune; generally a few strings snap.' For a time, spurred on by the extraordinary gathering of virtuosi in Paris before 1848, French manufacturers took the lead. That Liszt switched to Bösendorfer in his later years may have been simple opportunism; the great were besieged for testimonials, the less good, like Wagner, readily switched their allegiances. On the other hand, it may be evidence that Liszt, as befitted the venerable Abbé he became in later life, pounded less than he did as an *enfant terrible*.

With the new virtuoso there is not only a rapid development of style and technique: orchestras are expanding, and larger auditoria are built to cater to the growing concert audience, and for these reasons too, more and more power is demanded of the instrument. Women pianists, who were penalized if they showed too many signs of virility, found themselves disadvantaged, a situation all the crueller because the piano had begun by encouraging not just their self-expression but also their professionalization, in considerable number as teachers and accompanists, and a few as virtuosi.

The combined demands of virtuosity and acoustics elicited improvements in the construction of the frame and the stringing. Strings are now made from high-tensile steel wire produced by the latest smelting methods; bass strings are further strengthened by the introduction in the 1850s of a new technique of copper winding. These improvements also pay off by helping to solve the problem of producing an effective upright instrument for the domestic market, to replace the square which was Broadwoods' bread and butter. The original problem with the upright was simple: an up-ended grand was too tall to be practicable (though strange examples were produced, known from their shape as giraffes). The height was reduced a little by diagonal stringing, but the upright only really took off when Pape devised the idea of cross-stringing, which made it smaller by mounting the bass strings across the upper registers at an angle, over a higher bridge.

In Britain, by the mid-century, uprights comprised more than 80 per cent of the output of English factories, they were even cheaper than the French ones, and Broadwoods were in trouble for sticking to squares. Nevertheless improvements were still badly needed, especially since an upright piano action is not as effective as a horizontal one. The decisive impulse, the iron frame, came from new quarters across the seas. Iron was first used in pianos made in the United States as early as 1800, and even European makers adopted iron strengthening bars. In 1825, the Boston maker Alpheus Babcock came up with the first complete frame made in a single casting, designed for a square, and in the same city eighteen years later, Chickerings adapted it for a grand, and then for an upright.

After the mid-century, when the technology has been perfected, the centre of production moves to North America as new manufacturers emerge into dominance. They export very little, but quickly outclass the old firms in Europe in scale of production. They include Steinway in New York and Kimball in Chicago. Kimball's factory is sited to take advantage of a new source of primary materials and a new market. High-quality spruce, the best kind of wood for both soundboards and moving parts, traditionally obtained from the forests of Switzerland, has been discovered along the Northern Pacific Coast. A friend of Isaac Singer, inventor of the domestic lockstitch sewing machine, Kimball becomes the world's foremost manufacturer of uprights until the Japanese learn to outpace the Yankees in the 1960s. He discovers new buyers, like his friend, by offering his goods for sale throughout the West on the instalment plan. The Steinway family, émigrés from Germany, and better placed in New York to command the top of the market, produce a concert instrument incorporating several signal innovations, which by means of an expert publicity campaign, rapidly establishes a European reputation and a new universal standard. Both manufacturers further rationalize the organization of the labour process, and introduce appropriate machinery. The American System of Manufacture has come to the piano.

In Europe, the centre of production now moves back to Germany. The Germans adapt the American System to their own economy, and discover a special advantage in their late development. Arthur Loesser has shown that for all the improvements and developments in piano-making since the

1770s, productivity did not increase. In spite of economies of scale and the judicious introduction of machines (which combined to de-skill a large part of the workforce), in the 1850s it still took Erards 400 workers, Broadwoods 600, to turn out 1,500 and 2,300 instruments a year respectively, the same amount of labour power per piano as a harpsichord-maker and apprentices a century earlier needed to make eighteen or twenty. They still couldn't manage more than three or four instruments a year for each pair of hands. The important gain was that they could do it more cheaply. It was another thing, however, to pass to the Marxian world: to reduce the proportion of labour to plant and machinery, which is called improving the organic composition of capital. In Europe, the big manufacturers tended to diversify their investments rather than reinvest in their primary branch of trade, in order to spread their risks. It was more profitable at that time to build a concert hall and promote concerts than to instal machines when they were not yet reliable enough. Germany, however, because of its late development, still had a large dispersed body of small craftworkers. At the same time, with its rising economy, it produced the best steel and iron in Europe. In these circumstances, companies rapidly emerged to specialize in the mass production of the different aggregate parts of the piano — soundboards, actions, frames and strings — to supply a large cottage industry of assembled instruments, well built by experienced carpenters and cabinet-makers, standardized and cheap.

Perhaps the reader will have noticed that as the centre of production shifts backwards and forwards, the piano appears to follow the trajectory of capitalism itself. As Loesser remarks, 'The history of the piano does not coincide with the development of musical genius; it follows the development of industry and commerce.'[7] Not only that. It is also representative of capitalist development in other ways too. Marx himself argued that the worker's participation in cultural satisfactions is only possible economically because of an enlargement in the sphere of pleasures that society has to offer in the periods when business is good. The capitalist therefore searches for the means to spur on consumption, to give his wares new charms, to inspire the consumer with new needs by constant chatter. Here the piano is exemplary. How is the instrument developed? Rosa Luxemburg explained how small capitalists always played the role of pioneers of technical change. Indeed in a double sense, for they not only initiate new methods of production in well-established branches of industry, but are also instrumental in the creation of new branches of production not yet exploited by the big capitalist. The piano is the perfect illustration of the process.

Between 1851 and 1900 (according to the estimate of Cyril Ehrlich) world production of pianos increases tenfold, and reaches about 50,000 a year.[8] The best instruments remain expensive, but there are now increasing numbers of cheaper instruments on the market, uprights that are mostly sold on hire-purchase. By this means, pianos become a durable commodity within the reach of the better-off working classes. 'Don't you think the collier's pianoforte', asks a character in D.H. Lawrence's *Women in Love*, 'is a symbol for something very real, a real desire for something higher, in the collier's life?' 'Yes,' comes the cynical reply, 'amazing heights of upright grandeur.' But it was true. Social emulation was a powerful force in Victorian society, and a parliamentary report on life among miners in North-East England in the 1870s even found that pianos were rated 'a cut above' perambulators.

Meanwhile, the concert instrument reaches a new perfection, and around the turn of the century the art of piano composition achieves its apogee in the work of a most remarkable generation of composers, all of them born within twenty years of each other, between 1862 and 1882: Debussy and Ravel, Albeniz, Granados and de Falla, Busoni, Schoenberg, Bartók and Stravinsky. All are composing pianists, some of them are virtuosi in their own right, and in their hands, as we reach the twentieth century, the piano becomes a fully-fledged modernist instrument, a new percussiveness and unsuspected contrasts of tone colour incurring upon its Romantic *cantabile* and brilliance. The twentieth century also means a new commercial popular culture, and in the United States there follows another generation of composing pianists — all of them born before the turn of the century — but with this difference: white or black, they are mainly self-taught. Their world is popular entertainment, their primary forms are ragtime, jazz and blues, Tin Pan Alley and musical theatre. They include Scott Joplin, Jelly Roll Morton, Duke Ellington, Jerome Kern, Irving Berlin, Cole Porter and George Gershwin. As pianists some were shaky, others were accomplished performers, but all are pioneers of what is also a completely modern piano style.

The medium for the dissemination of their music becomes above all mechanical reproduction, even though the phonograph for its first fifty years was far too primitive to challenge the piano's supremacy, while cinema, because of its need of music as long as the screen was mute, gave it a great boost. The twentieth century thus begins with a buoyant market, a multitude of producers, and trade increasing practically up to the eve of the First World War, which in Europe threw the entire industry into disarray. It is not a coincidence, of course, that the same period witnessed a craze for mechanical player pianos, the old pianolas which fell out of use when radio and electrical recording arrived in the 1920s. The turning point has now been reached, before the recovery of pre-war levels of production. The cinema turns talkie, the leisure market becomes ever more consumerized, and for the piano a long decline sets in, although pianism is led by the recording industry into ever more prodigious realms. Nevertheless the instrument seems to be returning whence it came, to become once more an expensive luxury and a specialized instrument within the high-culture market, when a revolutionary jump in technology occurs, the result of electronification and the micro-chip. The 1970s and 1980s bring the keyboard synthesizer, and another shift in the centre of production takes place. Remarkably, Japanese manufacturers, who started making pianos at the turn of the century, take the lead not only in the new technology but also in the old, discovering that there is still enormous scope in the market for all kinds of music, and therefore all kinds of instruments. In fact, more than ever.

Until recently (up-to-date figures are unavailable), only one country in the world produced more pianos than Japan: the USSR. Most are of lower quality, but the best employ actions made to order by the Nottinghamshire firm of Herrburger Brooks, who also supply the actions for some of the best European grands. A specialist firm which originated in Paris in the 1850s, it became a British company in the 1920s; since 1965 it has been owned by the old US company of Kimballs, which itself passed under new ownership a few years after the Second World War. The new owners, a mid-West timber and furniture corporation, also took over the leading Austrian piano maker of Bösendorfer a year later. Steinways too have recently changed hands, twice. The company was acquired first by the media conglomerate CBS, who then, when they ran into trouble at the beginning of the 1980s, sold it to a group of Boston businessmen.

In the course of these developments, the performer, as Roland Barthes pointed out, has changed. Recording has made things different. Our music now comes to us overwhelmingly through loudspeakers, disembodied. Physical technique is taken more for granted. First, wrote Barthes, 'there was the performer, the *actor* of music, then the interpreter (the great romantic voice), finally the technician, who relieves the auditor of every activity, however vicarious . . .' Because musical amateurs, he says, are now so much rarer, there are no longer musicians like the pianist Lipatti or the singer Panzéra, who appeared like the perfect amateur because they stirred in us 'not satisfaction but desire — the desire to *make* such music'. Instead we have professionals with an esoteric training, and we are cast, as auditors, in the cold and objective role of judges. We listen differently in this condition.

Yet the situation is paradoxical. The piano itself has been transformed by electronic means, with the result that probably more people now play keyboards, after a fashion, that at any previous time. For although pianos are made in greater numbers than ever before an electronic synthesizer is cheaper, and even if the keyboard is usually shorter, it is always exactly in tune, no attention needed at all. The cheaper, more popular models are musically much more limited than the cheapest piano, and have too many automatic controls. The more sophisticated jobs, on the other hand, with proper touch-sensitive keys and multiple banks of programm-able oscillators, offer entirely new sonic worlds. They are not a replacement of the piano, but an entirely different instrument, which has had a major effect not only within popular music but in many areas of musical production where dissemination takes place through loudpseakers.

The Conquest of Equal Temperament

Orchestras are complex and contradictory organisms, bands of special-ized individuals who are required to suppress their individualism (and submit to an even bigger individualist). In order for the classical orchestra to emerge, it was necessary for the harmonic system to reach a high level of articulation, and then for factors like precision of pitch and conformity of phrasing to acquire precedence over individual tone colour. The orchestra is thus a product of the rationalization of timbre over the course of the evolution of Western harmonic music to produce another of what Max Weber regards as its essential features: the grouping of instruments into families — strings, woodwinds, brass — each comprising a balance of high, middle and low voices, and percussion to add colour.

Whereby hangs a tale, for in the early classical orchestra and the consort it grew out of, percussion is altogether absent; it is only after Berlioz that a limited range of percussion is reintroduced as a standard feature. This is another way in which music after the Renaissance contrasted with before. Medieval music, according to Christopher Small, 'made much use of non-harmonic sounds — not only percussion, such as bells, drums, rattles, tambourines and triangles, but also pitched instruments which produce sounds with a high proportion of non-harmonic noise — the crumhorn, racket, bagpipe, shawm and sackbut.' Not, he adds, 'because they did not know how to produce "smooth" sounds, but because they liked "rough" sounds.'[9] In a word, percussion instruments produce noises rather than tones: sounds that are unpitched or pitched only imprecisely. Even with pitched percussion like the timpani, the pitch may be muffled and unclear. The paradigmatic instruments of the classical orchestra, on the other hand, all produce sounds of clear and definite tone, appropriate to music based on logically ordered tonal relations.

The early-eighteenth-century orchestra consisted of an *ad hoc* or at least variable assembly of instruments grouped around the harpsichord, which provided the rhythmic pulse and the harmonic body of the music which the melodic instruments clothed and embellished. In theory the performance was subject to dual control by the principal violin (or leader) and the continuo player; in practice the harpsichord became predominant, because to read from a figured bass, fill in the harmonies and double for a missing instrument, was a prerogative the composer preferred not to relinquish. The instruments would be positioned round the keyboard in two groups: on one side the principal melody instruments (violins and oboes), on the other, those supporting the bass (cellos and bassoons). This placement reflected a concern to achieve a blended sound in the *tutti* passages, against which the *obbligato* instruments could project themselves. *Obbligato*, or obligatory, refers to the use of named instruments in a quasi-solo role playing a special part, as opposed to the band which consists of whatever instruments happen to be available. Opera particularly favoured the *obbligato*, where the instrument might be chosen for iconic reasons: pastoral scenes employing flutes to suggest shepherds' pipes, trumpets and drums for military imagery, and so forth. In the Concerto Grosso the *obbligato* instruments were grouped together into the *concertino*, the accompanying body into the *ripieno*. The possible combinations were considerable, and belie the suggestion that the early eighteenth century had little feeling for tone colour because all instruments were treated much alike. In this respect much has been regained in the restoration by the early music movement of original instruments (and tunings).

In the early orchestra, up to the time of Haydn, instrumentation remained partly arbitrary. There was considerable doubling of parts, and it was generally the woodwinds which doubled the strings rather than vice versa. The reasons are not obscure. In the first place, string players do not get out of breath, they can play continuously. In the second place, the tone of early wind instruments was both weaker and more irregular than modern instruments. In the third place, not all wind instruments were capable of playing all the notes; they were thus regarded as interchangeable according to need, or else their use was limited to specific effects and passages. This was especially the case with the brass, originally designated as *haut* instruments for outdoor use with military associations, which (except the trombone) needed considerable technical adaptation to become fully-paid-up members of the equally tempered symphony orchestra, a position they only secured after the invention of valve systems in the early part of the nineteenth century.

The conventional division of wind instruments into two main families, brass and woodwind, is in some ways misleading, since certain differences between them do not derive from the material they are made of. Although this certainly affects the timbre, there is another crucial difference: in woodwind instruments changes of pitch are attained by opening sound holes along the column of the instrument, which effectively shortens the column, while in the brass instruments the column remains closed and different notes are made primarily by varying the pressure of the lips against the mouthpiece. The instrument is therefore initially restricted by its dependence on the natural harmonics available within the tube, and is therefore made to be played in a particular key (or group of related keys with shared harmonics). Only the trombone, an instrument originally belonging to the church, was fully equipped to produce the complete range of notes of the chromatic scale, by means of a telescopic slide which enabled the player to adjust the length quickly and efficiently. Yet the trombone was slow to enter the orchestra. Apart from theatrical appearances to underline awesome moments like the statue of the Commendatore coming to supper in Mozart's *Don Giovanni*, it was not thought appropriate to secular music. It only became a standard orchestral instrument in the nineteenth century, once the other brass instruments had developed the means of chromatic playing, and they could take their place in a balanced family of instruments of equal capacities.

Brass instruments began to emerge from their medieval simplicity and acquire their modern configuration in the sixteenth century, with the growing availability of sheet brass and important developments in tooling — such as the introduction, in the 1570s, of the mandrel on which the metal was shaped. Until the seamless drawn tube of the twentieth century, sheet metal from rolling mills was bent around the mandrel, then brazed along the seam; the bell was made separately. Before hydraulic expansion, in order to curve the tube, it was filled with molten lead or other filler of a lower melting point, then bent round a shaped pattern, reheated, and the filler emptied out. The newer technologies have certain advantages, such as elimination of internal wrinkling caused by the molten lead method, but they are expensive industrial processes which only flourish under conditions of mass production like those of the North American market, and in any case the best instruments still use some of the older processes; the bell, for example, is still best shaped by hand.

Two methods were employed for achieving pitches additional to the harmonic series, depending on the instrument. One was by adding sections to the tube and thereby making a new set of notes available. This, however, was not a very practical thing to have to do in the middle of playing. Eighteenth-century horn players developed instead a technique of 'stopping' by placing the fist in the bell, which added a number of semitones to the scale. In the case of the trumpet, where this technique was unavailable because the bell was too small, the seventeenth century had already seen a different device, the addition of a sliding mouthpiece to extend the tube. Known as the 'flat trumpet' because it could play in minor ('flat') keys, it was used by Purcell in his *Funeral Music for Queen Mary* of 1690. Another solution, the 'key trumpet', which employed keys of the woodwind type to shorten the tube, elicited a concerto from Haydn; but too much brilliance was lost this way, and this instrument did not survive either.

In pre-logarithm days the bell curves were worked out by joining co-ordinates on paper, and generations of makers passed down profiles of the shape of the bell by which the harmonic series is accurately focused. However, loud playing still produced discordant, inharmonic overtones, partly due to turbulence in the air within the tube, and partly through vibration in the metal along which sound travels much faster than through the air. When greater volume came to be demanded, therefore, the bore was widened to allow for stronger blowing without the tone scattering in a flurry of powerful unwanted overtones. At the same time, the makers showed constant interest in improving the alloys employed and determining the best thickness of the metal (according to its reverberance).

The full liberation of brass instruments from the limitations of the harmonic series, however, had to await the development of the piston valve, jointly patented in Germany in 1818 by Heinrich Stölzel, horn player to the King of Prussia, and a mining-company bandsman called Friedrich Bluhmel; it was followed by the rotary valve, devised by Joseph Riedl of Vienna in 1832. The essence of the device is that not only must the piston be able to move up and down with perfect accuracy and lightning speed, but the whole assembly must be absolutely silent and airtight; the model for such a valve is the steam engine. Also the assembly involves small screws and springs, hardly possible before the age of precision engineering.

Precision engineering and exact calibration also play a crucial role in the positioning of the holes in woodwind instruments, where precise calculation of their emplacement was increasingly crucial to temperament. The process, called 'setting out', uses a short lathe in which the joints are mounted for turning and boring by a drill. The same improvements in technology, partly stimulated by developments in clock-making, which issued in the late seventeenth century in the first prototypes of the modern flute, oboe, and bassoon, also bore fruit in the appearance of a new instrument in the early eighteenth. The five-key clarinet, with its sweet, smooth, mellow and above all singing tone, which captured the imagination of Mozart, first appeared in a primitive two-key version at the same moment as the piano. The inventor is said to have been J.C. Denner, a renowned woodwind instrument maker of Nuremberg who died in 1707. The instrument is at first confused with the French chalumeau, a simple single-reed pipe, sometimes with two keys, which was made, like the recorder and the viol, in several sizes but without the distinctive feature introduced by Denner, the speaker hole. This small additional hole, also employed on the oboe, operates on the wind column to produce the harmonics required to play the higher part of the register, and helps to give the instrument its characteristic timbre. By the middle of the century the bell had been lengthened, more keys had been added, and the instrument was made in five or six sections.

The continual improvement of musical instruments is partly brought about by the instrument-makers' ready adoption of tools developed in other branches of production once their reliability was established. Bassoon-makers used a copying lathe modelled on a gun-stock lathe. Spear-point drills were replaced by high-speed steel drills. The introduction of machine tools served to reduce hand work to a minimum and make possible the standardization of components, thereby reducing costs and allowing mass production. Eventually the result would be the demise of the old type of master craftsman, who was also a performer of the highest standard. It was one of the last representatives of this tradition, Theobald Boehm, who was responsible for decisive improvements to the flute, above all to the mechanism of the keys, that were then taken up by other woodwinds. According to his own account, the reason he undertook this work was to bring the flute in line with equal temperament. He developed by stages a complex mechanism of keys, levers and screws made to tolerances of which nineteenth-century technology was only newly capable.

In large part, the decisive improvement of brass and reed instruments in the first half of the nineteenth century reflects the development of a new market, and thus of extended economic opportunity for the instrument-makers — the growth of military wind bands which began during the period of the Napoleonic Wars. It was partly the cut-throat competition between different Parisian manufacturers which brought about the bankruptcy of the most innovative of these instrument-makers, Adolphe Sax; the instrument named after him would never have been conceived without the wind band as a palette of sound, an experimental field ripe for the insertion of a new tone colour. The saxophone is a hybrid, combining the vigorous, noisy sound of the brass with the softer sonority of the woodwinds. It uses a conical metal tube with keys, attached to a single reed; somewhat like an ophicleide — a kind of bass-register keyed bugle — fitted with a clarinet mouthpiece. The result is a peculiar timbre of its own. Berlioz described the original instrument, a bass version, as 'full soft, vibrating, extremely powerful . . . easy to lower in intensity' and definitely superior to the ophicleide; he criticized it only for the difficulty in rendering rapid passages, a fault which subsequently Sax more than corrected.[10] The instrument was soon adopted into the wind band, where it added distinctive colour; the French musical showman Jullien began to feature saxophones in the 1850s. In the symphony orchestra, however, the metallic projection of the reed vibrato sounded so distinctive that even composers who recognized its beauty (many considered it downright ugly) only used it rarely (in the case of Berlioz himself, even though he liked it, never). Its tone was too unsettling, too easily disruptive, even subversive. It needed a new form of music altogether to bring this sensuous metallic oscillation, which Adorno calls 'sexually ambivalent', into its own.[11] But in jazz and the rest of the commercial music which replaces the old traditions of *musica practica*, it acquires symbolic value as the vibrant embodiment of the subjective excitement of the modern age, in place of the ethereal sound of the soaring violin.

The overriding factor in the modernization of the instruments of the orchestra was the need to bring them into conformity with equal temperament. Without the freedom granted by equal temperament, a continuous musical discourse able to modulate through the gamut of diatonic keys is impossible. That discourse is the classical sonata and symphony, with their primary media, the piano and the orchestra. The difficulty of extending the diatonic system to the remoter keys was not just a problem of instrumental technology, however; it was partly a question of calculation and mathematical values. In mean tone temperament, for example, the values for any given set of keys could be easily worked out, but what was good for C major, say, wasn't good for F minor, so as J.S. Bach's contemporary Marpurg put it, you made three scales ugly in order to make one beautiful. In the system of well temperament adopted by Bach and quickly superseded by equal temperament, the problem was resolved by adjusting the values to reduce the discrepancies and render the results more tolerable to the ear. In equal temperament, every semitone is given an equal value.

The general adoption of equal temperament followed the conquest of the piano. It accorded with the presence of the piano in chamber music and the piano concerto, which required that all instruments were tuned alike, and its universal employment to accompany solo and choral singing which demanded the same compliance by the voice. The more widely the piano spread, the more equal temperament became necessary, the more it imposed its needs, until every instrument in the full symphony orchestra of the late nineteenth century was capable of it, and for singers it became second nature.

At two crucial moments in the course of this history, the major manufacturers of the day demonstrated the spirit of modernization by taking a turn towards scientific research. The first, as we saw earlier, was when Broadwood in the 1780s investigated the problem of timbre. The harder and faster a string is struck, the more complex and richer the tone, because it includes more harmonics. It is therefore important what the string is struck with, and where. This was where the research carried out for Broadwood by Gray and Cavallo came in. They examined the nodes — the points along the string around which the partials oscillate. Now in equal temperament the harmonic corresponding to the interval of the minor seventh (C to B flat) is particularly critical. When Gray and Cavallo demonstrated that the best point to strike the string was about one-ninth along its speaking length, this is the point which corresponds to the node of the troublesome overtone. By striking on the node, the worrisome partial is suppressed, and the piano tone sounds smoother and purer.

The second scientific intervention was almost a hundred years later, following the introduction of the cast-iron frame, when decisive improvements were achieved by Theodore Steinway in New York. Most manufacturers now use the method he invented in the 1870s for bending the rim around the frame, which gives added strength to the sound. A further refinement to the iron frame itself finally clinched the superiority of the Steinway sound. Steinway was a German emigrant who maintained a correspondence with the physicist Hermann Helmholtz. Using what he learned from Helmholtz, he was able accurately to compute the vibrations of the short sections of string left over at either end of the speaking length. Bars were raised in the frame to divide these additional lengths further before they reached the pins, to create what is called the duplex scale: the piano had by this time become such a sensitive apparatus that these additional sections now vibrated harmonically with the overtones of the speaking length, and thus once more reinforced the tone. *Pace* Max Weber, this is perhaps the highest expression of rationalization in the construction of musical instruments. Everything is enlisted to reinforce the rationalized temperament with which the instrument is tuned.

The effect of the conquest of equal temperament was decisive. You can hear the result in the different sound of a piece of pre-classical music played on modern and on period instruments. Take a work like Purcell's famous Chacony. Played in a modern transcription on modern instruments, the most poignant dissonances and chromatics easily become either bland or cloying. When it is played, however, by a consort of recorders tuned historically, then it is liable at first to seem to the unsuspecting ear as if it were out of tune — although nowadays the early music movement has familiarized many listeners with these archaic sounds.

The nineteenth century made equal temperament an absolute. Indeed, according to Schoenberg, in moralizing mood, 'to be musical means to have an ear in the *musical* sense, not in the *natural* sense. A musical ear must have assimilated to the tempered scale . . . a singer who produces natural pitches is unmusical, just as someone who acts "naturally" on the streets may be immoral.'[12] Max Weber, however, suspected that equal temperament had created a negative effect. While it solved the problems of tuning, it exacted a heavy price in the atrophy of aural sensitivity. The process, he says, 'takes from our ears some of the delicacy which gave the decisive flavour to the melodious refinement of ancient music culture'. Or again, a few pages later, it has had 'an extensively dulling effect on the delicacy of listening ability'.[13] The result, in a nutshell, is that while piano tuners become musical ear specialists, the players they service suffer from ears whose acuity is blunted. The singer's capabilities too are corrupted, as equal temperament suppresses the microtonal differences in pitch that were characteristic of previous tuning systems, and Weber observed how singers trained at the modern keyboard are liable to imperfect intonation. The phenomenon is even noted by Grove's Dictionary of Music, but there it is hidden away in the entry on enharmonics.

But if this is true, then it means that music in the twentieth century is a story of the return of the repressed.

Notes

1. François Couperin, 'L'Art de toucher le Clavecin', quoted in David Wainwright, *The Piano Makers*, Hutchinson, London 1975, p. 21.

2. Arthur Loesser, *Men, Women and Pianos*, Simon & Schuster, New York 1954, p. 133.

3. Ibid., pp. 348–9.

4. Ibid., pp. 64ff.

5. Eric Blom, ed., *Mozart's Letters*, Penguin, London 1956, p. 54.

6. Harold Schonberg, *The Great Pianists*, Gollancz, London 1964, p. 43.

7. Arthur Loesser, p. 391.

8. See Cyril Ehrlich, *The Piano: A History*, Dent, London 1976.

9. Christopher Small, *Music, Society, Education*, John Calder, London 1980, p. 21.

10. See Wally Horwood, *Adolphe Sax 1814–1894, His Life and Legacy*, Bramley Books 1980, p. 33 and passim.

11. Quoted in Fredric Jameson, *Marxism and Form*, Princeton University Press, Princeton, NJ 1971, p. 15.

12. Quoted in Josef Rufer, *The Works of Arnold Schoenberg*, Faber & Faber, London 1962, p. 143.

13. Max Weber, *The Rational and Social Foundations of Music*, Southern Illinois University Press/Feffer & Simons, London 1977, pp. 102, 123.

PART V

Music in the Age of

Electro-acoustics

9

The Birth of Modernism

Modernization

Whether or not by accident — Adorno thinks not — modernism in music coincides with the emergence of recording. Edison's invention of the talking tin foil dates back to 1877, but in contrast to the cinematograph almost twenty years later, for which the North American inventor also shares some of the credit, its industrial development was relatively slow to get going.[1] It needed a variety of technical improvements, not to mention battles over patents, before the old twelve-inch 78 rpm shellac discs became internationally established as the standard product and the industry took off. The crucial problem was the absence of any method of replicating the cylinder on which the recording was made. Every record was its own original, and the only way of producing more than one at a time was to record simultaneously on a bank of machines, or use a pantograph to copy them a handful at a time. The invention which promised the repeatable recording but not its replication was able to capture the imagination of a potential market, but not to satisfy it.

It was Emile Berliner, a German immigrant to the USA, who achieved the improvements which, as he himself put it, made it possible to 'make as many copies as desired', and thus for singers and performers to 'derive an income from royalties on the sale of their phonautograms'.[2] His most crucial innovation was a method of duplication, by chemically etching the recording on to a metal disc, then producing a reverse metal matrix and using this to stamp the copies. (The 'golden discs' awarded to the best-selling recording artists are not merely symbolic: gold was eventually found to be the best metal for the master discs.) Berliner first demonstrated the technique in 1888. Flat discs, made of hard rubber, first appeared on the market in 1894: single-sided seven-inch plates, as they were called originally, lasting two minutes each; the hand-cranked machines to play them on sold for a mere $12. By the end of the century rubber was replaced by shellac and the size was increased. This solution to the problem of mass reproduction involved, on top of the spacio-temporal separation of listening from performing, the technical separation of the process of playback from that of recording. By 1901, when Berliner joined in the launch of the Victor Talking Machine Company, the gramophone — his word — had become an instrument for listening; a different machine, the cutter, was needed for recording, which was not marketed to domestic purchasers. Not until the spread of magnetic tape after the Second World War were the two functions reunited, and the recording process became even more readily available than 16mm film — an alternative format for low-budget commercial production, cheap enough to be taken up by non-commercial practitioners, and a new means of diffusion at the edges of the market and beyond it.

Fifty years earlier, when the record industry first took off, it was immediately — like the medium of film — international in character. A recording could be made anywhere and then transported across the ocean to be mass produced in a different location. Immigrant communities in North American cities, for example, provided a crucial market for records of operatic excerpts recorded back in Italy. A record made in Milan in 1904 by Enrico Caruso became the first gramophone record to sell a million copies, thus helping to establish the machine's credentials as a respectable form of diversion (at the same time that the other new medium, moving pictures, was evolving an aura of disrepute). This, suggests a writer celebrating the centenary of the invention, 'was the last occasion on which the classical European repertoire had a decisive influence on the development of the record industry'.[3] The claim is exaggerated — it ignores the role of the classical repertoire in the launch of new formats (the LP at the end of the 1940s, stereo ten years later, the compact disc introduced in the centenary year of 1977). But the drift which it indicates is correct, for the industry quickly learned to develop its own repertoire: above all, how to transform the 'raw' music of urban and ethnic popular culture into formulaic commodities of mass consumption. It is symptomatic that what by many accounts was the first jazz recording to sell a million copies, dating from 1917, was by a group of five white musicians calling themselves the Original Dixieland 'Jass' Band, who had journeyed north from New Orleans to reap the rewards of success in New York.

The invention of the phonograph was technically simpler than that of cinematography. Though both of them involved numerous contributing inventions, assorted precursors and rival claims for prior patents, Edison's phonograph used no new scientific knowledge and no new materials. The most frequently cited precursor is Léon Scott, a French amateur scientist who in 1855 invented an instrument to make a visual tracing of sound vibrations, which he called the phonautograph, or sound-writer; it was manufactured by a Paris firm for some years as a scientific instrument for laboratory research. The mechanism consisted in a membrane stretched over the small end of cone hinged to a wooden lever; at the other end of the lever a pig's bristle was suspended over glass or paper covered with lampblack, such that by speaking into the cone while the glass or paper was moved beneath the bristle, a tracing of the pattern of the sound waves would be produced. Scott's device belonged in turn to a long line of experiments concerned with acoustical analysis which would also issue in the telephone. Twenty years further on, another French amateur, Charles Cros, presented a paper to the French *Académie des Sciences* describing a process by which the same device could be made not only to trace a sound but to record and reproduce it; unfortunately he never succeeded in attracting the funds necessary to get it made.

Charles Cros was a poet, and the patron of a literary circle which met at the famous Parisian cabaret of the Chat Noir, which was also frequented by the young Claude Debussy, and where Debussy's friend Erik Satie was employed for a period as the pianist. The conception of a machine capable of fixing and reproducing the fleeting impressions of sound was no less symptomatic of the time and place than Debussy's fugitive music — the casual nature of the connection between them is an ironic touch of history. In this milieu, in the aftermath of the Paris Commune, artists and intellectuals cultivated a new sense of the uncertainty and disharmony of bourgeois existence and the contradictions of trying to satisfy a confused bourgeois audience. In the cafés, cabarets and salons they formed coteries and cliques, and increasingly became, as Walter Benjamin says of Baudelaire, secret agents — agents of the secret discontent of their class with its own rule. They became, in a word, iconoclasts, seeking, instead of the old formulae, the esoteric expression of their own estranged and isolated sensibilities. As another friend of Debussy, the poet Mallarmé, put it, 'In a society which lacks stability and unity it is impossible to create an art which is stable and well-defined.'[4] It is precisely this moment and this milieu to which the literary scholar Renato Poggioli has traced the emergence of the very term *avant-garde* (in which Baudelaire saw the predilection of the French for military metaphors) to describe a new socio-cultural phenomenon, 'the modern concept of culture as spiritual civil war'.[5] As for Debussy, a patriot but not very militaristic, he expressed his opposition to received ideas in his own characteristic image: 'Let us cultivate only the garden of our instincts, and trample disrespectfully upon the flower-beds in which ideas are all lined up symmetrically in full evening dress.'[6]

Modernity, according to Marx, was synonymous with the growing extent and feverish haste of industrial capitalism, 'its constant flinging of capital and labour from one sphere of production into another, and its newly-created connections with the markets of the whole world'.[7] It is no accident, for example, that the 1850s had seen both the rise of the telegraph and the systematic reorganization of stock and capital markets, which were brought under new legal codes and opened to general participation. The telegraph provided the means for the rapid and economical transmission of the information which generated the process, thereby creating a growing market for information which provided the first news agencies, Reuter's and Havas, set up to exploit the telegraph, with the largest portion of their business (for Reuter's, it still is).[8] Soon the telegraph also affected the production of news — when the telegraph came into use, Benjamin remarks, the cafés on the boulevards lost their function as a source of news copy — and fed directly into the massification of the press. The new principles of journalistic information which now emerged — its brevity, comprehensibility and freshness — were economically determined by the costs of telegraphic communication and ideologically angled to give the reader the impression of easily assimilating the information thus presented. But in fact they had quite the opposite effect, for they 'isolate what happens from the realm in which it could affect the experience of the reader'.[9] To this there is soon added the capacity to reproduce photographs in print. The result is a world that in its very modernity becomes increasingly fragmented and illusory; where the words and images that start flooding on to the market, juxtaposed to represent the world as actuality, only become a fragmented and disordered chaos. As Siegfried Kracauer has put it: 'In the illustrated magazines the public sees the world whose perception of it is hindered by the illustrated journals themselves.'[10]

The new technologies began to threaten chaos in the socio-economic infrastructure. A prosaic but symptomatic example was the confusion of railway timetables, which made long-distance travel impossibly complicated because train times were always given in local hours. In 1883, the American railroad companies became the first to adopt uniform time zones. In Europe the problem clearly called for international co-operation, and thus, the following year, representatives of twenty-five countries convened at the Prime Meridian Conference in Washington, and by an agreement which records the British imperial supremacy of the epoch, the standardization of time around the globe was indexed to London and the Royal Observatory in Greenwich. A symbolic moment in modern history. One would be tempted to say that this represented a definitive break with the past, a change in the very measure of history, except that it needed several decades before it was universally adopted, after the radio transmission of a time signal round the world from the Eiffel Tower in Paris in 1911.

In the view of the sociologist Georg Simmel, writing around the turn of the century, the effect of accelerated economic growth and the introduction of ever newer technologies was 'the preponderance that the technical side of life has obtained over its inner side'. It was 'as though the electric light raised man a stage nearer perfection, despite the fact that the objects more clearly seen by it are just as trivial, ugly, or unimportant as when looked at by the aid of petroleum'. This rapid development of 'external civilization' produced diverse and sometimes contradictory effects, such as the growing centralization of the state at the same time as increasing social anarchy, or a growing belief in the possibility of social justice — and the formation of powerful social-democratic movements — at the same time as an increase in individualism (with Nietzsche regarded by many as the prophet of the latter). In this milieu, individual consciousness became a search for security 'beyond all the oscillations and the fragmentariness of empirical existence', driven by a need to escape from life's 'constant unrest'. With the progressive erosion of religious convictions, this longing assumed for many an aesthetic character; and the aesthetic conception became a quest for 'release from the fragmentary and painful in real life'.[11] Hence the rise of a tendency which was linked to the cry of 'art for art's sake', labelled by some as decadent, and exemplified by the Symbolist movement, of which Baudelaire was the prophet, Mallarmé the high priest, and Debussy the bard.

The new technologies of transport and communication brought about the reduction of geographical space and the contraction of time — in a word, a transformation in the social chronotope. Ever newer inventions, from steamship and railway to telephone and wireless telegraphy, created a sense of acceleration and finally of the instantaneous, which implied the destruction of the old-established rhythms of living — and as a result, of the artistic forms that went with them. As David Harvey puts it, 'Modernization entails . . . the perpetual disruption of temporal and spatial rhythms, and modernism takes as one of its missions the production of new meanings for space and time in a world of ephemerality and fragmentation.'[12] The era that provided the technical means to shatter the physical bounds of space and time thus destroyed the conventions of traditional artistic forms. How could the old conventions survive when, as the modernist painter Léger was later to put it, 'A modern man registers a hundred times more sensory impressions than an eighteenth century artist'?[13] Debussy's music was symptomatic of the generation which was the first fully to feel the impact of these transformations, in the city which Walter Benjamin calls the capital of the nineteenth century.

Paris earns this accolade from the German-Jewish intellectual for already nourishing this sense of modernity well before the middle of the century. It was Paris, for example, where the commercial spirit first pioneered new forms of retail practice and urban entertainment. The Arcades of the 1830s and 1840s, built to serve the luxury goods trade, Benjamin calls the gateway to the 'primal landscape of consumption'; later came the *grands magasins* along the boulevards, 'temples of commodity capital' and precursors of modern department stores. To this world of anonymous and placid but eager crowds belonged the diorama, the café, operetta, and the great exhibitions. These exhibitions, initiated by the Great Exhibition in London in 1851, were festivals of capitalist production and the universal reach of nineteenth-century imperialism, 'places of pilgrimage to the fetish Commodity', with all the glitter to distract the masses.[14] Music did not escape inclusion. The exhibitions were invariably accompanied by music festivals, and included competitions for musical instruments. At the Paris Exhibition of 1867 the American piano firms of Chickering and Steinway each spent some $80,000 for brochures and advertising, entertainment, the engagement of pianists, and 'the judicious insinuation of favourable anecdotes and references into newspapers'.[15] An enormous sum for the day. Both manufacturers were rewarded with medals. News of these American successes were among the first messages to be transmitted over the new transatlantic telegraph cable.

Musically, however, by far the most important of the Paris Exhibitions was that of 1889. Indeed one could say that musically speaking this was where the twentieth century — the century of modernism — begins, when a number of young composers, including Debussy (who was then twenty-seven), first encountered the music of Africa and Asia. Debussy's response was a striking turnabout from that of Berlioz to the Far Eastern music he heard at the Great Exhibition in London less than forty years earlier. Instead of being dismissive, he was fascinated and seduced by the exotic orchestras, singers and dancers to be heard beneath the new tower built for the occasion by the military engineer Gustave Eiffel. The significance of this signal shift in perception is revealed in the setting. The Paris Exhibition of 1889 dramatized the official optimism with which the French government celebrated the centenary of the Revolution, boasting of the country's status as one of the great colonial powers. Yet as Max Raphael observed — concerning Picasso's discovery of African sculpture fifteen years later — in the wake of the very imperialism which was symbolized by the World Exhibitions comes 'a certain decomposition' in the unity of European consciousness and the hallowed Greek and Christian canons of its art.[16]

Debussy's response to the music he heard at the Exhibition is a variant on the characteristic complex of Western attitudes towards the Orient which Edward Said has so tellingly analysed in his study of Orientalism.[17] Europe's imaginary geography of the East is divided into two: on the one hand the Orient is dark and threatening, on the other seductive and enticing. On the one hand it is seen as a source of danger, wherein occidental rationality is undermined by Eastern excesses; on the other, these excesses become mysteriously attractive, precisely because they appear the opposite of Western values. Music exemplifies this condition, as if part of the

Western psyche has split off, and comes to fear the embrace of musics which manifest what its own idiom most represses, responding to them as if they were a veritable threat to civilization; while another part of the psyche responds with thrilled fascination, projecting on to these other musics all sorts of secret qualities which require a special effort of discernment. Napoleon, says Said, is a famous instance of this (usually selective) identification by sympathy. Mozart is another; both *Die Entführung aus dem Serail* and *Die Zauberflöte* (in which Masonic codes intermingle with visions of a benign Orient) 'locate a particularly magnanimous form of humanity in the Orient. And this, much more than the modish habits of "Turkish" music, drew Mozart sympathetically eastwards'.[18]

The same is true of Debussy, but where Mozart looked eastwards in philosophical spirit, Debussy was pulled by his ears. The French composer was particularly impressed by the Javanese gamelan orchestra and its complex counterpoint — non-diatonic and of great rhythmic subtlety — compared to which, he later wrote, that of Palestrina is child's play; a particularly significant comparison since he considered Palestrina and Lassus to be the very models of European church music. But when it comes to the gamelan, he said, 'if we listen, forgetting our European prejudices, to the charm of their percussion, we are forced to admit that ours sounds like the barbarous noise of a travelling circus'.[19]

In his youth Debussy had been a committed Wagnerian, and like Mahler in Vienna (his senior by only two years) eagerly adopted a creed of radical utopianism that shocked his teachers and even some of his fellow pupils at the Paris Conservatoire. But he returned from visits to Bayreuth in 1888 and 1889 shorn of his enthusiasm, repelled by the master's 'heroic showmanship' and 'that German mania for continually hammering on the same intellectual nail for fear of not being understood'. Although he never completely turned his back on him, he concluded that Wagner, 'if we may express it in suitably grandiloquent terms, was a fine sunset which might have been mistaken for the dawn'.[20]

In these circumstances, certain elements in the gamelan music he heard at the World Exhibition answered the need for a post-Wagnerian musical language, liberated from the taints of romantic pathos, bombast and gigantism. It was not a sudden conversion. It is said that while Debussy was a student at the Conservatoire during his teens he used to revel in improvising, for the benefit of bewildered fellow students, harmonies of a most unconventional kind. Then in the early 1880s, when he was engaged by Tchaikovsky's benefactress, Madame von Meck, as an accompanist and tutor to her children, he encountered the music of the Russian composers — which seemed to the Parisian audiences listening to the visiting Russian orchestras at the World Exhibition of 1889 to be the most modern of its day. Debussy was particularly impressed by the unconventional harmonies to be found in Moussorgsky. He was later to complain that Wagner was 'a slave to the major—minor diatonic system. His chromaticism is rudimentary, and he is not bold enough to be a real innovator.'[21]

Finally, three years after the 1889 Exhibition, he produced one of the most singular short pieces in the history of modern music, an orchestral work based on a poem by the symbolist Mallarmé, the *Prélude à l'Après-midi d'un Faune*. This extraordinary realization of the poet's sense of vague nostalgia turns out on analysis to do with the reinstatement of the interval known as the tritone: the interval which centuries earlier the Church fathers declared to be unacceptable and illegal, and which they called *diabolus in musica*, because it bluntly contradicted the emerging concepts of diatonic tonality, the tonic—dominant relationship and the triad. Debussy employed the tritone to create a shifting, ambiguous texture — which Mallarmé himself approved of — built around a unique whole-tone scale of his own devising, a scale that cannot function in conventional tonal fashion because it contains neither the interval of a fifth nor a fourth.

In spite of being shorter than many a movement in Beethoven, a snippet beside the gigantism of Wagner, Bruckner or Mahler, Debussy's orchestral prelude seems to float, purified, in a kind of timeless acoustic space. This is the moment when the surface of European music begins to dissolve, the established forms start to break up. Debussy abandons the structural function of triadic harmony. Since triadic harmony is the mark of the established chronotope of the civilized music of opera house, concert hall and salon, the *Prélude à l'Après-midi d'un Faune* prophesies the birth of a new musical chronotope.

No regular fourths and fifths, no tonic and dominant, therefore no modulation. No modulation, thus none of the emotional effusions of Romanticism. In Leonard Bernstein's view, 'this whole-tone scale is self-limiting, autistic, so to speak; in short, it is *atonal* — the first organized atonal material ever to appear in musical history. And because of its atonal nature, this new scale suddenly produces the most ambiguous sounds ever heard in music.'[22] Of course this is not yet full-blown atonality in the Schoenbergian sense. Firstly, because Debussy artfully provides continual tonal landmarks (including Wagnerian harmonies); and second because of an affinity between Debussy's new musical language and ancient modality. It is nonetheless in Paris, with Debussy, that modernism in music begins, just as it began in painting with the Impressionists, and in poetry with Mallarmé, if not Baudelaire before him (all of whom were similarly subject to the pull of the East). This is the moment when the transparent surface of high musical art first grows opaque. The critics who wrote disdainfully over the succeeding years that Debussy's music was formless were not entirely mistaken. The American J.G. Hunecker could even be regarded as distinctly perceptive when he commented:

Rémy de Gourmont has writtenof the 'disassociation of ideas'. Debussy puts the theory into practice, for in his peculiar idiom there seems to be no normal sequence ... The form itself is decomposed. Tonalities are vague, even violently unnatural to unaccustomed ears ... If the Western world ever adopted Eastern tonalities, Claude Debussy would be the one composer who would manage its system, with its quarter-tones and split quarters.[23]

The experience out of which Debussy arrived at this conception was not just some vague hankering after the exotic, however. At least no more so than in the case of the appeal to the Impressionist painters of Japanese art, in which they discovered, instead of the illusory depth of perspective, the value of colour on a flat pictorial surface; exactly as if they felt the same way about perspective painting as Debussy about functional harmony. Debussy himself signalled the affinity when he asked for a reproduction of Hokusai's print *The Hollow of the Wave off Kanagawa* to be placed on the cover of the score of *La Mer*. Affinities like this are symptoms of the increasing need which these artists felt for open forms of composition, both pictorial and musical, free from the congealed solidity of official academic art, its prescriptive attitudes, and the tendency to clothe itself in imitation historical garb which Baudelaire had criticized thirty years earlier.

The Disintegration of Tonality

According to Adorno, the introduction of the gramophone was a crucial determinant of the musical process in the twentieth century, just as photography was of painting. The liberation of painting from objective representation constituted a defence against the mechanization of representation by photography and the consequent cheapening of the image. In the same way, art music reacted against recording and the attendant commercial degradation of the traditional idiom by freeing itself from tonal harmony. Because the music industry was handed over almost entirely to the disposal of 'artistic trash and compromised cultural values', which catered to 'the socially determined predisposition of the listener', radical music was forced into complete isolation — Adorno is thinking essentially of Schoenberg, whose response to these conditions was the most thorough-going and uncompromising.[24] In this equation, the abandonment of tonality equals the abandonment of representation and atonality equals abstraction. Historical justification for this reading is ambiguous. It seems a little too neat. Walter Benjamin remarked how 'Earlier much futile thought had been devoted to the question of whether photography is an art. The primary question — whether the very invention of photography had not transformed the entire nature of art — was not raised.'[25] If the same might be said of recording — that it transformed the very nature of music

— then Schoenberg's solution is only one of several new directions in which music now develops. By defining the most extreme tendency, however, it doubtless played a predominant role in determining the dialogical response of all the others.

There were two phases in the emergence of modernism: the first, from the 1870s to the end of the century, was characterized by growing oedipal revolt, the second, after the turn of the century, by breakthrough and rupture with the past. In the transition between them, traditional categories lost their clarity and function; boundaries became indeterminate and artistic consciousness in the throes of crisis embraced the dissolution of the ego. Plural modes of vision which blimpish bourgeois aesthetics had blocked off were opened up. Time and space took on a new plasticity, leading to the transformation of artistic chronotopes.

Wagner is also a crucial figure for the composers of the so-called Second Viennese School, Schoenberg and his pupils Berg and Webern, and the gestation of the full-blown atonality which they launched upon the world shortly after the turn of the century. Here modernism enters its second phase, and the aesthetic surface which the first phase had already rendered opaque is shattered. It is no accident that the painter Kandinsky, who undertook the first essays in abstraction around the same time, found in Schoenberg a kindred spirit. When he and Franz Marc — fellow members of the group known as *Der Blaue Reiter* — first heard the music of Schoenberg at a chamber recital in Munich in 1911, Marc wrote to a third, August Macke: 'Can you imagine music in which tonality (that is, the maintenance of a key) is completely abandoned? . . . Schoenberg works on the principle that consonance and dissonance don't exist at all. So-called dissonance is only a consonance which has been stretched.' He added that like themselves, Schoenberg seemed convinced of the dissolution of the laws of European art and harmony.[26]

The critical element in Wagner was the intense chromaticism exemplified by *Tristan and Isolde,* and the famous Tristan chord which hangs in the air as a symbol of unresolved erotic desire. As the semiologist Jean-Jacques Nattiez has mentioned, it is possible to find the same chord in earlier works by Beethoven and Spohr, Mozart and Bach, indeed right back to Gesualdo and even Machaut. But in none of those cases does it count as a harmonic entity in its own right; in the Beethoven instance, for example, it occurs in a fast passage where it is immediately resolved in a perfectly expectable manner (Piano Sonata Op. 31 No. 3). What distinguishes the use which Wagner makes of it is its prominence. It occurs at the outset of the prelude, the tempo is *langsam und schmachtend* (slow and languishing), it is repeated three times in the space of half a dozen measures, it recurs frequently throughout the opera. Dramatically and harmonically it has the character of a statement.[27]

The point about the Tristan chord is its unresolved ambiguity. Leonard Bernstein gives a characteristically engaging description of it. As the Prelude starts we wonder what key we are in. Here is a rising interval of a minor sixth which ends with a deceptive cadence suggesting the key of A minor. There is a pause and the phrase is repeated, higher, more intense, with the rising minor sixth now stretched, transformed into a major sixth, suggesting a different key, only for the process to be repeated again and again, the resolution of the ambiguity always itself ambiguous, as if the mounting sense of fiercely unappeased sensual desire can no longer be contained in a tonal framework.[28] As the cultural historian Carl Schorske has put it, in *Tristan and Isolde* Eros returns in surging rhythms and chromatics to assert its claims against the established political and moral order of the state, whose authority is vested in firm metre and diatonic harmony.[29]

If *Tristan* played such a key role in the transformation of tonality, then according to Schoenberg it was no accident. Until the arrival of Wagner, nineteenth-century modern Western music was firmly rooted in the major—minor system. Not only the educated music of the concert hall and the salon but also that of the opera house and the streets, for the spread of the piano — and other pretuned instruments like the accordion — ensured that vocal and popular *musica practica* too succumbed to the hegemony of equal temperament. But with the adoption of equal temperament the art of composition began to juggle with a new formal tension: between the centripetal pull of the firm centre and the centrifugal pull of chromatics and remote keys. The first intimations of this tension can already be found in the late Beethoven String Quartets. Since nothing any more stood in the way of modulation from any key to any other, there began a process of exploration of ever more remote tonalities which corresponded to the Romantic predilection for the strange and unusual, the straining after effect and the oneiric. In Chopin, for example, a broadening sense of harmony combines with gliding modulations and deceptive progressions to produce distinctly unsettling results. These wandering or floating tonalities, this tonal instability, has the effect of undermining the clear and balanced alternation of harmonic centres. Because of this, the music comes to seem more 'subjective', or to some, more 'irrational'. At the same time, because the architectonic use of harmony is diminished, the accent falls on harmonic details: unusual harmonic progressions or even single chords, culminating in the Tristan chord itself.

In short, if triadic harmony had achieved a paradigmatic equilibrium in Vienna around 1800, it proceeded to self-destruct in much less time than it had taken to evolve; especially after the renewed disillusion which followed the failure of the European Revolutions of 1848. It is in *Tristan* that the exploitation of harmonic ambiguity reaches its peak, and the influence of the triad begins to dissolve. Nietzsche was right when he said that here was a new syntax which in Wagner himself is limited, but whose influence on the evolution of music was bound to be inescapable. After *Tristan and Isolde* there is indeed no progressive composer who is able to escape the struggle with the old harmonic vocabulary. Mahler is still producing previously unsuspected chords in his Ninth Symphony in 1910, and parallels to Schoenberg's own harmonic explorations can be found not only in Berg and Webern, but also in Debussy, Bartók and Puccini; not to mention lesser composers like Richard Strauss, Scriabin, Reger, Schreker and Dukas.

It was Schoenberg who theorized what was going on, much as Zarlino in the sixteenth century had theorized the emergence of the major and minor out of the decay of the church modes. To recapitulate what we discovered earlier: Schoenberg perceived the development of Western harmony as an evolutionary process built upon this decay, a product of the progressive articulation of the relation between consonance and dissonance. These apparent polar forces, he says, are really the opposite ends of a continuum. This continuum is the harmonic series, the sequence of overtones that accompanies the sounding of a musical note: the strong consonances are those which correspond to the predominant overtones, dissonances to tones which come higher up the series. Chromaticism and dissonance are therefore not an accident but an integral part of the system. (In other words, they are not the same as noise, which is constituted by inarticulate sounds that fall outside the system.) Moreover, unrecognized chords force themselves on the attention and progressively became articulate figures of musical speech — although never, of course, without resistance. (We also remember Schoenberg's acerbic comments about how his early string sextet *Verklärte Nacht* was rejected for performance because it contained a chord unrecognized by the theory of the day. Said Schoenberg: if there is no such thing as an inversion of a ninth chord, 'therefore there is no such thing as a performance of it, for one cannot perform something which does not exist. So I had to wait for several years.'[30] Today, of course, the chord in question seems innocuous, albeit highly expressive.)

Schoenberg's harmonic sensitivity was fully matched by his sensitivity towards timbre, and in this connection the attraction of the painters of the *Der Blaue Reiter* to his music is extremely telling. There is a deep affinity between Schoenberg's theory of the emancipation of dissonance and Kandinsky's concerning the emancipation of colour. Kandinsky spoke of certain visual effects in painting as *Farbenklänge* or colour-sounds, Schoenberg of the converse, *Klangfarben* or sound-colours, and thus arrived at the novel idea of *Klangfarbenmelodie*, or tone-colour-melody. Alma Mahler records in her *Memories* that he once discussed with Mahler 'the possibility of creating a melody from one note played successively on different instruments'. Mahler, she said, strenuously denied that it could be done. (In public, on the other hand, Mahler always supported Schoenberg, ever ready to align himself with the struggling young composer against the incomprehension of the philistine mob — on two occasions he took a prominent part in quelling disturbances at concerts.)

Schoenberg posited the idea of *Klangfarbenmelodie* in *Harmonielehre*, and pulled it off in the third of the *Five Pieces for Orchestra* of 1909, 'Summer morning by a lake (Colours)'. The piece consists in nothing but a shimmering series of atonal chords, each of which undergoes various transformations of timbre as the instruments playing them change. A footnote in the score says 'The chords must change so gently that no emphasis can be perceived at the instrumental entries, and so that the change is made apparent only through the new colour.' It was this score which Mahler, when Schoenberg showed it to him, said he couldn't read. It was so advanced that even Richard Strauss turned down Schoenberg's invitation to conduct it. Surprisingly, the first performance of the *Five Pieces for Orchestra* was given by Henry Wood at a Promenade Concert in London in 1912. Ernest Newman, the doyen of English music critics, wrote in his review of the occasion:

> It does not often happen that an English public hisses when it does not like a piece of music; but a good third of the people allowed themselves this luxury after the performance of the Five Orchestral Pieces by Schoenberg. Another third of the public did not hiss, because it was laughing, and the remaining third seemed too non-plussed either to laugh or to hiss . . . Nevertheless, I allow myself to say that Schoenberg is not the lunatic that he is generally taken for. Could it not be that the new composer sees a logic in tonal relations which amount to chaos for the rest of us at present, but whose connection could be clear enough to us one day?

Ten years later Schoenberg announced what he called his 'method of composition with twelve tones related only to each other', the infamous technique which Thomas Mann was later to parody in his novel *Doctor Faustus*.

Umberto Eco has described the situation Schoenberg found himself in very simply and directly:

> A musician becomes aware of the crisis of the tonal system the moment he realizes that certain sonic frequencies have so long been identified with particular psychological states that the listener can no longer hear them without instinctively relating them to a particular moral, ideological, or social reality, to a particular vision of the world. When, in order to escape this dead end, the avant-garde musician founds a new language, a new system of sonic

relationships, a new musical form that few people are ready to recognise as such, he condemns himself to noncommunication, to some sort of aristocratic distance. But he does it on purpose, to express his refusal of a system of communication that guarantees him an audience if, and only if, he is willing to submit to an obsolete value system.

So, the avant-garde musician rejects the tonal system not only because it alienates him to a conventional system of musical laws, but also because it alienates him to a social ethics and to a given vision of the world. Of course, the moment he breaks away from the accepted system of communication and renounces its advantages, he will inevitably appear to be involved in an antihuman activity, whereas in fact he has engaged in it in order to avoid mystifying and deceiving his public.[31]

By rejecting a musical model, says Eco, the avant-garde musician actually rejects (more or less consciously) a social model. This implicit rebellion incenses the protesting audience. But it would be wrong, he adds, to assume that this double rejection involves no affirmation.

There is another crucial current within modernism, more diffuse, less focused by theoretical discourse, but equally iconoclastic. For no sooner had internal pressures brought the European idiom of diatonic harmony to the point of collapse than a whole range of external influences began to break in upon European musical sensibilities from the outside. On the one hand, therefore, while the liberation of dissonance led to the negation of tonality in the Second Viennese School, others followed the lead of Paris and Debussy and bent their ears towards non-functional harmony and modal melody. On the other hand, because diatonic harmony had entailed the interdependent subservience of both melody and rhythm, the rupture of harmonic equilibrium also affected rhythmic sensibilities. This opened the door to the rhythmic diversity of 'exotic' musics, including the syncopation succoured by the new and fast-evolving form of jazz. Further, these trends combined, and produced a diversity of experiments in polyrhythms and polytonality, pioneered by composers like Stravinsky and Milhaud beginning around the time of the First World War.

Around the turn of the century, a number of investigators had become aware of non-diatonic inflections in the surviving folk music of the peripheries of Europe. Bartók and Kodály embarked on field trips in Eastern Europe armed not only with pen and paper but also, for the first time, with a phonograph and a supply of cylinders. In the course of analysing the recordings they brought back, they made their signal discovery that these inflections were not the chaotic result of untutored singing and playing, but the systematic product of self-conscious art. (Bartók, we remember, once said that listening to phonographic recordings was like examining musical objects under a microscope.) They also showed that the folk music of Eastern Europe employed both pentatonic and other 'archaic' scales. A high percentage of the melodies they collected were based on the ancient modes, both Greek and ecclesiastical. These discoveries had a profound effect on them as composers, especially Bartók. The results begin to appear in works like his Fourteen Bagatelles for piano of 1908, which contain some of the earliest examples of polytonality — music that is written in more than one key at the same time. In the very first piece of the set, the right hand is marked as being in the key of C sharp minor, with four sharps, and the left hand, with four flats, as F minor (which is close to the ancient Phrygian mode). This clash of keys is precisely calculated. It is the means by which Bartók creates the feel of the 'false' intonation or tuning of folk music.

This is not just a question of exotic effect. Bartók conceived of folk music as the voice of a world of freedom, close to nature, repressed by the tyrannies of conquerors and modern civilization. In Hungary at end of the First World War this had serious political implications, and in 1919, together with Dohnányi and Kodály, Bartók served on the Directorate of Music set up by the revolutionary government of Béla Kun. According to the testimony of the Marxist philosopher Gyorgy Lukács, who served under Béla Kun as a People's Commissar and knew Bartók personally, it was in Bartók's music that the revolutionary trend of the day 'reached its deepest expression and most exquisite manifestation'. Bartók, says Lukács, considered the peasant class 'a natural force' in the artistic struggle to transcend the alienation of modern society; as Lenin said to Gorky about Tolstoy, 'before this Count there was no real peasant in our literature' — except that Bartók, says Lukács, had more 'historical universality'.[32]

The effect of these techniques is again to weaken triadic harmony. Another of Bartók's Bagatelles is cited by Schoenberg in *Harmonielehre* as an example of a crucial tendency to be found 'in the works of some of us', in a passage which links Berg, Webern and himself not only with Bartók but also Debussy and the Viennese Franz Schreker, not to mention Dukas and even Puccini (whose idiom is close, of course, to Schoenberg's mentor, Mahler).[33] All of them were moving towards chords of seven notes and more which annulled the traditional pull of dissonances towards resolution.

In Bartók's case these chords were constructed out of the synthesis of the intervals in the melodic motifs he derived from folk music. It was Bartók himself who remarked that the same thing could be found in Stravinsky. The famous *Petrushka* chord, for instance, really a motif, is nothing more than a combination of the broken triads of C major and F sharp major, which produces a particularly striking effect because these two keys are separated by a tritone — the same forbidden interval which Debussy employed in *L'Après-midi d'un Faune*. Separately, these elements are tonally unexceptional, but superimposed the result is close to atonality, that is, the suspension of a tonal centre. We may call this tonal simultaneity, more akin to cubism than abstraction. It is the musical world not only of Bartók and Stravinsky but also of Ives, Prokofiev, Villa-Lobos, Milhaud, Hindemith, Weill, Revueltas and early Messiaen. In the twelve-tone music of Schoenberg, which leads through Webern to post-war serialism, the triad is wholly abolished. In these other composers the triad no longer reigns supreme in the old way but still operates. This polytonal sound was far more prevalent before the Second World War than twelve-tone music.

Nor is it an accident if composers like Stravinsky, Ravel and Milhaud became fascinated by jazz, which they first encountered by way of gramophone records. There were obvious features in jazz to attract them — the much-vaunted novelty of its rhythms, the techniques of syncopation, swing and polyrhythms — which at the same time eluded European musicologists because they lie outside notation. But as the creation of Afro-Americans, jazz was also crucially inflected by non-European scales of sub-Saharan provenance. Again we remember what we discovered earlier. The African scale has a natural temperament and its intervals are therefore pitched differently. The traces of these 'exotic' scales came across in alterations of timbre and sonority which produced totally new ways of playing what after all were traditional European instruments. A response by the black American to the tempered diatonic scales of European music, in jazz, the Western intervals of a third and a seventh become ambiguous, as the encounter with Afro-American musical sensibility flattens or sharpens them. The result is what are called the blue notes: around the interval of a third, the tone hovers between major and minor; at the seventh, it becomes distinctly modal. The effect is all the greater for syncopation, which strengthens the natural tendency to sharpen accented beats and flatten unaccented ones, so that the syncopated shift from strong beats to weak ones also tends to flatten the note. Bartók found analogous inflections in the folk music of Eastern Europe and the Mediterranean, with the result that on hearing live jazz at a speakeasy in Chicago during his first US tour in 1927 ('they played from a score but many times they improvised and this was fascinating'), he had no need, he said, to fling himself into its arms; essentially there was nothing there he hadn't already learnt about from his detailed studies of Eastern European and Mediterranean folk music.[34]

The New Acoustics

There was another current at work on the European ear at the turn of the century. Parallel with modernization, the scientific knowledge which helped to spawn it was itself modernized and transformed. Some disciplines, as T.S. Kuhn demonstrated in *The Structure of Scientific Revolutions*, threw up a crisis which was strangely analogous to that of modernism: established theories and old value systems collapsed, chaos and anarchy threatened, until new theoretical paradigms emerged and a semblance of order was re-established. The revolution in acoustics happened more quietly, but its long-term effects were equally profound.

The theory of vibrating bodies developed back in the eighteenth century gave little consideration to the role of the ear. It was Hermann Helmholtz who brought acoustics and physiognomy together, in a series of experiments in the late 1850s, which established that the analysis of consonance and dissonance required more than the physics of vibrating bodies but had to include the interaction of sound upon the ear, another vibrating structure which behaved according to its own rules and produced internal phenomena of its own.

Helmholtz effectively unified what before him had been a disparate history of investigation, in which attempts to analyse sound went in tandem with attempts to produce it. For example, according to Brian Winston in his important critique of the myths of modern technology, *Misunderstanding Media*, the idea of speech synthesis goes back to the eighteenth century, when the St Petersburg Academy offered a prize in 1779 for a device which could reproduce vowel sounds. (Interest in language was very much in the air; ten years earlier the Berlin Academy offered a prize for an essay on the origins of language − or what it called the 'invention' of language − which was won by the philosopher Herder.) Machines which could produce vowel sounds or even a few words, by means of the mechanical imitation of the human larynx, were demonstrated in Austria in 1791, America in 1843, and London in 1846.[35]

The relations that Helmholtz developed with instrument-makers were in no way incidental to this research. Learning the secrets of the organ-builder, he detected that with very low notes under certain conditions a fundamental can be heard when there isn't one; by analysing the phenomenon he discovered what he called combination tones and difference tones. These effects are the result of a critical difference in the beat between the combination of tones produced by the organ-builder with separate pipes. Helmholtz observed that combination tones produce beats where the cycles of vibrations strike against each other, and that this beating could be heard: hence we wince at the wolfs of the organ (or, for the modern reader, at high-pitched tones reproduced by stereophonic loudspeakers out of phase with each other). Acutely unpleasant beating is physically painful. Helmholtz thought he saw in this a physiological explanation for consonance and dissonance:

> When two musical tones are sounded at the same time, their united sound is
> generally disturbed by the beats of the upper partials, so that a greater or less
> part of the whole mass of sound is broken up into pulses of tone, and the joint
> effect is rough. This relation is called dissonance.
>
> But there are certain determinate ratios between frequency numbers, for
> which this rule suffers an exception, and either no beats at all are formed, or at
> least only such as have so little intensity that they produce no unpleasant
> disturbance of the united sound. These exceptional cases are called
> consonances.[36]

He also used these discoveries in the analysis of speech, thereby showing
that vowel sounds are made up of harmonic tones.

Later theorists have found the argument about musical consonance
unconvincing, although pragmatic people like piano tuners continue to
listen to the beats to find the right intervals. And pragmatically speaking
Helmholtz's heritage is huge, his work a vital contribution in every branch
of investigation to do with speech and hearing and the analysis and
reproduction of sound. As his own wide range of scientific interests reveals,
there was a continuum joining music and acoustics with the physiology of
hearing and speech and the transmission of sound in any form — the
same continuum that led Alexander Graham Bell, for example, from his
early involvement in teaching the deaf to speak to the invention of the
speaking telephone. The publication in 1862 of Helmholtz's seminal
work, *On the Sensations of Tone as a Physiological Basis for the Theory of Music*,
made a decisive contribution to all these fields, establishing a theoretical
paradigm on which all sorts of people could draw to equal advantage,
from Steinway and Bell and Edison to the Italian Futurists thirty years
later, not to mention subsequent researchers in areas like psycholinguistics. Not least, the heritage of Helmholtz is present in a succession of
initiatives to create electrophonic instruments — new instruments with
new sounds generated by electrical, electromagnetic and later electronic
means — from a device called the telharmonium, which made its debut
in the 1890s, to computerized electronic synthesizers like the Synclavier
a century later.

The link between sound and electromagnetism was first established in
the 1830s, with a device to convert electrical waves into sound credited to a
Dr C.G. Page of Massachusetts in 1837. The effect, which he called
'Galvanic Music', was achieved by revolving the armature of an
electromagnet in front of a negative and positive electrical pole: loud
sounds were emitted which could be varied by altering the strength of the
current in the poles. In 1846, a M. Froment in Paris showed a device
designed not to create sounds but to analyse those made by Page's effect.
Helmholtz himself demonstrated in the 1850s that electrical impulses could
be sent down a line and cause a tuning fork to resonate on the principle of

sympathetic vibration. This was the experiment that Bell began by reproducing when he started work in 1872 on the process that led to his first telephone patent of 1876. Meanwhile, in 1860, a German professor named Philip Reiss paired up Page's noise-emitting electromagnets with Scott's phonautograph to produce a prototype of the telephone. According to Bell's assistant Thomas Watson, 'Probably the physics laboratory of every well-equipped college in the world had one in 1870.'[37] Bell himself constructed a macabre version of the phonautograph in 1874, while immersed in the problem of producing a speaking telephone, using a dead man's ear attached to a metal horn for the cone.

Analogies with music were never far away. Many of the techniques devised in the nineteenth century to transmit or originate sound were given names that alluded to it: galvanic music, harp telephone, harmonic telephone. The terms indicate not only the close relation between the invention of the telephone and new musical technologies, but the curious circumstance that unlike most inventions, the word telephone was in use long before the device itself was achieved, as if sound-from-afar was a dream people had thought up long before the means existed. In fact this was no accident: according to Winston, the term was first introduced at the end of the eighteenth century by a German called Huth in order to distinguish theoretically between visual and acoustic methods of signalling. The former was known as semaphore, and Huth proposed a comparable derivation from the Greek for 'telegraphic communication by means of speaking tubes', or the system he himself proposed, which used megaphones. When the connection between signalling and electricity became evident soon afterwards and appropriated the term telegraphy, it left the word telephone for an idea that was constantly pursued but took till the last quarter of the century to reach fruition. Perhaps the musical metaphors mark the inventors' awareness that their inventions were only what Winston calls partial prototypes. Even the machine described in Bell's first patent was barely up to its intented function, and the patent application speaks of the transmission of 'musical notes differing in loudness as well as in pitch' but makes no specific mention of speech.[38]

But then the metaphor begins to be taken literally, and the idea of a new kind of musical instrument gradually takes shape — not, to begin with, among musicians, though they are not slow with their curiosity. The truth is that the changes that have revolutionized musical perception and practice over the past hundred years are part of a protracted dialogue between music and science, technology and the sonic imagination. The secrets of the instrument-makers guide the investigations of scientists. The imagination of the inventor discovers in the aesthetic domain of music a space for the free play of technical ideas. Then the musician begins to discover in the partial prototypes of the technological imagination a space for the free play of musical ideas.

The first effective musical prototype was probably the original device made by Bell's rival, Elisha Gray, in 1869, a harmonic or musical telephone which employed vibrating discs arranged in a diatonic scale, and for which he managed to sell the rights to Western Union. Doubtless Gray adopted this arrangement of discs because it was easier to accomplish than the transmission of speech — Bell also experimented for a time with tuned metal reeds; but the patent, filed in 1874, speaks of it explicitly as 'a new kind of instrument' which might be able to imitate an accordion or harmonium.[39] However, this was a prospect in which Western Union not surprisingly lost interest, and Grey lost out to Bell.

Twenty years later comes the 'telharmonium' or 'dynamophone' of Thaddeus Cahill, a gigantic musical instrument weighing some two hundred tons which generated sounds by means of dynamos and carried the signal on telephone wires. The second version of the instrument, which Cahill demonstrated in New York in 1906, incorporated switches allowing for changes of timbre by means of the varied combination of pure tones. It also had a volume control, and according to a contemporary report in *McClure's* magazine, it was able to produce any combination of notes and overtones at any dynamic level. With its lack of amplifier or loudspeaker, the telharmonium was like a giant damp squib, and nothing now survives of it but a photograph. However, to Ferruccio Busoni, an Italian composer and pianist living in Berlin and dreaming of a new sonic universe, the news of this device was highly suggestive, and he spoke of it in his *Sketch of a New Aesthetic of Music* of 1907. For Busoni, the telharmonium offered the promise of realizing new musical materials. In particular, an apparatus which allowed 'an infinite gradation of the octave . . . by the simple expedient of moving a lever corresponding to the pointer of a dial' would break the tyranny of the diatonic scale ('those stepping stones twelve in number' as John Cage later called them).

Busoni's enthusiasm was not naïve. 'Only after a long period of careful experimentation and training of the ear', he said, 'will this unfamiliar material become a useful and plastic tool of the art of the future.'[40] But his dream of a new sonic universe began to draw closer after the invention by the radio pioneer Lee de Forest of the valve oscillator in 1915. Based on his own prior invention (in the same year as Cahill's second telharmonium) of the radio valve, the oscillator led among other things to the new electronic pitched instruments of the 1920s, the Theremin, the Ondes Martenot and the Trautonium, with their novel and intriguing timbres which attracted the attention of composers like Honneger, Jolivet, Hindemith and above all, Messiaen.

Noise Redefined

The new instruments involved a redefinition of musical sounds in terms of sonic objects, or groups of elements that are not in themselves musical. It was already the mark of Schoenberg's revolution that thinking about the liberation of dissonance also implied a rethinking of timbre. But here the redefinition of timbre in turn implies the redefinition of noise. Like the symbiosis of consonance and dissonance, noise ceases to be a simple category — the opposite of music — but emerges as the other end of a continuum. This means there is no clear dividing line between a musical sound and a non-musical sound. The whole palette of sounds, including the noisiest instrumental timbres, is opened up.

Timbre is determined by the make-up of the overtones, but is not just an acoustic phenomenon. The textbooks sometimes mention that while overtones lie well within the range of human hearing (which goes up to a frequency of about 20,000 cycles per second) they cannot generally be heard independently, apart from special cases like the jangling sound of bells. We know they are there — if you silently depress the piano keys corresponding to the overtones and then strike the fundamental, you can hear them resonating. Schoenberg, however (who uses this effect in his *Three Piano Pieces*, Op. 11), declared that the overtones are perceived — and exert their influence on the development of music — subconsciously. Anton Ehrenzweig explains that normally the overtones are repressed and replaced by the experience of tone colour, which is projected on to the fundamental. In other words, the process of acoustic perception substitutes the conscious experience of tone colour for the repressed overtones in much the same way that visual perception replaces the continual variations of shape, perspective distortion and colour which strike the retina, with the constant appearance of real things. Ehrenzweig speaks by analogy of 'acoustic thing perception'.

The phenomenon of constant visual shape was already known to medieval students of optics, though it was not until the nineteenth century that visual constancy became an object of systematic study by psychologists, and only in the twentieth that the acoustic equivalents were fully analysed. The acoustic analysis of the components of sound has now shown how differences beneath the threshold of conscious detection play a crucial role in the perception of both music and speech. The biological purpose of such arrangements is quite clear. If adjustment of the visual field were not to be made automatically by the brain, it would hardly be possible for the organism to find its bearings in the world. But adjustment is accomplished and we thus remain unaware of the distortions which make up our raw sense data. (Except, as the art historian Ernst Gombrich has pointed out, when artists force us to pay attention to them.)[41]

Acoustic thing perception serves a similar function to the constancies of visual perception. It provides for recognition of the different tone colours corresponding to the composition of the overtones in different acoustic objects, beginning with the human voice. Hence the evolutionary advantage. The new-born baby is able to recognize its mother's voice within a day or two, long before it has managed to get its eyes into focus and establish constancy of vision; the mother is able equally rapidly to distinguish her own baby's crying. Every individual voice is capable of an infinite range of vocalizations, and in order to fulfil its biological purpose, the perception of constant tone colour in the acoustic object is so arranged that it generally sustains itself through changes in both volume and pitch. We are thereby able to recognize familiar voices across the whole range of vocal expression. In the same way, musical instruments are designed to retain their own characteristic tone colour whether they are played loudly or softly, higher or lower. The tone colour of different instruments is characterized by their formants, or the patterns of resonance within the sound-producing body. The material out of which the instrument is made also affects the distribution of partials in the split-second moment of onset.[42] It has always been a conscious part of musical art to use these properties, to refine them and release their expressive power. In the seventeenth century the violin set a new standard in this regard, and with the technological improvements of the industrial revolution, by the early nineteenth century even instruments like the trumpet had acquired great tonal consistency.

Modernism disrupted the constancy of tone colour. From Debussy on, composers developed techniques of instrumentation which so blend the orchestral palette as to destroy the colour constancy attaching to individual instruments. Where the lower register of one instrument, like the flute, is closer to the upper register of another but lower instrument, like the bassoon, than it is to the other end of its own register, then you can mix the registers up in order momentarily to exploit a 'thing-free' ambiguity which confounds the ear: you cannot tell what instrument is playing. Schoenberg, Berg and Webern were past masters at sharing out a continuous melodic line between different instruments so smoothly that there is no break in tone colour. On the other hand, nor were they afraid to use the kinds of timbre that staid Viennese audiences regarded as noisy but jazz musicians refer to approvingly as 'dirty'.

This sense of deep fascination with sound itself, the properties of the sonic object, is often what unites the otherwise disparate endeavours of composers like Schoenberg, Bartók, Stravinsky or Varèse. It also helps to explain the extraordinary power of their music to disturb, for it involves constant transgression. Ehrenzweig explains: the converse of stable acoustic thing perception is the de-differentiated 'thing-free' play of form which is not found just in modernist music but in any music which foregrounds Dionysian form elements. The new instrumental techniques developed by modernist composers bring with them a sense of danger towards the musical body, which gives their music a unique capacity to distress the listener. Such techniques, says Ehrenzweig, express a central drive towards 'thing destruction', shared by all modernist artists. 'The musician, by obliterating the sharp boundaries of tone colour differentiation . . . resembles the painter who pays no heed to the boundaries of visual things and fuses segments belonging to different thing forms into a phantastic "thing-free" apparition.'[43] Furthermore, by encouraging instruments to imitate each other they demonstrate not only powers of de-differentiation but also imitation and parody, another trait which Schoenberg, Bartók and Stravinsky share.

There were many ways to satisfy the drive to give music a new sound. Busoni, formulating his new aesthetic of music in 1907, dreamed of new electronic instruments and microtonal intervals. Bartók discovered the raw power of untutored folk musicians. Stravinsky, Ravel and Milhaud found themselves drawn to folk musics and to jazz. Varèse, abandoning linearity, thought in terms of acoustic objects, agglomerations of rhythms, timbres and dynamic intensities, which he likened to crystals and other organic growths; the handful of works he was to write between the wars are among the most visionary by any composer. There was also the case of Luigi Russolo, who dreamt the dream of noise-music.

The immediate inspiration for Russolo's ideas came from fellow Italian Futurists: Marinetti's concepts of performance and the music of Balilla Pratella, who published manifestos on Futurist music in 1910 and 1911, proclaiming a new art of noise based on the machine world. Russolo once called the concert hall 'a hospital for anaemic sounds'. As far as he was concerned, Pratella had successfully demonstrated the idea that machine sounds were a viable form of music. The noise instruments he proceeded to construct for concerts in Milan, Paris and London in 1913 consisted in buzzers, bursters, a thunderer, whistlers, rustlers, gurglers, a shatterer, a shriller and a snorter. His manifesto for these concerts, *The Art of Noises*, declares itself a logical extension of Pratella's innovations. The instruments he built were no mere proto-Dadaist gestures. They were derived, by way of Russolo's idiosyncratic form of reasoning, from the acoustic analysis of Helmholtz.

Sound is defined (wrote Russolo) as the result of a succession of regular and periodic vibrations, while noise is caused by irregular motion. Helmholtz declares that a musical sensation is a sound that is stable and uniform, but the distinction between what counts as sound and what counts as noise is not a sharp one. 'We know that the production of sound requires not only that a body vibrate regularly but also that these vibrations persist in the auditory nerve until the following vibration has arrived, so that the periodic vibrations blend to form a continuous musical sound. At least sixteen vibrations per second are needed for this. Now, if I succeed in producing a *noise* with this speed . . .'[44] Hence the rectangular wooden boxes which made up the Futurist Orchestra, containing mechanisms turned by a handle to produce a remarkable variety of distinguishable noises.

Russolo's idea was to create music out of the noise of the machine which typified modern life not by reproducing it directly but by organizing it. 'It is necessary', he wrote, 'that these noise timbres become *abstract materials* for works of art to be formed from them. *As it comes to us from life* . . . noise immediately reminds us of life itself, making us think of the things that produce the noises that we are hearing.' In practice, the results were only a partial prototype of a new kind of music. To the critic who reviewed the London concert in *The Times*, the noises produced by these 'weird funnel shaped instruments . . . resembled the sounds heard in the rigging of a channel-steamer during a bad crossing . . .'. Judging by a recent reconstruction of the event on the BBC music station Radio 3, the remark, although doubtless that of a conservative, was also a genuine attempt to describe what he'd heard. Even Varèse criticized the Futurists for reproducing 'all the agitation of life in the form of noise, which is merely life's most superficial and bothersome element'.[45] Nonetheless, as Jean-Jacques Nattiez has observed, Russolo's rationale amounts to a remarkable anticipation of ideas to be developed more than thirty years later by the pioneer of *musique concrète*, Pierre Schaeffer.

The New Music according to Adorno

At the end of the First World War Schoenberg's situation was critical. He had almost stopped composing and according to accounts like that of Stuckenschmidt, the introduction of the twelve-tone method in the early 1920s was a matter of sheer necessity. But it was also the outcome of an organic process.

Established musical conventions had been 'thrown overboard in a revolt of the collective unconscious', tonality, harmony, melody and rhythm all decomposed, 'eternal laws were revoked'.[46] This created a state of almost limitless freedom bordering on chaos and anarchy. Driven by sheer intensity of expression — usually welling up from the darkness of the unconscious — the music of this period was experienced as the psychopathology of inner disintegration. Adorno compared *Erwartung* to the first psychoanalytic case-studies: the unnamed heroine 'is consigned to music in the very same way as a patient is to analysis' and 'passions are no longer simulated, but rather genuine emotions of the unconscious — of shock, of trauma — are registered without disguise through the medium of music'.[47] Indeed the text was written by a young psychoanalyst, Marie Pappenheim. The more radical the music became, the more its social rejection: concerts would provoke hisses and boos, and on occasion, fisticuffs. Ridiculed by the greater part of the audience, composition became more and more difficult.

A profound need for psychic reconstruction generated a search for new means of organization, and for this it seemed that the only possible basis was the instinctive adherence which the composers involved all discovered in their work to the unconscious principles of motivic composition. Schoenberg, Berg and Webern all found themselves constructing their music through the manipulation of motivic cells. Simultaneously, the pull of chromaticism engendered the unwritten rule that no tone should be allowed to dominate by virtue of close repetition. The result was melodic lines and chords comprising all twelve semitones of the chromatic scale, in short, the special form of cacophony called dodecaphony (from the Greek, *dodeka*, meaning twelve). Schoenberg's method codified this situation (more rigorously than a similar method proposed a few years earlier by Josef Hauer). The whole composition is to be derived from the same tone row, by turning it into a type of magic square. Webern, writing to the poet Hildegard Jone, likens this to the old formula:

S	A	T	O	R
A	R	E	P	O
T	E	N	E	T
O	P	E	R	A
R	O	T	A	S

which reads the same horizontally and vertically both fowards and backwards. The composition is built from the combination of any of the individual rows which comprise the square (which in the musical version, given that the row comprises twelve tones, contains forty-eight versions, reading forwards, backwards, down and up).

But this, says Adorno, is rationalization with a vengeance, bordering on irrationality. 'The material transformation of those elements responsible for expression in music, which — according to Schoenberg — has gone on uninterruptedly throughout the entire history of music, has today [the mid-1940s] become so radical that the possibility of expression itself comes into question. In the process of pursuing its own inner logic, music is transformed more and more from something significant into something obscure — even to itself.'[48] In a word, the alienation of artistic technique becomes the very substance of the work, and the shock of incomprehension illuminates the surrounding mean-inglessness. 'Modern music . . . has taken upon itself all the darkness and guilt of this world. Its fortune lies in the perception of misfortune; all of its beauty is in denying itself the illusion of beauty . . . Modern music sees absolute oblivion as its goal. It is the surviving message of despair from the shipwrecked.'[49]

In 1943, when Adorno gave a copy of the manuscript with this account in it to Thomas Mann, the latter found it exactly what he needed to help him write the novel he had just begun, the story of a composer called Adrian Leverkühn. A sorry misunderstanding gave immediate notoriety to the novel when it was published in 1949. Mann ascribes to his fictional composer the invention of a technique of composition in all essentials identical to the twelve-tone method Schoenberg introduced a quarter century earlier. Schoenberg, in a letter to *The Saturday Review of Literature*, strongly objected, piqued to discover that the conductors Bruno Walter and Otto Klemperer were mentioned in the book by name, but not himself, who was the intellectual author of Leverkühn's compositional technique. Moreover, Leverkühn 'is depicted from beginning to end, as a lunatic. I am now seventy-four and I am not yet insane, and I have never acquired the disease from which this insanity stems. I consider this an insult . . .'.[50] As for Adorno, whom Schoenberg calls the author's 'informer' and 'a former pupil of my late friend Alban Berg', 'Mr Adorno is very well acquainted with all the extrinsic details of this technique and thus was capable of giving Mr Mann quite an accurate account of what a layman − the author − needs to tell another layman − the reader − to make him believe that he understands what it is about.'

The attack is doubly ironic. First of all, Adorno's study is actually a sustained defence of Schoenberg against his arch-rival Igor Stravinsky. Adorno asserts that the worldly success of the anti-hero to his own anti-hero is based on little more than growing sham, increasing sterility, and infantile regression. Secondly, the origin of this feud is Schoenberg himself, and dates from 1925, shortly after Schoenberg had adopted the serial method and Stravinsky had turned to neo-classicism.

Schoenberg even set his attack to music. The two composers were both present at the annual festival of the newly-founded International Society for Contemporary Music in Venice, but apparently failed to meet. Webern, writing to Berg a few weeks after the event, reported Schoenberg's comments thus: 'He told me about the disaster of "modern music", including Stravinsky, of whom he said he had had his hair cropped close', adding that 'he *bachelts*' − which might be translated as 'he Bachifies'.[51] On his return to Vienna, Schoenberg wrote a ditty and set it to music as one of his *Three Satires* for mixed chorus (Op. 28): 'Who's that coming along? /

Why, it's little Modernsky! / He's got himself a pigtail, / Which looks very pretty! / What *real* false hair! / What a wig, / Just (as little Modernsky imagines) / Like Papa Bach.' In a preface to the score, Schoenberg identifies those on whom he turns his mockery as the 'seeming tonalists', the 'back-to people', the 'folklorists' and all the other '-ists', who for him are only mannerists. Stravinsky commented many years later simply that 'in 1925, [Schoenberg] wrote a very nasty verse about me (though I almost forgive him, for setting it to such a remarkable mirror canon)'.[52]

Venice 1925, then, is the birthplace of a myth which Adorno sanctions at the end of the Second World War with the publication of his *Philosophy of Modern Music*. This is not to say that the charges against Stravinsky are unsustainable. According to Michael Tippett, on whom Stravinsky had a strong influence, in earlier works like *Petrushka*, *Le Sacre du Printemps* and *Les Noces*, Stravinsky's Dionysian tendencies were at their apogee. 'After *Les Noces* Stravinsky made an apparently final and quite voluntary sacrifice to Apollo. The Dionysian elements never return in the same force. Instead we get the fullest possible development of Stravinsky's passion for classical order, clarity of texture and precision of technique.'[53]

But we also get something else: Stravinsky's kleptomania. From the *Ars Nova* of the Italian Renaissance all the way to ragtime and jazz, by way of Lully, Handel, Bach, Pergolesi, Mozart, Rossini, Glinka, Tchaikovsky and Russian folk song, Stravinsky steals freely from the most diverse sources to provide himself with musical models and materials. This list, says André Boucourechliev (a composer himself), 'is enough to show the speed and the appetite with which [he] criss-crossed the whole of musical history ... abolishing the notion of history as chronology at a single stroke'.[54] According to Adorno 'the composition feeds upon the difference between its models and the use which it makes of them'. The concept of musical material contained within the work itself, a central idea for Schoenberg's school, can hardly be applied, he says, to Stravinsky, whose music 'continually directs its gaze towards other materials, which it then "consumes" ...'.[55]

What Stravinsky demonstrates here but Adorno misses is a prophetic answer to a radically different question: the challenge of what Bakhtin calls the heteroglot nature of contemporary culture. In short, the proliferation of competing and intersecting voices in contemporary time-space, the contradictions between the present and the past, between different epochs of the past, between different tendencies in the present. In the face of this anarchy of cultural codes, when the possibility of individual style all but evaporates, the composer's job sails perilously close to pastiche. But where Schoenberg decries, Stravinsky embraces the cultural polyphony of the times — including in the end the twelve-tone technique as well. He is like an oracle speaking in some new kind of pidgin, using what Jameson calls 'the masks and voices stored up in the imaginary museum of a now global culture'.[56] In this sense Stravinsky can be seen as a precursor of the peculiar kind of dissociation from history to be found in postmodernism. In short, it is Stravinsky, not Schoenberg, who stakes out the future.

Notes

1. On the invention of cinematography see Michael Chanan, *The Dream That Kicks*, Routledge & Kegan Paul, London 1980.

2. Quoted in ibid., p. 63.

3. Derek Jewell, 'Popular marriage begets golden children', *The Times*, 18 April 1977.

4. Stefan Jarocinski, *Debussy, Impressionism and Symbolism*, Eulenburg, London 1976, p. 31.

5. Renato Poggioli, *The Theory of the Avant-Garde*, Harvard University Press, Cambridge, MA 1968, p. 96.

6. Jarocinski, p. 94.

7. Marx, *Capital*, Vol. I, p. 384.

8. See Michael Chanan, 'The Reuter's Factor', in Colin Chant, ed., *Sources for the Study of Science, Technology and Everyday Life 1870–1950*, Vol. 2, Hodder & Stoughton, London 1988.

9. Walter Benjamin, *Charles Baudelaire: A Lyric Poet in the Era of High Capitalism*, Verso, London 1973, p. 112.

10. Quoted in David Frisby, *Fragments of Modernity*, Polity Press, Cambridge 1988, p. 154.

11. Georg Simmel, 'Tendencies in German Life and Thought Since 1870', quoted in ibid., pp. 42–5.

12. David Harvey, *The Condition of Postmodernity*, Basil Blackwell, Oxford 1990, p. 216.

13. Quoted in Stephen Kern, *The Culture of Time and Space 1880–1918*, Weidenfeld & Nicolson, London 1983, p. 118.

14. Benjamin, *Baudelaire*, p. 165.

15. Arthur Loesser, *Men, Women and Pianos*, Simon & Schuster, New York 1954, p. 512.

16. See Max Raphael, *Proudhon, Marx, Picasso*, Lawrence & Wishart, London 1980, pp. 130, 132.

17. See Edward Said, *Orientalism*, Penguin, London 1985.

18. Ibid., p. 118.

19. Quoted in Jarocinski, p. 95.

20. Ibid., p. 100.

21. Quoted in M.D. Calvocoressi, *Debussy*, Novello, undated, p. 7.

22. Leonard Bernstein, *The Unanswered Question*, Harvard University Press, Cambridge, MA 1985, p. 251.

23. Quoted in Nicholas Slonimsky, *Lexicon of Musical Invective*, University of Washington, Washington 1965, p. 92.

24. T.W. Adorno, *Philosophy of Modern Music*, Sheed & Ward, London 1973, pp. 5–6.

25. Walter Benjamin, 'The Work of Art in the Age of the Mechanical Reproduction', in *Illuminations*, ed., Hannah Arendt, Schocken, New York 1969, p. 227.

26. Letter of 14 January 1911, in Miesel, ed., *Voices of German Expressionism*, Prentice Hall, Englewood Cliffs 1970, pp. 67–8.

27. Jean-Jacques Nattiez, *Music and Discourse, Towards a Semiology of Music*, Princeton University Press, Princeton, NJ 1990, p. 219.

28. Bernstein, p. 233.

29. Carl Schorske, *Fin-de-siècle Vienna*, Weidenfeld & Nicolson, London 1980, p. 347.

30. Quoted in ibid., p. 233.

31. Umberto Eco, *The Open Work*, Hutchinson Radius, London 1989, p. 140.

32. Györy Lukács, 'El Mandarin Milagroso contra la alienacion' ('The Miraculous Mandarin against alienation'), in *Bela Bartók, Escritos sobre música popular*, Siglo Veintiuno, Mexico 1979, pp. 240ff.

33. Arnold Schoenberg, *Theory of Harmony*, Faber & Faber, London 1978, p. 407.

34. Hamish Milne, *Bartók*, Midas, London 1982, p. 73.

35. Brian Winston, *Misunderstanding Media*, Routledge & Kegan Paul, London 1986, p. 306.

36. Helmholtz, *On the Sensations of Tone as a Physiological Basic for the Theory of Music*, Longmans, London 1912.

37. Quoted in Winston, p. 215.

38. Ibid., p. 321.

39. Quoted in ibid., p. 316.

40. Ferruccio Busoni, 'Sketch of a New Aesthetic of Music' in *Three Classics in the Aesthetic of Music*, Dover, New York 1962, p. 95 (translation amended).

41. Ernst Gombrich, *Art and Illusion*, Phaidon, London 1962, p. 46.

42. In the case of the trumpet, for example, the first and second partials develop more rapidly, while the upper partials take longer to reach their full energy. This is why the trumpet sounds sharper and more clearly defined than the violin, where the upper partials come first, and the first two partials develop more slowly:

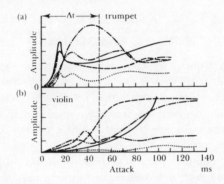

43. Anton Ehrenzweig, *The Psychoanalysis of Artistic Vision and Hearing*, Routledge & Kegan Paul, London 1953, pp. 156–7.

44. Quoted in Jean-Jacques Nattiez, *Music and Discourse, Toward a Semiology of Music*, Princeton University Press, Princeton, NJ 1990, p. 50.

45. Ibid., p. 51; italics in the original.

46. H.H. Stuckenschmidt, *Twentieth Century Music*, Weidenfeld & Nicolson, London 1969, p. 90.

47. Adorno, *Philosophy of Modern Music*, pp. 39, 42.

48. Ibid., p. 19.

49. Ibid., p. 133.

50. Quoted in Patrick Carnegy, *Faust as Musician. A Study of Thomas Mann's Novel Doctor Faustus*, Chatto & Windus, London 1973, pp. 168–70.

51. H.H. Stuckenschmidt, *Arnold Schoenberg*, John Calder, London 1977, p. 309.

52. Stravinsky and Craft, *Conversations with Igor Stravinsky*, Faber & Faber, London 1959, p. 69.

53. Michael Tippett, *Music of the Angels*, Eulenberg, London 1980, p. 89.

54. André Boucourechliev, *Stravinsky*, Gollancz, London 1987, p. 18. The works concerned include *Symphony of Psalms* and the *Mass* (Ars Nova), *The Soldier's Tale* and the *Ebony Concerto* (jazz), *Apollo Musagetes* (Lully), *Oedipus Rex* (Handel), *Pulcinella* (Pergolesi), *Dumbarton Oaks* (Bach), *The Rake's Progress* (Mozart), *Jeu de cartes* (Rossini), *Le Baiser de la fée* (Tchaikovsky). *Mavra* borrows from Glinka, Tchaikovsky and gypsy songs, while *Les Noces* takes its inspiration from Russian folklore, etc.

55. Adorno, *Philosophy of Modern Music*, p. 183.

56. Fredric Jameson, *Postmodernism or the Cultural Logic of Late Capitalism*, Verso, London 1991, p. 65.

10

Musica Practica Electronified

Music and Media

In the 1930s, confronted by the Great Depression, capitalism behaved substantially as Marx believed it did: it pursued the revival of the economy through the expansion of what he termed secondary production. That is, it sought to stimulate demand for consumer products, in order in turn to stimulate production in the primary sector (which comprises heavy industry and the production of the means of production). The new technologies of communication and the new media fully reinforced this process, and along with new brands of canned foods, domestic cleaning materials, toiletries and drugs, came the growth of advertising carried by radio and the mass circulation press, designed to succour the desire for consumption as much as to promote individual products. With cinema, radio and the record industry as major economic players, no insignificant part of this effort was directed towards consumption in the culture industry, including music. Indeed music was now involved in all three media.

Early in the century the gramophone had achieved its status as purveyor of mass culture through two moves. First it separated audition from performance − the effect to which Walter Benjamin drew attention. However, the early cylinder was almost impossible to duplicate − thereby stimulating a market it was unable to satisfy − and the second stage, the introduction of the disc, which provided the means for mass production, had the effect of separating playback from recording, marketing to the consumer the means for the former but not the latter. Thus, mechanical reproduction not only removed the performer from the presence of the listener, robbed the listener of participation in the act of performance, and deprived the performer of the listener's encouragement. It also made recording into an exclusively commercial business.

These developments had marked effects on both performance and listening. The former began to lose its spontaneity and became the art of the repeated take. The latter turned attention away from the excitement and risk of the act of performance, towards the reproduction and its surface sheen. The coming of radio, though it undoubtedly made music, good as well as bad, available to increasing numbers of listeners, reinforced the passivity of the listener and confirmed the growing emphasis on the consumption of music rather than its production. The 1920s and 1930s saw not only a dramatic fall in sheet-music sales, but a general reduction in public musical performance, both professional and amateur. Britain witnessed the collapse of several concert organizations, culminating in the demise of the British National Opera Company in 1929, while by 1935 the number of active music societies had fallen to under two thousand, or less than half the number a decade earlier.[1]

The introduction of the talkies also affected music profoundly, and not only because of the loss of employment for cinema musicians. Undertaken by the studios in order to counter competition by radio and the decline of cinema-going, the sound film lifted music out of the dark of the theatre pit and on to the screen, incorporating it for the first time directly into the process of film production. As a consequence, musicals began to play a significant role in the recovery of the record industry after the Great Depression. The sound film also provided new opportunities of employment for a small proportion of musicians equipped to meet its special demands, with the result, in America, that Hollywood soon began to rival New York as the primary centre of musical production in the United States. With its huge influence on musical taste, this deserves a special study of its own.

All this, from the point of view of capital investment, corresponded to the orthodox method of promoting technical innovation in order to reinvigorate a market. Quite different was the move in the 1930s by the film industry's own primary sector — the manufacturers of cameras and film stock — to develop a new market among non-commercial users. The spread of documentary and amateur cine are both results of the introduction of 16mm equipment, which the trade press labelled sub-standard and distributors kept off the cinema screens. The promotion of amateur cine, however, represented a radical shift in the focus of market exploitation: a turn towards a new form of consumer participation, in which capital proceeds to market not just cultural products but the technified means of cultural production itself.

The precedent for this process was the gambit pioneered by George Eastman back in 1888 with the introduction of the Kodak. It was a simple box camera using roll film, was advertised with the famous and novel slogan 'You press the button, we do the rest'; the brand-name was devised to be easily pronounceable in as many languages as possible (not originally because Eastman's ambitions were global but to reach the multilingual immigrant population of the United States itself). The first Kodaks were sent back to the factory where the film was removed, processed, and returned with the camera loaded up with a new roll of film (which also makes it one of the first examples of mass consumer mail order).

Camera and film, like gramophone and record, are linked commodities. This in itself is nothing new. There was always a link, for example, between the sale of musical instruments and the consumption of sheet music. What is new is the technification of the process on the one hand, and the capital-intensive nature of the necessary technical support industries; and on the other, the application of new techniques of advertising and market exploitation, themselves a product of the stimulus provided by the growth of the mass media. The promotion of 16mm film, for example, involved the creation of a tertiary consumer industry, including magazines, competitions and prizes catering for the amateur. The whole process, which has been repeated not only with 8mm, Super-8 and then video, but also with products like hi-fi and computers, was ideologically geared to containment of the activity, promoting it at the level of a harmless and inconsequential hobby, partly to keep it from encroaching on the domain of professional commercial production and partly because ever since the introduction of the printing press, the dominant ideology has always been suspicious of unvetted cultural activity. Indeed freedom of the press itself was not a right which was ever granted willingly, but was only achieved through defiance and struggle against power and authority. Music is not exempt from the ideological effects of this process just because it is lacking in articulate content. As one Joseph Klapper of CBS told a Congressional Committee inquiring into 'Modern Communications and Foreign Policy' in 1967, 'the broadcasting of popular music is not likely to have any immediate effect on the audience's political attitudes, but this kind of communication nevertheless provides a sort of entryway of Western ideas and Western concepts, even though these concepts may not be explicitly and completely stated at any one particular moment in the communication'.[2] And not just popular music either.

There is good reason to believe that without the effort of ideological control, new gear might always reveal a different character; for the same struggle takes place over and over again with every new medium and format of cultural production. The German writer Hans Magnus Enzensberger mentioned the example of duplicating machines in the Soviet Union, or rather the lack of them. The Soviet bureaucracy, he wrote in the 1970s, 'has to deny itself almost entirely an elementary piece of organizational equipment, the duplicating machine, because this instrument potentially makes everyone a printer. The political risk involved, the possibility of a leakage in the information network, is accepted only at the highest levels . . .'[3] The threat of non-approved uses is present in every piece of media technology because in the process of increasing the volume and circulation of cultural production it creates the space for more voices to be heard. Enzensberger holds that the danger is inherent in the technology, and everywhere, not just in totalitarian states, the media are subject to restraint by economic and administrative measures. Brecht observed something similar about radio back in the 1920s, when he asked why it was organized in the hierarchical form of broadcaster to audience, one to many, centre to periphery, when the technology of radio transmission permitted two-way traffic. But what happened to radio was the same thing that had happened with the gramophone: reception was separated from transmission in the same way as playback from recording.

The cheap new film gear of the 1930s was classed as amateur and substandard and separated from the commercial film industry, the means of production of cinema proper. Nevertheless it was used to produce alternative forms of film, especially in the shape of the documentary and workers' film movements. The same thing was to happen again with video in the 1970s and 1980s, but on an even wider scale, ranging from the experimental video of individual artists in Europe and North America, to political videos by anonymous groups in countries under dictatorship like Chile. Nowadays, with the multiplication of public media and private means of replication, the mechanism of the market has created a condition in which cultural products circulate more and more freely beyond its control − in the same way that *musica practica* has always done. In the new phase of postmodernism, the techniques of reproduction look set to become a parallel agency of cultural production, and threaten to nurture new creative potential of their own. And because this involves the increasing technification of communication, this potential inevitably extends the attack on the old traditions. Music, as we shall see, provides a paradigm for this development.

Electrophones

The equivalent in music to amateur cine or video is not just the technology of reproduction, whose primary effect is to boost the audience for recorded music, but new instruments. Records promoted musical knowledge but in crucial respects the evolution of style and technique had much more to do with new instruments − based on electromagnetic and electronic principles − which impact directly upon *musica practica*. Nothing now survives of Thadeus Cahill's Telharmonium of 1906 except a few photographs, but within a generation, and following the technological development of oscillators, amplifiers and loudspeakers, new electronic pitched instruments became legion, bearing fancy names like Aetherophon, Couplex Organ, Electrochord, Electronde, Electrone, Emicon, Hellertion, Klaviatur Sphaerophon, Magnetton, Ondes Martenot, Ondes Musicales, Orgatron,

Phototone, Pianotron, Radio-Synthetic Organ, Rangertone, Superpiano, Theremin and Wave Organ. Most of these instruments have become museum pieces, and one or two continue to make appearances on the concert platform, but their successor, the keyboard synthesizer, is now ubiquitous.

Technically, these instruments followed a number of different principles. Some were monophonic, like wind instruments or the violin family. Here one of the main problems was that of resonance. The rich overtones of the natural substances used in traditional instruments make for a plastic and malleable sound, which is focused by the design of the instrument. Too many unfocused resonances and the instrument sounds noisy, like the medieval shawm. Too diffuse, and the sound becomes muffled, like drums (though even in the case of drums the tone can be articulated and inflected in a number of ways; in African drum music different ways of striking the instrument produce pitches quite distinct enough to be able to articulate the 'syllables' of drum speech).

At the same time, different styles of playing will draw different kinds of sound out of any instrument (which will often, for reasons investigated earlier, remain beyond the powers of notation). This is a test which every new instrument must pass. And the consequences of these properties for the design of electrophonic instruments are considerable. Without a rich envelope of naturally produced partials, the sound of the electrophone is clearly synthetic. Most researchers pursued the model of the harmonium or organ, and tried to produce a band of tones controlled by a conventional-looking keyboard, although this is complicated. To produce such a complex timbre, the instrument must produce multiple tones which are overlaid, modulated, filtered and amplified in various ways before reaching the loudspeaker. Notwithstanding, the rate of experiment increased at the end of the First World War with the rapid dissemination of knowledge of radio technology, and assorted researchers in university laboratories engaged in a host of undocumented and half-remembered attempts to build their own instruments. The main obstacle to progress, the lack of an effective mechanism for varying the timbre, began to find solutions around the end of the 1920s. The American Lorens Hammond produced his first electric organ in 1929, the prototype for an electrical instrument cheap enough to be taken up in commercial popular music. Hammond employed a synchronous motor to drive a series of ninety-one tone-generators, using alternating current to produce the component tones from which the synthesis of timbre is built up. At the side of the manual a harmonic controller enables the player to set the timbre, providing eight harmonics in nine gradations of intensity. The Hammond organ was simple enough to play for it to be taken up after the Second World War by a new generation of amateurs and untutored pop musicians, who thus acquired enough keyboard technique to speed the adoption of the electronic keyboard synthesizer which began in the late 1960s.

The main problems with the synthetic sound of the electric organ were indifference to the touch of the player, sluggish response, distortion, and a monotonous timbre. It is one thing to synthesize a complex tone, quite another to give it the mobile character of the sound of the traditional instrument. Much more interesting for the experimental instinct among classically-trained musicians were a small number of monophonic instruments with a special affinity to the class of traditional instruments producing a continuous tone across their full range — in other words, where the pitch of the note is not mechanically fixed and limited to the equal-tempered scale.

The first of these instruments was built by the Russian Leon Theremin, who began giving demonstration concerts in the Soviet Union in 1920 and then took it abroad, arriving in America on a tour sponsored by the Wurlitzer company in 1927. The timbre of the instrument was somewhat eerie, somewhere between an out-of-tune violin and a strangled soprano. Its visual appearance was unprecedented (and much more 'futurist' than Marinetti's boxes): an oblong container with two metal antennae, one in the shape of a rod, the other a loop. These antennae are connected to high-frequency oscillators inside the box. The player, without touching the antennae, moves one hand up and down the rod to change the pitch, the other manipulates the space in front of the loop to control the volume, thus appearing to conjure sound from the very air. Learning to play the instrument is learning to control its continuous glides and portamento, but cannot be regarded as any more difficult in principle than learning to play a violin.

Theremin's career is a historical curiosity. In New York he was taken up by a rich artistic patron and established a studio where he trained performers and developed further versions of the instrument, but polite society dropped him when he married a black dancer. A few years later he disappeared — apparently kidnapped by Soviet agents and taken back to Moscow. Nothing more was known until the time of glasnost, when a story appeared in *Moscow News* reporting that he was alive and well. After an American documentarist tracked him down and interviewed him, it emerged that he had been set to work for the KGB in devising electronic eavesdropping technology for espionage purposes and had developed the first bug.[4] After Theremin disappeared, the instrument migrated to Hollywood, where it gradually became a favourite effect among film composers like Bernard Herrmann, with an ear for unusual sonorities. (He uses it, for example, to singular effect in the Hollywood science-fiction movie *The Day the Earth Stood Still* of 1951, which is scored for theremins with electric violin and bass.)

What determines the take-up of a new instrument is partly its timbre, and partly the musical space which opens up for it. A more advanced instrument based on similar principles to the theremin was built by the French musician Maurice Martenot in 1928. Known as the *ondes martenot* ('Martenot waves'), it improved on the theremin by extending the range to five octaves and introducing a wider spectrum of tone colours. Milhaud, Varèse and Honegger included it in orchestral works written in the 1930s. Messiaen's *Fête des belles eaux* of 1937 is scored for six of them, and he subsequently used the instrument several times. Messiaen, above all, is the reason why the instrument acquired its followers and makes regular, though sporadic, appearances on the concert platform. The most successful electric instrument, however, prior to the keyboard synthesizer, was neither of these, but the electric guitar.

In terms of technique the electric guitar was not so much a new instrument as an old one with knobs on, but in terms of timbre it provided radical new possibilities which were especially favoured by recording. Again the origins of the instrument are obscure, and written sources extremely thin on the ground, but it was born in response to demand from musicians in the popular music industry, where its locus has remained. According to a recent study of popular music culture by Richard Middleton, the idea of amplifying the guitar 'began in reponse to guitarists' demands for their solos to be heard through the sound of big bands'.[5] Middleton gives no details, but another recent source is more specific. 'Throughout the 1920s,' says the music journalist Jon Lewin, 'many guitarists and DIY enthusiasts tinkered with ways of making the guitar louder, producing prototype electric guitars and basses, and primitive amplifiers based on . . . valve radio technology, though none ever made it into production. The coil-and-magnet guitar pickup as used today was invented around 1930 [by George Beauchamp] and the first electric guitars (made by Rickenbacker and National) went on sale to the public in 1931.'[6]

The instrument was first taken up by jazz musicians, initially to strengthen the rhythmic backing and then for solos, with Eddie Durham apparently being the first jazz guitarist to take a solo on record, around 1933. Electrification began by encouraging traditional guitar techniques (like fast runs, vibrato and glissando). It also created wondrous new effects (like wah-wah and fuzz), doubtless many of them discovered by accident. When its electric twang became the dominant timbre of rock'n'roll after the war, it also provided crashing rhythms aimed at the solar plexus and the imitation of the wail and cry of the human voice. Above all, it became a symbol of masculine power. Another recent writer explains what any lead guitarist, he says, will tell you about the importance of feedback. 'Hold your guitar close to its loudspeaker, and the note will sustain, indefinitely if you want it to. The sound from the loudspeaker feeds back to the guitar's strings, which carry on vibrating.'[7] The guitarist will describe a feeling of power when playing this way — and heavy-metal fans will describe their feelings of identification with this demonstration of musical power.

From Reconstruction . . .

Post-war reconstruction rapidly picked up where the 1930s left off. Consumer expansion began with the relaunch of television and magnetic tape recording, which both made their first appearance in the 1930s, and the appearance of the LP and EP record formats. Then came the introduction of the transistor and the integrated circuit. Like radio at the end of the First World War, the rapid spread of television in the late 1940s and early 1950s came from the reconversion to consumer electronics of the huge productive capacity in electronics which had been developed to fight the war. New record formats were the record industry's fight-back against television, in the same way the sound movie had been cinema's response to radio. The development of the tape-recorder was a by-product of military victory, when entrepreneurs in the United States pounced upon German patents which their defeat made available as part of the spoils. As for transistors and transistorized circuits, the R&D was promoted by the space agencies' need for miniaturization, and the results benefited all branches of electronics: they were not only more reliable than valves but cheaper and easier to mass produce, leading to both a fall in price and increase in ease of use. They also required less power, and the appearance of battery-operated transistor radios which could be carried around anywhere ensured that radio broadcasting more than held its own against encroachment by television. Indeed in Third World countries it was only in the 1950s and 1960s that radio became the principal medium of mass diffusion. The transistor also helped to facilitate the development of computer technology, since the computer chip represents the miniaturization of the transistor.

In classical music, the initial impact of the tape-recorder after the war was partly a direct commercial challenge to the big monopolies on their own ground. As Roland Gelatt explains in his history of the gramophone:

> For an investment of a few thousand dollars one could buy a first-class tape-recorder, take it to Europe (where musicians were plentiful and low-salaried), and record great amounts of music; one could then bring the tapes back to America and have the 'custom record department' of either Columbia or RCA transfer them — at a reasonable fee — to microgroove records. One not only could, one did. Between August 1949 and August 1954 the number of companies in America publishing LP recordings increased from eleven to almost two hundred.[8]

In fact, a similar situation had developed in the 1920s: the technology of electrical 78rpm recording had permitted a good number of small and often local record companies to flourish, especially in the United States — the 'indies' or independent labels which promoted jazz and blues and the other popular musics upon which the monopolists brazenly fed.

These independent labels were wiped out by the Depression. When tape-recording arrived a new generation of independents sprang up, this time in both the popular and the classical music markets, and the monopolists had to renew their efforts to maintain control of the market. In due course they succeeded in taking over most of the new record companies, partly by grace of the Dutch transnational Philips, who conquered the emerging market for a portable tape format with the launch in 1963 of the audio cassette. Smaller than the rival cartridge formats introduced over the preceding few years, its operation could hardly have been simpler; to ensure its success, Philips handed out manufacturing rights to anyone who wanted to produce the cassettes, provided they used Philips's specifications. At first this stood to the monopolists' advantage, but as access to the necessary duplication plant expanded, more and more producers entered the scene. A dozen years later, when a new generation of independent record companies appeared, this time catering for alternative rock, punk and black music, the major record companies had to redouble their efforts. Over the course of time the new independents were duly swallowed up, but the same thing happened again in the late 1980s, this time in the classical sector, where the introduction of the CD encouraged a new generation of independent producers to cater for a range of specialist tastes ranging from early medieval to Californian New Age.[9]

The economic law which operates here is the ease with which small operators can take advantage of expensive new technologies whose research and development has been borne by the market leaders. A crucial aspect of this process, easily overlooked, is the link which is repeatedly forged between independent record producers and musicians at the forefront of renovation in *musica practica*, especially in the genres of popular music; which suggests that the growth of the market is not a purely passive affair. This would seem less true of companies who busy themselves with the top end of the classical market, yet this too is demand-driven, as the gradual absorption of these labels by the major companies attests. But the big monopolies cannot manage without the independents, for it is always the small capitalists who open up new areas of the market not yet exploited by big capital. In short, in the domain of cultural production the classic conditions described by Rosa Luxemburg continue to operate. The majors need the independents in the same way that industrial capital needed the small producers who play the role of pioneers towards technical change and new markets. But music manages in this way to loosen its subordination to the market and claim the space for original currents of expression.

At the end of the war, in the great hunger on the European continent for spiritual rebirth after the ravages of fascism, musical art showed its extraordinary resilience in the renewal of pre-fascist modernism and the rapid burgeoning of a new avant-garde. It happened, the music publisher Ernest Roth has recalled, virtually unassisted. The promotional support which publishers had been used to giving composers for a century had dried up in the economic and political troubles of the 1930s. When serial music rose from the ashes of the war, 'there was no publicity at all. Its . . . supporters were themselves surprised.'[10]

For the new generation of composers emerging at the end of the war, the choice of idiom was hardly in question. The post-war situation is neatly summarized by Umberto Eco when he compares Schoenberg's concert piece *A Survivor from Warsaw* of 1947 with the concerto written by Richard Addinsell for the film *Dangerous Moonlight* in 1940. Schoenberg, commemorating the Warsaw Ghetto, is able to express 'an entire culture's outrage at Nazi brutality' only because he is using a new musical language.

> Had Schoenberg used the tonal system he would have composed not the *Warsaw Survivor* but the *Warsaw Concerto*, which develops the . . . subject according to the most rigorous laws of tonality. Of course, Addinsell was not a Schoenberg, nor would all the twelve-tone series of this world suffice to turn him into one. On the other hand, we cannot attribute all the merit of a composition to the genius of its creator. The formal starting point of a work often determines what follows: a tonal discourse dealing with the bombing of Warsaw could not but lapse into sugary pathos and evolve along the paths of bad faith.[11]

The cultural establishment had no alternative but to fall back upon composers who in one form or another retained the pre-war idioms of chromaticism or polytonality, which now began to sound familiar. Rather than *A Survivor from Warsaw*, concert planners preferred to programme Richard Strauss's *Metamorphosen*, the private lament of the ageing one-time Nazi sympathizer for the bombing of his home city of Munich and its opera house, which from an ethical point of view is little better than Addinsell: a late example of chromatic expressionism incapable of registering the true scale of the Nazi horror.[12] Such patronage, apparently forgiving of past political indiscretions of both left and right — but not the indiscretions of the present — turned the best composers slowly but surely from *enfants terribles* into mainstays of tradition, thereby alienating them from the new generation, who now saw relatively little difference between Richard Strauss, Hindemith, Milhaud, Copland, Walton or even Benjamin Britten.

It was partly in order to save himself from this fate that Stravinsky, who was politically no radical and creatively a long-time servant of Apollo, now abandoned tonality and took up twelve-tone technique. A few of Europe's cultural radio stations, keen to re-establish their credentials, began to provide material support for experimental music, and in due course the resurgent avant-garde managed to eke advantage from the market growth of capitalist reconstruction — in spite of hostility in traditional cultural quarters, and the aggressive nature of the challenge which their music threw down to the audience.

The movement was associated with the famous summer school in Darmstadt. Set up at the end of the war to help rectify the isolation imposed in Germany by the years of Nazi Kulturpolitik, Darmstadt became an open forum which drew young composers from all over Western Europe, and in due course from further afield too. One of them, Luciano Berio, has described it as a place swarming with 'musical adventurers . . . merchants of sonic carpets . . . graphic extravaganzas, political gestures and musical cure-alls'; nevertheless 'those years were, to say the least, fundamental'.[13]

It was in Darmstadt that Olivier Messiaen composed his first serial work, with its impeccably objective title: *Mode de valeurs et d'intensités*, 'Mode of Values and Intensities' (the first of four Études de Rhythme for piano), which had such a strong influence on younger composers like Boulez, Nono, Pousseur, Stockhausen and Berio himself. One of the towering figures of twentieth-century music, Messiaen held the living of a church organist. This, in the grand scheme of musical ambition, is to stake out identification with Bach, apparently a backward-looking situation in which to locate oneself. But Bach — according to Adorno and Mann — was not a simple reactionary, more like a creative force sitting astride the cusp between an old and a modern musical idiom. Warning us that 'the controversy whether Bach belongs to the Middle Ages or already to the Modern Age is undialectical', Adorno considers the presence in Bach of a medieval tradition, which, like the absolutist state, did not bow unprotestingly to the demands of the rising bourgeoisie.[14] The stronghold of this tradition was the style of sacred music which Johann Sebastian made his own, and his problem — according to Adrian Leverkühn in *Doctor Faustus* (Adorno speaking through Thomas Mann) — was not how to write harmonically in the form of polyphony, but how to write polyphonically in a harmonic language. Not, in other words, how to write 'modern' music in an ancient style, but how to write the old music in the modern manner.

History does not repeat itself, but Messiaen's situation was quite similar. He chose the church because he refused to bow unprotestingly before the godlessness he witnessed in the most terrible of all wars. We know about this from his ominously entitled *Quatuor pour la fin du temps* ('Quartet for the End of Time'), written in a prisoner-of-war camp. His problem became how to write religious music in a time when, like belief itself, neither harmony nor polyphony seem possible any more. Forced to reinvent a devotional idiom from scratch, he turned towards Eastern philosophy and Eastern music, and to nature: he engaged in the most detailed study of birdsong anyone has ever undertaken. Marrying up these sources with a scheme of simple affirmative non-developing harmony in the monumental *Turangalila* Symphony, he created a unique musical discourse around the idea of love, both religious and erotic (this, according to his own testimony: metaphysical composers, distrusting words, often use them tokenistically). Musically, defying equally the prescriptions of left and right, he became not a centrist but a bridge between different realms of alienated experience. Messiaen's music is hugely restorative, and for as long as it lasts, returns to the non-believer the capacity to feel the deep consolation of mystical faith.

The new form of serial composition which Messiaen helped to define took the principle of the twelve-note series and applied it systematically to the other main musical parameters. In this way duration, and hence rhythm, along with key aspects of timbre like dynamics and attack, all come to be governed by the same rubric of mathematical coding as pitch. The result of this 'total' or 'integral' serialism is to regenerate the very sound of music as a kind of impersonal pointillism, which to youthful ears constituted an appropriate new paradigm for post-war sensibilities. 'What I was after', Boulez later said, 'was the most impersonal material. Personality had to be involved, of course, in bringing the mechanism into action, but then it could disappear after that. To have the personality not at all involved was a necessity for a while.'[15]

Boulez called this the 'zero point' of composing; the term evokes Roland Barthes's first book, *Writing Degree Zero* (published in 1953), where he begins his life-long task of dissecting the claims of literary style and narrative, and warns us that literature is like phosphorous, 'it shines with its maximum brilliance at the moment when it attempts to die'.[16] For most critics what Boulez provided was evidently a zero point of listening. A few felt forced to admit that the technique managed to generate its own special beauty — at least in the hands of a composer like Boulez, hailed by Stravinsky and Adorno alike — but there were also hostile attacks apparently motivated by Cold War ideology. It is the fashion, wrote the musicologist—composer Herbert Eimert in 1957, 'for empty-headed critics to make out that the systematic "management" of musical material is identical with the terrorist rule of force in totalitarian political systems'. One such 'social critic' held that serial technique produced the programme music of the concentration camps, or that of a Kafkaesque world of inhuman bureaucracy. But to hear in this music, says Eimert, 'the counterpart to political totalitarianism, is just as witless as to appeal to "Nature" when what one really means is textbook harmony'.[17]

Even for some of the survivors of pre-war modernism, however, total serialism was simply going too far. Stuckenschmidt, for example, wrote that the impression it made 'even on a listener who has read the commentaries beforehand' was one of chaos, in which melody and harmony were suppressed in favour of shock effects of dynamics and timbre. 'The fact that these shock effects were organized according to pre-chosen series was only of theoretical interest.'[18] Besides, the method was based on a fallacy, for the number twelve in any other parameter than pitch is arbitrary, perhaps even fetishistic. Another critic, this time of the post-war generation, wrote that the listener is 'faced with a strange anomaly, for *everything* in the music is significant to the composer, insofar as everything is subjected to some kind of serial necessity which he has established, yet *nothing* is significant to the listener, who is incapable of divining that necessity and hence of relating each entity to the morpohology of the whole. Consequently the music has nothing to offer but its surface.'[19] This was still some time before surface reflection and the exploration of its properties was identified as one of the characteristic modes of postmodernism.

Boulez acknowledged the risk of sterility when he used the title of painting by Klee, 'At the limit of the fertile country', as a motto at the head of a score with the characteristic title *Structures I*: in this direction there is nowhere further to go, all is barren. Thereafter he proceeded to redistribute his musical equations to achieve a breakthrough in expressivity, creating in the process a more personal style, at once diaphanous and veiled; among the first fruits of this breakthrough, *Le Marteau sans Maître*, dating from 1955, was hailed by Stravinsky as the best thing yet by a post-war composer. A setting for voice and ensemble of three symbolist poems by René Char, a few lines each of concentrated expression, the voice breaking into great leaps and strange melismatic acrobatics as the poet 'searches weeping for a habitable head' (*'Cherche en pleurant la tête habitable'*), it must stand in here for the work of a whole number of composers who demonstrated the cogency of this ear-bending new music.

Scored for female voice and small ensemble, *Le Marteau* betrays in its instrumentation a curious relationship to non-European musics not unlike that of Debussy, to whom Boulez has frequently declared his allegiance. The xylophone evokes the African balafon; the vibraphone, the Balinese gamelan; the guitar, the Japanese koto. This has nothing to do, says Boulez, with 'the clumsy appropriation of a "colonial" musical vocabulary' to be found in the numerous *rhapsodies malgaches* or *cambodgiennes* of the early years of the century; his aim was 'to enrich the European sound vocabulary by means of non-European listening habits, some of our traditional classical sound combinations having become so charged with "history" that we must open our windows wide in order to avoid being asphyxiated'.[20]

The same frustration is associated with the name of John Cage, and in the early 1950s drew Cage and Boulez together. Cage, who brought the example of American experimentalism to Darmstadt in 1956 and in the process helped to change the direction of the European avant-garde, also turned to the Orient, but in a very different way. For one thing, Cage was a child of California, a deceptive place where the frontier ends and the west points to the east, and where native intellectuals cultivate naïveté and dream of ancient oriental wisdom. As a student in Schoenberg's composition class at UCLA in the mid-1930s, Cage learned from the master that he had no talent for harmony.[21] According to one story, Schoenberg declared he was no composer — but an inventor of genius. The prediction is borne out in the series of works he produced between 1939 and 1952, using various novel combinations of percussion and electrics, which he called *Imaginary Landscapes*. The instrumentation speaks for itself: the first uses two microphones, to amplify a Chinese cymbal, a piano played on the inside, and variable-speed turntables playing radio-station frequency test records; Nos. 2 and 3 introduce the first use of contact microphones (derived from the electric guitar pickup) combining turntables and electrical sources with regular percussion; in other words, the invention of live electronic music — this was in 1942, *before* the advent of *musique concrète*. The most notorious is No. 4 for twelve radios, dating from 1951, while No. 5, completed the following year, is one of the first tape pieces, using material from fifty-two gramophone records.

By this time Cage had enrolled in the Japanese philosopher Daisetz Suzuki's class in Zen Buddhism 'back east' at Columbia University, and in 1951 began to use chance techniques derived from the Chinese *I Ching* to determine the values of the notes and sounds of his music. In *Imaginary Landscape No. 4*, each radio requires two players, one to regulate the tuning and the second the volume, according to a score which scrupulously notates loudness levels, duration and station tuning whose values Cage determined by chance operations. Chance here operates on two levels, since no two performances would ever capture the same sounds anyway. (The piece works best in fairly intimate sorroundings in a venue where reception is clear, in which case it becomes mesmerizing. In a large formal concert hall where reception is poor because the casing of the building blocks the signal, the piece falls flat.) His object was 'to free sound of all psychic intentionality . . . let sound be itself, rather than a vehicle of human theory and feeling'. This evacuation of the subject position of the composer, which pre-echoes the French literary theorists' idea of the death of the author, is clearly cousin to the impersonality sought by Boulez.[22]

Cage belongs, of course, to no tradition except that of the American eccentric — but this is a fraternity which makes a special showing in music. His confrères include figures like Ives and Ruggles; Henry Cowell and his tone clusters; Harry Partch with his forty-three-note scales; and Conlon Nancarrow, whose rhythmically intricate pieces for player-piano that are so beguiling were written in Mexico, where he settled after fighting in the International Brigade in Spain when the US authorities refused to renew his passport. Ruth Crawford Seeger shared much of this sensibility, Varèse, as an adoptive American, was an honorary member, and Satie their mascot. The eccentric, however, is by no means the innocent he or she may try to seem. To express the desire for spiritual liberation by rifling the conceptual apparatus of the great mystical philosophies of the East is perhaps only another symptom of the loss of selfhood in the West. It is therefore an ambiguous position, which combines (to follow Edward Said) certain habits of thought rooted in the mentality of the colonizer, typical of Orientalism, with the desperate need to escape from them. Cage, it must be said, succeeds in escaping.

However, when Boulez later criticized Cage for the 'adoption of a philosophy tinged with Orientalism serving to mask fundamental weaknesses of compositional technique', it was because the French composer had become worried that his own total serialism was only the obverse of throwing dice: both were forms of number fetishism, the one relying on arbitrary and mechanistic automatisms, the other on extreme nonchalance. Boulez, in attempting to distinguish serial music from chance music and distance himself from American experimentalism, advanced the term aleatoric (from the Latin *alea*, dice) to describe the use of controlled choice as an integral element of the musical structure, in contrast to the randomness cultivated by Cage. The term caught on for music that played with elements of chance and choice alike, ignoring the differences Boulez was trying to bring out. The same thing, of course, had happened with the word 'atonal', which in defiance of Schoenberg was widely used without differentiating between heavy chromaticism, polytonality and twelve-note music. Boulez similarly found himself lumped together in general awareness with diverse composers of different tendencies — Cage and other American experimentalists such as Morton Feldman; the Europeans Nono, Berio, Stockhausen, Ligeti, Penderecki, and Xenakis — nothwithstanding the often considerable contrasts in their compositional technique and the radically different-sounding music that resulted. Not everyone, however, denied the broad similarity between them. To Feldman, 'The fact that men like Boulez and Cage represent opposite extremes of modern methodology is not what is interesting. What is interesting is their similarity. In the music of both . . . what is heard is indistinguishable from its process. In fact, process itself might be called the Zeitgeist of our age.'[23]

Feldman is not of course alone in this opinion. The emphasis in music on process and impersonality prefigures the emergence of certain contemporary philosophies, especially in France, which are similarly focused. The structuralism of Barthes and Lévi-Strauss begins in the idea of language (or rather what Saussure called *langue*, the language system) as a structure, whose properties are structural properties. From this a picture emerges of the artistic composition as a text rather than (as in Bakhtin's view) an utterance, and the composer of this text as a machine for producing textual effects. In the end, the very idea of the author is seen as an 'effect' of the text, nothing more than the traces in the discourse of the act of generating that discourse. This idea, which always leaves a residue of doubt where literature is concerned, is nowhere so fully realized as in certain musical compositions of this period, on both sides of the Atlantic.

. . . to Deconstruction

For all these tendencies, the crucial catalyst was electro-acoustics, which was equally responsible for the transformation of popular music. The story is one of a variety of techniques affecting different areas of musical creation in different ways which then gradually converge, and in the process bring about a certain confluence, or at least interchange, between different musical camps and genres.

Serialism itself was forged in the electronic music lab. With the development of electronics, the phenomenon of sound, as a whole and in its parts, becomes susceptible to radical new forms of investigation, analysis and manipulation. However, confronted with a sonic world potentially unlimited but in the form of entirely abstract possibilities, not only are the traditional acoustic categories of music rendered inadequate and ineffective, but the reorganization of those categories becomes imperative. Although Webern's pre-war pointillism was seen in Darmstadt as the fountainhead of integral serialism, the full redefinition of the parameters of music was only achieved through the medium of electronics and in response to its exigencies: the very term 'parameter' was imported into musical terminology in the 1950s in the course of this process. Moreover, because much of the equipment which was employed came from scientists studying linguistics, acoustics and information theory, new theoretical categories were ready to hand, and new theoretical paradigms mushroomed. This process of redefinition was accomplished so rapidly that by 1955 Eimert was able to say that no longer was Webern to be found at the centre of the new music.

Part of Darmstadt's importance was its composite character as a workshop and an open forum for debate and performance, which made it like a testing laboratory for new music where experiments could be carried out in a quasi-scientific spirit. Hence the input from figures like Werner Meyer-Eppler, who ran the Institute for Phonetics and Communication Research at Bonn University. The first results of work carried out there by Eimert were presented at Darmstadt in 1951, the same year as a presentation of *musique concrète* by Pierre Schaeffer, who worked with the information theorist Abraham Moles.

Schaeffer's work built on attempts made during the 1930s to develop the musical use of noise. Following the introduction of optical film sound, experiments were carried out with film soundtracks by Norman McLaren in New York and the Whitney brothers in Los Angeles. At the same time, composers as diverse as Milhaud, Hindemith, Varèse and, at the end of the decade, John Cage, had all experimented with discs played on variable-speed turntables to create striking, though limited, transformations of sound. Schaeffer, a radio sound technician in Paris, began to experiment in 'scratching' records during the war and by 1948 had formulated a method of composition that freed the sonic material from association with its origins. Taking sounds from different sources, from pianos to railway trains, he produced a series of short pieces by playing them at different speeds, forwards or in reverse, isolating fragments and superimposing them. This was *musique concrète* — concrete music as opposed to abstract music made by putting notes on paper — and by the early 1950s Schaeffer had attracted around him a group of young musicians keen to know more, including Messiaen and his pupils Boulez and Stockhausen.

Moles, in his classic work on information theory and aesthetic perception, explained that there is no real difference between *noise* and *signal* except in intent. What intrigues him most (comments Eco) is the ambiguous message — by which he means the message which is at once particularly rich in information and yet very difficult to decode.[24] This not only describes the sensation enjoyed by partisans of the new music, it also explains their distaste for music in the traditional idiom: it was too easy to decode and very limited in what it said.

Information theory brought an immediate paradigm of order to the potential chaos of noise. Musical sound is now understood, both in theory and in practice, to include noise of all sorts, since all sound can be measured along the three fundamental parameters of frequency, duration and intensity. Pitch and timbre are now defined by means of frequency analysis; dynamics becomes intensity measured in decibels; and rhythm and tempo are dissolved into the duration of the notes or the sounds, measured in those days in the inches-per-second of the tape on which they were recorded. (Nowadays they are measured by computer clocks in milliseconds — and the number of memory bytes they occupy.) In the music of the past, the dominant parameters were pitch and duration, responsible for melody and rhythm; timbre and intensity were secondary. What electro-acoustic music achieves is to annul the hierarchy between these parameters: to dethrone pitch and rhythm, and to foreground colour and intensity. It then modulates them in order to create depth and to make the sounds move, which multi-channel sound projection renders palpable, creating new kinds of sonic landscapes. These soundscapes have the character Schaeffer called acousmatic — a sound without a source — recalling the Acousmatics of ancient Greece, initiates in the Pythagorean brotherhood who were required to listen in silence to lectures delivered from behind a curtain so that the lecturer could not be seen. The music that results is composed not of notes but of the sound-objects, disposed within the acoustic space of the soundscape and endowed with properties like the sound envelope, perspective and mobility. This operation involves a grammar so radically new that no one can say exactly what it consists in. Composition takes place at the level of how to quantify an amplitude vibrato accelerando.

The term acousmatic aptly describes the modern media, in which music (and all types of sounds and noise) come to us through loudspeakers, which are carriers, not sources. It is no accident that the first forms of electronic music were Cage's live electronics and *musique concrète*, which are both composed of the manipulated fragments of sound-objects, whether disguised or undisguised. *Musique concrète* came of age with the introduction of the tape-recorder; radio stations were the first centres of research and experiment, and different schools of thought quickly began to emerge about what this new kind of music could do. The first dedicated electronic music studio in Germany was set up by Herbert Eimert at the radio station in Cologne, where he was joined in 1952 by Stockhausen; here they set out to create not *musique concrète* but electronic music proper, in which 'natural' (i.e. recorded) sounds were taboo. Pretty soon Stockhausen started to incorporate them anyway, and in Italy in 1955, Luciano Berio and Bruno Maderna set up a studio at a radio station in Milan which brought the two compositional principles together from the outset. In the same year, at the University of Illinois, Lejaren Hillier and Leonard Isaacson began to programme a computer to compose a piece for string quartet; their efforts were oddly naïve but pointed in yet another direction, subsequently explored by Iannis Xenakis in Paris. Then in 1959 another electronic device made its musical debut when the Columbia-Princeton Electronic Music Center acquired the RCA synthesizer, which the corporation had begun to develop six years earlier as a research instrument for the synthesis of human speech.

Here in embryo, though not yet integrated into a single system, were all the means for the creation of a totally new acoustic universe, completely unrestrained by any existing order. Their integration only needed the computer. Even so, these means gave rise in no time to the most extraordinary and diverse music. By 1960, Pierre Henry had created extended meditational works, several of them for Maurice Béjart's dance company; Ussachevsky and Luening had produced their first pieces; Pousseur, Boucourechliev, Boulez and Xenakis had all composed studies; Cage had produced some more collage pieces. Louis and Bebe Barron had even created a soundtrack for a science-fiction movie version of *The Tempest* called *Forbidden Planet*. Above all, Varèse had composed his *Deserts* and *Poème électronique*, and Stockhausen, *Gesang der Jünglinge* and *Kontakte*.

The co-ordinates of this new musical universe are paradoxical. One of the most remarkable effects of electronic music is the transformation of the space in which it is heard. Composers quickly understood the value of multiphonic reproduction, and became involved in the construction of auditoria for electronic music. For the 1958 Brussels World Exhibition, Philips, Europe's leading electronics enterprise, commissioned a piece from Varèse; they gave him a studio at their headquarters in Eindhoven to compose it in, and from Le Corbusier a pavilion to play it in equipped with 350 loudspeakers. The experience prompted Le Corbusier's young assistant, Iannis Xenakis, to abandon architecture and devote himself to music. Later Stockhausen had a hand in designing a pavilion for an exhibition in Japan. The listener in such an environment, surrounded by sound, feels suspended in a space whose walls are alive, and which seems to contract and expand from the size of a womb to beyond the horizon. The effect can be felt even in halls poorly adapted to the purpose. Nor is it an accident that this is often music without beat or rhythm, whose movement is wholly organic and pulsating, and which therefore also transforms the experience of time. The result has been that major electronic works in the 1960s by composers like Stockhausen and Berio created new musical paradigms whose influence carried far beyond electronic composition itself, for they marked a radical shift in the musical chronotope.

There are differences, of course, between high serialism and Cagean experimentalism, just as there are between serialism and *musique concrète*, but this paradigm shift is overarching, with characteristic variation in emphasis within the experimental movements on either side of the Atlantic. In Europe, Boulez summed up for everyone when he wrote that 'Classical tonal thought is based on a world defined by gravitation and attraction; serial thought, on a world that is perpetually expanding'.[25] Eco offers another version of the same analogy when he explains that:

> The multiple polarity of a serial composition in music, where the listener is not faced by an absolute conditioning centre of reference, requires him to constitute his own system of auditory relationships. He must allow such a centre to emerge from the sound continuum. Here are no privileged points of view, and all

available perspectives are equally valid and rich in potential. Now, this multiple polarity is extremely close to the spatiotemporal conception of the universe which we owe to Einstein . . .[26]

No wonder the sound of a work like *Kontakte* suggested the constant soft whisper of the universe detected a few years earlier by radio telescopes, which the astronomers Penzias and Wilson, who first noted the phenomenon, suggested was a trace of the surviving energies of the Big Bang in which the universe was formed.

This music was utterly unprecedented. Mostly, these works seemed to escape all conventions of communicability and to operate without any recognizable codes, like a completely hermetic artificial language which was programmed to generate itself. A somewhat baffling condition for semiology and music critics alike — although perhaps no more so than music has always been. But it makes you wonder, as Eimert put it, 'whether perhaps it is not the symphony recorded on tape or disc that is the synthetic, and electronic music the genuine article'.[27]

Popular music underwent a parallel transformation which began with the introduction of magnetic tape-recording. Tape-recording shook up recording technique in both the classical and popular sides of the business, but differently. In classical music, tape editing meant it was no longer necessary to select between the best of several alternative takes of a complete item, but a 'perfect' version could be assembled from several imperfect ones. This affected the organization of the recording session partly by helping to take the pressure off and reduce recording time. (Later, studio time increased again when the introduction of stereo made the recording process more complicated.)

In popular music a whole new method of musical production evolved. The job of the engineer was split up as disc-cutting was removed from the studio to the record factory, leaving the recording engineer to concentrate more on the signal coming from the microphones rather than putting it down on the disc. The engineer became a mixer. At the same time, the control room came to house a proliferation of equipment to monitor and control the signal — delay lines and reverberation units, equalizers, filters, compressors and limiters. Then, hand in hand, came the multi-track tape-recorder and stereo; the first four-channel tape-recorders were introduced in 1958, and eight- and sixteen-track recorders were available by late 1960s. At this point pop music becomes a new form of musical construction. Direct recording — to disc or tape — relies on microphone placement, equalization, acoustics and mixing *before* recording. Multi-track recording allows mixing to take place afterwards, in the process of re-recording, known as mixing down or remixing. This, some commentators argue, is what distinguishes popular music from classical music. For example, according to Bruce Swedien, a recording engineer who has worked in both fields (and won Grammy awards for recordings by the likes of Quincy Jones and Michael Jackson),

> When I started recording classical music (I worked for RCA in Chicago, my gig was recording the Chicago Orchestra) I soon began to feel as if I was taking dictation, or something. In other words, the most that I could do in recording classical music was to re-create the original sound-field. On the other hand, in pop music (all types, rock, R&B, etc.), the only thing that limits the sound image that we create is our own imagination. Mix up those reverb formats, get crazy, don't try to rationalize anything.[28]

According to another, the remix 'is a unique artistic act whose artistry is produced through the technology', since the craft is in manipulating both the *sound* and the music'.[29] Indeed the rock critic Simon Frith has argued that tape-recording allowed producers and engineers to manipulate performances in the same way it allowed musicians to manipulate sound. With multi-track recording, not only could parts of different takes be edited together but individual parts could be altered without changing others played alongside (more or less). Each track can be manipulated separately, different effects can be added, the tracks can then be recombined and balanced with other tracks and the final mix sent to another recorder. As a result, multi-track recording puts the producer and recording engineer firmly in charge of the studio, but it also creates new musical possibilities; the new mode of production therefore begins to turn the recording engineer − the mixer − into a musical creator of a new kind.

In some cases, the remix has given birth to new genres. According to one account, the development of reggae is an example. Engineers, says the sociologist Dick Hebdige, experimented by mixing the tracks together on the final tape in different ways. 'For instance, ska and rocksteady records were mixed differently. In ska, the vocal track had been given prominence . . . but on the new rocksteady records, the singers' voices tended to be treated like any other instrument.' Pride of place was given instead to the 'dread ridims' of the bass guitar.[30]

Changes in recording technology seem to affect control-room procedure first, musicianly performance second. The 'action' moves from the floor of the studio to the control room, where the mixing and editing equipment is located. The problem for the performer is now more than the lack of an audience, but the altered status of interpretation, especially in a situation where performance becomes fragmented. This, however, is the same in popular and classical music alike. As one opera singer put it, 'You have to put over emotion in bits and pieces, and all the time you feel you're singing not just for an evening but for always.'[31] In a single act the performance is removed from an audience and from time, and expression and the impression of spontaneity become the objects of technique and control.

Paradoxically, however, recording also returns to *musica practica* something of its primacy, and this effect is also felt in different camps. In classical music, the record engenders the appearance of a new category, the 'historical recording', in which the qualities of performance are generally more important than what is performed: the resurrection of an old recording in a previous format, which now acquires, if not the aura then at least the sheen of authenticity. It was fostered originally by radio stations like BBC Radio 3, who were able to draw upon their own archives, and the record companies then began to follow suit. The whole business is now highly ecological. Every time a new format is introduced, the previous format becomes an archive to be recycled, by reprocessing old recordings and reissuing them. Not only that, but the archives seem to grow ever larger, as old unissued recordings are discovered and brought out for the first time. The result is to give back to us the history of recording as a history of interpretation.

In jazz, recording played a crucial role in the rapid and extremely wide diffusion of the music; many jazz musicians who grew up in the 1920s and 1930s have spoken of how they first developed their instrumental technique by copying records. But the role of the record was not to substitute for the written score; it communicated what cannot be indicated in any score, the nuances of articulation and timbre which are central stylistic concerns of jazz. The aim of jazz is to achieve a sense of the spontaneous through sophisticated and controlled improvisation, to be a music which never stands still; the record is a means to an end.

In the case of pop music, it becomes an end in itself. As Tin Pan Alley takes second place to Top Forty radio, and sheet music loses its position as the main distributed form of the pop song, it is the record as a musical object which becomes the text. Again, the untutored learn by playing along with the record and imitating it. But here this makes the precise style and intonation of the singer ever more important, often much more so than what is being sung. The record industry encourages this kind of naïve talent precisely because, in being untutored, non-professional and unorganized, it is easy to exploit.

By the 1960s the transformation of popular music had entered a new phase. To take up the account of a progressive DJ on a New York radio station, rock music had already incorporated the electric organ when two Americans, Moog and Buchla, took advantage of transistor technology to produce the first commercial synthesizers. Initially of limited capability and scarcely more interesting than the electronic instruments of the 1920s, these too became performing instruments equipped with keyboards and quickly attracted adherents. By the end of the decade, the synthesizer started being taken up by pop musicians; in 1969 the Beatles, who had already employed tape effects on their albums, incorporated some discreet synthesizer sounds in *Abbey Road*, 'and electronic rock was off and running'.[32] It was this incorporation of electronics into rock and pop which provided the market that stimulated the integration of the various technologies of musical production into a unified system.

Revolver, released in 1966, had already used backward tapes and splicing techniques derived from *musique concrète* and the electronic music studio. Before *Sergeant Pepper* was released in 1967, the Beatles quit touring and pronounced themselves a studio band. Paul McCartney declared that the Beatles were working not only on new songs but on new sounds, and all was ready for *Sergeant Pepper* to be received as the first of a new kind of studio rock album, composed for recording not performance. The Beatles were not the first to use these techniques (and anyway they share the credit for the creativity of these albums with their producer George Martin, as they themselves were happy to admit), but being the most visible, these two albums became the pivot of a new brand of 'art rock', by exponents like Yes, Electric Light Orchestra, King Crimson, Steve Miller Band, Pink Floyd and Jimi Hendrix. For many people, this was when rock music first achieved the same claim to serious musical consideration as jazz, and the fusion of the two in the kind of jazz-rock pioneered by Miles Davis was only a logical development.

Cage had called for an art which imitated nature in its mode of operation. Like Boulez reaching for impersonality, he wanted to remove all trace of subjectivity from the creation of music. In composition degree zero *à la* Cage, the rigorous pursuit of chance produces music 'free of individual taste and memory (psychology) and also of the literature and "traditions" of the art'.[33] One of the reasons this worked is that although apparently denying dialogical content, it opens the ear to the sound of the surrounding world. The ultimate example is the infamous and paradoxical *4'33"*, four minutes and thirty-three seconds of silence, dating from 1952. Originally intended for a solo pianist, the piece consists in a span of total inactivity — except for a silent action like raising and lowering the piano lid in order to mark the three 'movements'. Michael Nyman has called it the most empty work of its kind and therefore the most full of possibilities: 'It is a well-known fact that the silences of *4'33"* were not, after all, silences, since silence is a state which it is physically impossible to achieve.'[34] The piece is both theatrical and self-reflexive (in a small hall in London, one found oneself listening intently to every scuffling foot and every suppressed snigger). What Cage proposes here is that what we have been in the habit of calling silence is in reality non-intentional sound (that is, not intended or prescribed by the composer); reverse the relationship and build the music out of it, and it is quite capable of exercising a mesmeric effect. Paul Griffiths sums up that 'Cage's great achievement here . . . is to claim silence for his own. If one is not listening to anything else, and maybe even if one is, then one is listening to Cage.'[35] The same goes for what is conventionally called noise, and the pieces Cage created for acousmatic instruments like turntables and radio sets.

In general, the introduction of chance techniques into musical performance has the consequence that each version of the work is unique: performance is replaced by realization or actualization, in defiance of the frozen form imposed on performance by recording. At the same time, it calls on the performer to develop a new discipline, the cultivation of a frame of mind similar to Zen which was described by Cage's close associate, the pianist David Tudor: 'You can't carry over any emotional impediments, though at the same time you have to be ready to accept them each instant, as they arise . . . I had to learn how to be able to cancel my consciousness of any previous moment, in order to be able to produce the next one. What this did for me was to bring about freedom, the freedom to do anything, and that's how I learned to be free for a whole hour at a time.'[36] Earle Brown wrote that 'the emancipation of time is far more important than the emancipation of sound'.[37] Christian Wolff explained 'It is not a question of getting anywhere, of making progress, or of having come from anywhere in particular, or of tradition or futurism. There is neither nostalgia nor anticipation.'[38] Morton Feldman spoke of working with time 'in its unstructured existence . . . how Time exists before we put our paws on it . . . our minds, our imagination, into it'.[39] His formula for composition was simple: 'I make one sound and then I move on to the next.'

The result of this American experimentalism is the cousin of what Eco, citing examples by European composers, calls the open work, and in particular, the mobile work (or 'work in movement'), which can never be the same twice.[40] The classical composition, says Eco, is a balanced and unified organic whole which the composer has completed and brought to a close. That does not prevent it at the same time being open on the level of interpretation and performance, but the new approach is qualitatively different. It rejects 'the definitive concluded message' and organizes the elements of the music into multiple permutations from which the performer is invited to choose. Stockhausen's Piano Piece XI, Berio's *Sequenza* for solo flute, Pousseur's *Scambi* and Boulez's Third Piano Sonata, which all date from the late 1950s, are Eco's examples of works which thus engage the performer's initiative. They each leave the arrangement of some of their components to the performer and the moment, abandoning the idea that the artwork has a single definitive version.

These works go further than the open mode long since explored by modernism, ranging from Mallarmé's experiments in poetry to Brecht's refusal of dramatic closure at the end of his plays. The paradigm of the classic open modernist mode for Eco is James Joyce. The reader of *Finnegans Wake*, he says, is in a similar position to that of the person listening to serial music in the striking description of Pousseur: 'Since the phenomena are no longer tied to one another by a one-to-one determination it is up to the listener to place himself deliberately in the midst of an inexhaustible network of relationships and choose ... his own mode of approach, his reference point and his scale, and to try and use as many dimensions as possible at the same time and thus dynamize, multiply and extend to the utmost degree his perceptual faculties.'[41] The composers of mobile works, consisting of independent structural units whose order is unplanned, take this process a stage further. This has the effect on the listener of making uncertainty a positive feature of the musical experience — though much more abstractly than in jazz — and of calling for a new form of mental collaboration with the music.

In America, where composers found their own ways to favour the prerogatives of the performer, these procedures quickly led to a new kind of game music, where the score of the work consists not in notes but in a set of rules the players are instructed to follow. Christian Wolff's *Duet II*, for example, consists of a series of musical fragments and instructions to the players about how to put them together and what to do in certain situations. Fellow composer David Berhman described the result in terms of table-tennis: 'The player's situation might be compared to that of a ping-pong player awaiting his opponent's fast serve: he knows what is coming (the serve) and knows what he must do when it comes (return it); but the details of how and when these take place are determined only at the moment of their occurrence.'[42] Musical games like these not only appeased the composer's desire for anonymity, they engaged the audience less through their sound than through their theatricality. And thus, by merging the gestures of play with libertarian philosophies, they became metaphors or symbolic representations of certain human behaviour patterns — including the behaviour of the audience. The tendency began by turning the game of notes inside out, it ended by returning the ball to the audience's court. In a number of 'audience pieces' by LaMonte Young and the New York group Fluxus dating from 1960, the audience is told that they can do anything they wish for a specific length of time and that this is the composition; or else the performers watch the audience in the same way the audience usually watches the performers. In London a few years later similar things were done by Cornelius Cardew and the Scratch Orchestra;

in Germany, Stockhausen adopted a rather more mystical version of the same ideas.

Traditionalists and the unprepared found these trends intensely frustrating in their total refusal of common-sense musical comprehension. But the logic by which aleatoric music led to this outcome is not mysterious. In the first place, to sacrifice the classic unity of the work is to re-establish the uniqueness of the act of music making itself. A music which then goes one stage further, and operates without given notes at all, is the ultimate expression of the singularity of the moment in which music comes into being in the listener's ear (an experience which is close to that of free jazz improvisation). The act of making music now becomes what the jargon of the time called a happening. The politics of the whole tendency is opposition to the generalized passivity of consumption, which is based in replication and repetition. Cage is explicit about this: 'Most people think that when they hear a piece of music, they're not doing anything but that something is being done to them. Now this is not true, and we must arrange our music, we must arrange our art, we must arrange everything, I believe, so that people realize that they themselves are doing it, and not that something is being done to them.'[43]

It cannot be said that these developments meant very much to the wider concert audience. Research findings suggested that the class composition of the post-war audience was not substantially different from what it was at the time of the first flowering of modernism before the First World War. According to the North American economists, Baumol and Bowen, opera and concert audiences in both the USA and the UK in the mid-1960s remained dominantly middle-class ('white-collar'), just as they had been since middle-class patrons began to outnumber the upper classes in the 1830s and 1840s.[44] Their findings serve to confirm that, despite the efforts of the experimentalists, the concert hall was no longer a dominant space in the formation of musical taste. Under the impact of records, radio and television, the social space represented in the concert hall contracted, and became reduced to little more than what Walter Benjamin called 'a school for asocial behaviour'. At the same time, however, a new and more diversified audience began to emerge, but beyond the concert hall's confines, whose tastes were determined by different criteria. 'Just think', says the Italian composer Luciano Berio in an interview dating from 1981, 'of the wave of interest in music that there's been over the past ten years or so among young people.' They find themselves, he says, in a complex and dramatic world which they lack the means, including the ideological means, to decipher. They are attracted to music because they sense, however dimly, that it can symbolize the possibility of consolation, even of a utopian interpretation of the world. It provides an alternative space, 'though not necessarily a reassuring and optimistic one'. This youthful audience, continues Berio, will listen to anything and everything. 'Clearly the mass media and a different way of organising musical life have made music more accessible. But it's too easy just to attribute the current phenomenon of a great, indiscriminate move towards music to industry's desire for a wider market.' It is a phenomenon which escapes precise analysis, 'including the marxist type, which, in musical matters, tends to be dogmatic and simplistic'.[45]

What is missing in such approaches is the sense of music as an arena of social controversy, with all the richness that Bakhtin's dialogical approach discovers in the contemporary cultural process: the heteroglossia of voices, which do not fuse into a single *Zeitgeist* at all but are constantly counterposed. This heterophony, amplified by the media, attacks the aesthetic hierarchy which places educated art at the summit and trashes popular culture. The process took a decisive turn in the 1960s, when just as post-war recovery arrived at the high point in the economic cycle, a new phenomenon appeared. Instead of compliant mass consumption, the 1960s created a new counterculture, the expression of a profound disenchantment which refused subordination and set about exposing the mendacious claims of the dominant ideology, and which fused a novel brand of political protest with the claims of autonomous imagination.

The music usually associated with the 1960s is one or other variety of rock music. According to one account, groups like the Beatles and the Rolling Stones provided their whole generation with a narrative of its journey from compliance to opposition. Progressive rock told of the alienation of suburbia and the inner city, the disillusion of student life, the arrogance of power so fiercely castigated in the songs of Bob Dylan, 'and, in obviously coded lyrics, the saga of the subterranean drug culture'. These developments did not add up to a coherent movement, however. On the one hand lay a new sense of communitarian ideals, which connected with libertarian socialism, the movements for civil rights and women's liberation, and against the war in Vietnam; on the other appeared a new mysticism which the media dubbed 'flower power' and confused with something called psychedelics.[46]

Perhaps because of the very confusion of this hubbub, the authors of this account — the American editors of an anthology entitled *The 60s Without Apology* — begin their introduction to this momentous decade by citing as an emblem of the time a work of the European musical avant-garde: Berio's *Sinfonia*. This musical tapestry for symphony orchestra and voices has multiple overlapping texts — including passages from Lévi-Strauss and Samuel Beckett — distributed among the voices of the Swingle Singers, for whom the work was written. The incorporation of a vocal group that made it to the charts with swung vocalizations of Bach was a minor scandal which signals Berio's rejection of dogma and his dialogical attitude towards all realms of musical experience. The heart of the work is in the central movements, the second a short simple sung memorial to Martin Luther King, the third an extraordinary collage of music and spoken voices in which the musical backbone is the Scherzo from Mahler's Second Symphony, *The Resurrection*, but overlaid with fragments of Bach, Brahms, Boulez, Berlioz, Schoenberg, Stravinsky, Strauss, Stockhausen, etc. The rich intertextuality of the music is matched by the verbal dimension, which comprises 'bits of the 60s — fragments from May 1968 in France, conversations about art and music, references to other events, chatter'. Whatever Berio is trying to do here, there is no attempt at congruity: the movement hangs together only by its statement about non-synchronicity, the contrast 'between the time when the symphonic form was strained by the breakup of the familiar narratives, and the contemporary moment when formal coherence is abandoned'. The music of Mahler here tells us that there is *no* resurrection of the past, which recedes as the noise of the everyday gains ground. Berio reminds us 'of discontinuous time and space, where the old distinctions between speech and poetry disappear, where narratives lose their endings as well as their origins . . .'. In short, where the past is present but impossible, while the present is ungraspable except as an anarchy of conflicting utterances.

In an important sense, this is metamusic — music about music. Here, not just the history of the tradition, but the traditions of history and the historicist attitude, have been transformed into an enormous field of stylistic icons waiting to be wrenched from their historical referents and cannibalized. This process is only superficially like collage (Berio declares 'I'm not interested in *collages*, and they amuse me only when I'm doing them with my children: then they become an exercise in relativising and "decontextualising" images . . .').[47] The territory has been mapped by Fredric Jameson. Recent criticism, he says, has been concerned to stress the heterogeneity and discontinuities which have come to characterize the postmodernist work of art, which is now no longer unified or organic but a 'virtual grab-bag or lumber room of disjointed sub-systems and random raw materials and impulses of all kinds. The former work of art, in other words, has now turned out to be a text, whose reading proceeds by differentiation rather than by unification.' These theories of difference, associated especially with the name of Jacques Derrida, have tended to stress disjunction to the point where the text falls apart into mere fragments. (Derrida calls this *différance* in French, meaning to indicate with the odd spelling that this is not a passive condition but an active process.) In the most interesting postmodernist works, says Jameson, one can detect a much more positive conception of relationship, which restores the proper tension to the notion of difference itself, and the result is 'something for which the word *collage* is still only a very feeble name'. *Sinfonia* is such a work, whose very disjointedness and discontinuity demonstrates what Jameson calls 'a paradoxical slogan': 'the proposition that "difference relates" '.[48]

This relationship between music and philosophy should not surprise us. It has been present throughout the history of both. At the same time, the affirmation of aesthetic disunity, which can also be found in composers like Peter Maxwell Davies and Mauricio Kagel, is cousin to the attack of 1960s counterculture on conventional politics: both engaged in the deconstruction of dominant ideological discourses. But this deconstruction is not the dispassionate affair advanced by the academics. Robert Stam, writing about the growing resonance of the ideas of Bakhtin, reminds us how politics in the 1960s became carnivalized, as 'demonstrations incorporated colorful elements of music, dance, costume and guerrilla theatre' to create a spectacle in which the line between performer and demonstrator was often blurred, with the same political import as the carnivalesque in Bakhtin.[49] It is part of the definition of carnival, for Bakhtin, that it provides a taste of freedom in which the revellers play out imaginary roles corresponding to their deepest desires. It offers a temporary suspension of hierarchy, authority and prohibition, which not only echoes the preoccupations of the musical avant-garde, but also describes the celebration of utopian revolutionism which exploded in Paris in 1968.

As the carnivalesque spirit began to invade the concert hall, it had two main effects. It brought a new sense of theatricality to the act of performance, and with it, the whiff of politics.[50] The new music theatre harked back to the politically didactic pieces called *Lehrstücke*, which Brecht wrote with Hindemith and Weill, and to Brecht and Weill's *Little Mahagonny*, as well as the Stravinsky of *The Soldier's Tale* and *Renard*, all of which were revived at this time. In this context Peter Maxwell Davies came up with his most celebrated work of the period, *Eight Songs for a Mad King*, in which a singing actor impersonated the mad George III trying to teach caged birds to sing with the aid of a mechanical organ. Written for a small ensemble, the musicians were placed within outsize cages, and taunted by the screeching singer with fragments of Handel's *Messiah*. Dating from 1969, the *Eight Songs* readily evoked the attack on orthodox concepts of madness by radical 'anti-psychiatrists' like R.D. Laing. In short, it was a piece of black comedy which evoked the kind of dissociated schizophrenic speech which David Cooper spoke of when he remarked that his schizophrenic patients seemed to him like the strangled poets of the age.

In the case of Mauricio Kagel we are dealing not only with a particularly absurdist streak of music theatre but also with films, for Kagel is a cross between a composer and an experimental film maker, a latter-day surrealist who composes his films and films his music. *Match*, for example, dating from 1964 and filmed two years later, is a trio in which two cellos hold a competition with the percussionist as referee until, provoked by the percussionist's inconsistent behaviour, they turn against him. In 1970 comes *Ludwig van*, which also exists in two versions, a concert piece and a film for Beethoven's bicentenary. The latter is done as a spoof using the techniques of a Godard. A central scene in this film shows the interior of the music room in Beethoven's house, guarded by life-size cardboard cut-outs of Beethoven, Mozart and Haydn, in which every available surface is covered by sheets of his music. For ten minutes the camera pans around the room, while the soundtrack was recorded by taking the musicians into the dubbing theatre, projecting the film, and asking them to play whatever their eyes alighted upon. The concert piece extends the idea on the model of Beethoven's *33 Variations on a Waltz by Diabelli*, but without a recurring theme. The result is a prime instance of deconstruction, or what Kagel in this case calls the 'analytical synthesis' of the chosen material. It is also another example of something which is more than collage but, in Kagel's word, 'meta-collage', or what he describes as 'a contribution by Beethoven to the music of our time'.[51]

As for the overall impression left by the images of Kagel's films — a technician locked in combat with miles and miles of unspooled recording tape; strangled sounds that come from the horns of inert acoustic gramophones; the big close-up of three different forefingers plucking the same cello strings; a pianist wearing nothing more than a pair of shorts, playing a Beethoven sonata, while the camera pulls back to reveal wires which link him to a machine that records every movement of his muscles — these are images that belong to the inventory of the postmodernist subconscious.

Musical space thus became a site of ideological engagement and skirmishing, but of a character quite different from the demonstrations that accompanied new music in the years before the First World War (most famously in the case of the riot at the Paris premiere of *The Rite of Spring*). When the first performance of Stockhausen's *Stimmung* took place in Paris in December 1968, the newspapers described it as a 'hippies' camp fire'. In a *tour de force* of meditative music, six singers sit cross-legged, yoga-style, in a circle and intone a few almost unchanging notes, interpolated with magic names and mystical verses. The piece calls for a special vocal technique, which Stockhausen borrowed from LaMonte Young, who discovered it in Tibetan chant: the singer must use the resonating chamber of the mouth to bring out the harmonics of a series of vowel sounds. But as Stockhausen later recalled, a number of those hippies took umbrage with it, and in the Amsterdam Concertgebouw during the Holland Festival the following year, the performance 'was so severely interrupted after about twenty minutes by caterwaulings from some dozen "Provos" (so-called "students of the radical left") that we had to abandon it . . . the agitators included some "modern" Dutch composers; and in a subsequent . . . public discussion some of them explained they had wanted to "join in", and that if this music excluded that possibility then it must be "authoritarian". The incident was the subject of such distorted and blown-up publicity that in the end the German Radio was broadcasting the news that this work was "lacking in social necessity" '.[52]

It is probably from this experience that we can date Stockhausen's alienation from radical politics. This is not to suggest, as in the title of the book by Cornelius Cardew, simply that 'Stockhausen Serves Imperialism'. An English follower of Cage and Fluxus, Cardew came to this conclusion after undergoing a political conversion to Maoism, which led him to reject his own experimentalism in favour of the crudest tonality. But the born-again Cardew was unconvincing, while Stockhausen's trajectory had the merit of a process of rediscovery, even if it led in the end to mysticism and mystification. *Stimmung* was a signal that the carefully constructed exclusions of serialism were beginning to collapse. The musical discourse of the work is built up from six basic tones with strong triadic affiliations — the overtones of an absent B fundamental. In short, the chord intoned by the singers had a tonal character. This act of provocation heralded another return of the repressed — the restoration of tonality.

Other composers arrived at the same point by different routes, such as Steve Reich, the most singular of the so-called minimalists. Like the alternative label of systems music, the term is a misnomer; process music is nearer the mark. Minimalism fits the music practised in the circles around LaMonte Young and Fluxus in New York in the early 1960s, where a piece might consist of nothing but a quiet drone played by a very precisely tuned violin. Nothing more. When this isolated sound succeeds in fixating the ear it begins to regenerate the feeling of the natural untempered harmonic relations of the overtones. But this only turns into a new sense of tonality when these potentially harmonic sound objects begin to generate motivic cells which are then set in motion against each other according to simple but far-reaching procedures (not unlike computer programs, which use fractals to generate complex and unpredictable graphic patterns).

The huge success of the composers of process music, who also include Terry Riley, Philip Glass, and in England, Michael Nyman, was to bring them a new audience beyond the traditional adherents of the avant-garde — and the disparagement of suspicious critics. The American Samuel Lipman, for example, calls this music 'the aesthetics of the cafeteria', and traces its source to the rise of radical youth culture. 'The social sex appeal of the educated young masses, so seductive when exhibited in front of the Pentagon, seemed to provide both an irresistible inspiration and a tempting market'; the result was quickly to tame the vein of experimentation, and produce a kind of 'pop music for intellectuals'.[53] Doubtless Adorno would agree. Nevertheless, this newly recovered sense of tonality is in crucial respects quite different from the functional harmony of the preceding four centuries. It is not hierarchical in character, but cyclical; the drive towards closure and finality is replaced by a quasi-modal feel which represents a different chronotope.

This is why Reich's pieces do not come to an end, they just stop. There is no sense of completion and closure because Reich, like Stockhausen, is indifferent to the tonic (which is less true of Terry Riley or Philip Glass). Reich goes even further. He transposes the same process to the domain of rhythm by means of phase-shifting, a technique originating in two works using tape loops from the middle 1960s, *It's Gonna Rain* and *Come Out*. The first takes a fragment from a recording of a black preacher in a San Francisco square, the second, the words of a black protester in Harlem who had been beaten by the police and accused of murder. By making these fragments into loops, re-recording them and playing the identical loops just slightly out of phase, the result is a thickening texture which obliterates the original words and produces complex and mesmerizing cross-rhythms; these are not easy pieces to listen to, but they carry a powerful charge.

When the same technique is transferred to instrumentalists, who phase-shift repeating rhythmic or melodic motifs, the effect is to displace the stress which Western music since the Renaissance places firmly on the first beat of the bar; not to lose it like Debussy or Boulez, but to distribute it between the ensemble of players in the form of constantly permutating cross-rhythms. In a word, where *Stimmung* floats, Reich's music takes off.

Implosion

When Fredric Jameson speaks of postmodernism as 'the cultural logic of late capitalism', he is referring to the syndrome first described by Adorno and Horkheimer in their critique of the culture industry of the 1930s, but now writ large and multiplied by an economic process which goes far beyond that of classic monopoly capitalism. It is a logic which by virtue of intricate economic processes penetrates every corner of cultural life. The monopolies and cartels of the early years of the century have given way to new patterns of corporate organization in the form of the multinational corporation, the transnational, and most recent to emerge, the global network. In the course of this process, the culture industry becomes a branch of the communications industry, which in turn is a huge outgrowth of the military—industrial complex; where defence research and space exploration produce techniques whose real pay-off is in the form of new commodities for the mass market, from transistors to computer chips. The result is the electronification, integration and now the computerization of the production, processing and distribution of information, entertainment, education, and cultural activity in general, which washes daily over the atomized consumer from cradle unto grave. A condition of continuous overload takes over, where an ideology of technical rationality produces streamlined irrationality and high-tech paranoia; and the devices of advertising burst the bounds of the media and force themselves upon the most traditional sectors of cultural production.

In this situation, the fate of artistic endeavour is significantly influenced by global interrelations between the different branches of the media and the judgement of a hugely bloated advertising industry. It doesn't matter who thought up the idea of the World Cup Three Tenors' concert. The effect, to borrow Jameson's formula, is 'the penetration of commodity fetishism into those realms of the imagination and the psyche which had . . . always been taken as the last impregnable stronghold against the instrumental logic of capital'.[54]

On this reading, postmodernism is an effect encouraged by radical neo-liberalism like the regimes of Thatcher and Reagan, with their monetarism and deregulation. Deregulation, as the sociologist Armand Mattelart has pointed out, does not mean the removal of regulation but the exchange of one set of regulations for another; and contrary to what is often supposed, it is not the fruit of spontaneous development but the result of political will. The purpose, as with privatization (or denationalization), is not only the restructuring of industry but the wholescale rearrangement of public space, including the transformation of the media, in favour of supposedly unsullied market economics. Hence the ascendancy of advertising, which now becomes a veritable philosophy.[55] It is no coincidence that Thatcherism was linked with the rise of the advertisers who handled the Tory election campaign, Saatchi & Saatchi, to become the world's foremost advertising agency network. The new style of aggressive advertising which propelled Saatchis to the top invaded every domain through application of the novel concept of 'lifestyle', which allowed the advertisers to modernize the old method of social classification (the advertisers' ABC) based on class. The most highbrow musical tradition did not escape the advertisers' paws. They talked about the benefits of linking products with musical classics in order to increase brand-name recognition: of enlisting Elgar to sell Royal Doulton china, or more bizarrely, Mahler for motor oil and the Grand Chorus from *Aida* for computers. (But did anyone know, when the electricity board chose the *Eroica* for their TV spots, that Beethoven once declared himself 'electrical by nature'?) The process only extends the dissipation of the musical tradition as it is cut even further adrift from its origins.

Another effect of the way advertising culture permeates public space is in attaching brand names to sports tournaments and opera productions with equal ease. The proud tradition of classical music is reduced to a small subsector of a vast industry, in which it is no longer able to maintain a separate identity. But this also means that the exploitation of classical music can be hitched to multifarious forms of marketing, with the result that in 1991, the bicentenary of his death, Mozart became an octopus with an infinite number of tentacles. Like it or not, commoditized cultural space has become so pervasive that it becomes impossible to continue thinking of any part of the cultural domain as a reserved and uncontaminated territory.

That the same incongruities can be found in the use of music in political campaigning is no accident, but an index of how deeply the ethos of advertising has penetrated the public sphere. The adulteration of the cultural tradition is matched here by alienation from political culture. As reported by a newspaper article on British election day 1987, the party pieces were out of tune with their composers. Purcell's trumpet voluntary succeeded in serving the Alliance parties as an icon of the national quintessence, although his politics are unknown, and anyway he died in 1695. Labour's choice of Brahms, however, extolled as Neil Kinnock's favourite composer, was even more incongruous, and not just because he was German: born in a slum, the son of a harberdasher and a bass player in a brothel band, Brahms had became a staunch follower of the notorious reactionary Bismarck. As for the Tories using *The Planets* as the background to a speech by Thatcher, here again the wires had been crossed: Holst, a pioneer socialist and follower of William Morris, would probably have wanted to sue them for violation of his moral rights.[56]

This kind of dissociation is not just incidental, but an ideological product of the creation of what the German philosopher Habermas calls 'societies of generalised public relations'.[57] The process has its roots between the wars, when advertising began to shift its methods from the offer of enticing information to a supposedly rational consumer towards the increasing manipulation of the irrational. In the virtuoso effusions of its highest form, the television commercial — which Jean Baudrillard calls the simulation of a communication which seems more real than reality — cultural signifiers of every kind are pulled loose and float around in a suspended space, which Baudrillard calls hyper-reality, where they sometimes attach themselves to commodities and sometimes to buzzwords.[58] The advertising message is a pretence which addresses a subject who is thrown off balance by the disappearance of the real into the illusory. It is fantasy, caprice and whim at the service of contrived desire. The commercial creates a subject in its own image, a dependent spectator, pure consumer, whose every desire is catered for on one condition: the price to be paid. Every product is a bait, every real and possible need is weakness which leads the fly to the gluepot, every wish an opportunity for the advertiser to assume a posture of amiability and announce (as Marx put it 150 years ago), 'Dear friend, I give you what you need, but you know the *conditio sine qua non*; you know the ink in which you have to sign yourself over to me; in providing for your pleasure, I fleece you.'[59] Here traditional cultural values are not so much subverted as simply vaporized.

Music and information behave in similar ways. Mark Poster observes that information as a commodity is endowed with a quality which capital can only regard as anomalous: 'unlike material goods information is not exhausted in its consumption . . . Scarcity of material resources, the prime axiom of capitalist economic theory, does not apply to information.' Nor to music. Moreover, in both cases the new technologies allow the consumer to become his or her own reproducer. What this implies for popular culture and education ought to be a great boon, for as Poster puts it: 'The Enlightenment dream of an educated society, wherein all knowledge is available to the least individual, is now technically feasible.'[60]

This anomaly represents a fissure in the established systems of power, domination and authority, who resist the democratization of music almost as much as genuine freedom of information. Ideologues on the right talk about the 'free flow of information' while authority tries to control it. The same thing appears to happen with music, especially in the hands of programme editors who divide it into streams according to the concepts of niche marketing. In a country as sophisticated as France in the early 1980s, a group of music producers on the cultural radio programme were fired because they began mixing up musics from different levels of the hierarchy of styles − ethnic music and jazz, for example, alongside chamber music and opera excerpts, in the same programmes. The newspaper *Libération*, which knew of course that this is the way people really listen to music nowadays, protested about their removal on its front page. Within a few years, even the BBC's serious music station recognized the phenomenon, but ghettoized it in a special late-night programme called 'Mixing It'.

Actions like these have hardly stopped the breadth of musics within general awareness from constantly growing. And nor has music been depoliticized. On the contrary, the question of music became a live political issue in Britain in the lead-up to the 1992 general election, when the leaders of the musical community protested angrily at Tory government proposals for the new national curriculum for music in schools. Ideologically in line with the order to eliminate the contemporary period from the history curriculum, Education Minister Kenneth Clarke overruled his own working party and called for the reinstatement of appreciation and theory − at the cost of a drastic reduction in the practical component. In other words, in *musica practica*. Newspaper correspondents accused him of 'failing to comprehend what every professional musician takes to be self-evident — that we only come to know about and understand music by doing it'.[61] A letter of protest was sent to the Prime Minister by a score of singers, pianists, conductors and composers. The *Guardian* reported that 'Simon Rattle, Sir Colin Davis, Sir Charles Groves and others are this week writing to John Major, whose tastes on yesterday's *Desert Island Discs* ranged from George Gershwin to Diana Ross.'[62] The conductor Mark Elder warned the press of the serious danger 'that music will be forced to become an academic subject rather than a creative, imaginative pursuit . . . We want as many children as possible to find a place for music in their lives.'[63]

Even the music industry has come to share this opinion, as it complains about the lack of training available for good recording producers. A recent study of the music business by Andrew Blake, a London-based sociologist and sometime member of the band Man Jumping, explains the issue: Britain is the most educationally backward country in Western Europe — proportionately fewer youth stay in education after the age of sixteen; fewer complete technical apprenticeships or enter higher education. Worthy people come up with the argument that the workforce is lacking competitive skills and that music is one of the ways the youth can be trained in microcomputer use. Besides, popular music is a major earner of invisible exports.[64] That this is not just a local question is evident from the example of the Yamaha Music Foundation, which operates worldwide, publishing songbooks and music textbooks, running schools to provide instruments, teachers and classes, sponsoring competitions, concerts and recordings. The commercial spin-off from this kind of marketing is huge.

The musicians' angry response to the rejection of the proposed curriculum was the result of a year's campaigning, which built on the frustrations suffered since Margaret Thatcher became Prime Minister in 1979. The rejected report had also warned of the depletion in staffing and tuition in many local authorities, the result of reductions in local authority education budgets; music teaching was hit especially hard because of the large amount of peripatetic music teaching in many of the counties. The peripatetic system was one of the gains created by the post-war expansion of education: it allowed as wide a range of instrumental tuition in as many schools as possible, with teachers spending time in each in turn. The vitality of school orchestras across the whole country demonstrated the success of this approach, which Thatcherism seriously undermined. After ten years in which the politicians in power refused to understand that they were destroying the foundations on which the musical culture of the country was built, the action of the Education Minister had the effect of raising the stakes.

Blake describes the build-up to the protests. The working party included educationalists, music administrators, civil servants, and a professional composer who wrote for television and children. Their report laid stress on giving children opportunities to pursue all types of music, and mentioned several types from which children could learn the basics — reggae, West African drumming and Indian ragas — as well as they could from notated music. 'There was an explosion of anger . . . in the right-wing press' from people 'outraged that children might no longer be taught to venerate music written by dead Europeans'; they were 'not at all interested in either cultural or economic reasons for giving children creative musical skills of their own', and a right-wing lobby formed.[65]

Remarkably, the musical community at large did not this time shrink back from the ideological agenda. The working party had imagined a sixteen-year-old who might be singing in a gospel choir, playing a prepared solo in a jazz combo, harmonizing a pop song, or practising West African drumming patterns.[66] When Kenneth Clarke ordered that all this should be cut out, the protests came flying. According to one writer, 'The dismissal of non-Western styles betrays a profound ignorance of how European music developed'; in the words of another, 'To ignore the music of cultures other than the Western European is to impoverish the subject; more seriously, many students in our schools are deeply rooted in such cultures.' The *Guardian* announced: 'Composer James Macmillan accuses education secretary and his supporters of paranoid disdain for non-European musical cultures.' Macmillan berated them for creating 'an unwarranted confrontation between eurocentricity and multiculturalism. Whether this has been a calculated political ploy or simply the defensive knee-jerk instincts of cultural reactionaries, one cannot be completely sure. What is certain is the blinkered nature of their ideological position.'[67]

Politicians are not unaware of the symbolic power of music. They know their image is enhanced by association with music, and suitable picture opportunities are now provided in every election campaign almost as a matter of course — the most popular role is of course that of conductor, an image which is supposed to spell leadership and harmony. But they cannot help shrinking away from the strength within music which lies behind this image of benign power, the utopian dream of community and reconciliation which demands that everyone's voice is equally valued.

Music, at the same time a direct and a symbolic expression of social relations, retains the power of affirmation. Through a century of transformation by electronic technology, it responded with enormous and often anarchic energy, and in the process has only renewed its utopian dreams. True, one cannot say that these dreams seem to get any closer. But the powerful conviction is there that music and society are not indifferent to each other. Attali even says that many errors in sociology might have been avoided if scholars had paid more attention to music. Music, as definitive a human proclivity as speech itself, and which we know no society to have lacked, is a barometer of the social order, in which we can not only listen to the past but, if we know how, also take soundings of the future.

The presentiments that music offers us are expressed as well as anyone has expressed them in the words of a thirty-year-old worker in Czechoslovakia, whose formal education ended with secondary school, on being asked as part of a survey in 1966 to give his response to a piece of electronic music:

It was as if musicians were improvising and discovering unknown worlds. I have the feeling of being an explorer. Through music I perceive something newly discovered which cannot yet be precisely defined — something not yet restricted by any canon, prescription, arrangement or regulation. In the face of this new land all those who would lay claim to determining the point of view towards it or what one should take possession of within it are impotent. Before this unknown region the powerful cannot immediately know whether Lenin would have found it in order or not and for that reason they are silent . . . When I hear music like this, I begin to hope that tomorrow or in one or two years this new discovery . . . will become reality, and, in so doing, further influence our daily life . . . and perhaps then the kingdom of humanity and reason will arrive sooner than hoped for. Art must move ahead of life and indicate the direction which life is to take. Music such as this — as in the case of all modern art — affirms that this is possible even in the twentieth century.[68]

Notes

1. See Paddy Scannell, 'Music for the Multitude? The Dilemmas of the BBC's Music Policy, 1925–1946', in *Media Culture & Society*, London, Vol. 3, no. 3, July 1981.

2. Quoted in Herbert Schiller, *Mass Communications and American Empire*, Beacon Press, Boston, MA 1971, p. 106.

3. Hans Magnus Enzensberger, 'Constituents of a Theory of the Media', in *Raids and Reconstructions*, Pluto, London 1976, pp. 24–5.

4. 'Theremin — An Electronic Odyssy', Channel Four, 2 November 1993. A few days after the transmission of this film, Theremin died.

5. Richard Middleton, *Studying Popular Music*, Open University Press, Buckingham 1990, p. 90.

6. Jon Lewin in Notes & Queries, *The Guardian*, 30 December 1991.

7. Andrew Blake, *The Music Business*, Batsford, London 1992, p. 16.

8. Roland Gelatt, *The Fabulous Phonograph 1877–1977*, Cassell, London 1977, pp. 299–300.

9. This necessarily condensed account is greatly expanded in my forthcoming study *Repeated Takes, a Short History of Recording and its Effects on Musical Culture*, to be published by Verso.

10. Ernest Roth, *The Business of Music*, Cassell, London 1969, p. 67.

11. Umberto Eco, *The Open Work*, Hutchinson Radius, UK 1989, p. 143.

12. As far as the debate about Strauss's politics is concerned, I agree with the Italian musicologist Andrea Lanza: 'The void created by Nazism, not least in cultural matters, allows

no excuses: nothing remains of the culture of the Nazi epoch, and even its most prestigious exponents, like Richard Strauss, Wilhelm Furtwängler, Martin Heidegger and others, sympathisers before the establishment of the regime, came to feel the heavy shadow of tragic complicity.' Andrea Lanza, *Historia de la Musica*, Vol. 12, 'El siglo XX', Third Part, Spanish edition, Ediciones Turner, Madrid 1980, p. 58.

13. Luciano Berio, *Two Interviews*, Marion Boyars, London 1985, p. 61.

14. T.W. Adorno, *Introduction to the Sociology of Music*, Seabury Press, New York 1976, p. 158.

15. Joan Peyser, *Boulez*, Cassell, London 1977, p. 67.

16. Roland Barthes, *Barthes: Selected Writings*, ed. Susan Sontag, Fontana, London 1983, p. 51.

17. H. Eimert, 'The Composer's Freedom of Choice', *Die Reihe* 3.

18. H.H. Stuckenschmidt, *Twentieth Century Music*, Weidenfeld & Nicolson, London 1969, p. 214.

19. David Drew, 'Modern French Music', in Howard Hartog, ed., *European Music in the Twentieth Century*, Penguin, London 1961, p. 309.

20. Boulez, *Orientations*, Faber & Faber, London 1986, p. 341.

21. John Cage, speaking at the Almeida Festival in London, July 1990. This was his last visit to England before his death in 1992.

22. Quoted in Wim Mertens, *American Minimal Music*, Kahn & Averill, London 1988, p. 106.

23. Quoted in Michael Nyman, *Experimental Music*, Studio Vista, London 1974, p. 2.

24. Eco, p. 63.

25. Boulez, *Relevés d'apprenti*, Seuil, Paris 1966, p. 297.

26. Eco, *The Open Work*, p. 18.

27. Herbert Eimert, 'What is Electronic Music?' *Die Reihe* 1, p. 10.

28. Quoted in Steve Jones, *Rock Formation — Music, Technology and Mass Communication*, Sage, London 1992, p. 173.

29. Jones, p. 171, citing J.D. Tankel, 'The Practice of Recording Music: Remixing as Recoding', *Journal of Communication*, Vol. 40, No. 3.

30. Dick Hebdige, *Cut 'n' Mix*, Methuen, London 1987, pp. 71–2, 82.

31. Leonard Warren cited in 'Recording in Italy', *Time*, 29 July 1957.

32. John Schaeffer, *New Sounds, The Virgin Guide to New Music*, Virgin, London 1990, p. 5.

33. Cage, *Silence*, Calder & Boyars, London 1968, p. 59.

34. Nyman, pp. 2 and 22.

35. Paul Griffiths, *Modern Music*, Dent, London 1981, p. 70.

36. Quoted in Nyman, p. 52.

37. Quoted in Mertens, p. 106.

38. Quoted in Nyman, p. 23.

39. Quoted in ibid., p. 12.

40. Eco, chapter 1.

41. Quoted in ibid., pp. 10–11.

42. Quoted in Nyman, p. 16.

43. Quoted in ibid., p. 21.

44. William J. Baumol and William G. Bowen, *Performing Arts — The Economic Dilemma*, MIT Press, Cambridge, MA 1968, chapter IV.

45. Berio, pp. 29–30.

46. Sohnya Sayres, Anders Stephanson, Stanley Araonowitz and Fredric Jameson, Introduction to *The 60s Without Apology*, University of Minnesota Press, 1984, pp. 5–6.

47. Berio, p. 106.

48. Jameson, *Postmodernism*, p. 76.

49. Robert Stam, 'Bakhtin and Left Cultural Critique' in E. Ann Kaplan, ed., *Postmodernism and its Discontents*, Verso, London 1988, p. 136.

50. Anyone who doubts that the composers I am speaking about were as politicized as I am suggesting should consult the names listed in the advertisement which appeared in the leading British newspapers protesting the very heavy sentences handed down to the anarchist group known as the Angry Brigade.

51. Mauricio Kagel, programme note to the recording of *Ludwig van*, DGG 2530 014.

52. Stockhausen in Karl Wörner, *Stockhausen: Life and Work*, University of California Press, Berkeley and Los Angeles 1976, pp. 66–7.

53. Samuel Lipman, *The House of Music*, David R. Godine, Boston, MA 1984, pp. 31–48.

54. Fredric Jameson, Foreword to J.-F. Lyotard, *The Postmodern Condition: A Report on Knowledge*, Manchester University Press, Manchester 1984, p. xv.

55. See Armand Mattelart, *Advertising International*, Routledge, London 1991.

56. Martin Linton, *Guardian*, election day 1987.

57. Jürgen Habermas, 'The Public Sphere', in Mattelart and Sieglaub, eds, *Communication and Class Struggle*, Vol. I, International General, 1979.

58. Jean Baudrillard, *Simulations*, Semiotext(e), 1983.

59. Karl Marx, *The Economic and Philosophic Manuscripts of 1844*, ed. Struik, International Publishers, New York 1964, p. 148.

60. Mark Poster, *The Mode of Information*, Polity Press, Cambridge 1990, p. 73.

61. Richard McNichol, 'Crotchets and quavers in school music debate', *Guardian*, 27 February 1992.

62. *Guardian*, 27 January 1992.

63. Ibid.

64. Andrew Blake, *The Music Business*, Batsford, London 1992, p. 100.

65. Ibid., p. 101.

66. *Guardian*, 15 February 1991.

67. James Macmillan, 'Baton charge of blinkered ideologues', *Guardian*, 30 January 1992.

68. Quoted in Wes Blomster, 'Electronic Music', *Telos*, No. 32, Summer 1977, p. 78.

Index

sonata form 97, 99—100, 101, 195
Songspiel 130
Sony 30
sound, link with
  electromagnetism 238—9
sounds
  non-harmonic 179
  redefined 241—4
space, in music 49—50
speech synthesis 237
Spohr, Louis 158, 159, 230
Stanislavsky, K.S. 42
Stein, Johann 201, 203
Stein, Nanette 201
Steinway piano 206, 209
Steinway, Theodore 216, 238
stereotyping, music printing 120
Steve Miller Band 272
Stockhausen, Karlheinz 69, 260,
  264, 266, 267, 275, 277, 281
  Gesang der Jünglinge 268
  Kontakte 268, 269
  Piano Piece XI 273
  Stimmung 279—80, 281
Stokowski, Leopold 74
Stradivarius, Antonio 183
Strauss, Richard 149, 159, 232, 233,
  277
  Metamorphosen 259
Stravinsky, Igor 16, 23, 69, 97, 104,
  105, 132, 142, 234, 236, 242, 243,
  246, 261, 277
  composer-pianist 208
  Les Noces 247
  Petrushka 84—5, 235, 247
  The Firebird 154
  The Rite of Spring 71, 105, 247
  Threni 104
  twelve-tone method 260
string instruments 169, 174
string quartet 49—50
structural linguistics 82—5
Stuckenschmidt, H.H. 244, 262
subconscious, musical 103—6
Sutherland, Joan 190
swing 236

Swingle Singers 276
symphony 40, 49—50, 135—6, 157,
  195
symphony orchestras 139, 157, 158,
  160—61, 211, 214—15
syncopation 186, 234, 236
synthesizers 209, 210, 254, 255, 267,
  272
syrinx 170, 173

Table Music 111
Tallis, Thomas 64, 113, 123, 124,
  189
tape-recorder 257—8, 267, 269
Tartini, Giuseppe 183
  Devil's Trill Sonata 104
Tchaikovsky, Peter Ilyich 97, 161,
  227
  Fourth Smphony 100
technology, music and 14—16
telegraphy 224, 239
telephone 238, 239
television 29, 30, 257, 275
  commercials 283—4
Telharmonium 240, 253
temperament
  equal 177, 182, 210—17, 231
  just 181
  mean-tone 181—2
  see also tuning
tetrachord 175
Thatcher, Margaret 282, 285
thematic transformation 100—04
theremin 255
Theremin, Leon 255
Thompson, J. Walter 156
thorough-bass 70
timbre 85—6, 186, 210, 212, 215,
  237, 241, 254, 255, 266
time
  in music 49—50
  standardization 224
Tinctoris 78
Tippett, Michael 247
tonal music, generative theory 83—4